MODERN HINDUISM

MODERN HINDUISM

Being An Account of the Religion And Life of the Hindus in Northern India

William Joseph Wilkins

GYAN

Published by

Gyan Publishing House
5, Ansari Road
Daryaganj, New Delhi-110002
Phone: 011-47034999, 9811692060
E-mail: books@gyanbooks.com

Distribution Network
gyanbooks.com
India, USA, Canada, UK, Australia, France

ISBN : 978-81-212-2363-8 (PB)
First Published, 1887

2nd Impression 2021

Printed at: Gyan Press, Delhi.

Modern Hinduism
Author: William Joseph Wilkins

INTRODUCTION.

In a former work,* I have given, as far as possible in the language of the sacred books, an account of the deities commonly worshipped by the Hindus of Northern India. In this I propose to give an account of the life of the Hindus, which is largely the result of the worship of those deities. Having lived for many years in India, and met with all classes of the community in the cities and in the villages, and having conversed with them in their own language, I have learned much that is not to be found in books written on this most interesting subject. I have read much that has been written by Europeans and Bengalis concerning the faiths and practices of the people; and in conversation with priests and pundits have tested the accuracy of many of the statements made in these works, so that what is found in these pages may be received with confidence as a trustworthy account of the religious life of the Hindu community. In this book, as in my former one, I have abstained from comment on the character of these practices; my work here is rather that of a chronicler than of a preacher. In writing of the mythology

* "Hindu Mythology—Vedic and Purānic." Thacker and Co., Newgate Street; and Thacker, Spink, and Co., Calcutta.

of the Hindus, I felt that the most powerful refutation of Hinduism was a fair statement of what their books themselves teach concerning the character and conduct of the beings whom they worship as divine; and in describing the every-day life of the Hindus, which is the practical outcome of such worship, there seems to me to be but little necessity for comment.

It may perhaps appear strange to some readers to see several subjects treated of in this book which professes to be an account of the Hindu religion; but it must ever be borne in mind that, with the Hindu, religion is not a thing for times and seasons only, but professes to regulate his life in all its many relations. It orders ceremonies to be performed on behalf of a man before he is born, and gives instructions to his descendants, which they must follow in order that his happiness may be secured after death. It regulates the ceremonies attendant on his birth, his early training, his food and its cooking, his style of dress and its manufacture, his employment, marriage, amusements—his whole life from before his birth until generations after his death. Religion seeks to regulate not only the private life of the Hindu, but also his domestic and national relations, and no contingencies are possible for which it has not provided laws. To treat, then, of the ordinary life of the Hindu is to describe the Hindu religion.

It should also be remembered that descriptions absolutely true of certain classes or of certain districts may not be strictly correct of other classes or other districts; and also that some classes are grossly ignorant of the customs of other classes, and the residents of one district, whilst familiar with the practices common there, are totally ignorant of what prevails in other parts of the country. This can scarcely be wondered at when we consider the number of books which are believed by the people to be divinely given as authorities on matters concerning the gods and the religious life. The people of one district are familiar only with perhaps a small part of one of these books, whilst those of other districts found their religious faiths on other books or different parts of the same, the religious teachers of the people as a rule knowing only a small part of one or other of these large volumes. In addition to this it must not be forgotten that until a couple of generations back there was no prose literature, no newspapers or magazines, no novels; whilst the theatrical representations which the people so dearly love were almost entirely confined to mythological representations. It is no uncommon thing to find some custom in the home, or some ceremony in worship, supported by quite different authorities by different people. When, therefore, hearing or reading of certain things being believed or done by Hindus, we are inclined to deny the accuracy of these statements, it is well to inquire whether it is not our limited knowledge that is at fault rather than the accuracy of the writer or speaker. The sacred writings are full of contradictions, and naturally the beliefs and practices of the people differ widely.

Many books have already been written on this subject, but it is not by any means exhausted. Any one living amongst the people with the seeing eye and inquiring mind may see and hear much that has never been described in print. And it is the duty of the observant to note these things, as it is true to-day in India as elsewhere that "the old order changeth, giving place to new;" and certainly more true now than it has been in the past. As Hinduism loses its hold upon the popular heart, and purer faiths are adopted and more reasonable practices followed by the millions of India, many things now patent to the observer will cease to be done, and it will be only as old men's tales that they can then be known. Men visiting certain isles of the Pacific search in vain for any traces of the old idolatries that once prevailed there, and can learn of the religion of olden time only from the descendants of those who once followed this faith; men can nowadays visit the scenes of child murder and sati in India, but are dependent upon the stories of eye-witnesses, who have passed away, for descriptions of these obsolete customs; so will it be, doubtless, with many of the common forms of Hinduism. In the meantime, that those who cannot visit India may know what its people believe and do in their religious worship, and that those who come after us may know what was the form the religious life of the past assumed, it is the duty of those who have seen this gigantic system in its full force and activity faithfully to describe what their "eyes have seen, and their ears have heard."

CONTENTS.

EARLY LIFE.

HINDU SECTS.

CASTE.

WORSHIP.

WOMAN.

MORALS.

DEATH, SHRĀDHA, AND FUTURE JUDGMENT.

THE EARLY LIFE OF THE HINDUS.

CHAPTER I.

BIRTH AND ITS CEREMONIES.

The well-known lines of Wordsworth—

> "Our birth is but a sleep and a forgetting;
> The soul that rises with us, our life's star
> Hath had elsewhere its setting,
> And cometh from afar;
> Not in entire forgetfulness,
> And not in utter nakedness,
> But trailing clouds of glory do we come
> From God who is our home,"

are in perfect harmony with the spirit of Hinduism; hence it teaches that even before a child is ushered into the world certain ceremonies should be performed on its behalf. About four months before its birth there is the ceremony called The Uncooked Food (Kācha Sād). The astrologer having been consulted on this, as on all other important occasions, and a suitable day having been fixed by him, all restrictions respecting food, which at other times are most rigorously observed by the expectant mother, are removed, and she is permitted to eat all kinds of fruits, preserves, pickles, &c., rice and grain of all kinds only being prohibited. Two months later comes the Cooked Food (Bhājā Sād) ceremony, when the lady with a few friends, whose husbands and children are living, is permitted to eat parched peas, rice, and cooked sweetmeats. A month later still the Panchāmrita festival is held. This name is given because on this occasion the five delicacies supposed to form the food of the gods, viz., milk, ghi, curds, honey, and cow-dung, are set before her, though she is permitted to eat only fruits and sweetmeats, a little of which are put into her mouth by the officiating priest. She is gaily dressed in a red-bordered sāri, or cloth, which is afterwards most carefully preserved, lest any unfortunate mother who has lost her children from jealousy should cut it, or take away any part of it, as any injury coming to it would be ominous of evil to her child. At this time a day is fixed as near as possible to the expected day of birth for the final and more elaborate feast.

At the concluding festival before the birth of the child, all the lady relatives of the family are invited, and a liberal supply of varied kinds of food provided. In order to make the day as lively as possible, singing and dancing girls are engaged. In former years (and in some places even now) the songs and dances were of a most indecent character, but nowadays this objectionable element of the feast is generally absent. When all is ready, the lady on whose behalf it is given, beautifully dressed, and adorned with her jewels, walks to her seat, which is painted white, and placed in the centre of the apartment, whilst her guests sit in rows on either side of her. A light burns in front of her, the sacred conch shell is sounded, and a rupee which has touched her forehead is offered on her behalf to the gods to ensure her a safe issue from her coming trouble. The guests then partake of the sumptuous feast, and, as soon as it is over, hurry away to their homes in order that they may reach them before darkness sets in. As the giver of the feast is expected to provide palanquins and other conveyances to bring her guests and also to take them home, and as there are not sufficient to take more than a small number of them at once, there is often a rather lively scene as the ladies try to get the first use of these conveyances. It is customary for those who have participated in the feast to send presents to the lady whom they came to congratulate.

So great is the mortality of Hindu women at childbirth,

that this event has obtained the name of the Hundredfold-dreaded (Satasanka); and many of the friends, in making presents to the hostess, give them as farewell gifts. According to a Hindu proverb, the ordinary life of a woman being sedentary, and comparatively idle, is preferable to that of a man; the dread of motherhood, however, is regarded as an equivalent to the cares and toils of manhood, so that men are content with their lot and willing to remain men.

It may here be mentioned that, excepting on these high days of festival, the Hindu wife, until her child is born, is under many restrictions respecting food, dress, movements, &c., and generally her fear of the dangers of the coming event is sufficiently great to lead her carefully to observe them. As a rule, a Hindu wife is not more than thirteen or fourteen years of age when her first child is born, sometimes she is even younger, and at such times is attended only by some ignorant person, who is quite unable to render her any real assistance when there may be special need. A skilled doctor save in the rarest cases, would not be admitted into a Hindu home; and when they have been sent for, attempts have been made to prevent them from seeing more than the hand and tongue of the patient. It occasions no surprise, therefore, that there should be great fear experienced by the young wife; the uncertainty whether she will survive the event being assigned as the reason for celebrating the festivals referred to. Amongst the many regulations imposed upon the wife for months before her child is born, the following may be mentioned. She must not wear any clothes over which birds have flown. She must always wear a knot in her dress (sāri) where it is fastened round her waist. In order to avoid the contact of evil spirits, she must not walk or sit in the open courtyard of her house, and must wear a thin reed five inches long tied in the knot of her hair. As a means of easily getting through her trouble, she has to wear an amulet (māduli) round her neck, containing flowers consecrated to Baba Thākur, a deity worshipped chiefly by the lower orders of the people; and she must daily drink a few drops of water that have been touched by this amulet.

When the hour of birth draws near, as a mother is regarded ceremonially unclean for three weeks after childbirth if she have given birth to a son, and for a month if her child be a girl, and as her touch is defiling for this period, she cannot remain in the house. A shed is therefore provided as her temporary home. In the homes of the poor the lumber room is generally emptied; in other places a mat hut is set up; whilst in the larger houses a room is kept for this purpose. These rooms are generally quite destitute of furniture, a little straw only being spread for the woman to lie upon. In this wretched place she must remain until the day of her purification, and although it is admitted that under the most favourable circumstances there is great risk to her life, the proceedings in this shed seem calculated to largely increase this danger. Before the lady enters the room the skull of a cow smeared with red paint is reared up against the wall to drive away evil spirits. An image of Sasthi, the goddess who presides over married women and children, is made of cow-dung, and placed in a conspicuous position and specially honoured until the time when the mother can rejoin the family. And during all this time neither husband nor father, sister nor mother, must enter the shed lest they be defiled, the poor mother being left entirely to the tender mercies of the Barber's wife, whose reign is supreme over both mother and child. When European ladies visiting the homes of the people have expostulated with them on this cruel treatment, and tried to induce the friends to show a little more consideration to the invalid, all their arguments and entreaties are met by the assurance that any departure from the custom of past ages would only anger Sasthi, and lead her to increase the evils and dangers of any one who was bold enough to dare to introduce reforms amongst those over whom she reigns. Sasthi is all-powerful over the superstitious minds of the

Hindu woman. If a child die soon after its birth, it is Sasthi who has removed it; if a mother is blessed with many living sons, it is Sasthi who must be praised.

As so much is said in this chapter about Sasthi, it will not be out of place to give a brief account of this all-powerful deity, as many of the Hindus regard her. She is called "Sasthi, or the Sixth," because she is believed to be the sixth part of the Divine essence of *Pradhāna Prakriti*, the male and female creative principles by whose influence this universe has been generated. The following legend is related in connection with her worship: "Priyavrata, the son of Svayambhū Manu, who had spent many years in enthusiastic and solitary devotion, was at last persuaded by Brahmā to contract the bonds of matrimony. But as his wife did not for a long time present him with offspring, he desired the divine sage Kasyapa to celebrate the *putreshti-yāga*, on the completion of which the sage gave her to eat the sacrificial charm (rice cooked in clarified butter), on swallowing which she became *enceinte*. In due time she brought forth into the world a son as bright as gold, but unfortunately still-born. The king with a sad heart took the dead child and laid it on the funeral pile, with a view to cremation. On a sudden, however, there appeared overhead in the sky a goddess of surpassing beauty, radiant in the summer sun. The king, entranced with her heavenly grace, asked her who she was. The goddess said, 'I am the wife of Kartikheya, the chief of mothers, and as I am the sixth part of *Prakriti*, men call me Sasthi.' So saying, the bright goddess took hold of the child, gave it breath and life, and made a gesture as if she was going to take it away with her to the realms of glory. The king, petrified with fear, addressed many a fervent prayer, beseeching her to restore the infant to him. The goddess, pleased with the incense of praise, said, 'O thou son of Svayambhū Manu, thou art the lord of the three worlds. If thou promise to celebrate my praise as long as thou livest, I will give the child to thee.' As a grateful return for her favour he celebrated the worship of Sasthi with the utmost pomp. From that time the worship of Sasthi became one of the most popular institutions in the land of Bharat (India). The proper image of Sasthi is a woman of matronly appearance, painted yellow, riding on a cat, and nursing a child; but usually she is represented by a rude stone, not bigger than a man's head, painted with red-lead, and placed under a *vata* tree in the outskirts of the village; whilst not unfrequently she is worshipped in the form of a branch of the *vata* tree stuck in the yard of a house." *

If the room sacred to Sasthi, in which the young mother is placed, is bare and uncomfortable, the means of restoration of her devotees are most painful too. A drink called jhāl (hot) is made of pepper, chillies, &c., and given her to drink; and even in the hottest months of the year a fire is lighted, near which she is made to lie; and until the fifth day after the birth of the child no attempt is made to clean this place. The child, too, has a warm reception; for from head to foot it is smeared with hot mustard oil, and for hours daily is placed in the bright sunshine. In former times, if the child did not thrive under this treatment, and refused to take nourishment from its mother, it was a common practice to hang it in a basket on a tree to die. It is said that the great Hindu reformer, Chaitanya, was exposed in this manner, and would most probably have died had he not been seen by a passing pilgrim, who declared him to be an incarnation of Vishnu, and prophesied that he would grow up to be a great leader of men.

There is another mode of treatment coming into fashion at the present time, though for the most part it is amongst the worshippers of Vishnu, and as it too can claim authority from the sacred writings, as well as the approval of common sense, it is to be hoped it soon will be universal. It is believed that this plan has the special approval of the god Krishna, and is successful on this account. According to

* "Bengal Peasant Life," p. 44.

this system no hot and spicy drinks are forced upon the mother, nor is a fire made to scorch her in her cheerless room. She is allowed to drink cooling draughts, and but little restriction is placed upon her diet. A day or two after the birth of the child, Hari (Krishna) is worshipped by the grateful mother, and sweetmeats are distributed to the children of the neighbourhood. It is said that those who adopt this method come through their troubles without harm: when this is generally known by the people it will not be at all surprising if the Krishna method altogether supplants the Sasthi.

The earnest desire of every Hindu wife is that she may have a son. According to the popular idea, whilst daughters are a source of anxiety and expense to their parents, sons form their strength and support. One of their proverbs expresses this idea clearly, "Blind sons support their parents, but a prince's daughters extort money from them." Perhaps the deepest root of this desire for sons lies in the fact that the last religious rites of the Hindus can be most successfully performed by their male descendants. In the Mahābhārata is a story conveying this lesson most forcibly. A Hindu had remained unmarried for years after he had attained to manhood. Passing into the spirit-world, he came upon a number of men hanging by their heels from the branch of a tree, with their heads overhanging a deep precipice, whilst rats were gnawing at the ropes which bound them, in momentary fear of being dashed to pieces. Inquiring whom they were, he was told that they were his ancestors for several generations, who were doomed thus to suffer because he had not married, and so failed to procure a son whose proper performance of their funeral ceremonies would have saved them from this pain, and secured entrance for them into heaven. Doubtless this, though not the only one, is the strongest reason which leads all classes of the Hindu community so earnestly to welcome the advent of a son into the family. The words of Jesus are true in an extraordinary degree in

India, when He said that a mother no more remembers the anguish for joy that a man is born into the world. A childless mother is an object of ridicule, whilst a mother of girls only is regarded as having in some special manner given offence to the gods; hence it is that the young wife is buoyed up with the hope that she will soon have a son in her arms; and when, instead of this, a girl is born, though for a little time she may be deceived, very soon the truth comes out; for on the birth of a son the conch shell gives forth its trumpet-like notes to call upon the whole neighbourhood to rejoice with the happy parents; whereas when a daughter is born the shell is silent, and, instead of congratulation, condolences are offered. Though at first the sense of disappointment is very keen, maternal instincts prevail, and the little daughter is welcomed to the mother's heart, and is as dear to the father in the Hindu home as in homes in other lands.

The food to be eaten by the mother whilst occupying the lying-in room (Sutika ghar) is all arranged by laws, even to the one grain of boiled rice that she is permitted to have on the third day after her child's birth; but nothing of importance takes place until the fifth day, when the room is properly cleaned, and its occupant made a little more comfortable than was possible before. On the following day Sasthi is worshipped, and praises are presented to her for her goodness in preserving and giving life. On the night of this day a far more important event is supposed to take place, viz., the fixing of the child's destiny, the arranging of its future life. At this time Vidhātā, a form of Brahmā, is supposed to visit the room, and write upon its forehead the main events of its life. Before the sun goes down various things have to be placed ready for this important visit. There must be a palm leaf, pen and ink, a snake's skin, a brick from a temple of Siva, fruit, wool, money: these are all placed in readiness, and as some one must remain awake during the night, lest the deity should feel slighted, and in anger write a long list of calamities upon the forehead of the unconscious babe, it generally devolves upon the midwife to keep this solemn vigil. If Vidhātā is propitious, a life of prosperity will be arranged; if he is angry, suffering and loss will be the characteristic of the child's experience through life. And it is the belief of the mass of the people that at this time the whole plan of their life's history was written in ineradicable lines. "It is written on my forehead," is a sufficient reason for the greatest calamities and troubles in after life. This superstitious belief largely accounts for the stoical endurance of physical pain, disappointment, and loss, that is so noticeable in the Hindu. What Vidhātā (Fate) has written must come to pass; it is useless, therefore, to attempt to oppose the inevitable.

In his book called "Bengal Peasant Life," Mr. L. B. Dey gives a typical account that the midwives relate of what takes place on this eventful night. "I heard the sound of footsteps at the door, especially on that side where the pen and ink were. The same sound of footfall was heard all along the passage from the door to where the baby was sleeping by his mother. Immediately after, I heard a sound similar to that which is made by a man when writing, but I saw no figure. By the light of the fire, however, I saw a smile playing on the lips of the baby. Shortly after, I heard the sound of retreating footsteps, and I rushed towards the door and said, '*Thākur!* I hope you have written favourably.' The god knew me well, as he had often seen me, and told me what he had written on the forehead of the child, but on condition of the strictest secrecy. I dare not disclose it to you, for if I disclose it, Vidhātā will be angry with me, and will kill me outright by twisting my neck; but rejoice, for the child's forehead is good."

When the child is eight days old, the Atkauri ceremony takes place, so called because eight kinds of peas, rice, &c., are distributed. Children from the neighbourhood come with winnowing fans near the room where the mother and her child are lying, and, after knocking at the door with the fan, inquire after the child's health; and on being told that all is well, they reply, "Let it rest in peace in its mother's arms." Led on by the elder folk, they indulge in a little joking at the father's expense, after which they are regaled with sweetmeats.

When the three weeks (or, in the case of girls, a month) have passed by, the ceremonies for the purification of the mother are proceeded with. Sasthi is again worshipped, her representative being a small branch of the vata (Indian fig) tree. Miss Leslie, in the "Dawn of Light," gives the following account of the purification of a Hindu woman: "Her nails were cut, her hair tied up; she was put in a palanquin, the bedding having been taken out, and carried to the river, a distance of six miles. The bearers waded into the stream with their burden as far as they could go, and the sacred waters gushed in, around, and upon her, shut up in her dark box. She was then carried back all those six miles in her wet clothes, and such was the efficacy of the bath, that from that time she was reckoned ceremonially clean. The neighbours were feasted with sweetmeats, and puja (worship) was offered to the goddess Sasthi." In addition to the feasting at the house as part of this ceremony, twenty-one small baskets, filled with parched rice, plantains, sugar-cane, &c., are sent to as many married women whose husbands are still living. And also the goddess Subhachini, who is said to be a form of Durgā, is worshipped. The reason of this worship is found in the following legend. In a certain village there lived a poor Brāhman boy, who on one occasion, seeing a fishwoman with some beautiful fish, cried because he could not purchase them. The fishwife, seeing his grief, left some of the fish at his house, saying she would call for the money on her way home. In the meantime the mother cooked the fish, but before it was eaten the woman called for her money, and, as the mother of the boy could not pay for it, she consented to take it back, although it had been cooked. Though the boy lost the fish, he tasted the water in which it had been cooked, and was so delighted with its flavour, that he could not resist the temptation of stealing a lame duck belonging to the king, and quietly eating it. The duck was missed, investigation made, and the culprit being discovered, was tried, condemned, and imprisoned. Upon this the boy's mother was almost beside herself with grief. When in this distress Durgā, in the form of Subhachini, appeared to her in a dream, and advised her to worship her under this name. She did so, and as part of her worship made seventeen ducks of rice paste, one of which had a lame leg. The worship was completed, the burnt-offering made, when some of the holy water that had been brought for the sacrifice falling upon the feathers of the stolen duck, brought it back to life; and though its flesh had been eaten by the boy, the living bird was sent back to the king. He, hearing this wonderful event, sent for the mother, who told him the whole story; whereupon, seeing how great a favourite this family must be of the powerful goddess, he ordered the release of the boy, and, acting upon the advice of his ministers, gave him his daughter in marriage. Subhachini is associated with Sasthi in this worship, in the hope that she will take the child, on whose behalf her worship is celebrated, under her especial care, and rescue him from the difficulties that may beset him in his life.

When a boy is six months old, the ceremony of *naming* takes place, and at the same time a festival called Anna prāsan, or rice-eating. On this occasion the child, beautifully dressed and decorated with jewels, is brought into the guest-chamber, and a few grains of cooked rice are put into his mouth. In some families it is the custom to purchase this rice from the priests of some of the great temples; when this is not done, Brāhmans are fed, and laden with presents to purchase their goodwill. As a part of this important feast, the father performs a sort of thanksgiving service called the Vridhi Shrād, in which he makes offerings for the benefit of his ancestors. It will be noticed that these gifts for the good of their ancestors are frequently given by the Hindus, it being believed by them that it is by this means that those who have passed away are supported.

The name-giving, however, is the important event on this occasion. The father proclaims the selected name, though generally it is the mother who has chosen it. "What's in a name?" asks Shakespeare; but often a history of years of disappointment and weary waiting, as well as of present joy, is written in the name a Hindu child bears through life. As Hannah of old, by calling her son Samuel, proclaimed that she had spent years of sadness and deferred hope, and then the gladness with which she welcomed her babe to her bosom; so by the name a Hindu mother gives to her boy, a life's history is often suggested. One story from thousands of similar ones will illustrate this. A Brâhman and his wife had lived together most happily for many years, but remained childless. Their bliss was very greatly marred by this circumstance. The husband had hinted that the time had come for him to supersede the wife of his youth by a second, in the hope that by this means a son might gladden his home. Many prayers had been offered and gifts bestowed; but still no child was given. As a last resource, a long pilgrimage to Kālighat was made, and a vow registered that if a son were given within a certain time, money should be given to the shrine. In due course, as they believed in answer to their prayer, and as a reward for their faith, a son was given; and when the naming-day came, in the name Kāli Prasād (given by the favour of Kāli), the history of the many years of sorrowful waiting, and then of the fulfilment of their desires, is clearly written. There are thousands of Hindus to-day bearing the name of Siva Prasād, Durgā Prasād, Tāra Prasād, &c., because it is the belief of the parents that it was through the bounty of these deities that their sons were given to them.

As a rule the names chosen are those of some of the deities or deified heroes whose deeds of prowess are written in the Rāmāyana and Mahābhārata. Sometimes the humility of the parents is seen as they call their children the servants of some of the gods or goddesses, as, *e.g.*, Durga Dāss, Kāli Dāss. A child never bears the same name as his father. Girls are named after goddesses, as Lakshmi, Ganga, &c.; or after flowers, as Padma (a lotus) and Kāmini. A strange practice prevails where a number of children have been taken away by death. Instead of calling them by the names of the deities they are called Dukhi (pain), Tiu Kauri (three cowry shells), Hāran (the lost one), &c., the idea being that when Yama, the god of Death, stalks along with his noose in his hand, and asks, Who goes there?—hearing such names as these, he will pass them by as unworthy of his notice, and so their lives are prolonged. In after years sometimes other names may be added, when it is seen that these have served the purpose of saving their children from Yama's noose.

In addition to the name chosen by the parents, and given during infancy, another name is selected by the astrologer who casts the horoscope of the child, which has as its initial a letter from the particular star that ruled at the hour of its birth. A child, *e.g.*, born in the last division of Virgo's rule, whose ordinary name is Gopāl, appears in ceremonial documents, say, as Thākur Dāss, because Th is the last letter of the Sanskrit word for Virgo. Whilst speaking of names it may be stated here that though the Hindus of course bear the family name in addition to those selected by their parents, they are not generally known by them. Excepting in places where European customs prevail, a man named Hari Narāyana Banerjea would seldom or never be called so, but Hari Narāyana Bābu, the family name being usually dropped in ordinary conversation. And when a student obtains a title from the Sanskrit colleges, the title is taken as a surname in place of the family name.

Perhaps the most important ceremony connected with the birth of a Hindu child is the preparation of his horoscope. The precise moment of birth is noted and given to the astrologer, who, according to the fee paid, prepares a more or less elaborate forecast of the child's fate. The chief real service that this document serves in after life, where births are not registered by government officials, is to determine the exact age of its owner, and in disputes that are carried into the law courts this document is considered of equal value with a register of birth as kept in the police registers in England. Where evils are indicated or good foretold in this prophetic scroll, the Hindu seeks to obtain deliverance from the one, and to obtain the other by liberal donations to the gods. It seems strange at first, perhaps, that men should trust to these guesses, but the desire to penetrate into the darkness of the future seems to be almost universal. Most important events sometimes hang upon what has been written by the astrologers; marriage arrangements that would have been satisfactorily completed are broken off when, on the horoscopes of the intended bride and bridegroom being compared, it is found that they were born under mutually hostile stars.

CHAPTER II.

THE HINDU HOME.

After describing the ceremonies attendant upon the birth of a Hindu we naturally pass on to consider the character of the dwelling-place in which he will live. In order to understand this it will be necessary to dismiss at once and entirely from the mind all notions that cling round the word home as the word is used in England, for there is nothing at all answering to this in the Hindu home. I shall first speak of the dwellings, and then of those who occupy them.

Amongst the middle and upper classes, no Hindu about to marry would think, as we do here, of having a home of his own. It would be quite contrary to his ideas of propriety to leave his wife alone in a house whilst he went about his ordinary work; neither, if his duties called him to a distance, would he think of taking his wife to live with him there. When he marries he considers that his father's house is the safest and best place for his wife to dwell in; consequently there is no house to be built or rented; he simply conducts his bride to the family house where a room is prepared for her reception.

The typical Hindu family house is built in the form of a quadrangle, with an open courtyard in the centre. Opposite to the entrance gate is a platform built to receive the images that are made for the periodic religious festivals that are held in honour of the various deities. On the ground floor the rooms to right and left of the courtyard are used largely as store-rooms, offices, &c.; whilst over these are the public reception rooms, well lighted and generally well furnished, some of them having chairs, &c., for the convenience of European visitors. Here also is a room in which the family idol is kept, before which the priest performs service generally twice a day. All these apartments are used by the male members of the family only. Excepting at feasts the meals are not taken here, unless there may happen to be a number of visitors other than members of the family who are not admitted into the more private portion of the house.. From the back of the courtyard a passage conducts into a second and smaller yard which is also surrounded by rooms in which the lady members of the family live. Here the meals are eaten, and here the sleeping apartments of the family are to be found. The guests sleep in the rooms adjoining the outer courtyard. These inner rooms are generally much smaller than those in the more public part of the house; and the windows are also smaller and placed high in the walls, for Manu distinctly declared that it was not right for a "woman to look out of the windows." During the day the gentlemen generally occupy the more public rooms, as they may be transacting business, or amusing themselves in various ways, whilst the women are engaged in household duties or in their own forms of recreation. As it is considered indecorous for a man to speak to his wife during the day, their only time for conversation is when they retire to their own apartment for the night. And as it is not considered right for a married woman to look at or address her husband's elder brothers, it will be clearly realized that anything like the social home-life of an English house is impossible under such conditions. It is more like hotel life than that of a home. As during the day the men usually associate with the men, and the women with the women, and even during the meals the husband sits down to his food with his wife attending on him as a servant, and not eating with him as an equal, there is, there can be nothing at all answering to the pleasant sociality of an English dinner-table. When further it is remembered that in some of these immense houses over three hundred people live together it will be still more clearly seen how vast is the difference between the Hindu and the English home. Few things in England seem to please the Hindus who come over here more than the sociability of an English home.

Of course the bulk of the people do not live in these palatial dwellings. I shall now give a description of the typical home of the ryots, the rural classes who answer to our very small farmers in England, and with slight modifications this would be a true description of the homes of the artizans—of all, in fact, excepting the very poor, who are unable to keep their wives in any way secluded, great though their desire is to do so. This account is taken from Mr. Dey's book on "Bengal Peasant Life" (p. 28): "You enter the house with your face to the East, through a small door of mango wood in the street, and you go at once to the *uthàn*, or open yard, which is indispensable to the house of every peasant in the country. On the west side of the yard, on the same side as the gate, . . . stands the *bara ghar*, or big hut. This is the biggest, the neatest, and most elaborately finished of all Badan's huts. Its walls, which are of mud, are of great thickness; the thatch, which is of the straw of paddy, is more than a cubit deep; the bamboo framework, on which the thatch is laid, is well compacted together, every interstice being filled with the long and slender reed called sărā, alternating with another of red colour; the middle beam, which supports the thatch, though it is not made of the costly teak or săl, is made of the palmyra, and the floor is raised at least five feet from the ground. The hut is about 16 cubits long, and 12 broad, including the verandah, which faces the yard, and which is supported by props of palmyra. It is divided into two compartments of unequal size, the bigger one being Badan's sleeping-room, and the smaller one being the store-room of the family. . . . The verandah is the parlour of the family. There friends and acquaintances sit on mats. In Badan's sleeping-room are kept the brass vessels of the house and other valuables. There is no bedstead in it, for Badan sleeps on the mud floor, a mat and a quilt stuffed with cotton interposing between his body and mother earth. There is not much light in the room, for the thatch of the verandah [coming down very near the ground] prevents its admission, while there is but one small window high up in the wall towards the street. I need scarcely add that there is no furniture in the room: . . . there is only, in one corner, a solitary box. In one side of the room two whole bamboos are stuck into the walls, on which clothes are hung, and on which the bedding is put up in the day.

"On the south side of the yard, and at right angles to the big hut, is a smaller hut of far inferior construction, which . . . is used as a lumber-room, or rather as a tool-room, for keeping the implements of husbandry. . . . In the verandah of this little hut is placed the *dhenki*, or rice-husking pedal. From this circumstance the little hut is called the *Dhenki-sālā*.

"In the south-east corner of the yard, and at right angles to the Dhenkisālā, is another hut of somewhat better construction, in which Gayarāma (Badan's brother) sleeps, and a verandah which serves the purpose of a kitchen. . . . The only other hut on the premises is the cow-house, . . . situated to the north of the yard, nearly parallel to the big hut. . . . The eastern side of the premises opens on a tank."

As the houses differ in arrangement from our own, the Hindu family system is even more unlike anything that prevails amongst us. It is a patriarchal system pure and simple, as the head of the family rules supreme in the home, and all the money earned by each member of the family, with some few exceptions, comes into his hands, and is disbursed according to his commands. How long this style has been in vogue it is impossible to say, but it was probably brought with the Aryan immigrants into India from their home in Central Asia. It has all the force of a religious institution. "Religion shaped itself according to the wishes of the legislator, and thus what was intrinsically useful became a legal and religious institution of the land." And it is interesting to see how in this, as in so many instances, sacred texts can be found to support a system which, but for this, would long ago have passed away. The text of Manu, which is held to teach authoritatively on this subject, is the following: "Three persons, a wife, a son, and a slave, are declared by law to have in general no wealth of their own; the wealth which they may earn is regularly acquired for the man to whom they belong." And Nārada, another authority, declares of a son: "He is of age and independent in case his parents be dead; during their lifetime he is dependent, even though he is grown old."

The Hindu family system may be described as a sort of Joint Stock Company, in which the head of the family is managing director, with almost unlimited powers; or as a little kingdom, in which he is an almost absolute sovereign. The sons, grandsons, nephews, who form the family, regard all their earnings as belonging to the common treasury; and their expenditure is under the direct control of the karta, or head. Thus it happens that when several members of the family are absent from home engaged in various ways, the balance of their salaries or profits must be remitted to the karta. This has its advantages and its disadvantages. There is a home in which a man can leave his wife with confidence when he is hundreds of miles away engaged in business, or filling some government appointment. This, to the Hindu who would not regard it as a safe procedure to have his family with him in an ordinary house, is a source of immense comfort. Once a year, if his business is distant from his home, he takes leave, that he may have a few days with his family. There is also the certainty of support in case of sickness or permanent incapacity for work. But it has its drawbacks too. An idle, worthless son has no necessity laid upon him to work; he can obtain all the necessaries of life without it; and many a family has one or more members who are mere parasites, doing nothing whatever to increase the income of the family; and, according to our ideas of life, it is destructive of the most sacred institution, the home. Often, however, the idle son is not altogether without his place in society. If he will not or cannot go out to earn money as the other members of the family do, it is something if he remain at home to look after the domestic and other affairs, and to afford protection to the ladies who live there. Where all are workers, if the head of the family is growing old, the sons take it in turn to remain at home, perhaps for a year at a time; or the one who has the worst prospects of advancement will resign his appointment at a distance and devote all his time to the care of the family.

In a description of the members of the Hindu home, the karta, or head, must first be considered. This will be the father, or grandfather, of the present generations of workers. Until recent years *all* the earnings of the family were under his absolute control, and without his sanction no important transaction of any member of the family would be considered as settled. All sales and purchases of property would be in his name, and it is he who arranges for the marriage of the children. The following description of the typical orthodox Hindu karta is given by a Hindu gentleman, Mr. B. Mulleck, in his account of the Hindu family (p. 18, ff.): "In his habiliments he is all simplicity. An ordinary cloth of five yards in length constitutes his usual costume. When he goes out he takes an additional piece of cloth to wrap his trunk with. To wear heeled shoes or boots is inconsistent with his venerable position, and he prefers loose slippers. It is his habit to shave his head and face clean, leaving only a tuft of hair about the centre of his head unshaved. This and a bead necklace mark him as a Hindu, and are prized by him as Hindu distinctions. The only perfumery he uses is mustard oil. . . . His education is not of a high order. He can read and write. At all times he is a lover of learning, and such of his children as are mindful of their studies are his especial favourites. Devoid of a liberal education himself, he is possessed of strong common sense, and his judgments generally smack of practical wisdom. . . . The authors of the Rāmāyana and Mahābhārata are his great pets, and the stories contained in those works delight his imagination.

"For literary and philosophical culture he greatly depends on the priest, versed in ancient lore. He accepts the truths enunciated by him without question or cavil, and stores them up in his mind. . . . The only science he cares for is arithmetic, in the knowledge of which he is generally profound. . . . In bookkeeping, too, he has some experience.

"In regard to morals, the karta knows that falsehood is a sin. Evasion and equivocation sometimes are his practices when direct falsehood is impossible. To avert loss or injury he may tell an untruth. His self-love verges on selfishness, though he is just and fair in his dealings. . . . Servile obedience is constitutional with him when he has to deal with superiors in office. Flattery is the oil he uses to soften their minds. He is possessed of plenty of gratitude to those who have benefitted him; but his hatred towards his enemies is implacable." Of course, it is the Bengali of the old school whose picture has here been drawn, the young men of the present generation, when their turn comes to reign in the Hindu homes, will manifest a very different character.

When the head of the family dies his younger brother may take his place; or if he has no brother, his eldest son will rise to this dignity; but as a rule it is not until a man has attained to a good age that he becomes a karta. And such is the respect shown to the person holding this position that an elder brother will exercise as much authority over his brothers, who may be but a year or two younger than himself, as his father had done before him. In the present age, where the younger members of the family will not submit to the authority of an elder brother, a partition of the property is made; but frequently before this is agreed upon a good part of the estate has been squandered in useless litigation.

Next in authority to the karta is the grihini, or chief wife in the family. This may be the wife, or it may be the mother of the karta. In all matters relating to the management of the house and to the conduct of the female members of the family, her influence is as great as that of the karta in all that concerns the men. She may occasionally consult the head of the family; but this is by no means the invariable rule with her. And as his power is felt in the more public concerns of the family, so hers is not without influence in the domestic arrangements. She superintends if she does not actually do all the cooking, and it is quite possible for her to make the home a happy or miserable one for the younger women. "The grihini leads a life of self-denial. Her personal comforts are few [when, as frequently happens, she is a widow]. She lives upon the coarsest of meals and wears the commonest of raiment. She works from morn till night. She fasts twice or thrice a month, and keeps vigils for securing the blessing of the gods towards her children, and, to make assurance doubly sure, commands her daughters and daughters-in-law to do the same. . . . It is her pride to enforce purity and cleanliness with the utmost rigour. She bathes and changes her clothes half-a-dozen times a day. If she is cooking, she must wear clothes that have been washed and dried in the sun. When in the store-room she must have another suit to wear. Should she be preparing the offerings for the household god there is another change of her habiliments. . . . The house is washed many times a day, and the cooking utensils undergo the pangs of constant friction." . . . And other members of the family must follow her lead in this respect. Added to all this is a great number of religious festivals which she observes, the main object of which is to obtain the prosperity of the family.

In cases where the husband is dead it sometimes happens that the widow has charge to a large extent of the family property, and all the legal affairs are conducted in her name.

Next to the karta and grihini come the sons and their wives. It is evident, from what has gone before, that in the home their position is a subordinate one. The sons may earn the money by which the family is supported, and their wives may have a fair share of the daily work of the home, but in the management of affairs they have little power. The only resource that is open to a son's wife when her husband's family make things unpleasant is to complain at night to her husband, and to go for a longer or shorter visit to her father's house. And if all one hears of these matters is correct, when the husband is absent from home for a year or two at a time the position of some of these women is anything but enviable. The bulk of them being totally uneducated cannot even apprise their husbands of what is troubling them at home; but many of the present generation having learned to write are able to get some relief in pouring out their griefs to their husbands and in receiving their cheering letters in reply.

In addition to these the ordinary members of the family, in cases where a girl has married a Kulin Brahman, or where her father is rich and her husband poor, the girls remain in their father's house, and their husbands become members of the family. In these cases, as a rule, they are drones in the hive, feeding upon the generosity of their wives' relations. These by swelling the numbers of the family tend to destroy altogether the privacy of the home.

There is, however, one thing to be said in favour of this family system: there is no poor law, and there are no poorhouses in India. The idle and the weaker members of the family find shelter and maintenance at the expense of their more industrious and healthy relatives. Occasionally men are to be found wandering about leading a beggar's life; but though the idle are not always treated kindly, it would be considered a disgrace for them to be in actual want; and, to avoid this scandal, food and home are given to many who would doubtless be better were they forced to toil.

A notice of the Hindu family would be incomplete were no notice taken of some other members.

First of all there is the family priest. Every well-appointed house has its shrine with its image or some representation of the family god. The father, unless he be a Brāhman, cannot officiate; for this purpose he must either have a priest supported from the common fund, or he must share his services with some other family. The priest's work is to bathe and anoint the idol, recite the ritual, and make the offerings of fruits and flowers that the family present. Occasionally the head and other members of the family may be present during the performance of this worship; but as a rule the priest is there alone, and receives as his perquisite the offerings that are given to the idol. In some cases there may also be a piece of land assigned for this expense which some pious ancestor has bequeathed. The priest is also present at all the important events, such as birth, marriage, and funeral ceremonies, for which he obtains additional presents as fees for the service he renders. Generally a room in the house is assigned for the priest's use, for, being of a higher caste than the family in whose house he lives, of course he does not take his food with them.

Next to the priest, though not second in importance, may be mentioned the guru, or religious guide. Every Hindu must have his guru, as it is by him that he is initiated into the privileges of the Hindu religion. The power of these men over their disciples is almost unparalleled in history. It is even taught in the Hindu scriptures that it is better for a man to offend the gods than his guru, because if he offend the gods his guru can intercede with the gods on his behalf and win their favour; but if a man offend the guru, there is none can appease his wrath; the curse of a guru will condemn a man to untold miseries in hell. It should be noticed that neither the guru nor the astrologer live in the family houses of those to whom they minister.

Then comes the astrologer, whose work it is to determine the proper time for the initiation and completion of any important work of the family. If the season be inopportune, no skill, no care in its execution, can ensure success. It is he who fixes the hour for weddings, religious festivals, starting on a journey, commencing a new business, &c.; and without his advice nothing is attempted.

We have now considered the chief persons in the Hindu home, and shall pass on to consider the ceremony of initiation into the Hindu community.

CHAPTER III.

THE GURU, AND INITIATION INTO HINDUISM.

WHEN a Hindu boy is about eight years of age, in some castes not until he is about twelve, the important ceremony of initiation takes place. It is a strange coincidence that as in the Christian Church there is the Sacrament of Confirmation, by which the person is formally received into the Christian fold, so in Hinduism there is a rite administered by which the child is supposed to enter the sacred pale. This rite is performed by the guru, a man altogether distinct from, and having no connection at all with, the priest. In some sects—and the Hindu community at the present time is just a conglomeration of sects—the guru need not be a Brāhman, but the office may be assumed by any who desire it. At this ceremony, in the case of the Brāhman, Kihshetriya, and Vaisya castes, who are regarded as twice born, the sacred poitra, or thread, is put on for the first time. This is a simple necklace made of a few strains of thread, which is the mark of the spiritual aristocracy of India; and in most cases an earl is not more proud of his coronet than is the Hindu of this thread which marks him as a special favourite of the gods.

On an appointed day the guru of the family calls, and the youth who is to receive the Seed text (Vij mantra) must fast, bathe, and appear in the most spotless of garments. The youth is then left alone with the guru, who selects for him some special deity, whom he is to regard as his chief object of worship amongst the many thousands that form the Hindu Pantheon. The teacher then teaches the child a text; it may be simply the name of the selected deity, or some few Sanskrit words that have a similar sound, which must be kept a profound secret in after life, and which it is the duty of the disciple to repeat mentally or in whispers an hundred and eight times every day. The members of many of the Hindu sects carry a rosary, which they use to count the times they repeat this mantra; and as a sign of their humility some carry this in a bag, that it may not be seen by others; but, Pharisee-like, they do not object to this bag being seen, nor do they hide the movement of their fingers in counting their beads as they stand in the market and other conspicuous places muttering this charm. So strong is the superstition regarding the necessity for secrecy in connection with the guru's mantra that I have known some Christian converts shrink from making public the phrase taught to them when they were initiated, lest the anger of the gods should somehow vent itself upon them. From those that I have heard it it is clear that as a rule they are meaningless words strung together with a rhyming sound.

The person receiving the mantra is regarded ever after as the disciple of the teacher who gives it. This relationship continues through life, the son of a guru often taking up his father's disciples when he dies. In many cases this is a most lucrative post, as, influenced by superstitious fears, the Hindus give largely to these men who are believed to wield almost divine powers. The guru visits his disciples about once a year, and if he be a really earnest man, as some undoubtedly are, he avails himself of this opportunity to teach them some portions of Hindu mythology, or other lessons in religion. I have often seen the guru with two or three disciples sitting at his feet listening most earnestly as he read a few lines from some of their sacred books, and then expounded them for their benefit. As a rule, however, they are ignorant and selfish men, their chief object in visiting their disciples being to obtain the customary fee. The following account of the guru from the pen of a Hindu gentleman * will show the general opinion of these men by the more enlightened of the community:—

"Akin to the priest is the guru. The guru is the medium of salvation, and therefore his position is higher than that of the priest. Woe to the Hindu whose body and soul have not been purified by the spiritual counsels of the guru! He lives and dies a veritable beast on earth, with no hope of immortal bliss. However charitable may be his gifts, however spotless his character, be his faith in the gods ever so strong, his salvation is impossible without the guru.† Both the guru and the priest vie with each other in ignorance and conceit. Both are covetous, unprincipled, and up to every vice; but the guru is much more revered than his adversary, owing to the former being a less frequent visitor, and the speculative and mysterious nature of his avocations. The guru's sway over the family is complete. His visits are generally annual, unless he be in a fix [for money] on account of an impending matrimonial or funeral ceremony in his house, when he certainly comes to you for his ghostly fee." There are many who simply pass their time in the disciples' houses, going from one to another and remaining as long as they wish, imposing on the hospitality and trading on the superstitious fears of their hosts.

"At one time these visits were regarded as auspicious events. Paterfamilias would consider the morn to have auspiciously dawned which brought with it the radiant face of his guru. . . . Dame Nature has selected him for his precious physiological and anatomical gifts. Picture to yourself a fat, short man having what the doctors call "an apoplectic make," of pretty fair complexion, round face, short nose, long ears, and eyes protruding from their sockets. Picture that face as sleek

* "The Hindu Family in Bengal," p. 156.

† In the chapters on the Hindu sects it will be seen that in many of them respect for the guru forms a most prominent feature of the religious life.

and soft, shorn of hairy vegetation, and the crown of the head perpetually kept in artificial baldness save a long tuft of hair in the centre. . . . His countenance does not show the least sign of worldly care; plenty and ease have always been his environment. . . . He comes with half-a-dozen famished beggars, each of whom has an important part to play in his lord's drama. One prepares his food, another his hemp smoking and opium pills, a third looks after his treasure, a fourth shaves him and anoints his body, whilst the sixth helps him in his amatory transactions. These are not paid servants, but mere hirelings, who follow him through fire and through water for anything 'that hath a stomach in it.'

"At the sight of the guru and his crew the whole house is thrown into commotion, and even the inmates of the Zenana for the nonce lose their equanimity. 'The lord has come' is the alarm given by the karta, and it is echoed and re-echoed in the whole household. Preparations for his entertainment on an extensive scale are immediately ordered; all the while the wily guru laughs in his sleeve with the thought that so long as there are cunning men in the world there must be fools. The karta is seen to reach the doorpost of his house and fall prostrate before the guru, who compliments him by coolly putting his foot on the devotee's head as if it was a stepping-stone to the attainment of higher honours in store for him. It is habitual with the guru to enter the house with a sorry face and cold demeanour. There is a vein of policy in it—viz., to terrify the karta, and extort from him a higher fee. This attempt sometimes causes unpleasantness. We have seen gurus insulting their spiritual disciples, cursing and swearing, and exhibiting conduct as would, under any other circumstances, justify his immediate expulsion from the house.

"On entering the house the guru is escorted to a sitting-chamber, furnished with new carpets (for it is sacrilegious to make him sit on used ones), and is requested to be seated. He will not sit at first till the fascination of large promises becomes irresistible, and he yields. Large demands are sometimes made, which are generally acceded to by the terrified disciples. After this the members of the family are inquired after, and are dismissed with the touch of the holy man's foot. After his bath the guru is regaled with the choicest food, and the whole family and their neighbours esteem it a great privilege to partake of what he may leave."

Some of these men are very rich, and make a great show of wealth as they travel in state from village to village. It is rather a surprising thing that, notwithstanding this great display of wealth and comfort, they should continue to retain their hold of the Hindu mind; for, as a rule, it is asceticism in their religious teachers rather than enjoyment, that seems to have the greatest influence over them. The sacred writings abound with stories of the way in which men, by hard and long-continued penance, have prevailed over the gods even; it is seldom that the self-indulgent are described as wielding superhuman power.

It is in the Tantras, probably the latest of all the religious writings of the Hindus, that the powers of the guru are set forth with the greatest extravagance. According to these books, as the following quotation shows, his power is almost infinite:—"Of this word (guru), the *g* is the cause of friction, the *r* destroys sin, the *u* is Siva himself, the whole word is the Eternal Brahmā excellent and inexplicable. He whose lips pronounce the sound guru, with what sin is he chargeable. The articulation of *g* annihilates the sin even of killing a Brāhman; the sins of the present birth are removed by pronouncing *u*, of ten thousand births by the pronunciation of *ru*. Parasurāma murdered his mother, and Indra destroyed a Brāhman, yet they both obtained absolution by pronouncing the word guru." Though this is the teaching of the form of religion which, it is said, Siva sent his son Ganesa from heaven purposely to teach, the gurus may be and are guilty of the grossest immorality without any very great loss of respect amongst the more ignorant classes of the community.

Having spoken of the *initiation* of a Hindu into the system, it naturally follows that we speak of the religious sects into one of which he must be initiated. Strictly speaking, there is now no grand division of what may be called orthodox and heterodox systems ; but the whole community of the Hindus is divided into a great number of sects, all to a greater or less degree differing in faith and practice from each other, and also from the Hinduism of their forefathers before it had been modified by the teaching of Buddha and his disciples.

HINDU SECTS.

CHAPTER I.

GENERAL CHANGES OF HINDUISM.

Before passing on to notice minutely the peculiarities of the many sects into which the Hindus are divided, it will not be out of place to give a very brief sketch of the phases through which Hinduism has passed.

When the Indian branch of the great Āryan family migrated to India, the people brought with them the general religious ideas and mythology common to the whole. The deities of the Vedic age differ little from those of the older forms of the Greek and Latin; whilst the forms of worship were almost identical. After settling down in India the Rishis or Sages developed the ideas they brought with them; and the form of this development was largely determined by the character of the country into which they had come, and the manifestations of the natural world by which they were surrounded. The beliefs and practices of the original inhabitants of the country also very largely tended to modify the forms Hinduism assumed after the Hindus had resided for a lengthened period in India. As this religious system, with its elaborate ritual, developed, as the restrictions it imposed upon its adherents increased in severity, as the distinctions of caste became more marked, and the privileges claimed by the higher rendered the position of the despised classes more intolerable, the people became prepared to listen to the teaching of Buddha, who rose as a great Reformer, teaching the equality and brotherhood of man, and pointing out how the highest good was attainable by all. For a long time this work of preparation must have been going on; the dissatisfaction with the Hinduism of the day must have been very general, otherwise Buddha's immense success would not have been possible. The great teacher commenced his work as a Reformer about B.C. 600; by B.C. 300 his system had become almost universal in North India.

Gautama at first did not manifest antagonism to Hinduism; he was trained in its tenets and followed its teaching, and the larger part of his doctrine is to be found in the beliefs of the ascetics with whom he associated. What he did was to select, modify, and emphasize certain parts that appeared to him of supreme importance. He found Hinduism existing, and his system was in itself a modified form of it.

Before his death Gautama had gained an immense number of disciples, for from the first his was a proselytizing religion, and on his death a council was held for the purpose of appointing a leader. A century later, a second council met, and almost a century later, a third council. These councils had a two-fold purpose: the revision of the creed, and the selection of methods by which the teaching of the system could be spread. Missionaries were sent far and wide, and this religion became "established" in several Hindu States. As a result of this there is no doubt that from, say, the 2nd century B.C., to, say, the 4th or 5th A.D., Buddhism was very largely embraced by the people as well as the accepted religion of the rulers.

What was there in Buddhism that will at all account for its rapid spread throughout India? It exalted kings. Previously kings had existed, but they were controlled by the Brāhmans. Buddha's teaching undermined the power of the Brāhmans. It repudiated caste. Gradually the chains of this slavery were forged and rivetted on the Hindu mind; and when Buddha proclaimed that all were alike free, his words were sweet to the low caste and down-trodden races. It taught each man to use his various powers; that he was an integral part of the great system of the universe, and not a mere machine.

Great was its popularity we know; but how its doctrines gradually spread; how the Hindus, who were partial to the old system of things, gradually came to see in Buddhism an enemy and not a friend; how the two at length came to an open rupture; how they carried on mutual warfare, a struggle to the death—these most important and deeply interesting questions at present must be left without any intelligible answer, for the conquering Hinduism has left but few ruins to mark the places where once its powerful and most popular rival had gathered its devotees. The first record of persecution is about A.D. 196. "King Sadraca destroyed the workers of iniquity." This, however, could be but a partial persecution, as in the fifth century Buddhism was still supreme in many places. Kumarila Bhatta is said to have been the chief leader of the persecution, for it was at his instigation that the decree went forth, "Let those who slay not be slain, the old men amongst the Buddhists, and the babe from the Bridge of Rāma to the Snowy Mountains." And Kumarila worked for the accomplishment of his great purpose of conquest, not merely by the use of the civil power, but by presenting Hinduism in a far more attractive character than it had previously assumed. He appealed to the Vedas as the divine authority, and employed all his skill and learning to controvert the tenets of Buddhism. At the end of the fifth century the hierarchs of Buddhism found an asylum in China; and numbers of the people migrated eastward to lands where the doctrines, now persecuted in India, had found a home; or to countries where as yet its doctrines had not been promulgated. As late as the twelfth century, it is known that a few Buddhists remained in certain parts of the country, but now none are to be seen. A more complete change of religion in a country the world has seldom seen.*

* For a fuller account of Buddhism and its history, see Dr. Rhys Davids' book published by the Society for Promoting Christian Knowedge.

But though Buddhism became the fashionable religion of India, there must have been a large number still adhering to the older forms, who, though suppressed for a time, had been gradually recovering their strength. After struggles, extending probably over centuries, Saivaism (the worship of Siva) became common, and it again in its turn had largely to give way to Vaishnavism. Saivaism was started in Benares by Paramatma Kalanola; Vaishnavism at Kanchi by Lakshman Acharjya. In the eighth century a great impulse was given to Saivaism by Sankarācharjya, a great Vedantist. Though himself a Deist, he encouraged idolatry in the case of the ignorant. It is recorded that one of his last sayings was this: "O Lord, pardon my three sins; I have in contemplation clothed Thee who art shapeless with a shape; I have in praise described Thee who art indescribable; and by visiting the Tirthas (shrines) I have ignored Thine omnipresence."

From this brief sketch it will be noticed that the religion of the Hindus has assumed three distinct forms: the Vedic, the Buddhistic, and the present Brāhmanic; the transitions from one to another probably being centuries in duration.

CHAPTER II.

*GENERAL REMARKS ON THE HINDU SECTS.**

To a cursory observer Hinduism appears to be a compact system, and the people themselves are under the impression that their present forms of religious worship have existed from time immemorial. They know of little change, because their learned pundits have not excelled in writing history. And as there is no so-called orthodox church persecuting those who may differ from them, and at the present time no mutual jealousies and rival factions fighting against each other, but a general indifference regarding the beliefs of other than those of their own sects, any one living amongst them may imagine that this has been the usual state of affairs in religious matters. But a closer examination shows that there is as great (if not even greater) diversity of opinion and practice amongst the peoples of India as amongst those of Christendom: the persecuting spirit, however, being absent because of the general want of earnestness in matters religious. They cannot proselytize to any large extent because the great blessings to be enjoyed through the Hindu religion can, according to a fundamental belief common to all classes, only be obtained by those who are born in Hindu families. Where some of the aboriginal tribes have of late years been absorbed into the Hindu community, they form only the very lowest caste, and have as their chief hope the possibility of rising in future births into the higher and more favoured ones. And

* For the materials of this chapter I am largely indebted to the book on Hindu sects by Dr. H. H. Wilson.

so latitudinarian are the leaders of Hindu society in this wicked age, the Kali Yuga, that they believe they are only fulfilling the prophecies of degeneration that have been made centuries gone by, when they teach that it does not matter what a man believes so long as he observes the rules of the particular caste to which he may belong.

So far does the liberality of the Hindu go, that whilst firmly believing in the divine origin of his own religion, he will freely admit that Mahometanism may be also given by God for those who embrace that system, and that Christianity may be given by the same Being for those who worship Him according to its teaching. And further, that it is the duty of those who have received these differing forms to continue in the system in which they were born. In the bazaars in Calcutta are to be found pictures which clearly illustrate this phase of Hindu contemporary thought. There is a figure of a man with eight arms, each of a different colour, as the representatives of the gods of the universe. These arms indicate Brahmā, Vishnu, Siva, Rāma, Kāli and Durgā, the most popular of the Hindu deities; the remaining two, each holding a book in hand, are to represent Mahomet with the Korān, and Jesus with the Bible. The Hindu knows that only birth can admit a man into the privileged classes of Hindu society, and therefore believes that it would be worse than casting pearls before swine to preach to and attempt to proselytize other nations; he does not seek to interfere with men of other religions, nor to molest those who as Hindus may differ in creed from himself. He lets other people alone to walk on in their own way, whilst he asks in like manner that they would not attempt to disturb him in his religious beliefs. Quite as earnestly as the Christian child sings, "I thank the goodness and the grace that on my birth have smiled" in making me a Christian, the Hindu thanks the gods that he is a Hindu; and the best wish he can express on behalf of those not so highly privileged is that in some future birth they may appear on the earth as Hindus.

There are gods many and lords many recognized by the Hindus, and though each has his own chosen deity, *one* whose name is on his lips many times every day, one to whom the larger part of his offerings are made, he recognizes the godhead of all the rest, and when the proper day for their worship comes will generally take a more or less enthusiastic part with their most earnest devotees. I say *generally*, for there are some practices common to the worship of Siva and the various forms of his consort Kāli which the devout worshippers of Vishnu regard with abhorrence. There can be no doubt whatever in the minds of those who read the Purānas, which are largely occupied with the praise of one particular deity, and to anathematizing those who neglect him, that however free from sectarian bigotry the present generation of Hindus may be, this was not always the temper they cherished. There was as bitter animosity, as burning jealousy, and as fierce conflicts between the worshippers of the rival deities as the world has seen. But with the general deterioration of the people, religious earnestness has given place to indifference, and the Hindu of to-day will calmly look on, though he may not actually join in religious rites that he believes his own particular object of worship regards with detestation. Nay, many of the priests who officiate at the worship of the goddess Durgā, which worship is celebrated by the offering of sacrifices of buffaloes and goats, are in private the worshippers of Vishnu, one great characteristic of whose worship is the sacredness of life. An old Brāhman pundit and priest, with whom I frequently conversed on these subjects, told me that in his own daily worship he first made an offering to his own chosen deity, Nārāyana (Vishnu), and when this was done, he threw a handful of rice broadcast for the other deities to scramble for it, and it was his hope that by thus recognizing the existence and authority of these, though there were no clear notion in his mind respecting any one of them, that he would keep them in good humour towards himself. He further assured me that the general idea of the Hindu was this: we must worship our own chosen deity with earnestness and devotion; but in order not to be disrespectful to the others, and bring upon ourselves their resentment, we must give a general acknowledgment of their existence and authority. Stories are to be found in the Purānas clearly teaching that the most earnest devotee of one deity is not at all safe from evils that others may bring upon him—hence arises this practice of a general acknowledgment of the other beings who claim the worship of the people.

In the following sketch of the many sects into which the Hindu community is divided, we shall see that human nature is the same in India as elsewhere; that pride and jealousy have played their parts in causing rival sects to war against each other; and also that some heretical sectarians have sprung up whose teaching has been distinctly opposed to that which is found in the older religious writings. Some have taught that the Vedas themselves were obsolete, and have tried to lessen the authority of the Brāhmans. In the case of Buddha this effort was most successful for centuries; and there is no doubt that it is largely owing to the teaching of that great reformer and his followers that the worship of Vishnu in some of his many incarnations, which is, in some respects, entirely opposed to that of Siva and his wife, is so very general at the present time. Buddhism was almost entirely obliterated, and its followers exiled; but it still lives, with some modifications, under the various forms of Vaishnavism.

One marked distinction of the popular Hinduism of the present day is the substitution of deities that were entirely unknown in the Vedic age for those then commonly worshipped. The gods of the old Pantheon are almost entirely forgotten, whilst others to whose praise the Purānas are devoted have quite taken their place in the popular faith. Attempts with very partial success have been made, it is true, to connect these present-day gods with the gods of the olden time, but it is not difficult to see that this is a mere trick of the writers of the Purānas to catch the faith of the people who would not willingly have departed from the faiths of their fathers. So great has been the change in the objects of worship, that the older deities are scarcely known to the common people, the names even of some being quite forgotten. As a result of the growth of sectarianism, the exclusive laudation of particular deities in the Purānas, and the conflicts to which this rivalry gave rise, "the worship of Brahmā has (almost entirely) disappeared, as that of the whole Pantheon, except Vishnu, Siva, and Sakti, or their modifications: with respect to the two former, in fact, the representatives have borne away the palm from the prototypes, and Krishna, Rāma, or the Linga, are almost the only forms under which Vishnu and Siva are now adored in most parts of India." As an illustration of the way in which the Purānas are devoted to the special lauding of one deity to the disparagement of the others, Siva, a god who in some of the other Purānas is made the supreme, is in the Padma Purāna represented as saying that "those who adore other gods than Vishnu, or who hold that others are his equals, and all Brāhmans who are not Vaishnavas (worshippers of Vishnu) are not to be looked at, touched, or spoken to." Siva, in acknowledging that the distinguishing marks of his votaries—the skull, tiger's skin, and ashes, are reprobated by the Vedas—states that he was directed by Vishnu to inculcate their adoption purposely to lead those who adopted them into error. Nāmuchi and other demons had become so powerful by the purity of their devotious that Indra and the other gods were unable to oppose them. The gods in their distress had recourse to Vishnu, who instructed Siva to introduce the Saiva tenets and practices, by which the demons were beguiled, and thereby rendered wicked and weak.

Again the Bhāgavata says, "Those who worship Siva (Bhava) and those who follow their doctrines are heretics and enemies of the sacred Sastras;" whilst the Padma Purāna declares "from even looking at Vishnu the wrath of Siva is kindled, and from his wrath we fall assuredly into a horrible hell: let not, therefore, the name of Vishnu even be pronounced."

As a further illustration of the sectarian character of the Purānas, in the Padma Purāna the eighteen books are classified as follows: six of them which have a general bias in favour of Siva, and inculcate his peculiar worship, are said to be imbued with the spirit of Tāmasa, or darkness, and the study of them condemns a man to hell; six are imbued with Sātivika, or truth, and are devoted to the praise of Vishnu: the study of these is said to procure Mukti—*i.e.*, final deliverance from the evils of life and absorption into the Deity; and six are said to be imbued with Rājasa, or passion: these are devoted to the praise of Sakti, or the female principle in nature, and their study will ensure entrance into Swarga, or heaven; a less goodly boon than "*mukti*," because its bliss is but temporary; for when a person has enjoyed all the bliss his good deeds have procured for him there, he has to be re-born into the world and again suffer all the ills of life on earth. I shall never forget the lesson I learned from some Brāhmans on this subject. After preaching in a village the priests of a neighbouring temple invited me to their home, and in a confidential manner asked me to tell them in a few words the essence of the religion I was trying to set up in India. After speaking of Jesus and His work, and assuring them that His disciples were by Him made pure and then admitted into (Swarga) heaven—after a little consideration they said if that was all I had to offer, Christianity had no attraction for them; they wished for *mukti*, absorption into Deity, not merely entrance into heaven, the blessedness of which they believed to be terminable.

It should be noticed here that the more intelligent and thoughtful of the Hindus would generally repudiate the idea of being connected with any sect. If asked to describe themselves they would say they are Hindus and Vedantists. And there can be hardly any doubt that they come nearer in belief and worship to their old Āryan forefathers. We may therefore take them as perhaps the most orthodox section, and the others as more or less heterodox. The number of theso is very small; and whilst it is true that they repudiate many of the grosser forms of Hinduism that prevail amongst their more ignorant neighbours, they do not attempt to instruct or raise them to their own higher level. They say that though the more popular forms of Hinduism are not good for themselves, they are suited to the condition of the ignorant masses. And further, though an outsider might be disposed to regard the Vedantist as more in harmony with the older form of the Hindu faith, the people would not for a moment be disposed to acknowledge their superiority in this respect. And certainly authority in the older or more modern Scriptures is to be found for all, even the grossest forms of Hinduism that now prevail.

CHAPTER III.

VEDANTISM, OR THE RELIGION OF THE MORE INTELLIGENT OF THE COMMUNITY.

To speak correctly, this is rather a system of philosophy than of religion; and whilst there are some Vedantists in philosophy who are really and truly polytheists and idolaters, still in the case of many it is their form of religion, and, as said above, may be taken as perhaps the form nearest to orthodox Hinduism from which the teaching of the sects has more or less departed.

What polytheism and the popular forms of Hinduism in their grosser forms are to the mass of the Hindus, Vedantism is to the educated and more intelligent and thoughtful. This system is generally ascribed to Vyasa, the great compiler of the Hindu scriptures, but was probably put into form about 500 B.C. The Mahābhārata gives an account of the way in which it was taught by Krishna to his friend Arjuna. Its main doctrines are as follows :—

1. The nature and attributes of the Divine Being. The Vedanta teaches the unity of God. It speaks of Him as light, and declares that He is eternal, self-existent, immutable, perfect, incomprehensible, omniscient, almighty, formless, supremely happy, and the sustainer of all things. It is most curious to notice how the Hindus can hold these ideas respecting God, and yet at the same time entertain such directly opposite views respecting the various incarnations. Often have I heard men who were worshipping some of the

gross representations of Deity declare Him to be formless, perfect, and pure. This string of the attributes of God is often on the lips of the Hindus, even the very ignorant, though their practice shows conclusively that they cannot realize their true meaning. Vedantism never speaks of God as possessing power except when united to matter. It teaches that He is "within and without everything." The words of Vyasa are, "The Supreme Being is the material as well as the efficient cause of the universe;" and further, "an effect is not other than its cause." In showing that the supreme Brahma is at once cause and effect, he uses the following amongst other illustrations: "Hair and nails which are insensible grow from a sensible animal body." "The sea and its waters are one, yet waves, foam, froth, &c., differ from each other." "As milk changes to curd, and water to ice, so is Brahma variously transformed and diversified."

2. *Creation.* As the Divine Being is essentially connected with matter, everything visible and invisible in the universe is but an emanation from the Supreme. Brahma is the first cause. He educes from himself the materials of creation, as the spider draws out the web from its own body. At first the work is carried on with only partial success by himself; afterwards he works through the Prajāpatis, or progenitors.

3. *Man.* Man is said to consist of three parts: spirit, which is an essential part of the Supreme Being; and two bodies, a grosser and a more sublimated or refined one. When the grosser body dies, the spirit still continues to inhabit the finer one, and by it the consciousness of its identity is preserved, and the person recognized after death. When the spirit is re-absorbed into Brahma, or re-born into the world, this finer body is supposed to vanish.

It should be noticed here that the idea of recognition after death is not at all commonly received by the Hindus generally. Their books teach, and the people generally believe, that as they bring no reminiscences of past lives into their present life, so they carry with them no memory of the present into any future life.

4. *The Universe.* The universe has three main divisions: —earth, heaven, and hades. Regarding the earth as the centre, the seven parts of heaven are above, the seven of hades below. Of the seven above the earth, six are to continue for longer or shorter though definite periods, but the highest of all, called Satya Lok (the abode of truth), is eternal, in which there are four kinds of blessedness: Sālokya, dwelling with God; Sārupya, likeness to God; Sājugya, union with God; and Nirvāna, absorption into God. Of the parts under the earth, the lowest of all is called Pātāl, or hell, and is divided by some into twenty-one, by others into twenty-eight parts, the names of which correspond with the peculiar punishment inflicted there, or with the vices that there find their peculiar punishment.

In this, as in other systems of Hinduism, a great deal is made of Māyā, or illusion. It is owing to this *illusion* that men imagine themselves to be free agents, able to think and speak and act as they desire; whereas they are impelled by the divine forces to act as their Maker desires. All men are more or less under the influence of this Māyā, and fancy themselves to be free; whilst in reality they are but parts of God, and are impelled by His subtle power to act in harmony with His will. All enjoyment and suffering is simply the result of illusion. And as a natural consequence it is taught that the universe will continue only for a limited time, after which it will be re-absorbed into the great Brahma from whom it emanated.

Salvation is gained through a recognition of the relation existing between the soul and God; when its identity with God is realized, absorption into the Deity will follow. Hence it is no uncommon thing to see Hindus continuing, through weeks and months, meditating on nothing; making the mind a complete blank under the impression that they are qualifying for the highest blessedness man can attain unto. Works of merit are inculcated because a certain amount of happiness in heaven is attached to their performance; whilst evil deeds will send a man to hell to suffer the penalties an almighty fiat has attached to them. But in both cases there will be the endurance of other lives on earth until the highest excellence is attained—viz., realization of oneness with the Supreme.

There is no *moral law* given in this system. Some acts are said to be good, others mixed, and others, again, evil; but these are not moral distinctions. Its followers are exhorted to be truthful, continent, careful of all forms of life, and forbidden to steal; but inasmuch as the Vedantists of the present day acknowledge deities worshipped as the incarnations of God, though they may not take an active part in the ordinary worship, it is evident that their moral nature cannot be well trained, for nearly all of these popular deities were guilty of the very acts that are forbidden by their system.

Having glanced at the tenets of what may, to a certain extent, be regarded as the ordinary creed of the orthodox Hindu, before passing on to notice the peculiarities of some of the more commonly known sects, to one or other of which the great mass of the Hindus belong, I shall give a very brief account of the sects that were in existence before the fourteenth century. It is a most interesting fact that there have come down to us two works, written about that time, with the express object of refuting the errors of these sects, from which we learn their peculiar tenets. It is interesting to notice how similar the history of religious faiths in India has been to that of other lands. The sects that in the fourteenth century were regarded as heterodox, with the exception of those concerned mainly in the worship of the female energies, are now regarded by the Hindus generally as orthodox.

CHAPTER IV.

THE SECTS EXISTING ABOUT THE FOURTEENTH CENTURY A.D.

THESE may be divided into three classes :—

1. *Vaishnava sects; i.e.*, sects by whom Vishnu was regarded as the Supreme.

The *Bhākta* worshipped Vishnu in the form of Vāsudeva, *i.e.*, the son of Vasudeva, but there were no peculiar sectarial marks, nor was there anything peculiar in their worship. A few years later the term Bhākta became common to denote those who, like the Pharisees, professed to be more earnest in religion than their neighbours.

The *Bhāgavatas* worshipped their deity under the name of Bhagavān (the mighty one), and wore the usual distinguishing marks of his followers—viz., the discus, club, &c. They also reverenced the Sālgrāma, an Ammonite from the rivers in Nepāl, a common representative of Vishnu, and the Tulsi plant, into which his favourite mistress was transformed. The name remains, but it is doubtful if any members of the sect are now to be found.

The *Vaishnavas* worshipped Vishnu as Nārāyana (he who moved upon the waters), and, wearing the common sectarial marks, looked for a very sensual kind of bliss in the heaven of their chief deity.

The *Chakrinas* were the Saktis of the Vaishnava sects, worshipping almost exclusively the female personifications of the energy of Vishnu, and their descendants are to be found in the worshippers of Krishna and Rāma, or of Saktī or Devi.

The *Karmahinas*, as their name implies, abstained from all ritual observances and professed to know Vishnu as the sole source and sum of the universe. These can hardly be said to exist as a sect at the present time, though their peculiar tenets are accepted by many in other sects.

It is worthy of notice that at the time these polemical works were written no allusion is made to the separate worship of Krishna, or of the infantine forms under which he is so popular in the North-West Provinces of India; nor are the names of Rāma and Sita, of Lakshman or Hanumān, once particularized as enjoying any portion of distinct and specific adoration.

2. The *Saiva sects; i.e.*, sects amongst whom Siva was worshipped as the Supreme Being. These were six in number, but as they do not appear to have had anything peculiar, excepting sectarial marks, they do not call for special mention.

3. The *Saktas; i.e.*, sects whose chief object of worship were the Saktis, or female personifications of the Divine power. These sects were probably as numerous as they are at present, and appear to have worshipped some of the same objects as Bhavāni, Lakshmi, and Sarasvati; but Sitā, Rādhā, either alone or in conjunction with Rāma and Krishna, never appear. These were divided then, as now, into a right hand, or purer, and a left hand, or impurer order. Probably the more licentious rites with which these deities were worshipped have been modified; at any rate, they are not openly indulged in at the present time. But Bhairava (Siva) is still worshipped by the Saktas and Jogis, though the naked mendicant, smeared with funeral ashes, armed with a trident and sword, carrying a skull in his hand, and half-intoxicated with the spirits he has quaffed from that disgusting wine-cup, is not so frequently met with as he was in past times. This class of men was called Kāpālikas (skullmen) at the time of the writers of these works.

Speaking generally of the objects of worship then popular,

it will be seen that whilst most of the deities now worshipped were also worshipped then, other deities that are only addressed in common with some of the great gods were then exclusively adored by a larger or smaller number of devotees. Amongst these may be mentioned Brahmā, who, though not publicly worshipped, save in one or two temples in India, had then some followers who were exclusively devoted to him. In like manner, Surjya (the sun) was far more commonly worshipped as a separate and special deity than he is at present; the rising sun representing Brahmā, the sun in mid-heaven being regarded as Siva, whilst the setting sun was the prototype of Vishnu. Others, again, worshipped the sun, not as visible in the heavens, but through a mental image, and they had marks to remind them of him burned upon their skin. Others, again, regarded Ganesa as the supreme deity.

In addition to these, several other sects are mentioned, and their opinions controverted, which do not demand any notice here. It is interesting, however, to find that the opinions of the Buddhists and the Jains are condemned as heretical; also the evil doings of those are condemned who, though really more orthodox than their critics, gave exclusive reverence to some of the old Vedic gods who had at that time dropped into almost complete oblivion. Of these are Indra (the king of the gods, the lord of the firmament), Kuvera (the god of wealth), Yama (the king of the dead), Varuna (the Neptune of India), Garuda (the being half bird and half man, who was the devoted servant of Vishnu), Sesha (the serpent god, representing the end), Soma (the intoxicating plant whose praises were so constantly sung in the Vedic hymns), and last, though not least, Kāma (the Indian Cupid). And "it is a feature that singularly characterizes the present state of the Hindu religion, that if in some instances it is less ferocious, in others it has ceased to address itself to the amiable propensities of the human character, or the spontaneous and comparatively innocent feelings of youthful natures. The buffoonery of the Holi, and the barbarity of the Charak Puja, but ill express the sympathies which man in all countries feels with the vernal season, and which formerly gave rise to the festive Vasantasava of the Hindus; and the licentious homage paid to Sakti and Bhairava has little in common with the worship that might be supposed acceptable to Kāma and his lovely bride Rati, and which, it would appear, they formerly enjoyed." *

In describing the sects as they exist at the present day it will be seen that in most cases they are but modified forms of those already mentioned as existing five centuries back. It is a most interesting fact that Sankara, the great authority on Hinduism, himself a staunch believer in the supreme Brahma as distinct from his three-fold manifestation as Brahmā, Vishnu, and Siva, sent forth disciples to teach the more popular forms of faith. He professed to explain this inconsistency by the fact that the mass of the people were not qualified to receive the more intellectual and refined forms of religion. It is said that it was on his authority that the Saiva faith was promulgated at Benares, and the Vaishnava at Conjeveram; that others of his disciples taught men to worship the Sun, the Saktis (female deities), and also the more dreadful form of Bhairava. The outward unity of Hinduism is affirmed, as it is declared that one who had himself no faith in these acknowledged lower forms, authorized his disciples to teach them because he considered them better suited to the capacities of the more ignorant masses. There is of course another explanation of what appears to be a most glaring inconsistency—viz., that the teachers of these more objectionable forms of worship borrowed the name of this great teacher in order to obtain respect for their really heretical teaching.

The same general divisions will be retained in describing the sects of the present day as in speaking of the older ones. It will be evident to the reader, as he notices the practices of

* Wilson's "Hindu Sects," p. 17.

some of them, that they are in direct opposition to what may be termed orthodox Hinduism, as, *e.g.*, where caste rules are disregarded at feasts; men of all classes being encouraged to eat of food prepared by men of a different caste from themselves. And it is evident that some of these sects have arisen through the desire to lower the pretensions and lessen the influence of the Brāhmans. Where, as it has frequently happened, Brāhmans have joined some of these sects, they have been gladly welcomed, but have had to pay the cost of this relinquishment of their privileges by being treated as outcasts by their stricter brethren. At the same time the members of these sects are regarded as good Hindus even by those who themselves have kept aloof from them. And it often happens that when a man, for some violation of caste rules, is put out of caste by his old associates, he joins some one of these heretical sects, where he is sure of a hearty welcome, and finds companions there to take the place of those who have driven him from their midst. Even prostitutes, who on taking to an immoral life as a profession are cut off at once from their family and caste, can easily enter some of these sects, and by their generous gifts purchase the sympathies of their fellow-sectaries, and hope to possess at death similar blessings to those whose lives have been more pure. The more one looks into it the more clearly is it seen that Hinduism is a most expansive and inclusive system; those who have most carefully studied the question find it most difficult to define clearly what Hinduism is—who may and who may not rightly be classed as Hindus. Thus in the Bengal Census Report of 1881 Mr. Beverley asks, "What is a Hindu? is a question which has often been asked without eliciting any satisfactory reply. No answer, in fact, exists, for the term in its modern acceptation denotes neither a creed nor a race, neither a church nor a people, but a general expression devoid of precision, and embracing alike the most punctilious disciples of pure Vedantism, the Agnostic youth who is the product of Western education, and the semi-barbarous hill-man who eats without scruple anything he can procure, and is as ignorant of the Hindu mythology as the stone he worships in times of sickness and danger." Sir Alfred Lyall, quoted in the same Report, says "that the religion of the non-Mahommedan population of India is as a tangled jungle of disorderly superstitions, ghosts and demons, demi-gods and deified saints, household gods, local gods, tribal gods, universal gods, with their countless shrines and temples, and the din of their discordant rites; deities who abhor a fly's death; those who still delight in human sacrifices." In the account of the fifty-three out of the ninety-six sects into which the Hindus say their co-religionists are divided, will be given the peculiar forms of worship which prevail amongst the great majority of the Hindu people.

The authorities on this subject are two works—one by the Munshi to the Rāja of Benares, the other by the librarian of the college of that city. These books contain merely a sort of catalogue of names and drawings of the sectarial marks which the members wear, the legendary part being taken from a very popular Hindi work called the Bhakta Māla, or Garland of the Faithful. This book was originally written about two and a half centuries ago by a man named Nabharji, a Dom, *i.e.*, a member of one of the lowest and most despised of the Hindu castes, whose occupation consists in making baskets and burying the dead. It is said that he was born blind, but when he was about five years of age, two worshippers of Vishnu happening to pass by saw his pitiable condition, and bathing his eyes with water from their drinking vessel, sight was given to him. They then took him with them to their monastery and received him into their fellowship. This work, originally written in prose, Tulsi Dāss has rendered most popular by putting it into a poetic form. Tulsi Dāss, a Brāhman by birth, through the influence of his wife became a most ardent worshipper of Rāma. He lived the greater part of his life at Benares, where he made an immortal name by translating the Rāmāyana into Hindu. He also built a temple sacred to Sita and Rāma, and a monastery adjoining, both of which continue to this day. Another poet, named Jayadeva, is described in the Bhakta Māla, concerning whom the following wonderful legend is recorded. When Jayadeva was leading the life of an ascetic, a Brāhman, on his way to Puri to dedicate his daughter to Jagannātha, whose worship is there celebrated, saw that deity and received from him a command to give his child in marriage to Jayadeva. At first the sage refused, but on her appealing to his kindness he consented to take her. He then set up house and became a poet. Wishing on one occasion to write a poem descriptive of Rādha's virtues, as he could not find terms sufficiently strong, he went down to the river to bathe and find inspiration. During his absence Krishna himself came and, taking up the poet's pen, wrote what the poor man had been unable to do. On another occasion, when in the forest, he was attacked by Thugs, who cut off his feet and hands. Some time afterwards these men came to the king's palace disguised as mendicants; but Jayadeva saw through their disguise and treated them most kindly. As they were departing some of the attendants asked them how it was that the poet had treated them so kindly; they replying that they had saved his life from robbers who had thus mutilated him, the earth opened and swallowed them, whilst the hands and feet of Jayadeva were restored, and he was enabled to write the book from which the writers of the works on the Hindu sects have drawn so largely.

We shall now pass on to notice the sects of the Hindus as they exist at the present day.

CHAPTER V.

THE VAISHNAVA SECTS, OR THOSE IN WHICH VISHNU IS REGARDED AS THE SUPREME DEITY.

MOST of these, as also those of the other classes, have distinguishing marks, which it is the duty of those who are initiated to wear. A most important duty at the great festivals, when the ceremony of bathing is completed, is to have these sectarial marks freshly painted on the forehead, breast, and arms. All the Vaishnavas use for their marks a white earth called gopichandana, which, to be of the purest description, must be brought from a pool in Dwaraka, in which the gopis, or milkmaids, drowned themselves when Krishna forsook them. A common calcareous clay is, however, often substituted for this.

1. *The Sri Sampradayis, or Rāmānujas.*

[Marks: Two perpendicular white lines from the roots of the hair to the eyebrows, and a transverse line connecting them across the root of the nose. In the centre there is a transverse streak of red made with roli, *i.e.*, turmeric and lime; also patches of gopichandana, with a red central streak on the breast and on each arm. These marks are supposed to represent the lotus, conch shell, discus, and club, which Vishnu bears in his four hands, the central streak of red representing Sri, or Lakshmi, his wife. The members of this sect also wear a necklace made of the seeds of the Tulsi plant, and carry a rosary made of the same seeds, or from those of the lotus.]

This is the oldest and most respectable of the Vaishnava sects, having been founded about the middle of the twelfth century by Rāmānuja Achārjya. This man is said to have been an incarnation of the great serpent Sesha, whilst his chief companions and disciples are said to have been the embodied discus, shell, lotus, club, &c., the insignia of Vishnu. He taught the tenets of his creed at Conjeveram and afterwards visited Sri Ranga and other places, reclaiming men and recovering temples from the Saiva faith.

On his return to Sri Ranga the dispute between the rival sects of Vishnu and Siva rose to such a height that the king, a devout Saivite, ordered all the Brāhmans in his kingdom to sign an acknowledgment of the superiority of his chosen deity, and by bribery and fear was successful with the greater number. Rāmānuja refusing to sign this document, the king sent an armed force to seize him; but the Brāhman escaped, and took refuge in Mysore. Whilst there he is said to have expelled an evil spirit from a daughter of the king, who thereupon embraced the doctrines of his holy guest. On the death of the king of Sri Ranga, after a stay of twelve years in Mysore, Rāmānuja returned to his former home. The headquarters of this sect are now in the Deccan, and although the founder is said to have set up seven hundred monasteries (maths), four only exist at the present time.

The worship of Rāmānuja's followers is addressed to Vishnu and his consort Lakshmi and their incarnations either singly or conjointly. The teachers are usually Brāhmans, but the disciples may be of any caste. Besides the worship offered in the temples of either of these gods, or their incarnations, images of metal and stone are set up in the houses, and the Sālgrāma and Tulsi are also generally worshipped. The name by which the members are most commonly known is Sri Vaishnavas. The chief ceremony of initiation into the sect is the communication of the mantra by the guru to the disciple. The initiatory mantra is said to be "Om Rāmāya namah;" *i.e.*, Om salutation to Rāma; but there is always great reluctance on the part of the Hindus to give any real information respecting the mantras; the most reliable source of information is that of those once initiated who, having become Christians, are free from the fear of evil consequences following the betrayal of the secret.

The chief religious tenet of the Rāmānuja sect is the assertion that Vishnu is Brahma, the Supreme Being. By a mere wish he created the universe, which is an emanation from himself. He has manifested himself to men in five forms—in images, in his incarnations, in certain forms, as Krishna, Baharaiva, &c., in certain qualities, and in the human soul. He is to be worshipped in five ways corresponding to these forms: by cleaning the images and temples, by providing flowers and perfumes for religious rites, by the presentation of these as offerings (bloody sacrifices are hateful to Vishnu), repeating the name of the deity, and by meditation, the object of which is to unite the soul with the deity; the proper performance of which, it is believed, will give entrance in Vaikuntha, the heaven of Vishnu.

2. *Rāmānandis, or Ramawats.*

[As this is regarded as a branch of the preceding sect, the marks differ only in this—the red streaks are narrower.]

Ramanand, the founder, is said by some to have been a disciple of Rāmānuja, but more probably he was a disciple of a disciple in the fifth descent from that leader. As far as can be definitely known, he flourished about the end of the fourteenth or the beginning of the fifteenth century. The worship of this sect is devoted to Rāmachandra (one of the great incarnations of Vishnu), together with Sita his wife, his half-brother Lakshman, and his faithful friend Hanumān, the commander-in-chief of the monkey army that was raised to assist Rāma to rescue his wife from the great demon Rāvana, who had carried her to Ceylon. Some of the members regard Rāma as their supreme deity, others prefer Sita; whilst others, again, give equal adoration to the two. The other forms of Vishnu are treated with profound respect by these people, and the Sālgrāma, as his special representation, is worshipped by them.

This sect originated in a very simple manner. Rāmānand, in obedience to his superior, is said to have gone from place to place inculcating the doctrines of his sect. On his return to the math, or monastery, of his leader, some of his fellow-disciples accused him of having violated, in the course of his travels, one of their vital doctrines—viz., the observance of the closest privacy in partaking of his food. On the matter being referred to the head of the math, he agreed with the disciples. This so incensed Rāmānand that he at once left the monastery and started a sect of his own. He lived chiefly at Benares, at the Pancha Ganga Ghat, where, it is believed, his math continued until it was destroyed by the Mussulmāns. At present there is a stone platform, which is said to retain the impression of his feet. In the vicinity of Benares are several maths of this order, and it is there the chief council meets to settle all questions connected with the order.

The members of each of these sects are divided into two main classes, which answer very nearly to the two divisions in the Christian church called cleric and lay; the clerics, again, are subdivided into monastic and secular. It is in India that we find the home of the belief of the superior sanctity of the celibate life which was transferred to the Christian church. In most cases the celibate is regarded as of greater sanctity than the married, and the larger part of these, for a longer or shorter period of their lives, wander from place to place visiting shrines and collecting offerings, which, after deducting necessary expenses, are given to the math to which they belong. In order to provide a home for the celibates who do not wish to travel, as well as for those who wander, these monasteries are supported, each with its own mahant, or superior, who sometimes obtains the position by inheritance, sometimes is chosen by the members of the order, and sometimes the appointment is made by royal patrons, in whose country the math is situated. In fact in their main features these monasteries and their uses and government differ very little from similar institutions in the Christian church of the West. The whole scheme appears to have been borrowed from the East. There are some mahants who exercise a sort of authority over others, much in the same way as the archbishop exercises authority over the bishops under his jurisdiction.

Rāmānand, having been driven from his own sect owing to its many restrictions, laid few burdens on his disciples; in fact, he gave them the name Avadhuta, *i.e.*, liberated; meaning that they were freed from many of the trying ordinances that prevailed in other classes. With respect to eating and bathing he left them free to follow their own inclination. The most important innovation was the virtual abolition of caste. Amongst his most illustrious disciples were a Rājput, a weaver, and a chamār (currier), and a barber. He taught that God and his worshippers are one; and as Bhagavān (Vishnu) appeared in inferior forms as a fish, boar, &c., so his worshippers may be born in the inferior as well as superior castes. And what is equally remarkable is this, that though the founder of this system did not write any works himself, his followers wrote religious works; not as Rāmānuja and Sankara had done—commentaries on the Vedas for the use of the Brāhmans only—but in the common dialects of the people, and in a popular style, so that they were suited to the capacities of all. Further, it is possible for any of the members, whatever his caste, to rise to the position of a vairāgi (ascetic), a guru (teacher), or mahant (head of a monastery). From the success which attended the efforts of this teacher there is every encouragement to work for the spread of Christian truth. Multitudes at his call left their own particular castes and joined his brotherhood, in which Brāhmans and Chamārs associated as brethren.

There are said to be *twelve* chief disciples of Rāmānand, some of whom, having founded new sects, will be mentioned separately; but a few facts respecting one of the less conspicuous will not be uninteresting.

Pīpa, the Rājput mentioned above, originally worshipped Devi (Siva's wife), but wishful to become a worshipper of Vishnu, he placed himself under Rāmānand's instruction at Benares. Coming at an inopportune moment, the sage angrily wished that his visitor might fall into a well close by. Pīpa immediately threw himself in, that his teacher's wish might be fulfilled. This act of submission so pleased the onlookers that they at once gave him the title of Rāja. On a visit to Dwaraka with his master, he plunged into the sea and paid a visit to Vishnu in his submarine shrine, where he was hospitably received. On a journey his wife was carried off by some Pathāns, but Rāma appearing, rescued the wife and slew the robbers. On another occasion, meeting an angry lion in the forest, he placed his rosary on its neck, and whispering the mantra of the sect (Sri Rāma), made him tranquil in a moment.

3. *Kabir Panthis.*

[Outward signs are regarded by this sect as of little importance. Some do not wear any, others have the same as the Rāmānandis, others, again, have a streak of sandal wood ashes or gopichandana along the ridge of the nose. They also wear the necklace of Tulsi seed and use the rosary.]

Of all Rāmānand's disciples, Kabir is the most celebrated. With immense boldness he attacked the whole system of idolatrous worship, ridiculed the learning of the Pundits and the teaching of the Sāstras, and, what is even more remarkable, addressed his remarks to Mussulmāns as well as Hindus, making the Korān equally with the Hindu Scriptures an object of ridicule. It is said that the writings of this man more than any others influenced Nānak, the founder of the Sikh faith.

There are two legends connected with the birth of this leader. It is said in the Bhakta Māla that his mother, a Brāhman virgin widow, was taken by her father to see his guru Rāmānand, when the great teacher saluted her with the wish that she might have a son. His words could not be recalled; but as the birth of a son could only be a source of shame, she was privately delivered of her child, which was exposed at its birth. Being found by a weaver and his wife, this child was brought up as their own. The common belief ignores all this part of the story, and says that a weaver's wife named Nīmā found the child, which was an incarnate deity, floating on a lotus in a lake near Benares. As soon as the child was in her arms it asked to be carried to the holy city. Hearing an infant speak, the woman and her husband thought it must be a demon, and, casting it down, ran as fast as they could to the city; but the child ran faster than they. At length they agreed to take it and bring it up as their own.

Kabir flourished about the beginning of the fifteenth century, and a curious story is told of his initiation, which must have taken place before Rāmānand had developed his system. Kabir was again and again refused admission into the sects because of his being of low caste. Standing one day on the Ghāt by which Rāmānand went to bathe, he touched the sage's foot, who, as a sort of expiatory measure, cried "Rāma, Rāma," the initiatory mantra: from that moment Kabir asserted that he was admitted into the fraternity by the involuntary utterance of the text.

Both Hindus and Mussulmāns claimed Kabir as one of their creed. A story is told to the effect that his mother (in this case said to be a Mussulmani) complained to the Emperor Sekandah, who sent for the son and ordered him to make the usual salām. This young man said, "I know none but Rāma—why should I bow down before a king?" Upon this the emperor ordered him to be cast into the river, but the waters would not drown him. He tried to burn him to death, but fire had no effect upon him. He next ordered his elephants to trample him to death, but they dared not approach him. At last the king on his own elephant went to slay him, but Kabir transformed himself into a lion, and the king then gave up the attempt. At his death the Hindus wished to burn, and the Mussulmāns to bury his body. As they were quarrelling about this, Kabir himself appeared and told them to look under the cloth which was supposed to be covering his dead body. They did so, and found only a heap of flowers. Part the Rāja of Benares took and burnt, and the spot where they were burnt is now known as Kabir Chaura; part the Mussulmāns buried at Magar, near Gorukhpore, where he died.

As Kabir was a disciple of Rāmānand, this sect is regarded as belonging to the Vaishnavas, though the members need not worship any of the Hindu deities; and where they are found doing so it is more out of compliance to the wishes of others than from any good they expect from it for themselves. One of their leader's maxims was, "Associate and mix with all, and take the names of all; say to every one, 'Yes, sir; yes, sir;' and abide in your own abode." This certainly is rather a free rendering of the apostolic resolve to be "all things to all men." They do not join much in the outward worship of the deities; their chief religious exercise is singing hymns to the invisible Kabir.

The doctrines of this sect are not very easily learned; but as far as can be seen they do not differ very much from what is taught in the Purānas, though the way of stating them is somewhat original. They say there is but one God, the Creator of the world, and the pure man, the Sādhu of the Kabirs, is His living resemblance, and after death His associate and equal. All that is has come out from God, is a part of Him, therefore God and man are not only the same, but they together form everything that lives and moves. The Paramapurush (the Supreme Being) was alone for seventy-two ages. Desiring to renew the world, the female Māyā sprang forth from whom all errors among men have arisen. From her union with the Supreme the three great gods, Brahmā, Vishnu, and Siva have come; and from union with them their brides, Saraswati, Lakshmi, and Umā were born. Life is the same in all beings; the great object is to learn the source ; for as long as ignorance of this continues, new births must be experienced. Heaven and hell do not actually exist, but are simply some of the delusions of Māyā.

The moral code of this sect is rather worthy of praise. It teaches that all life is sacred; humanity is therefore a cardinal virtue, whether the object be man or animals. Truth is necessary, and retirement from the world is advantageous to piety; absolute obedience and profound reverence for the guru is especially insisted on. Their abhorrence of violence, love of truth, and unobtrusiveness of life make them most inoffensive members of the community. In North India their numbers are great: those choosing the wandering life do not *beg* for alms.

There are a few other sects similar to those already described which require but a brief notice.

The *Khakis*, founded by Kil, perhaps, in the fourth generation from Rāmānand. No mention of this sect is found in the Bhakta Mālā, hence it may be inferred that it is of modern origin. Most of its members seem to adopt the wandering ascetic life, and are distinguished by the use of clay and ashes on their bodies. They also wear the Jātā, or braided hair, which they appear to have copied from the Saiva sectaries. They worship Sitā, and are especially devoted to Hanumān.

The *Maluk Dāsis* [mark: a shorter streak of red than is common with the other Vaishnavas; otherwise their sectarial marks are similar] take their name from Maluk Dāss; their gurus and most of their members remain in their homes, and do not wander about as do the *Khakis*. The principal establishment is situated near a temple of Rāma Chandra, at Kara, Manikpore, the birthplace of the founder, and the present mahant is reckoned as the eighth in descent from him. There are six other maths in different places.

The *Dādu Panthis* [mark: the members of this sect wear no peculiar frontal mark, nor do they wear a Mālā, or necklace ; they carry the rosary and wear a round white cap with a flap hanging down behind] are an offshoot from Kabir ; their worship is also addressed to Rāma, but is restricted to what is called *Japa, i.e.*, the mere repetition of his name. The founder of the sect, Dādu, a cotton cleaner, was born at Āhmedabād, whence he travelled to other places. At Narama it is said he heard a voice from heaven calling upon him to live a religious life; accordingly he retired to the Baherana mountain, and, no traces of him being left, he is believed to have been absorbed into the deity. His followers burn their dead at early dawn; but the more religious among them order that their bodies be left exposed in the open country to be devoured by birds and beasts, as in the funeral pile insect life is apt to be destroyed.

The Rāi Dasis are the followers of Rai Dās, a Chamār, one of the lowest castes of the Hindus, and his followers generally belong to the same caste. He must have been a man of considerable influence, as the following legend from the Bhakta Mālā will show. It was owing to an imprecation of Rāmānand that a Brahmachāri (student) was born in a Chamār family. When born he refused to take nourishment until Rāmānand, recognizing in this infant the young man he had cursed, breathed the mantra into his ears and thus admitted him into his sect. From that moment he began to thrive. When he grew up to manhood he worked at his trade, and devoted all he could spare to feeding the poor. One day Vishnu, pleased with his devotion at a time of great distress, came and offered him the philosopher's stone; but Rai Dās disregarded the gift, as he was so well satisfied with the knowledge of Hari (Vishnu). Some months afterwards Vishnu paid him another visit, and seeing that the stone had not been used, caused a number of gold pieces to lie all round him. With these Rai Dās erected a temple of which he became the priest. Again Vishnu caused his glory to became widely known by inciting the Brāhmans in the district to persecute him. But again Vishnu came to the rescue and wrought a miracle on behalf of his servant in the presence of the king and court.

Sena Panthis are the followers of Sena, a barber; but of the peculiar tenets of this sect little is known. In connection with him a story is told similar in spirit to that in Miss Proctor's "Legend of Provence." This barber being intensely devotional sometimes forgot his professional duties as barber to the king. Vishnu seeing the sovereign's anger, in order to save him from punishment, took the poor barber's place, and did his work so well that the king recognized the god, and made his barber his guru.

4. *Vallbhācharis, or Rudra Sampradayis.*

[Marks: Two red perpendicular lines on the forehead meeting in a semicircle at the root of the nose, and a round spot of red between them, with the same as those of the Sri Vaishnavas on the breast and arms. Some make the central spot of black. Their necklace and rosary are made of the stem of the Tulasi.]

Perhaps as numerous as the worshippers of Vishnu under the forms of Krishna and Rādhā, or Rāma and Sitā, are those who are devoted to him as the infant Gopāl. Krishna, in order to escape from the anger and jealousy of his uncle Kansa, immediately after his birth was transferred to the house of a cowherd named Nanda, who brought him up as his own child: the name Gopal, or the cowkeeper, attaches to him from that circumstance. This sect owes its origin to Vallabha Ācharjya, and is commonly known as the religion of the Gokula Gosains.

The original founder of the sect was a Brāhman named Vishnu Swāmi, who admitted Brāhmans only into his society, and imposed on all a vow to lead a life of asceticism. But Vallabha greatly extended the sect by communicating the mantra (or initiatory text) to men of other castes. This man was a Sanyasi himself, and flourished about the sixteenth century. Originally he resided at Gokul, near Mathura, then at Vrindāvana, where he lived under a pipul-tree, which is still shown to pilgrims. At Mathura, too, there are traces of him to be found: all these places being connected with various scenes in the life of Krishna. It was at Vrindāvana that he is said to have been honoured by a visit from Krishna himself, who enjoined him to extend his worship under the form of Bala Gopāl (the boy Gopāl). Vallabha is said to have gone to heaven from Benares in a miraculous manner. The popular story is as follows: Entering the river at Hanumān Ghāt, and stooping down to worship, he suddenly disappeared: a brilliant flame arose from the spot, and in the presence of a host of spectators he ascended into heaven, and was lost to sight in the firmament.

Although some of the other Purānas speak of the childhood of Krishna, it is in Brahmā Vaivartha that the fullest particulars are found; and though the worship of the infant Krishna is not distinctly commanded there, yet, as it speaks of the Creator as a young man, and dwells upon the miraculous doings of his youth, its authority is claimed for this form of worship. According to this authority, Krishna has a heaven of his own called Goloka, situated high above the heavens of Vishnu and Siva. In the centre of this beautiful home lives Krishna in the bloom of youth, in colour like a dark cloud, and clad in yellow garments, playing on his flute. Being alone, he meditated on the world; then Māyā, a female form arose, from whom and himself all beings came. Vishnu sprang from his right side, Siva from his left, Brahmā from his hand, Dharma from his breath, Saraswati from his mouth, Lakshmi from his mind, Durgā from his understanding, and Rādhā from his *left side*. Three hundred millions of gopis (*female* cowherds) exuded from the pores of her skin, and the same number of gopas (cowherds) from his.

Vallabha introduced one most remarkable innovation for a Sanyasi, which showed that Epicureanism was not at all confined to Greece. He taught that as privation formed no part of sanctity, God should be worshipped, not by nudity and hunger, but by costly apparel and good food; not in solitude and with mortification of the body, but in the pleasures of society and in the enjoyment of the world.

With the founding of the sect Vallabha at once gave up his ascetic life, and marrying, advised all his disciples to do the same. The gosains, or gurus, have great influence over their disciples, and are well cared for as they travel from shrine to shrine, from disciple to disciple. The mass of the adherents of this sect are merchants, and the gosains themselves are not above joining in mercantile transactions. The images of Gopāl that they worship are generally made of metal, and, in the same temple with those of Rādhā and Krishna, Gopāl's representations are also to be seen. The most celebrated temple of Gopāl is in Ājmere. It is said that the image there worshipped transported itself to that place from Mathura. It is the duty of every member of this sect, at least once in their life, to visit this shrine, and a certificate is given to each pilgrim who goes there by the chief gosain. There are several temples at Vrindāvana and other places.

5. *Mīrā Bais.*

This is really a subdivision of the preceding, found almost exclusively in the west of India; and Mīrā Bāi and Rānachor, a form of Krishna, are held in great veneration by the followers of Vallabha.

Mīrā Bāi is the authoress of several poems addressed to Krishna, which are read, with those of Nānak and Kabir, by members of other sects. She was the daughter of a petty Rāja, and became the wife of the Nānā of Udaypore. As her mother-in-law was a devout worshipper of Devi, Siva's consort, and Mīrā as devout a worshipper of Krishna, quarrels arose, the result being that the younger lady had a separate establishment, in which she was free to carry on her religious practices unmolested. She continued to adore Rānachor, and, as part of her worship, visited the scenes of Krishna's exploits, and became the protector of his followers throughout her husband's kingdom. During her absence from home, a persecution of Krishna's worshippers breaking out, a number of Brāhmans were despatched to bring her home. Before leaving Dwaraka she went to visit Rānachor's temple; the deity was so pleased with her that the image opened; she threw herself into it, and was never seen again. At Udaypore an image of Mīrā is to be seen beside one of Krishna.

6. *Madhwacharis.*

[In dress and general appearance they are like the Dandis. The Brāhmans who join cast off the poitra; all carry a staff and water-pot, go bareheaded, and wear a single cloth of a dirty yellow colour. They also have the symbols of Vishnu stamped with a hot iron on their shoulders or breast. Their frontal marks are the same as those of the Sri Vaishnavas, excepting that in place of the red centre streak they have one made of sandal-wood charcoal, which has been burned as incense before an image of Vishnu as Nārāyana, terminating with a patch of turmeric.]

This sect forms a sort of connecting link between the Vaishnavas and Saivas. Their founder, Mādhava, who is said to have been an incarnation of the god Vāyu, was born about the twelfth century. At first he appears to have been a member of a Saiva sect, but afterwards forsook that for the Vaishnavas. Unlike most men who change their beliefs, he was no bigot; hence in the temples frequented by the members of this sect we find images of Siva, Durgā, and Ganesa, side by side with those of Vishnu. One great peculiarity of his teaching was that the human spirit (Jivātma), though united to and dependent on the Paramātma, or Divine Spirit, is yet distinct from it; hence final absorption into the Godhead is impossible. This is a most marked departure from the orthodox creed.

7. *The Vaishnavas of Bengal.*

[Marks: Two white perpendicular lines on the forehead, made either with sandal-wood or gopichandana, which are joined together at the root, and extended to near the end of the nose. They have also the name Rādhā-Krishna stamped on the temples, breast, and arms. They wear a tight-fitting necklace made of three strings of beads of Tulsi stalk, and carry a rosary of the same.]

By far the greater part of the Vaishnavas of Bengal, about 8,000,000 in number, and forming, according to some authorities, at least one-fifth of the Hindu community, belong to the sect of which Chaitanya, a Brāhman of Nadiya, was the founder. This man developed and proclaimed with singular earnestness a system which had been partially elaborated by two men named Adaityananda and Nityānanda. Being householders, and indisposed to lead an ascetic life, they needed an active co-labourer to propagate their doctrines throughout the country. And in selecting Chaitanya they certainly made a most happy choice; for a more earnest and self-denying man than he has not been often seen. Whilst the success which to this day attends the proclamation of his peculiar views, affords a notable example of the great innovations in faith and practice that an earnest-minded man can produce amongst the religiously conservative people of India.

According to popular belief, and this will partly account for the immense success that followed his work, he was an incarnation of Krishna, who appeared in this form for the special purpose of leading men to worship him. In the temples of Nadiya, the head-quarters of the sect, the images of Chaitanya are of large size, whilst those of Krishna, in the same shrines, being small and insignificant, are regarded as of secondary importance. But Chaitanya, having left his family and lived the life of an ascetic, whilst Krishna is always worshipped in conjunction with his favourite mistress Rādhā, it is said that he is the manifestation of both Krishna and Rādhā combined. A few facts connected with the life of this great reformer will not be without interest. The book of the sect is the Chaitanya Charitāmrita, a work most highly valued by the members. It is written in a sort of jingling rhyme, in the Bengali language, with a large number of Sanskrit, Urdu, and Uriya words interspersed.

Chaitanya was born in the year 1485, just two years after Luther. It is stated in the book just mentioned that before and at his birth his parents had many indications that the child was no ordinary mortal, and that the heavenly deities came down to earth to visit him who was the incarnation of the second person of the Hindu Triad. Numerous stories of his miraculous knowledge and power are told, and others illustrating the character of his teaching in after life. One day, when his mother gave him sweetmeats to eat, he took up clay, which he ate in preference, as he said that there was no difference between them. When his attention was called to the fact that he was standing in an unclean place, and ordered to wash in the Bhagirathi river, he refused, because all places were alike holy.

When a boy he was well taught in the village school, and himself became a teacher, and, when his father died, performed the funeral ceremonies according to the ritual. But very soon after this the lessons of a book he had carefully read, the Sri Bhāgavata, which is largely taken up with the account of Krishna, were realized by him in an extraordinary degree, so that for hours together he would meditate on Krishna, and, becoming ecstatic in his love to him, was impelled by a mighty enthusiasm to preach to others of the intense joy he found in the contemplation of and devotion to that deity. It is a most curious fact that whilst Chaitanya himself was an ardent worshipper of Krishna, he should now be regarded by his followers as an incarnation of that deity. At times his followers declare that he changed his bodily form and appeared as the four-armed Krishna, to the great delight of his disciples.

The Vaishnavas, with Chaitanya at their head, were in the habit of meeting at night and spending hours together in talking over the life and singing songs in honour of Krishna, until earth became as heaven. On one of these occasions Chaitanya urged his companions to go from house to house in Nadiya, until all the inhabitants should know the bliss that was within their reach. This was too hard a task for the new disciples, so on the following morning a procession was formed with Chaitanya at the head, and the whole company marched singing through the streets with their music accompaniment. All came out to see and hear, and amongst others, two noted enemies of the Vaishnava worship. Seeing them, Chaitanya prayed that the divine weapon Sudarshan might destroy them; but on being asked by a follower to show love rather than hate, the order was countermanded, and through heavenly blessings the hearts of these opponents were melted, and they became followers of the new faith. The conversion of these two opponents, perhaps as much as anything, led to greater earnestness on the part of the disciples, and also to the conviction on the part of the Hindus generally that it was their interest to regard this new movement with favour rather than opposition.

When he was twenty-four years of age Chaitanya forsook his family and assumed the position of an ascetic. It was his duty, he felt, to visit the great shrines of India, and to preach the tenets of his system to all men. As he was travelling towards Puri, the shrine of Jagannātha, he was so overpowered with a sense of the ignorance and sin of men, that he was almost ready to drown himself. On arriving at the great temple of Jagannātha, he sat for hours before the image and "saw" him and all his glory—a sure sign that he at least was pure, as it is only to the eyes of the pure that this deity is said to manifest himself. Whilst at Puri he spent his time largely in speaking of the glories of Krishna, and many of the pilgrims who visited that shrine went back to their homes with their hearts fired with love to Chaitanya's chosen deity. From Puri he went to the extreme south of India, to the places rendered sacred as the scene of Rāma's labours and exploits. On his way he gained many disciples, and on some occasions even manifested his divine form to confirm the faith of his disciples.

On his return to Puri the people were greatly delighted, and at the next Rath Jātra (the great Car Festival held there in July) his influence was most marked. He divided his followers into four companies, who sang, danced, and played their music on the four sides of the great car as it moved along; but the leader himself was said to be present in all four companies at once, and it is declared that the god looked down with great delight at the devotion of his servant. At the close of the day, when the powers of elephants and men, who had been drawing the car, were exhausted, and it was found impossible for them to move it further, Chaitanya touched the back of it with his head, and it then moved easily along.

After remaining some four years at Puri, Chaitanya returned to Bengal, where he confirmed the faith of his many disciples, and then started for Vrindāvana and Mathura, the scene of Krishna's life on earth. Most marvellous are the accounts given of the power the name of Krishna exerted on beasts and men when uttered by him. "The lord passed through herds of tigers, elephants, rhinoceroses, and wild boars." The simple Bala Bhadra (his companion) was astonished to see those furious beasts keep a respectful distance from the Mahāprabhu. One day his foot touched a tiger that was sleeping by the side of the road. The lord said, "Krishna, Krishna," at the sound of which the tiger, rising up, danced for joy. On another occasion, as he was bathing in a river, a number of wild elephants came there to drink. Chaitanya, throwing water at them, said, "Repeat the name of Krishna;" on which, all the elephants shouted "Krishna! Krishṇa!" and, moved by faith and love, danced and sang. As he sang flocks of deer attended him on either side to hear the delightful sound. Some tigers then joined the company, and when the lord said, "Say Krishna," deer and tigers with this name on their lips danced with joy. Tigers and deer embraced each other, and forgot their natural animosity. Peacocks attended him on his journey, and even plants, vegetables, and minerals were glad, and showed signs of rejoicing as he sang the praises of Krishna. At Benares and Allahabad he made converts; whilst at Mathura, the home of Krishna, the animal and vegetable worlds were convulsed with joy, and manifested their pleasure in a marvellous manner. The writer of the book declares that "ten millions of volumes will not suffice to describe the transports of Mahāprabhu in Vrindāvana." After this journey he returned to Puri, where he remained for the rest of his life. During the years that followed it is clear that he had periodic fits of insanity, in which he fancied himself to be Krishna, and in imagination went through many of the incidents in that hero's life. Now he was dancing with the milkmaids, now conversing with Rādhā, and at last, in one of these fits, walked into the sea under the impression that it was the river Jumna, the scene of Krishna's amusements, and was drowned.

The two chief co-workers with Chaitanya were Nityānanda and Adaityananda; the former of whom is sometimes worshipped along with his master. The descendants of these men are now regarded as the leaders of the sect.

The following is an outline of the theology of the Vaishnavas who follow Chaitanya's teaching.

Krishna is the Paramātma, the supreme soul, and he is the supreme object of worship. There is but one substance in the universe, viz., Krishna, the earth being only a modification of him. The peculiarity of the Vaishnavas of Bengal is their belief that Chaitanya is a manifestation of deity. The followers of this sect say that Siva and Brahmā manifested a *part* only of the Divine Being, but Krishna is God Himself. Another peculiarity of the theology lies in the stress placed upon *bhakti*, or faith. The Vedantists teach that knowledge is all, and will save; other more popular systems say, "Perform penance," meditate, "Do good works;" *do* something; but Chaitanya said, "Trust Krishna." "The efficacy of good works, austerity, and knowledge, is nothing compared with that of bhakti. Without bhakti there can be no deliverance." Simple bhakti without knowledge, whatever be the object of this blind and implicit faith, will ensure salvation. The Vaishnavas maintain that anything, a log of wood, a plant, &c., believed by the devotee to be Krishna or Chaitanya, becomes to him such, and ensures to him happiness in the realms of heaven. Vedantism supposes knowledge and power of thought; Purānism prescribes a round of difficult and expensive rites and duties; but Vaishnavism is simple and inexpensive; hence we find that it is fast becoming the prevailing system amongst the poor. There are five degrees of this bhakti: 1st, *Sānta*, or peace. This, the lowest form, is the calm, unimpassioned contemplation of the deity. 2nd, *Dāsya*, or servitude. When this is attained, the heart is more animated, the mind is more active, and the affections are warmer. This leads to a vow of service, and the position of him who offers it is as that of a slave to his master. 3rd, *Sākya*, or friendship. When he attains to this height, the devotee no longer regards Krishna as his master, but as his personal friend, whom he is impelled to please because of the love he bears towards him. 4th, *Bātsālya*, or filial affection, is that degree of affection which is recognized as natural in a child towards its father; the childlike trust which leads its possessor to look up to Krishna and say, Thou art my father. The 5th and last form of this bhakti is called *Mādhurya*, or sweetness; and the illustration given of this is that love which the milkmaids of Vrindāvana bore towards the hero when he was residing in their midst, the highest type of all being that which Rādhā had for her lord.

Vaikantha is the heaven of the Vaishnavas wherein they hope to be united to, or rather identified with, Krishna, and then reign as divine for ever. Others seem rather to expect to enjoy a separate existence in heaven.

Amongst the most important duties as taught by the Vaishnavas is that of "*Guru Pādāsraya*," or the taking refuge under the guru. The gurus in Vaishnava sects are not necessarily Brāhmans, but the adoration claimed by them is even greater than that demanded by ordinary Brāhmans. The chief work of the guru is *giving the mantra*, or text, which it is the duty of the disciple to repeat 108 times before he eats or drinks anything. The following texts teach the authority of the guru. "The mantra is manifest in the guru, and the guru is Hari himself." Krishna says, "The guru is first to be worshipped, and then I am to be worshipped." "When Hari is angry, the guru is our protector; when the guru is angry, we have no protector."

The gurus, or, as they are often called, gosains, travel about with considerable state; and when they come to a disciple's house expect to be well treated, and on their departure well paid. The water in which their feet have been washed is drunk by the disciples and their family, whilst the food that has been placed before so sacred a person is greedily devoured by all the followers of the sect. Already there is rebellion in the camp; some of the Vaishnavas are throwing off this adoration of the gurus.

The next important duty is *Nāma Kirton*, *i.e.*, the repetition of the name of the deity. The common formula in Bengal is this: Hari Krishna, Hari Krishna Krishna, Krishna Hari, Hari Hari Rāma, Hari Rāma Rāma, Rāma Hari Hari. The rosary of 108 seeds is often to be seen in the hands of the Vaishnavas, or the hand and rosary are concealed in a bag, as the process of counting may not be seen by ordinary onlookers.

Next in order is the *Sankirtān*. This is a public act, in which a number join in singing the praises of Krishna. It is noisy, irreverent, often indecent; the singing is frequently accompanied by dancing.

One of the most important duties is the *Mahastab* (great joy). This is a feast which is held at the death of some gosain or mahanta, or any great personage amongst the community. At these feasts no *caste* regulations are observed. All who come to the feast eat together. The gosain takes a little food from a dish; what is left is mixed with the other food that is prepared, and the whole becomes *prasād*, or sacred. To eat of this is a work of great merit. But the most valued food of the whole feast is that which has been left by the gosain on his plate, a few grains of which is given to those only who are considered specially holy and devout.

It is a great work of merit to hear the Bhāgavata read by the kathaks, or professional readers, and it is amongst the Vaishnavas especially that the kathaks find employment. What Benares is to the ordinary Hindu, Mathura is to the Vaishnava; residence there is believed to be productive of indescribable benefits.

The Vairāgis, or ascetic Vaishnavas, can marry at a trifling cost, and obtain a divorce for as little; they are generally considered to be most immoral. This class as a rule bury, not burn their dead.

The chief *tendency* of Chaitanya's teaching was to break down caste. Men of all castes can receive the mantra, and even Mussulmāns have been received into the community. The Vairāgis, of whatever caste, eat together, but the secular members as a rule, except on the festival days, do not eat with those of other castes.

From the main body of Chaitanya's followers are two classes that may be regarded as seceders from it. 1. The *Spashtha Dyāks.* These differ chiefly with respect to the authority of the gurus. They deny their divinity. Men and women live together in convents professedly in the relation of brothers and sisters. The men act as gurus to each other, and the women are gurus to the female members of the community. All the members of this branch lead the ascetic life. 2. The *Kartha Bhojas.* This is a very modern sect founded by Rāma Taran Pāl of Ghoshpāra. Its teaching goes to the other extreme on this question. It teaches that the gurus are none other than Krishna himself, and he in the person of the gurus becomes the Ishta Deva, the chosen deity, of his followers. Its main teaching is summed up in the following: "Attach yourself to your guru, speak the truth, follow the counsels of your guru."

8. We now come to notice a few of the less influential sects connected with the Vaishnava worship, and shall simply

notice the particulars in which they differ from the large masses of the Hindus who are Vishnu's worshippers.

a. Rādhā Vallabhis are those who whilst worshipping Krishna, prefer to give their chief adoration to Rādhā, his chief mistress according to some, or his heavenly bride according to others. It is said that it was owing to a curse that Rādhā his celestial spouse became a milkmaid upon earth, and on this ground Krishna's criminal intercourse with her is defended.

b. Sakhi Bhavas. The teaching of this sect differs little from that of the preceding; but the members, in order to show their great regard for Rādhā in preference to her husband, not only adopt woman's dress, but also the manners and occupation of women. The members of this sect are few in number, and not very respectable.

c. Charan Dāsis. This sect was founded at Dehli, where its head-quarters are at the present time, by a merchant named Charan Dās. At first this man taught that no representative of deity should be worshipped; he even repudiated the Sālgrām and Tulsi. Gradually, however, innovations have been made, and the objects common to other Vaishnavas are now freely worshipped. He taught, further, that good works are of equal value with faith; that a man's works determine his final condition. There are a few ascetic members of this sect who wear yellow garments, and have a single streak of sandal-wood or gopichandana down the forehead. They also wear a small pointed cap and a yellow turban.

d. Sanyasis. This name, though usually employed to denote ascetics of the Saivya faith, is also used with the qualifying word Tridandi for a class of Vaishnavas of the Rāmānuja sect who have passed through the first two stages of the Brāhmanical order, and have entered upon the ascetic life. The word *danda* signifies a staff, and the Tridandi Sanyasis are those who have taken up the three-fold staff; *i.e.*, have exercised a three-fold restraint of speech, body, and

7

mind, or word, deed, and thought. These men do not touch metals or fire, and cannot, therefore, cook their food, but depend upon the generosity of the pious Brāhmans of the other orders of the Sri Vaishnava sect.

e. Vairāgis. These are the ascetics of the Rāmānand sect described above. They have no employment and no fixed abode, but wander from shrine to shrine, and from one monastery to another, dependent upon the gifts of the faithful.

f. Nāgas. All the great Hindu sects have a division of nāgas, *i.e.*, those who profess to carry their religious earnestness to an extreme length. These men discard all clothing; and though regarded as holy (saints) by the community, are known to be a most dissolute set of men. At some religious festivals hundreds of these men walk in procession absolutely naked, in the presence of thousands of men and women.

CHAPTER VI.

THE SAIVITE SECTS; OR THOSE WHO REGARD SIVA AS THE SUPREME DEITY.

[The distinguishing marks of these sects are horizontal instead of perpendicular, the differing widths and colours marking the difference of sect.]

The worship of Siva has little of the popular and attractive element that we have noticed in connection with the Vaishnava worship. It is mostly confined to the Brāhmans and those who are immediately influenced by them. In North India there are no legends of an attractive kind to lead men to choose him as their Ishta Deva (chosen deity); no popular works written to lead men to direct their worship to him; no breaking down of the strict caste rules as an inducement for those of the more despised classes to unite themselves with the Saivite sects. There are many temples sacred to Siva, in which he is represented by the Linga; but as a rule they are not popular shrines, as are those of Krishna, Jagannātha, &c. It is different, however, with the temples of his consort Parvati, Durgā, Kāli, in the many forms under which she is worshipped. Siva is rather a repulsive, dreadful being, and it is certain that it is fear only which impels men to worship him. It is as the husband of Parvati that men approach him with their gifts, rather than for anything that is attractive in his character and conduct. Krishna appeals to the human instincts of men, and his worship is a bright and joyous thing; whilst Siva is the embodiment of that which is stern, cruel, and powerful only.

There are no great sects, in one sense of the word, similar to those connected with the worship of Vishnu; the worshippers of Siva for the most part agree with each other in faith and practice. There are, however, classes of ascetics whose precepts differ somewhat from those of the great mass of Saivites which call for a brief notice. It is evident that Vaishnavism is a much more recent form of Hinduism than that of Saivism; and having broken away from the older and more stereotyped forms, there has been greater latitude in their creed and ritual than is seen amongst those who adhere to the older forms.

The great authority in matters connected with Siva-worship is Sankara Ācharjya. This man was born at Kerala, or Malabar, and by some is declared to have been an incarnation of Siva. Others, again, say that he was the child of an adulterous union, for which his mother was outcasted. He divided the people into seventy-two classes, eighteen of which he assigned to each of the four great Hindu castes. For some reason he appears to have been unpopular with the people of his day; and when he returned from a pilgrimage, his mother happening to die, the Brāhmans of the neighbourhood would not attend her funeral ceremonies, or give him any sacred fire wherewith he might burn her body. Sankara obtained fire by simply rubbing his arm, and having burned the body in the courtyard of the house, declared that Brāhmans should no longer read the Vedas there, that religious mendicants should not obtain alms, and that the dead should always be burned near to the house where they had lived. After this he lived an ascetic life, and was engaged in controversy with the leaders of other sects. His chief work is a commentary on the Bhāgavata Gita. He established several monasteries, lived for some time in Kashmir, and died when only thirty-two years of age at Kedarnāth, in the Himalayahs.

a. The Dandis, or Staff-bearers. These, and the Tridandtis mentioned before, are the legitimate representatives of the fourth Āsrama, or mendicant life, into which the orthodox Brāhman's life is divided. Each Brāhman's life, according to the Sāstras, ought to be divided as follows:—First, the Student stage; secondly, the Householder stage; thirdly, the Hermit stage; and fourthly, the Ascetic stage. As a student, he learned the Vedas; as a householder, he obtained sons; as a hermit, he taught students; and as an ascetic, he had opportunity for reflection and thought to prepare him for entering into the next stage of existence. Nowadays this the orthodox way of spending their days is not followed by many, though it is no uncommon thing for Brāhmans, when old age comes, to leave their home and take up their residence in Benares and other sacred places, that, being freed from the cares of a family, their minds may be fitted by contemplation to pass into the presence of the Judge. It is competent for any who may be disposed to take up the ascetic life to commence this at any period of their lives without going through the previous stages of student, householder, and hermit.

The Dandi is generally known by his staff, with a piece of red cloth attached in which his Brāhmanical cord is carried. He wears only a small cloth round his waist, and has his head and face cleanly shaven; his food he begs from the houses of Brāhmans, and ought to live alone, near to, though not inside, a city. They have no particular time for or form of worship, and their chief employment is meditation. I have frequently seen these men, and, when trying to converse with them, have found them to be almost idiotic. Not using their mind, it seems as though neglect had almost destroyed it. Some destroy their bodily organs, and certainly the mental faculties of many of them are impaired, as they pass their time in idleness, and try not to think; it is mere existence, not life, that they regard as the perfect state. Siva, under the name of Bhairava (the terrible), is their chief deity, and the mantra they receive is the one common to the Saivites. They are initiated into the worship of this deity by a small incision being made under the arm, the blood that flows from the wound being offered to the deity. The Dandis do not burn, but bury their dead, or throw them into sacred streams.

Originally the profession of the Dandi was open to men of the three highest castes only; now many of the lowest castes assume the dress, symbols, and life of the ascetic. To an outsider it seems to be a most idle and miserable life. More sleepy and dirty specimens of humanity than these *holy* men one has never seen. But it is evident that the honours given to them in this life, and the hopes of heavenly rewards, are sufficient to allure men from their work and home and families in order to lead this wandering life. These blessings have an attraction that the uninitiated cannot understand. At certain festivals, such as the Charak Puja, many of the low caste people assume this garb and profession for a few days only, and wander about the streets begging; but this is a part of the fun and frolic of the time.

b. The Dasnāmi Dandis. The name of this sect is given because the members are divided into *ten* classes after the ten chief disciples of Sankara, and are regarded as the legitimate descendants of the fraternities founded by him. The chief difference between them and the Dandis lies in the fact that at first they admitted Brāhmans only to their fellowship. Of the ten classes, now four only are regarded as true to their founder's doctrine. The chief deviation of the other six classes, who bear the name of atits, or guests, is this: they have given up the use of the staff; they wear clothes and ornaments, prepare their own food, and admit other than Brāhmans to their order.

c. The Yogis. This is another class of religious mendicants. The name signifies one who meditates, and meditation has been always regarded by the Hindus as the most sacred of religious duties. The Yogis of the present day profess to be the descendants of men who in olden time possessed immense influence over the people. The object of the Yogi was to concentrate his attention until he had come to regard himself as one with the supreme spirit. Methods by which this state of perfection could be attained are carefully taught in the Hindu Scriptures. The Yogi must breathe in a particular manner, sit in eighty-four different postures, fix the eye on the tip of the nose, and meditate on Siva until he and they become one. And these Scriptures go on to describe most marvellous effects which follow this complete mental abstraction. In this state they declare the Yogis can make themselves lighter than the lightest, and heavier than the heaviest substances; can magnify or lessen their forms at will, can instantaneously travel immense distances, reanimate corpses by breathing their own spirit into them, render themselves invisible, and know the past, present, and future at a glance. Such high pretensions are made of this profession in the past. Nowadays these men go about the country as fortune-tellers and conjurors, and often impose upon the ignorance and credulity of the people. No doubt many of them are clever jugglers. The founder of the sect was named Goraknātha, and his disciples are called Kānphati, because at their initiation they have their ears pierced. Traces of this sect are to be found at Peshawar, and at Gorakhpore there is a temple and a math of the order. Tradition says that the original temple was erected by Siva himself in the Treta age of the Hindus, which answers to the silver age of the classics. The present temple is of modern date, and in the adjacent math the superior or mahant of the order resides. Besides the regular members, there are many who simply for gain assume their dress and manners, and practise as conjurors without taking any religious vows, or making any pretensions to a religious life.

d. Jangamas. This class of Saivites is distinguished by the fact that they all wear a representation of the Linga, the emblem of Siva, on their bodies or in their dress: these are often made of copper or silver, and either worn round the neck or in the turban. In North India occasionally the members of this sect are to be seen leading about a bull to represent Siva's favourite animal Nandi; but in South India, where their numbers are very large, they are known by the name of Lingayets, and priests of the Siva temples generally belong to it. The founder of this sect, or the restorer of the worship of Siva in these parts, was named Bāsava, who was said to be an incarnation of Nandi, the bull of Siva. At Siva's command this faithful servant came to earth to resuscitate the worship of his master. He lived at Kalyān, where he was Minister of Police.

The Bāsava Purāna, as the book is called in which the history of this revival of Siva-worship is given, contains some wonderful legends of the benefits of Linga-worship, and is very different from the works on this subject in North India. On one occasion Bāsava, who had been profuse in his gifts to other members of his sect, was accused to the king of embezzlement; but when the treasury was opened it was found that all the minister's gifts had not in any way diminished the treasures. A fellow-casteman, living with a dancing-girl, sent to Bāsava's house for his daily supply of rice. The servant on his return spoke so strongly of the richness of the dress of the minister's wife that the cupidity of this dancing-girl was excited. Her lord, therefore, went to ask Bāsava for it. The minister ordered his wife to give it up; but, as she took it off, another equally beautiful sprang from her body, which was also given to the Jangama. It is also taught that Bāsava was escorted to heaven by Siva and Parvati themselves, who came from heaven thus to show their respect. It is supposed, as far as can be told, that the revival or institution of Siva-worship occurred in the early part of the eleventh century.

e. Paramhansa. The Sanyasi is of four kinds, the Kutichara, the Bahudaka, the Hansa, and the Paramhansa, the difference between whom, however, is only one of graduated intensity of self-mortification and abstraction. Of these the Paramhansa is the most eminent, and denotes the ascetic who is solely occupied with his meditations on the deity, and who is indifferent to pleasure or pain, insensible to heat or cold, and incapable of satiety or want. Some of those who profess to have attained to this excellence are to be met with. In proof of this they go naked, never speak, and never ask for anything they may want. They have attendants, who collect what is necessary, and feed them as they would a child. Of course there are some who make a gain by their professed sanctity, but some, so far as one can see, have come to believe that they are right in adopting this mode of life.

f. Aghoris. These differ from the former in this respect: that whilst the Paramhansa does not parade his virtues, the Aghoris make their supposed sanctity a reason for liberal alms-giving. The original Aghori-worship seems to have been devoted to the female powers, or Devi, in one of her many forms, and to have demanded human victims. The votaries of this sect carried a staff set with bones, and a human skull for a drinking pot. Though the regular worship of this kind has been suppressed a few miserable wretches go about the country professing to belong to the sect; and, as a proof of their utter indifference about worldly objects, eat whatever is given them, even carrion. In order to extort money they gash their limbs, that the crime of blood-letting may rest upon those who refuse to give them alms. Moor in the "Hindu Pantheon" speaks of the Paramhansas being seen sitting on a corpse as it floated down the Ganges, and eating the decomposing body; but he must have been misled; the Paramhansas, though professedly perfect, would not do this; it must have been one of this class of Aghoris that was seen in this disgusting attitude, probably as a means of extorting money from the bystanders.

g. In addition to the above are a few less known ascetics which may just be mentioned, men who practise austerities of various kinds, from which their names are taken. The *Urddhabāhus* (holders up of arms) are those who stand in one posture for years, holding one or both of their arms above the head until the muscles become contracted and they cannot bring them down again to their side. Some also close their fists, and allow their nails to grow until they completely pass through the hands. These men generally travel alone, and wander from shrine to shrine. The *Akāsmukhis* are those who turn their faces towards the sky until the muscles of the neck become fixed, and they cannot alter this most painful position. The peculiarity of the *Nakhis* is that they allow their nails to grow without being cut. The *Gūdaras* travel about with a small pan of metal, in which they burn sandal and other scented wood in the houses they may visit collecting alms; their method of asking alms being the mere repetition of the work Alakh, meaning that God's nature is incapable of being described; He is without any marks or distinctive features. The *Sūkharas*, *Rūkharas*, and *Ukharas* have nothing distinctive save their dress, excepting the last-named, who drink spirituous liquors and eat meat. The *Nāgas* are those who go about naked, allow their hair and beards to grow, use arms, and seem to be ready to take part in any rows that may arise; a sort of professional vagabond life is that which these men elect; but when tired of this it is open for them to re-enter any of the more respectable sects from which they may have come. It will be noticed that *all* the Sanyasi or ascetic sects of the Saivas are celibates; it is, in fact, a much harsher and more repulsive form of religious life than that followed by the Vaishnavas.

CHAPTER VII.

THE SAKTAS; OR THOSE SECTS EXCLUSIVELY DEVOTED TO THE WORSHIP OF THE FEMALE DEITIES.

It has been estimated that of the Hindus in Bengal about three-fourths are devoted to the worship of Sakti; *i.e.*, the power or energy of the God as represented in some of the many female forms. Of the remaining quarter, three parts are Vaishnavas, and the remaining quarter are mostly Saivas. Each deity has his consort, to whom the worship of the people is in some cases more freely given than to her husband. Thus Brahmā, the creator, is now almost entirely neglected; but Saraswati, his wife, is regularly worshipped as the patroness of learning. Lakshmi, Rādhā, and Sitā, are, to say the least, as popular as their lords; whilst the many forms of Parvati, Durgā, Kāli, are of all deities the most commonly worshipped by the masses of Bengal. And as the worshipper of Vishnu, or Siva, declares that his particular object of worship is the supreme from whom all the other gods derive their origin, the devotees of the goddesses have no hesitation in saying that they are the cause of all created things. Thus they are likened to the active energy of the soul, and to the power of burning in the fire. These goddesses are regarded as the divine force or energy of the god personified. The explanation commonly given is as follows: The Supreme Being wishing to create, divided himself into two parts; the one became Brahmā, the other Prākriti, or nature; and as from Brahmā all males, so from

Prākriti all females sprung. But as without the female the male is unproductive, the female is regarded as the real force in nature, and hence the almost exclusive adoration that is paid to the female deities by so many of the Hindus. In some of the Purānas the adoration of Prākriti or Sakti, the energy of the gods, who is worshipped under the forms of Saraswati, Lakshmi, Durgā, &c., the wives of the gods, is authorized to some extent; but it is in the more modern books called Tantras that this worship is chiefly upheld. It is probable some of these books were written almost as early as some of the later Purānas, but most of them are certainly not older than the eleventh century. There are two main divisions of this sect, the Dakshinas, or right-hand worshippers, and the Vāmācharis, or left-hand worshippers. But perhaps less is known of these sects than of any others, because as yet the Tantras have been kept in greater secrecy than most of the other books of the Hindus.

1. The *Dakshinas*, or right-hand worshippers, are those who worship the female deities and regard them as the supreme in an open, public manner, in accordance with the Purānic ritual, and free from the gross impurities connected with the Vāmāchari form of worship. The great difference in this worship from that which is offered to Vishnu, in any of his various forms, consists in the offering of *Bali*, or bloody sacrifices. On the great festival days at Kāli Ghāt, near Calcutta, and other popular shrines, the courtyard literally streams with the blood of the hundred of kids, and the many buffaloes that have been offered in sacrifice. And in the courtyards of the Hindu homes it is customary to offer up in sacrifice kids and buffaloes when the festivals of Durgā in any of her forms are held. One of the Purrānas declares that whilst it is true that animal sacrifices gratify Durgā, it is also true that this act subjects the sacrificer to the sin which attaches to the destruction of animal life. This teaching is the result of the Vaishnava faith, one prominent article of which is the sacredness

of all life; and to the earnest follower of Vishnu the scenes commonly witnessed at a Durgā or Kāli Puja must necessarily be most repulsive, and the worshippers cannot but be regarded by him as most guilty. The offerers of sacrifice can plead the authority of the Vedas and the customs of their remote ancestors, and it is probably the sanction that is given in those works to animal sacrifices that has led many of the Vaishnava sects to regard them with but little respect. The general worship of the Saktas is similar to that of the other Hindus, with the addition of the offering of these bloody sacrifices. The reason assigned for the presentation of blood to these deities is said to be this. When the goddess was weary in her great conflict with the demons she came on earth to destroy, as there was nothing else at hand to sustain her strength, she drank of the blood of her slaughtered foes. By the presentation of blood it is believed that the satisfaction she had when refreshed by that draught is brought to mind, and, being in a benignant mood, she will bestow blessings upon her worshippers. It should be noticed that it is only to the consort of Siva in her many forms that animal sacrifices are offered; Saraswati, Lakshmi, Rādhā, and Sitā, &c., the wives of Brahmā, and Vishnu in his incarnations, are never worshipped in this manner.

2. The *Vāmāchāris*. [When in public the members of this sect generally wear the sectarial marks of some other sect, because it is regarded by the more respectable Hindus as disgraceful to be connected with it. A few, however, are met with who glory in their shame, and boldly proclaim themselves Vāmācharis by their marks. These signs are the following: a semicircular line or lines of vermilion on the forehead, or a perpendicular line of red in the middle of the forehead, with a round red spot at the root of the nose. They use a small rosary of Rudrāksha, or coral shells, small enough to be concealed in the hand, or carried in a purse. At the time of worship they wear a strip of scarlet silk round the loins, and a garland of scarlet flowers round the neck.]

This sect worships the goddesses not in accordance with the teaching of the Purānas, but follow the instructions of the Tantras. Their services are carried on in secret, only the initiated being admitted to them. They worship Devi, the Sakti of Siva, Lakshmi, Saraswati, the Mātris (*i.e.*, the mothers), Yoginis, and Dākinis (a sort of ghost, or demon), Siva himself, under the form of Bhairava, being sometimes joined with his consort at their feasts. The aim of the worshippers is, by the reverence paid to Sakti, to obtain supernatural powers in this life, and to obtain a reunion with the deity after death. Their worship varies, of course, with the object to whom it is directed, but it generally includes one or all of the following: the offering of flesh, fish, wine, union with women, and mystical gesticulation.

When the object desired is to interview a spirit, a corpse is necessary. The inquirer must visit a cemetery or burning ghāt alone at midnight, and, seated upon the corpse, make the necessary offerings. If he can do this without fear, the Bhutas (spirits), Yoginis, and other imaginary goblins, both male and female, become his slaves.

The principal ceremonies connected with this worship are not, however, performed in solitude, but by the members of the sect together, a naked woman being worshipped by them as the representative of Sakti. The men present regard themselves as the representation of Bhairava (Siva), and the women as Bhairavis (Devis). The ceremony is followed by drunken and sensual orgies. The members are numerous, especially amongst the Brāhmans. The following is one form of the ritual as far as it can be published. The object of worship at the ceremony must be a dancing-girl, a female devotee, a harlot, a washerwoman, a barber's wife, a female of the Brāhmanical or Sudra caste, a flower girl, or a milkmaid. The worship is to commence at midnight with a party of eight, nine, or eleven couples of men and women. According to the person selected for the Sakti, appropriate mantras, or texts, are fixed by the ritual. She must be disrobed, but richly adorned with jewels, &c., and then is rendered pure by the repetition of certain mantras. After this, with its appropriate formula, she is sprinkled with wine, and, if not previously initiated, now receives the initiatory text. The rites then proceed, but if the reports given of them are at all correct, they are quite unfit for publication. It is only right, however, to say that the Hindus generally repudiate the doings of this sect, and regard them as evil; at the same time it is beyond dispute that it exists, and in certain parts of the country has a considerable number of members. A great deal of the teaching is not *written*, its precepts being taught verbally to the initiated, who in their turn become the instructors of the new members.

3. The *Kiratis*. These are the worshippers of Devi in her most terrible form as Kapālika, who in former times was propitiated by human victims. As these cannot now be offered to her, her votaries seek to please her by making offerings of their own blood. They pierce their flesh with hooks, cut themselves with knives, lance their tongues and cheeks, and, as long as the law permitted, swung from bamboos with hooks fastened into their bodies, and threw themselves from platforms upon knives fixed upright upon the ground. At the present time these practices are resorted to after a fashion; cords are tied round the waist in which the hooks are caught, and the knives are so arranged that as the man falls upon them, they lie flat upon the ground. Before the Government interfered, these cruel rites were freely practised, and many were seriously injured by them. Whenever I have seen these men thus lacerating themselves it has appeared to me that it was more from the hope of gain than from devotion that they did it. In every case they were quite intoxicated with a preparation of hemp that is common in India, which has the effect of exciting the brain, and at the same time lessening the pain they would otherwise suffer. But whatever the motive, it is certain that at these festivals there are plenty of men to be found who are ready to suffer, and, were it per-

mitted, would gladly run the risk of permanent injury to themselves from these frightful modes of worship. The true Kirati is thus described: His body is smeared with ashes from a funeral pile, around his neck is a garland of human skulls, his hair is matted, his forehead streaked with a black line, his loins are covered with a tiger's skin, in his left hand he carries a skull, and in his right a bell, which he rings as he walks, shouting, "Ho! Sambha Bhairava"; "Ho! Lord of Kāli." It will be noticed from this description that, as the name implies, the members of this sect try to imitate the dress and general appearance of Siva.

CHAPTER VIII.

MISCELLANEOUS SECTS.

1. *Saurapatas.* These are Hindus who regard Surya (the sun) as the supreme deity. Nowadays there are few of them to be met with, though at one time they were more numerous. On Sundays, and also on the days when the sun passes from one zodiacal sign to another, they eat but one meal, and that without salt. They must never eat until they have seen the sun.

2. *Ganapatyas* are those who regard Ganesa as the supreme. All the Hindus worship Ganesa, along with the other deities; but there are a few who place him as head over all, and direct their worship almost exclusively to him. It is difficult to see why this should be done; for although Ganesa is regarded as the god of wisdom, he is not credited with many very marvellous works in the Hindu scriptures.

3. *Sikhs.* The religion of the Sikhs is an offshoot from Hinduism, and as such calls for a brief notice. The word Sikh is simply a corruption of the word Sishya, meaning a disciple. The founder of the religion was Nānak, who was born at Lahore, in the year 1469. To him succeeded nine Pontiffs, of whom Govinda was the most influential. The aim of Nānak was to lead Hindus and Mussulmāns to recognize what was essential in the religion of each, and to reject or treat with indifference non-essentials. In order to this, whilst he recognized the divinity of the Hindu deities, he also acknowledged the inspiration of Mahomet. The chief

tenets of the system as taught by Govinda were these: To worship one supreme being, to eschew superstition, to practise strict morality, and to live by the sword. This last doctrine greatly influenced his followers, and moulded them into one of the bravest people of the East, enabling them to form themselves into a nation and fight until they gained their freedom. The gurus claimed to be true Kshetriyas. There are seven classes of Sikhs, each with some slight modification of creed and ritual; the following only need special mention:—

a. The *Udāsis* (solitary), as their name implies, profess to be indifferent to worldly vicissitudes, and dwell apart from the world in sangats, or colleges. They regard themselves as the true and genuine followers of Nānak. They do not, however, think it incumbent upon them to despise good food and clothing; nor is celibacy a necessary ordinance, though many of them are unmarried. Their office consists largely in reading and expounding the works of Nānak and Govinda, as collected in the Ādi Grantha and Dās Padshali Ki Grantha; they also read the works of Kabir, Sur Dāss, and others that have been previously mentioned in the description of the Vaishnava sects. The books of their religion are worshipped, and at the close of the services in which they have been read the presiding Udāsi gives a feast from the prasād, *i.e.*, food offered to the idols which were worshipped along with the books. The main object to be effected by this worship is benevolence and self-denial, and, in common with most of the Hindus, they look for deliverance from the delusions of Māyā, through whose influence it is that they regard themselves as distinct from the Godhead. Generally speaking, the creed of the Sikhs is very similar to that of the disciples of Kabir.

b. The *Rāmrāyis* take their name from their leader, Rāma Rāya, who disputed with Hari Krishna for the position of Pontift. He was unsuccessful in his attempt, but, as many thought him entitled to the office, they and their descendants are known as his adherents.

c. The *Suthreh Shahis* are a wandering set, who carry two sticks in their hands, which they strike together as a means of asking alms. Generally they are a dissolute set of men, and are regarded as a disgrace to the community by the genuine Sikhs.

d. Govinda Singhas. It was the leader of this sect who entirely changed the Sikh religion and made it a strong political institution. He welcomed Hindus and Mussulmāns alike who discarded their faith in the Hindu deities and Mahomet, and took up the sword in his cause. He professedly ignored the distinctions of the Hindu castes, though great reverence was paid to Brāhmans, and they continued to worship the Hindu deities. His followers, however, declare that they have given up their faith in the Hindu Scriptures, and regard the work of their leader, the Das Padshali Ki Grantha as their authority in religious matters.

e. The *Nirmalas* are an ascetic, contemplative class, who live alone generally, but who are to be found at the great Hindu shrines. They will give part of their prasād to Christians even, as several writers speak of having partaken of it.

f. The *Nāgas* differ little from the preceding class, excepting in the fact that they wander about the country naked.

g. There are a few followers of a Kshetriya namod Prān Nāth who tried to form a religious system on the same lines as Nānak, but his followers are now nearly all merged into the other sects of the Sikhs.

4. The *Jains.* The leading tenets of the Jains, and those which distinguish them from the main body of the Hindus, are the following: They deny the divine origin and infallible authority of the Vedas; they hold that certain saints have, by a life of purity and self-mortification, attained not only to an equality with, but even superiority over, the deities commonly worshipped by the Hindus; and they show excessive regard for all forms of animal life. It will be noticed that in the first two articles of their creed they agree with the Buddhists, though the calendar of saints who have attained to this

exalted position differs in the two great sects. The disregard which both the Jains and Buddhists manifest for the Vedas leads to the neglect of the rites they prescribe. The chief reason assigned for this is the fact that the Vedas sanctioned animal sacrifices; and the Homa, or burnt-offering of ghi, is repugnant to their feelings, because it is possible that by it animal life is destroyed, as insects may be crawling on the ground where the offering is made, or may exist in the ghi itself.

The Jains (*i.e.* the worshippers of the Jinas) profess to reverence twenty-four Tirthankaras, or deified mortals of a past age, twenty-four of the present, and twenty-four who have as yet to attain this honour. These they declare to be greater than even the chief deities of the Hindu Pantheon. Statues of these beings in black and white marble are to be seen in their temples. They are all of the same style of feature, quietness and calmness being their chief characteristic; nothing at all approaching to the grotesque, as appears in many of the ordinary Hindu objects of worship; and the Jain temples for beauty and cleanliness are in every way superior to those of the orthodox Hindus. The saints most generally worshipped by the Jains of North India are Parisnātha and Mahavir, the twenty-third and twenty-fourth of the present race of saints. The following epithets applied to the saints will show the profound reverence that is paid to them. They are called Jagatprabhus (lords of the world), Kshina-karma (free from ceremonial acts), Sarvagna (omniscient), Adiswara (supreme lord), Devādideva (god of gods), Tirthankaras (those who have passed over the sea of life), and Jina (victors over all human passions and infirmities).

The previous jinas, or saints, are said to have been of colossal height, and to have lived for millions of years; but as the two last mentioned alone are believed to have been of ordinary size, and to have lived for the ordinary term of life, it is generally admitted that they were historical personages, the others being the offspring of a fertile imagination, employed to carry back the origin of the sect into a remote antiquity. It is taught that these deified saints lived on earth as ordinary mortals through several lives until they finally attained to union with the supreme. It is uncertain when the sect was formed originally, but there are many reasons for believing that it is of later origin than Buddhism.

The Jains hold that all existences are divisible into two classes, Jiva and Ajiva; *i.e.*, life and not-life. Their forms may change, but they remain imperishable. They continue for a time in a certain form, undergo some change, and then return eventually to their previous state.

1. *Jiva* (life). All beings possessed of jiva are of two kinds: those that can move and those which cannot. In the first class are included men, animals, demons, and gods; in the second are the four elements, earth, water, fire, air, and the whole of the vegetable kingdom. According to the actions of each living thing during the continuance of its present life will the next be higher or lower. A man, *e.g.*, through his sins in his present life, in his next life is born as an animal. If his life be made up of virtue and vice, he will be born again as a man; if his life is virtuous only, and unmixed with vice, he ascends to heaven, and passing through various stages of probation, finally obtains emancipation from future separate existence. This is in accord generally with the teaching of the Hindu system.

2. *Ajiva.* In this class we find time, religion, &c., enumerated. Religion, again, is composed of many elements, the chief of which are the following:—*Punya*, religious merit—whatever is of benefit to human beings. As the nearest approach to this may be mentioned the works of supererogation of the Romish Church; *i.e.*, works not essential to salvation, but the performance of which will greatly conduce to the spiritual advancement of the doer of them. *Pāp* (sin), the opposite of Punya. Of these there are 1,082; but it is noticeable that generally these are not moral offences, but the violation of some arbitrary caste rules. For although in some

parts of India caste rules are partially disregarded by them, in other parts, the Jains are as scrupulous in caste matters as are the orthodox Hindus. *Asrava.* This signifies the organs of sense, passion, &c., the source whence evil in man proceeds. *Saṁvara; i.e.,* the power by which acts are aided or hindered, as attention, secrecy, patience, asceticism, conviction of truth, &c. *Nirjara; i.e.,* penance, such as fasting, repentance, study, &c. *Banda* (union); *i.e.,* the union of life with acts, as milk with water. *Moksha,* or liberation of the vital spirit from the bonds of action; exemption from the necessity of being again born into the world. It is not at all clear in what state the liberated spirit will continue to live. It is, however, not incompatible, in the opinion of the Jains, with the enjoyment of Nirvāna, which means "gone out," as a fire; "set," as a sun; "defunct," as a saint who has passed away enjoys repose. "It is not annihilation, but unceasing apathy, which they regard as supreme felicity, worthy to be sought by the practice of mortification as well as by the acquisition of knowledge."

The Jains are divided into two classes: Yatis, the clerical, and Srāvakas, or lay members. Implicit belief in the teaching and life of the Tirthankaras is considered a necessary part of their religious system. Their moral code is summed up in five laws: refraining from injury to life, truth, honesty, chastity, and freedom from worldly desires. There are four dharmas, or works of merit: liberality, gentleness, piety, and penance; and three kinds of restraint, viz., that of the mind, tongue, and person. It is a clear evidence of the lack of power of the system over the conduct of its members that some of the most religious of the Jains are amongst the most immoral of men. Some minor instructions are somewhat ludicrous. At certain seasons of the year abstinence from salt, flowers, green fruit, roots, honey, grapes, and tobacco must be observed. Water must be twice strained before it is drunk, lest any living creature should be in it; and no liquid must be left uncovered, lest an insect should fall into it and be drowned. And that they may not happen to swallow a fly, they must never eat in the dark. The very religious members of the sect generally wear a piece of gauze over their lips, lest in breathing they should kill any insect; and for the same reason a brush is used to sweep a seat before sitting down upon it. It is a system of quietism, which renders its followers harmless members of the community; but generally it produces indifference respecting the world to come.

The ritual of the Jains is very simple. The Yātis, or devotees, can worship in the temples or not; but the laymen must visit a temple at least once a day, and walk three times round the building; they then bow to the image, and offer a flower, and repeat a short mantra, or text. In ordinary life they certainly are not purer than their Hindu neighbours. The builder of one of their most beautiful temples, which is situated in a splendid garden, has his own house decorated in a most indecent manner. This house is most expensively furnished, but its ornamental parts are of the worst conceivable form. The officiating priests at the temples are generally Brāhmans, and whilst acknowledging the deity of the Hindu gods, they devote their chief worship to the deified saints. Sometimes the images of Bhairavas and Bhairavis, the attendants of Siva and Kali, are found in these temples, and the ritual differs but little from that of the Saiva and Sakta worship.

The mythology of the Jains is generally wilder even than that of the Hindus; and from this it seems pretty clear that their books are of later date. It is possible that the Jains were a sect of the Buddhists, but it seems more likely that they are a remnant of that sect, whose leaders at a time of religious toleration formulated their creed and gathered a few disciples long after the Buddhists had been banished from the country. The effect of Hinduism upon the Jains, is seen in the fact that in the South, where caste prejudices are stronger, the Jains carefully observe the caste regulations; but in North India, where the regulations of caste are not so stringently observed, they generally regard themselves as all belonging to the Vaisbyas, the third of the great castes.

The main body of the Jains is divided into two great classes, the Swetambaras, or white-robed; and the Digambaras, or air-clad, *i.e.*, naked. Between these the most bitter animosity prevails. Probably the Digambaras went about naked, or nearly so; now they simply divest themselves of their upper garment, a many-coloured one, during meals; the Swetambaras, on the other hand, retain their clothes during their meals. This, however, does not constitute the only or main difference between them. The Swetambaras decorate their images with jewels; their opponents consider this action to be wrong. The gurus of the Swetambaras eat their food from vessels; those of the Digambaras must take it from the hands of their disciples. The Swetambaras assert that the angas (Scriptures) were the work of the immediate disciples of the Tirthaukaras; the Digambaras affirm a much later origin for them. The Swetambaras assert that women can obtain nirvāna; the Digambaras deny this.

In addition to these two main divisions, there are a few insignificant sects, some of which discard the use of images altogether.

5. *Sādhus.* The term Sādhu (saint) is commonly applied to any Hindu ascetic, but there is a sect who accept it as their own proper name, which was founded by a man named Birbhān, who was born in the neighbourhood of Dehli, in the year 1658. This man declared that he received his teaching in a miraculous manner from the Satguru (the true teacher), Udāya Dās. The doctrine held by these people does not materially differ from that of Kabir and Nānak. Their great hope is final emancipation from living. They have no temples, but declare that the true shrine is the meeting of the faithful. At certain times the members meet together, read the writings of their leaders, sing songs, and partake of a common meal. They speak of God as the

Satnāma (the true name), and differ but little from the following sect.

6. The *Satnāmis*. This sect was originated by a man named Rohidās, a disciple and developer of the system of Rāmānanda. Rāmānanda taught that any of the three highest castes could enter the ascetic order; his followers freely admitted men of lower castes; whilst at the present time nearly all the members of the sect are Chamārs, one of the lowest and most despised of all the Hindu castes. It is possible, however, that those joining the sect from other castes have been regarded as Chamārs, because they associated with such people. It is a noticeable fact that whilst, as their name implies, they profess to be worshippers of the one true God, many of the people worship the many Hindu deities just as their neighbours do. As a rule, however, the members differ from the rest of the Chamārs in this: they are a quiet, industrious, sober people, who regard it to be a duty to abstain from meat of all kinds, intoxicating drinks, and tobacco. Their necklaces having been touched by the guru are regarded with especial reverence. They hate the orthodox Hindus; Brāhmans most of all.

7. The *Siva Narāyanas* are the followers of a Rājput named Siva Narāyana, who lived in the eighteenth century. His teaching was pure theism. All classes of Hindus, and Mussulmāns too, are welcomed to join the sect. Truth, temperance, and mercy form its main tenets, and its members are enjoined to observe the outward social observance of the community from which they came, though they repudiate the religious rites and faiths.

CHAPTER IX.

THE DEISTIC SECTS FORMED DURING THE PRESENT CENTURY.

Any account of the Hindu sects would be very incomplete if those were omitted that have arisen during the present century, and which are receiving accessions from the educated classes every year. The aim of the leaders of these sects has professedly been to lead back the Hindus to the primitive worship of their Āryan forefathers, although it is evident to all unprejudiced students of their doctrines that it is in many respects the teaching of the Vedas, very largely modified by that of the Christian Scriptures, that is prevailing amongst them. This will become more clear as we consider the development of these sects from their commencement. There is no doubt, as Augustine declared, that if Stephen had not prayed, the church would not have had Paul; if Christian missions had not been established in India, the various deistic Samājes would not have sprung up in her midst.

1. The Brahma Samāj, founded by Rāma Mohun Rai.*

Rāja Rāma Mohun Rai, the founder of the Brahma Samāj, or Divine Society, was born in the year 1774. His father and grandfather being attached to the Mohamedan princes at Moorshedabad, he early learned Arabic and Persian, and

* For a fuller account of the rise and development of the modern Theistic sects, see "Life of Babu Keshub Chundra Sen," by Rev. T. E. Slater, Bangalore.

thus gained some knowledge of the teachings of the Korān and the Persian poets. As a Brāhman he was educated in the mythology of Hinduism; but at the early age of sixteen his mind revolted against the heathen practices of his household, and as a result of his persistent opposition to the religious worship of his family he was persecuted, and left his home. When about twenty years old his father invited him to return; he did so, and, in order to qualify himself for employment under the East India Company, studied English, and was successful in obtaining a position of influence for several years under the East India Company. In 1814 he settled down in Calcutta, where he purchased a house, and, again speaking freely of the evils of the Hindu religious and social customs, was openly repudiated by his father. On the death of his father he became still more bold, and, purchasing a printing-press, published a number of pamphlets in various languages against prevailing errors. "This raised such a feeling against me," he says in an autobiographical sketch, "that I was at last deserted by every person except two or three Scotch friends, to whom, and to the nation to which they belong, I always feel grateful. The ground which I took in all my controversies was not that of opposition to Brāhmanism, but to a perversion of it; and I endeavoured to show that their idolatry was contrary to the practice of their ancestors and the principles of the ancient books and authorities which they profess to revere and obey." In 1819, after publishing several pamphlets containing religious lessons as taught by some of the Hindu scriptures, he published a tract called "The Precepts of Jesus, the Guide to Peace and Happiness." It is interesting to see how the modern reformer availed himself of the improved methods of communicating truth. In the case of the leaders of the sects previously considered, it was by a life of penance that they gained attention, and by wandering from city to city that they spread their views; but Rāja Rāma Mohun Rai could live in his own house, and by the use of his press speak to far greater numbers by means of the pamphlets his loving heart and fertile brain prepared.

In the year 1828 the Sabhā was founded. A few friends had been in the habit of meeting with their leader since 1815, but as the numbers increased it was agreed to hire a room in the Chitpore Road, Calcutta, where this monotheistic Church was founded under the name of the Brahma Samāj. In 1830 the numbers had so increased, and money having been given, a new house suitable for the purpose was built; and the following extract from the trust deed will show the purpose of this building: it was "for a place of public meeting of all sorts and descriptions of people as shall behave and conduct themselves in an orderly, sober, religious, and devout manner, for the worship and adoration of the Eternal, Unsearchable, and Immutable Being who is the Author and Preserver of the Universe." His object in founding the church was declared to be this—"to persuade my countrymen to forsake idolatry and to become monotheists."

Rāma Mohun Rai did not himself give up caste observances, neither did he teach others to do so; and though he was himself largely indebted to the Bible for his religious knowledge and impulse, he did not have it introduced into the meetings of this Theistic Church. The Hindu scriptures were read and expounded. Soon after the opening of this building the Rāja visited Europe, and died in Bristol. Though he never openly avowed himself a Christian, those who were most intimate with him speak most strongly of his belief in the divine authority of Jesus Christ, in His miracles, and in His resurrection.

The next great step in advance was made by Devendra Nāth Tagore, who was born in 1818. When twenty years of age this gentleman was brought under deep religious impressions. At this time he spent days in silent meditation, seeking light from heaven. At length "the Friend of the sinner, the Protector of the helpless, destitute, and castaway, vouchsafed in His infinite mercy to appear in my corrupt heart to heal me and chasten me." The result of this was that after a long struggle "the world lost its attractions, and God became my only comfort and delight in this world of sorrow and sin." Unlike Rāja Rāma Mohun Rai, his successor does not appear to have gone farther than the Hindu scriptures for light. In 1839 he formed a society called the Tattvabodini Sabha, a society for the knowledge of truth, which in 1843 united with the Brahma Samāj, and soon afterwards developments appear.

Up to this time the profession of Brahmist doctrine did not necessarily involve the giving up of all share in idolatrous worship. Many who in the meetings of the Samāj and elsewhere were most eloquent in denouncing the idolatrous worship of the people were themselves found, when the idols were worshipped in the home, joining openly in their worship. To prevent this a covenant was drawn up, which the members of the Samāj were expected to sign, containing a promise to abstain from idolatry, and cultivate the habit of prayer. About twenty signed this covenant at the first, and by doing so brought upon themselves considerable persecution. Still their doctrine spread, and in 1847 the number of "covenanted" Brahmas was 767, whilst many more, who verbally professed to hold the same views, were not bold enough to sign the covenant.

Very soon another onward movement is seen. Up to this time the members of the Samāj had regarded the Vedas as divinely inspired, and therefore as a supreme authority in religious matters. But as doubts had arisen in the minds of some of the members, learned Pundits were sent to Benares to copy and study these books. On their return the matter was most carefully considered by the members, and at last it was decided that the teaching of the Vedas was not in accordance with their religious views, and though regarded as valuable guides, their infallibility was denied. Soon after this decision had been arrived at, the society was re-organized, and a clearer and fuller form of covenant drawn up, the substance of which was as follows: "That there is but one God; that He is the Creator of all things, that love to Him, and the doing of what He loves, is worship; and that such worship alone ensures all present and future bliss."

This theistic movement was not confined to Bengal. In North India a sect called the Ārya Samāj was founded by Pundit Dayānanda Sarasvati. He, however, continued to repose an implicit faith in the divine authority of the Vedas; at the same time he "opposed idol worship, repudiated caste, advocated female education, and the re-marriage of widows, and secured hundreds of followers, and a much larger number of sympathisers." *

The next important event in the history of religious activity amongst the Hindus was the accession to the ranks of the Brahma Samāj of Babu Keshub Chundra Sen. It will have been noticed that the history of this movement is largely the history of its leaders. As they advanced, their followers advanced too; when they remained stationary, or took a retrograde step, they were not left alone. Rāja Rāma Mohun Rai groped after the light, and the members of the Samāj in his day moved slowly on. Rāja Devendra Nāth Tagore went a little farther in giving up implicit faith in the Vedas. And now it will be seen that, led on by Babu Keshub Chundra Sen, a further advance was made. In 1858, when he was twenty years of age, Keshub Babu joined the Samāj, and very soon made himself leader of the community. For three years he continued as a clerk in the Bank of Bengal, but afterwards, wishing to be free from secular employment, he resigned his post and devoted his whole time to the work of the Samāj. In 1862 he was chosen Minister, and soon after this, because he took his wife to dine with his friend, Devendra Nāth Tagore, who was regarded as an excommunicated Brāhman, mainly because he had the marriage of his daughter celebrated without the usual idolatrous ceremonies, he was cut off from intercourse with his family for six months.

* "Keshub Chundra Sen," by Rev T. E. Slater, p. 29.

For a time all went on well, but soon it became evident that the new Minister was progressing in thought too rapidly for many of the older members. He was thoroughly opposed to the restrictions of caste, and was wishful that all who took part in the services of the Samāj should hold similar views. He advocated a still further violation of Hindu customs, viz., the intermarriage of people of differing castes. When such a marriage took place a great outcry was raised, and the more progressive separated from the Samāj. The older and more conservative of the members held that the Samāj should concern itself only with religious reforms, and continue to respect the social customs of Hinduism, Keshub Babu and his party protesting that the two could not be separated. Before the separation took place the progressive party put their views into the following shape :—

1. That the external signs of caste distinctions such as the Brāhmanical thread should be no longer used.

2. That none but Brahmas of sufficient ability and good moral character, who lived consistently with their profession, should be allowed to conduct the services of the Samāj.

3. That nothing should be said in the Samāj expressive of hatred or contempt for other religions.

These simple regulations not being accepted, the progressive party left the Samāj, and established what was afterwards called the Brahma Samāj of India; the Society they left afterwards took the name of the Ādi, or original, Samāj. Since this separation the Ādi Samāj has not made any advance in theistic faith, but has rather gone back towards Hinduism.

From this time the history of the Brahma Samāj of India is really the history of the phases of faith of Keshub Chundra Sen. At the anniversary meetings of the Society he generally gave an address in English to an immense audience in the Town Hall of Calcutta, from which the theological position of the Society can be learned.

Before passing on to notice the progress of the Brahma Samāj of India, I will give the covenant of the Ādi Samāj :—

1. God alone existed in the beginning, and He created this universe.

2. He is intelligent, infinite, benevolent, eternal, governor of the universe, all-knowing, omnipresent, refuge of all, devoid of limbs, immutable, alone, without a second, all-powerful, self-existent, and beyond comparison.

3. By worshipping Him, and Him alone, we can attain the highest good in this life and in the next.

4. To love Him and to do the works He loves constitute His worship.

By declaring my belief in the above-mentioned four fundamental principles of Brāhmanism, I accept it as my faith.

2. The Brahma Samāj of India.

The most conspicuous feature of this Samāj in its earlier days was the reverence shown to Jesus Christ, and the unique position assigned to Him by the leader in his public utterances as well as in his own private faith. In almost the first public lecture that he delivered he claimed Jesus as belonging to India and the East more than to Europe, and there can be no doubt that it was largely owing to Keshub Babu's teaching that the educated Hindus generally regarded Jesus with very different feelings from those which had generally been common to that class. At the public services of the Samāj, which were held soon after the secession in a mandir, or church, that was built for this purpose, selections from the Bible were read along with parts of the Vedas, Korān, and other sacred writings. That fact is the key to understand this sect. It professes to draw its religious light from all quarters, whilst it gives exclusive reverence to none. Whilst admitting the inspiration of all great writers and the benefit of all good books, it teaches that there is a present inspiration for those who will receive it; and that this divine light being available to each, its teaching is the test of truth. The individual conscience is regarded as the final test of truth, from whatever source it may come.

In the history of this Samāj under Keshub's leadership, there are two main chapters—viz., the earlier efforts to adapt the older forms of Hindu faith and practice, and the attempt to introduce, in a Hindu form, some of the distinctive rites of Christianity. Amongst the Hindu forms of worship are *yoga*, or meditation, *i.e.*, the study of the divine nature, as taught in the writings of the old Vedic sages. In Hinduism this was carried to great extremes; in the public services of the Brahmas silent meditation finds a prominent place. Then bhakti, the loving trust of the Vaishnavas, is most earnestly commended, and Chaitanya, as the apostle of this doctrine, is held in high esteem by the members of this sect. The great peculiarity of the religious life of this Samāj lies in the fact that it seeks to awaken the emotional as well as appeals to the intellectual side of human nature. And many in its religious exercises profess to have found the truest bliss.

Annual festivals called Brahmatsavas were also instituted. For days together religious meetings with music and other festivities were arranged for, and by this means, as by the Hindu festivals, the faith of the members was strengthened and their zeal fired. Added to this were religious processions with music and singing, and later on a tendency set in favourable to Vairāgya, *i.e.*, the practice of asceticism. This, it will be seen, is in perfect harmony with the genius of Hinduism, as nearly all the other sects have had their vairāgis, or religious ascetics, who were regarded by the rest of the community as the perfected members of the community. This teaching of the benefits of asceticism as much as anything else shows the close affinity of Brāhmaism with Hinduism.

But Brāhmaism, whilst holding out one hand to Hinduism, holds out another to Christianity. Keshub Bābu never failed to express his love to Jesus Christ and his loyalty to His commands; and the spirit of Jesus is seen in nearly all his teaching. He began by claiming Him as an

9

Asiatic, and offers India to Him as a people. He next professes to show in the "Future Church" that whilst the dogmatic teaching of the Christian Church is not acceptable to India, the true Church is one which will embrace Christians and Hindus, and a few years later proclaims the fact that a new "dispensation" has been inaugurated by God through him and his apostles. As God appointed the Jewish, then the Christian, now He has also appointed this newer all-comprehensive Church, and the whole world is invited to enter. Long before this, efforts of a missionary character had been made by the leader and his more eminent followers, and by men solemnly set apart for this special work. Addresses were given in various parts of India commending their doctrine to others, and, as a result, branch Samājes have been formed in many places; but with the formation of the "New Dispensation" the offer went beyond India to men of all nations, and the blessings of this newly-given light were offered freely unto all men. It is interesting to note, too, that the distinctive rites of the Christian Church were adopted by Keshub Bābu. Baptism was administered in the tank in the grounds of his house; the Lord's Supper was observed, rice and water being used instead of bread and wine; and later on a religious dance was inaugurated. The following is the proclamation of the New Dispensation to the world:—

"THE NEW DISPENSATION.

"*Extraordinary*.

"NEW YEAR'S DAY.

"1st *January*, 1883.

"Keshub Chunder Sen, a servant of God, called to be an apostle of the Church of the New Dispensation which is in the holy city of Calcutta, the metropolis of Aryavarta.

"To all the great nations in the world, and to the chief religious sects in the East and the West.

"To the followers of Moses, of Jesus, of Buddha, of Confucius, of Zoroaster, of Mahomet, of Nanac, and to the various branches of the Hindu Church.

"To the saints and the sages, the bishops and the elders, the ministers and the missionaries of all these religious bodies:

"Grace be unto you and peace everlasting.

"Whereas sectarian discord and strife, schisms and enmities, prevail in our Father's family, causing much bitterness and unhappiness, impurity and unrighteousness, and even war, carnage, and bloodshed.

"Whereas this setting of brother against brother and sister against sister, in the name of religion, has proved a fruitful source of evils, and is itself a sin against God and man.

"It has pleased the Holy God to send unto the world a message of peace and love, of harmony and reconciliation.

"This New Dispensation hath He, in boundless mercy, vouchsafed to us in the East, and we have been commanded to bear witness unto it among the nations of the earth.

"Thus said the Lord: Sectarianism is an abomination unto me, and unbrotherliness I will not tolerate.

"I desire love and unity, and my children shall be of one heart, even as I am one.

"At sundry times have I spoken through my prophets, and though many and various my dispensations, there is unity in them.

"But the followers of these, my prophets, have quarrelled and fought, and they hate and exclude each other.

"The unity of Heaven's messages have they denied, and the science that binds and harmonizes them their eyes see not and their hearts ignore.

"Hear, ye men, there is one music, but many instruments; one body, but many limbs; one spirit, but diverse gifts; one blood, yet many nations; one church, yet many churches.

"Blessed are the peace-makers who reconcile differences and establish peace, goodwill, and brotherhood in the name of the Father.

"These words hath the Lord our God spoken unto us, and His new gospel that He hath revealed unto us, is a gospel of exceeding joy.

"The Church Universal hath He already planted in this land, and therein are all prophets and all scriptures harmonized in beautiful synthesis.

"And these blessed tidings the Loving Father hath charged me and my brother apostles to declare unto all the nations of the world, that being of one blood they may also be of one faith and rejoice in one Lord.

"Thus shall all discord be over, saith the Lord, and peace shall reign on earth.

"Humbly, therefore, I exhort you, brethren, to accept this new message of universal love.

"Hate not, but love ye one another, and be ye one in spirit and in truth, even as the Father is one.

"All errors and impurities ye shall eschew, in whatever church or nation they may be found, but ye shall hate no Scripture, no prophet, no church.

"Renounce all manner of superstition and error, infidelity and scepticism, vice and sensuality, and be ye pure and perfect.

"Every saint, every prophet, and every martyr ye shall honour and love as a man of God.

"Gather ye the wisdom of the East and the West, and accept and assimilate the examples of the saints of all ages,

"So that the most fervent devotion, the deepest communion, the most self-denying asceticism, the warmest philanthropy, the strictest justice and veracity, and the highest purity of the best men in the world may be yours.

"Above all love one another, and merge all difference in universal brotherhood.

"Beloved brethren, accept our love and give us yours, and let the East and the West with one heart celebrate the jubilee of the New Dispensation.

"Let Asia, Europe, Africa, and America, with diverse

instruments, praise the New Dispensation, and sing the Fatherhood of God and the Brotherhood of man."

The later years of Keshub Bābu's life were given rather to the development of the religious than the social improvement of his followers; for, owing to a departure in practice from his previous teaching, there was a split in his community, and the more progressive part left and formed another Samāj called the Sādhāran Samāj. The ground of offence was the marriage of Keshub Bābu's daughter to the young Rāja of Cooch Behar when she was below the age at which he had taught that marriages should be celebrated; and, further, that idolatrous practices were permitted in connection with the marriage ceremony.

Keshub Bābu died in Calcutta in January, 1884, and great was the lamentation made over him. He was a noble man, and one who was greatly beloved by all classes of the community. After his death his family and the Apostolic Durbar, as the council of the apostles of the New Dispensation was called, refused to allow the platform from which he had taught to be used, it being declared that Keshub, though absent in body, was still the leader of the society This *may* be the first step towards the deification of their great leader. And when this Durbar declares that their conscience authorizes them to take this position, it is difficult to set aside their decision. In the matter of Keshub's daughter's marriage, it was the result of a supposed inspiration that led him to go against his own teaching. His disciples, in making conscience the test of truth, are but following their great leader's example.

The covenant of this New Dispensation, which is far fuller and more comprehensive than that of the Ādi Samāj, is as follows:—

"One God, one Scripture, one Church.

Eternal progress of the soul.

Communion of prophets and saints.

Fatherhood and motherhood of God.
Brotherhood of man and sisterhood of woman.
Harmony of knowledge and holiness, love and work.
Yoga and asceticism in their highest development.
Loyalty to sovereign." *

Among the numerous objects in view are the following:—

To reduce the truths of all Scriptures to one eternal and unwritten Scripture. To preach Christ's kingdom of heaven. To kill idolatry by taking its life and spirit out of it. To explain the mystery of the Trinity, and to show Unity in Trinity. To reconcile ancient faith and modern science. To reconcile pure Christianity and pure Hinduism. To turn men's hearts from physical to moral miracles. To make science supersede supernaturalism. To preach Christ as the Son of God, as the Logos in all prophets before and after Him. To put down all manner of sin, and promote all manner of purity by the power of prayer.

3. The Sādhāran (Universal) Samāj.

This, the most active and socially powerful of the three, originated in 1878. The *occasion* of the secession, as noticed above, was the marriage of Keshub Bābu's daughter at an earlier age than he had taught was right; the *cause*, however, lay a little deeper. It was a growing dissatisfaction with the autocratic rule of the leader and the claim to an almost infallible inspiration. The greater number of the Calcutta members of the Brahmā Samāj forsook their old leader, and their action was approved by twenty-nine of the country branches, altogether 425 of the recognized Brahmas and Brāhmicās, *i.e.*, lady members of the Samāj, condemning his conduct.

The covenant of this sect, which largely agrees with that of the New Dispensation, is as follows:—

1. There is only one God, who is the Creator, Preserver, and Saviour of the world. He is a Spirit, infinite in wisdom, love, justice, and holiness; omnipotent, eternal, and blissful.

* "Keshub Chundra Sen," p. 107.

2. The human soul is immortal, and capable of infinite progress, and is responsible to God for its doings.

3. God must be worshipped in spirit and in truth. Divine worship is necessary for attaining true felicity and salvation.

4. Love to God, and carrying out His will in all the concerns of life, constitute true worship.

5. Prayer, and dependence on God, and a constant realization of His presence, are the means of attaining spiritual strength.

6. No created object is to be worshipped as God, nor any person or book to be considered as infallible and the sole means of salvation.

7. The Fatherhood of God and the brotherhood of man.

8. God rewards virtue and punishes sin. His punishments are remedial, and not eternal.

9. Cessation from sin, accompanied by sincere repentance, is the only atonement for it; and union with God in wisdom, goodness, and holiness, is true salvation.

In order to prevent the undue influence of any one man in this Samāj, a form of government somewhat of Presbyterian form has been adopted. The society is ruled by officers elected for this purpose by the members. "These officers are four in number, and are elected annually; they act in conjunction with a general committee of forty members, also elected annually, and a certain number of representatives of branch Samājes in the country towns; and this committee in its turn appoints an executive of twelve persons for the year." *

This latest sect has built for itself a meeting-house that will seat 1,200 people, at a cost of Rs. 40,000, and is most active in its efforts in Calcutta and Bengal. There are more "covenanted" Brahmas in connection with it than with the other two, and its organs in the press are always on the side of social progress. It has its prayer-meetings and Philanthropic Society, a first-class college, and a night school, for the benefit of working men. It is part of the con-

* "Keshub Chundra Sen," p. 87.

stitution of the society that "only those who have discarded idolatry and caste in their private lives as well as in public can be office-bearers, ministers, missionaries, or members of the Executive Committee of the Samāj." In 1880 there were 514 full members of this sect in India, and from the earnestness of those who have joined, and the self-sacrificing character of the missionaries they employ, there appears to be reason to believe that their numbers will quickly and largely increase. Taking all these sects together, in 1884 there were 173 Samājes, 1,500 enrolled members, and about 8,000 adherents.

The census returns of 1882, however, do not give quite so large a number, as the following extract from the Census Report will show; but at the same time it suggests the explanation of the apparent discrepancy :—"In 1872 the Brahmas were included among Hindus, and the figures seem to indicate that a large proportion of them have again been shown in the same manner. The adherents of the sect are almost entirely educated Bengalis, with, sometimes, their wives and families; and they are therefore chiefly found in large towns, and at the headquarters of districts, at few of which are they unrepresented. The census tables, however, only show 788 in the whole of Bengal, out of whom 763 are in Bengal proper, and from thirty-six districts none at all have been returned. It is beyond doubt that they have described themselves, or been described, in many cases as Hindus—a course which is not remarkable when we consider that many persons rank them as a puritanical monotheistic sect of the Hindus; while the fact that the sect is in many places looked on with disfavour would be enough to induce many to shrink from avowing the principles which they really entertain. Two-thirds of the whole number returned are to be found in Calcutta."

CASTE.

CHAPTER I.

*GENERAL REMARKS ON CASTE.**

Pride of birth is not by any means confined to the Hindus. Wherever there has been the belief that the gods have been incarnated, and dwelt on earth amongst mortals, there has been an endeavour to show that *some* of the residents in those lands are their direct descendants, and consequently entitled to greater honour and privilege than the masses of their fellow-countrymen. In order to secure reverence for their ancestry, their origin is ascribed, with more or less consistency, to one or other of these deities. A man who could trace his descent from a god naturally expected and generally received a greater share of the reverence and riches of his fellows than ordinary mortals who were fashioned by his hands. In modern times, great though the privileges of the nobility have been as compared with those of the commons, the privileges claimed and generally conceded to them, compared with those of the caste families of India, are as nothing. "The existence of a common brotherhood in the human family and the practice of a common sympathy and succour have, by the majority of men, been grievously overlooked. Tyranny, mischief, and cruelty have been most extensively the consequence of anti-social presumption and pretension. The constant experience of the general observer of human nature has been not unlike that of the Hebrew sage Agur, the son of Jakeh :—

* For this book I am largely indebted to Dr. Muir's "Original Sanskrit Texts" and Dr. Wilson's "Caste."

"'There is a generation that are pure in their own eyes,
And yet is not washed from their filthiness.
There is a generation, O how lofty are their eyes!
And their eyelids are lifted up.
There is a generation whose teeth are as swords,
And their jaw-teeth as knives,
To devour the poor from off the earth,
And the needy from among men.' *

"It is among the Hindus, however, that the imagination of natural and positive distinction in humanity has been brought to the most fearful and pernicious development ever exhibited on the face of the globe. The doctrine and practice of what is called caste, as held and observed by this people, has been only dimly shadowed by the worst social arrangements which were of old to be witnessed amongst the proudest nations, and among the proudest orders of men in those nations. The Egyptians, who, according to Herodotus, considered themselves 'the most ancient of all nations,' and who are described by him as excessively religious beyond any other people,' and 'too much addicted to their ancestorial customs to adopt any other,' most nearly approached them in their national and family pretensions, and the privilege and customs of priests and people viewed in reference to descent and occupation; but in the multitude, diversity, complication, and burdensomeness of their religious and social distinction, the Hindus have left the Egyptians far behind. Indian caste is the condensation of all the pride, jealousy, and tyranny of an ancient and predominant people dealing with the tribes which they have subjected, and over which they have ruled, often without the sympathies of a recognized common humanity." † According to native testimony, "it is by means of these caste distinctions that the Hindu religion has been so well preserved; they are its chief support; and when this support is removed there can be no doubt that it will sink to destruction."

Caste is a Portuguese word "signifying cast, mould, race,

* Prov. xxx. 12–14. † Wilson, p. 11.

kind, and quality. It was applied originally by the Portuguese, when they arrived in the East, to designate the peculiar system of religious and social distinctions which they observed among the Hindu people, particularly as founded on race. The Indian word which partially corresponds with caste is *Jāti* = gens, and γένος, 'race or nation'; while *Jāti-bheda*, the representative of the foundations of the caste system, means the distinctions of race. Varna, another word used for it by the Hindus, originally meant a difference in 'colour.' Gradually these Indian words, conveniently rendered by caste, have come to represent not only varieties of race and colour, but every original, hereditary, religious, instituted, and conventional distinction which it is possible to conceive." To give some idea of the minute regulations of this system of caste, and how its laws are framed to regulate the life of its slaves, it may be mentioned that "it has for infancy, pupilage, and manhood its ordained methods of sucking, sipping, drinking, and eating; of washing, anointing; of clothing and ornamenting the body; of sitting, rising, reclining; of moving, visiting, travelling; of speaking, reading, listening, and reciting; and of meditating, singing, working, and fighting. It has its laws for social and religious rights, privileges and occupations; for education, duty, religious service; for errors, sins, transgressions; for intercommunion, avoidance, and excommunication; for defilement and purification; for fines and other punishments. It unfolds the ways of committing what it calls sins, accumulating sin, and of putting away sin; of acquiring, dispensing, and losing merit. It treats of inheritance, conveyance, possession, and dispossession of property; and of bargains, gains, loss, and ruin. It deals with death, burial, and burning; and with commemoration, assistance, and injury after death. It interferes, in short, with all the relations and events of life, and with what precedes and follows, or what is supposed to precede and follow, life. It reigns supreme in the innumerable classes and divisions of the Hindus, whether they originate in family descent, in religious opinions, in civil or sacred occupations, or in local residence; and it professes to regulate all their interests, affairs, and relationships. Caste is the guiding principle of each of the classes and divisions of the Hindus viewed in their distinct and associated capacity. A caste is any of the classes or divisions of Hindu society. The authority of caste rests partly on written laws, partly on legendary fables and narratives, partly on the injunctions of instructors and priests, party on custom and usage, and partly on the caprice and convenience of its votaries. 'The roots of the law,' says Manu, 'are the whole Veda, the ordinances and observances of such as perfectly understand it, the immemorial customs of good men, and self-satisfaction.' No doubt that man who shall follow the rules prescribed in the Shruti (what was heard from the Veda) and in the Smriti (what was remembered from the laws) will acquire fame in this life, and in the next inexpressible happiness."

Most of the castes have peculiar marks which those initiated have to wear, but there is one common to all. "The great index of Hinduism is the tuft of hair on the crown of the head" (by which, according to the popular notion, the wearer is to be raised to heaven), "which is left there on the performance of the sacrament of tonsure, on the first or third year after birth in the case of the three great classes of the Hindus; and in the eighth year after the conception of a Brāhman, in the eleventh from that of a Kshatriya, and in the twelfth from that of a Vaishya, the investiture with the sacred cord should occur."

CHAPTER II.

CASTE DISTINCTIONS AS TAUGHT IN THE SACRED BOOKS.

I shall now proceed to give a general account of the four principal castes, their duties and privileges, as taught in the sacred writings of the Hindus.

The following account from Manu's Dharma Sāstra of the creation of man may be taken as the commonly received law on the subject of the duties of each caste: "For the sake of preserving the universe, the Being supremely glorious allotted separate duties to those who sprang respectively from his mouth, his arm, his thigh, and his foot. To Brāhmans he assigned the duties of reading (the Veda) and teaching, of sacrificing, of assisting others to sacrifice, of giving alms, and of receiving gifts. To defend the people, to give alms, to sacrifice, to read (the Veda), to shun the allurements of sexual gratification, are in a few words the duties of a Kshatriya. To keep herds of cattle, to bestow largesses, to sacrifice, to read the Scriptures, to carry on trade, to lend at interest, are the duties of a Vaishya. One principal duty the Supreme Ruler assigns to a Sudra, viz., to serve the before-mentioned classes, without depreciating their worth." This may be taken as the typical teaching on the subject, and it is that which is generally received at the present time; and though the phraseology of other books is in some respects opposed to it, it is twisted, and made, as far as it is possible, to harmonize with it.

The position of the Brāhman as taught by the Sāstras.

The Brāhman being the first-born, having sprung from the mouth of the Supreme, and being the rightful possessor of the Veda, is the chief of the whole creation. The birth of a Brāhman is said to be a constant incarnation of Dharma (religion); for a Brāhman is born to promote religion, and to procure ultimate happiness. Whatever exists in the universe is all in effect the wealth of the Brāhman, since he is entitled to all by his primogeniture and pre-eminence; and it is through his benevolence that other mortals enjoy life. His ideal inherent qualities are quiescence, self-control, devotion, purity, patience, rectitude, secular and sacred knowledge, the recognition of spiritual existence and the inborn disposition to serve Brahmā. Power and glory reside in every part of his body: the Ganges is in his right ear; his mouth is that of God Himself; the tirthas, or sacred places of pilgrimage, are in his right foot; the cow of plenty (kāmdhenu), from whom all desires may be satisfied, are the hairs of his body. The Brāhman is the *first-born* by nature, the twice-born by the sacrament of investiture with the sacred thread, the deity on earth by his divine status, and the intelligent one by his innate comprehension.

According to the same scripture, the Brāhman is superior to law, even to moral law, when it clashes with his worldly interests; and though it is disgraceful for him to live as a hired servant, he may without hesitation take the property of a Sudra. The gradations of punishment for offences according to the caste of the offender is most startling to one trained under just and equitable laws; *e.g.*, a priest shall be fined five hundred (panas) if he slander a Kshatriya, twenty-five if he slander a Vaishya, twelve only if he slander a Sudra. In like manner a crime against a man of his own caste by a Sudra is a venial offence; but a similar offence committed against a man of a higher caste is proportionally greater. And should a Sudra through pride venture to give instructions to priests concerning their duty, let the king order some hot oil to be dropped into his mouth and ears. An adulterer of the Brāhman class might suffer the loss of his hair; but a similar offender, if a Sudra, might be made to forfeit his life. Whatever a Brāhman's offence, the king must on no account put him to death; he may, at the most, banish him, allowing him to take his property with him. And it will be remembered how great was the astonishment of all India, owing to the general idea of the sacredness of life of the Brāhmans, when it was known that by order of the Governor-General a Brāhman was executed in Calcutta. Further, in case of wrong-doing against him, a Brāhman need not have recourse to the civil power, but is free to take vengeance upon the offender.

It will be borne in mind that the books in which their own order is so exalted were written by the Brāhmans themselves, in which stories most marvellous are to be found to lead the people to believe in the superhuman, and in some cases super-divine, power of some of their number. One of them is declared to be the father of the sun, and another the father of the moon. Brihaspati is said to have reduced the moon to a cinder; Visvakarma cut off the hands and feet of the sun; and Manu seems to acknowledge their truthfulness, as he says, "Who without perishing could provoke those holy men by whom the all-devouring fire was created, the sea with waters not drinkable, and the moon with its wane and increase? What prince could gain wealth by opposing those, who, if angry, could frame other worlds, and regents of worlds, and could give being to new gods and mortals? What man, desirous of life, would injure those by the aid of whom worlds and gods perpetually exist?" The following lines sum up in a few words the popular idea of the power of the Brāhman:—

"The whole world is under the power of the gods.

The gods are under the power of the mantras (charms used by Brāhmans);

The mantras are under the power of the Brāhmans.

The Brāhman is therefore our god."

As a deterrent from injuring a Brāhman, and as an inducement to bestow gifts upon him, the following texts are inserted in Manu: "A man who basely assaults a Brāhman, with an intention to hurt him, shall be whirled about for a century in a hell called Tāmisri; but having smitten him in anger and by design, even with a blade of grass, he shall be born in one-and-twenty transmigrations from the wombs of impure animals." "If a man sell his cow he will go to hell; if he give her to a Brāhman he will go to heaven." "If on Ganga's (the river Ganges) anniversary whole villages be given to Brāhmans, the person presenting them will acquire all the merit that can be obtained; his body will be a million times more glorious than the sun, he will have a million virgins, many carriages, and palanquins with jewels, and he will live in heaven with his father as many years as there are particles in the land given to Brāhmans." A proper gift to a Brāhman on a deathbed will secure heaven to a malefactor. The Brāhmans confer a favour on the people of other castes when they receive their presents.

The authority for the almost divine honours, which are even now paid by the more superstitious of the lower orders of the people, is found in such passages as the following, from the more recent Purānas: "Whatever good man bows to a Brāhman, reverencing him as Vishnu, is blessed with long life, sons, renown, and prosperity. But whatever foolish man does not bow down to a Brāhman on earth, Kesava (Vishnu) desires to strike off his head with his discus. Whosoever bears but a drop of water which has been in contact with a Brāhman's foot, all the sins of his body are immediately destroyed. Whosoever carries on his head the holy things touched by a Brāhman's foot is freed from all sins. Whatever good man worships a Brāhman by walking round him obtains the merit of going round the world with its seven continents."

The Brāhmans, though thus highly favoured amongst mortals, had not a position of ease and idleness. According to the Laws of Manu, their life was divided into four parts, in each of which there were special duties for them to discharge; and it is no doubt partly owing to the idea of their superior goodness, and to the supposed holiness of their life, that they were held in almost divine reverence. I shall briefly state the duties peculiar to these states through which it is taught that they ought to pass. It will be borne in mind that it was by their efforts that the sacred scriptures were written and then transmitted to posterity.

1. The first order is that of Brahmāchāri, or pupil. In this order the Brāhman boy is to render the greatest reverence and pay the greatest attention to his instructor. His religious exercises must commence with the early dawn, and, excepting during the times appointed for eating and study, must be continued throughout the day. He is ordered to collect wood for the holy fire, beg food from his relations, sleep on a low bed, and perform such offices as may please his preceptor. He must carefully study the Veda, abstain from honey, flesh, perfumes, garlands, women, unguents for his limbs, sandals; must not use an umbrella, indulge in sensual desires, wrath, covetousness, dancing, singing, dice, disputes, detraction, falsehood. He is ordered to sleep alone, and to perform the duties of a religious mendicant.

2. The second order is that of the Ghrihastha, or householder. He enters this when he has chosen, or has had chosen for him, a wife, whose qualities are carefully described. She must have an agreeable name, but no bodily defect; she must walk like a goose or a young elephant; her hair moderate in quantity; her body soft, and who, in the first marriage at least, must be of a Brāhman family. He must live with her in the strictest fidelity, give her elegant attire, seek to raise up a family, or, at any rate, to have a son, without whom, natural or adopted, the salvation of the father cannot be effected. He has to practise unceasingly various minute and burdensome rites and ceremonies, such as study, the offering of oblations to fire, the presentation of

food to spirits through living beings, particularly the "twice-born," the entertainment of guests, and the offering of water and rice to the manes of his ancestors. At the Shrāddhas, or ceremonies performed for the benefit of the departed, he has to avoid inviting and holding intercourse with any who may be diseased, or ceremonially unclean, or who may be following pursuits forbidden to Brāhmans. During the feasting his mind must be kept in perfect composure, for the shedding of a tear would send the food to restless spirits; anger would send it to foes; falsehood to dogs; touching it with his foot to Rākshasas; and agitation of mind to scoundrels. At the same time he must read for the edification of the guests from various Hindu scriptures. At these feasts, in the earlier writings, it is stated that animal food avails more in the work of propitiation than vegetable—a passage that the Brāhmans of the present day utterly ignore. His ordinary mode of life is most carefully marked out for him. He must not have long nails or beard; he must neither eat with his wife, nor see her eat; he must keep his passions under control. He must not sing, dance, or play with dice. He must carefully observe all religious festivals. Moral duties, too, are carefully ordered. If he sin, either himself or his descendants will suffer for it; by falsehood, sacrifice becomes vain, pride nullifies the effect of austerities; by the dishonour of priests life is diminished, by the *display* of charity its fruit is destroyed. Strange as it may appear to those who know the strong objection the orthodox Brāhmans of the present day have to eating flesh, it is distinctly stated that "no sin is committed by him who, having honoured the deities and manes, eats flesh meat which he has bought, himself acquired, or had presented to him by another." The touch of a person ceremonially unclean, or of a low caste man, is pollution; so that, in addition to the positive duties of his calling, which are many, he has ever to be on his guard lest pollution come to him through others.

3. The third order is that of the Vānaprastha, *i.e.*, the hermit.

in the wilderness. When the Brāhman enters this order his self-denial must be far greater than in that of either the student or householder. At the approach of old age he must leave his family and worldly affairs, feed on herbs, fruits, and roots only. He must wear a black antelope's hide, or the bark of a tree, and suffer his nails and beard to grow. He must be constantly engaged in the reading of the Vedas, or engaged in acts of penance, of which the following are to form part: Let him slide backwards and forwards on the ground, stand a whole day on tip-toe, continue in motion, rising and sitting alternately; but at sunrise, noon, and sunset, he must bathe. In the hot season let him expose himself to five fires; in the rains let him stand uncovered where the clouds pour the heaviest showers; in the cold season (when the evaporation caused by the dry air is excessive) let him wear damp clothes; and let him increase by degrees the severity of his austerities. Abandoning the use of all means of gratification, he must engage in meditation, for he is assured that if he is attacked by disease through the use of these means, his soul will unite with the Divine Spirit, and all his troubles be over for ever.

4. The fourth order is that of the Sanyāsi, or anchorite. For those in this class also austerities are enjoined, but their chief employment is meditation. Delighted with meditating on the Supreme Spirit, free from all sensual desires, let him live in this world, seeking bliss in the next by absorption into the Deity. He is ordered to wander from place to place, asking but one meal a day, giving pain to no living being. Meditating on the identity of his spirit with that of the Supreme, he is ready cheerfully to leave the cumbersome and miserable body.

Dr. Wilson wisely adds here, "The profession of the Brāhmans, that with certain non-essential modifications they have still this sacred character, and that they follow these injunctions esteemed divine, gives them a powerful hold upon the mind of India, quite independently of their pretensions to pre-eminence through their origin from Brahmā's mouth. With Brāhmanical discipline and pursuits there is real sympathy even on the part of those large portions of the community who are legally debarred from participating in them. There is an admiration and approval of the Brāhman among the people, as well as much dread and distrust of him, and contempt for his extravagant claims. Hence the attempt, in late centuries especially, of multitudes precluded from all priestly service, to become wandering saints, and devotees of various orders and grades. There is very great deference shown to the Brāhman even in view of the fact that he is now left without a legal remedy for enforcing on his own behalf the unjust laws which he has made connected with his own life, honour, and support. I add another observation. I have a strong impression that a great deal of the Brāhmanical legislation was from the first intended only for effect, and that it was never designed to be carried into execution as far as the priestly practice itself was concerned." In harmony with this last suggestion is the opinion of a native writer in the *Calcutta Review*:* "Those who arrogate to themselves great honours must at least profess to be guided by a more elevated standard of duty than their neighbours. A man who prides himself on the greatness of his origin must admit that it behoveth him to observe higher principles of morality than those over whom he affects superiority. The Brāhmans have accordingly laid down severe rules for the government of their order. Whether the authors of the Sāstras intended that their austere rules should be followed out in practice, or whether they merely proposed to exhibit their idea of priestly dignity without intending to realize it, it is not easy to determine. One thing, however, is certain, that as the Brāhman acknowledged no earthly superior, he had little apprehension of his delinquencies being severely visited. He could not be called to account for departing from his maxims, because no one

* *Calcutta Review*, 1851, p. 53.

was at liberty to judge him. An austere rule of life could therefore prove no greater restraint on his inclinations than he himself chose to allow."

Having given at some length the teaching of the Scriptures respecting the status and employment of the Brāhman, I shall now in a few words describe the position of the second great caste of Hindus, viz., the Kshatriya, or warrior.

The Kshatriya is generally held to have been produced from the *arms* of Brahmā, and is described as the great dispenser of justice, particularly as the one whose duty it is to punish offenders, the civil power to whose tender mercies the Brāhmans could hand over law-breakers. He it is who has to see that the various castes attend to their prescribed duties; but in doing this work he must abide by the decisions of the learned Brāhmans. He must cultivate humility, and is warned by the example of kings, who, through the absence of this virtue, have been ruined. He is enjoined to seek sacred and secular knowledge from the Brāhmans, and to avoid various kinds of immorality and sensuality. Of his eight ministers, some are to be versed in the art of war, some in the doctrines of religion. He should have for a wife a woman of his own caste, and appoint a domestic purahit, or priest, and be liberal in his gifts to the Brāhmans, for "an offering in the mouth of a Brāhman is far better than offerings to holy fires; it never drops, or dries, or is consumed." In battle he must be brave, resolute, and generous; but at the same time self-preservation is carefully taught. "Against misfortune let him preserve his wealth, at the expense of his wealth let him preserve his wife, but at all events let him preserve himself, even at the hazard of his wife and riches." This latter instruction ha been embodied by Brāhmans in the following proverb:

"Preserve your wife, preserve your pelf,
But give them both to save yourself;
There's other wealth, another wife,
But where is there another life?"

His duties for morn, noon, and night are most carefully prescribed for him, as are those of the Brāhman; nothing that a man can have to do but he will find some definite instruction given concerning it: the men to form his army; the time and manner of march; how to attack and how to defend, and the method of dealing with a conquered foe. When unable to attend to his state duties himself, he is advised to appoint a Brāhman substitute; and if at any time he is in need of advice, it is to the Brāhman, and not to the Sudra, that he must turn. The king is the guardian of all property; all treasure trove is to be divided equally between him and the Brāhmans; and whilst all wealth that may be left by any of the other castes dying intestate, goes to the king, the Brāhmans claim what was so left by Brāhmans. Sir W. Jones says of this legislation, by which the members of the several castes are to be guided, that it is "a system of despotism and priestcraft, both indeed limited by law, but artfully conspiring to give mutual support, though with mutual checks." And we shall see, later on, how these two highest castes came to entertain the bitterest hatred towards each other, and tried their best to wrest from each other the privileges each had enjoyed in harmony with these laws. There is one important statement respecting the effect of punishment by a king. "Men who have committed crimes, and have received from kings the punishment due to them, go to heaven pure, and become as clean as those who have done well." "This dictum," says Dr. Wilson, "which removes man from his responsibility to God, has taken a great hold of the popular mind of India. Native musicians attend the capital executions of the vilest criminals throughout the country, seeking to introduce them into the other world with joy and rejoicing, simply because they view their death by the public sentence of the law as an atonement for all their transgressions." It is also the duty of the Kshatriya to keep the castes below him to the works prescribed for them, to regulate all market prices with a due regard to the interests of buyer and seller, and to aid the male community in maintaining its lordship over the female.

3. We now come to note the third of the chief castes, the Vaishya. This comprises the merchant, agriculturalist, and keeper of cattle. This caste, springing from the thigh of Brahmā, is naturally inferior both to the Brāhman and Kshatriya. After performing the initiatory sacraments, ending with that of the sacrificial thread, and marrying a wife of his own caste, he should be attentive to his own proper work, which is chiefly that of keeping cattle; for God has committed cattle to Vaishya's care, as He has committed men to the care of the Brāhman and Kshatriya. He must acquaint himself with the prices of goods, learn to sow and reap, be able to distinguish good land from bad—in fact, he has to study the various branches of the subjects which tend to make him a good farmer or merchant.

4. The fourth class is the Sudra, or servants' caste, which is said to have sprung from the feet of Brahmā. As the Sudra has been created especially to minister to the comfort of the three higher castes, of course his duty lies in doing anything and everything that will in any way tend to their well-being. He is spoken of as a slave, his property, as well as his person, being at the disposal of his master. His religious degradation, too, is complete. According to Manu, a Brāhman is forbidden to give advice or food to a Sudra, the ghî portion of which, having been offered to the gods, must not therefore be eaten by him. Further, the Brāhman must not give "spiritual counsel to him," nor inform him of the legal expiation of his sin. He who declares the law to a servile man, and he who instructs him in the mode of expiating sin, sinks with that very man into the hell named Asamvrita. A Brāhman should never be the preceptor of a Sudra. "While the first part of a Brāhman's name should indicate holiness, that of a Kshatriya's power, and that of a Vaishya's wealth, that of a Sudra should indicate contempt. The Veda is never to be read in the presence of a Sudra, and

for him no sacrifice is to be performed. He has no business with solemn rites."

The privileges of a Sudra are very limited. He must not marry a woman of the higher castes, or their offspring will sink into a class even lower than his own. He must not aid in carrying the corpse of a Brāhman, even of his own master, that obstructions to the dead man's entrance into heaven may not result. He is allowed to carry his dead only through the southern gate of the city where he may live. His morals are not to be strictly looked after. The murder of a Sudra by a Brāhman is equal only to killing a cat, or a frog, or a crow. "Servile attendance on the Brāhmans learned in the Vedas, chiefly on such as keep house, and are famed for virtue, is of itself the highest duty of a Sudra, and leads him to future beatitude. Pure, humbly serving the higher classes, sweet in speech, never arrogant, ever seeking refuge in the Brāhmans, he may attain the highest class" in another birth.

CHAPTER III.

HISTORY OF THE GROWTH OF CASTE.

HAVING sketched the peculiarities of the four chief castes as they are described in the Law Books, and considered their ideal characteristics, I shall now give a few quotations from other Hindu sacred books, as far as possible in chronological order, so that some idea may be formed respecting the origin and growth of this most elaborate system. Dr. Muir,* reviewing the texts which he had cited on this subject, says, "First, we have the set of accounts in which the four castes are said to have sprung from progenitors who were separately created; but in regard to the manner of their creation we find the greatest diversity of statement. The most common story is that the castes issued from the mouth, arms, thighs, and feet of Purusha, or Brahmā. The oldest extant passage in which this idea occurs, and from which all the later myths of a similar tenor have no doubt been borrowed, is to be found in the Purusha Sūkta; but it is doubtful whether, in the form in which it is there represented, this representation is anything more than an allegory. In some of the texts from the Bhāgavata Purāna traces of the same allegorical character may be perceived; but in Manu and the Purānas the mystical import of the Vedic text disappears, and the figurative narration is hardened into a literal statement of fact. In the chapters of the Vishnu, Vāyu, and Mārkandeya Purānas, where castes are described as coeval with creation, and as

* "Old Sanskrit Texts," vol. i. p. 159.

having been naturally distinguished by different *gunas*, or qualities, involving varieties of moral character, we are nevertheless allowed to infer that those qualities exerted no influence on the classes in which they were inherent, as the condition of the whole race during the Krita age is described as one of uniform perfection and happiness ; while the actual separation into castes did not take place, according to the Vāyu Purāna, until men had become deteriorated in the Treta age.

" Second, in various passages from the Brāhmanas, epic poems, and Purānas, the creation of mankind is described without the least allusion to any separate production of the progenitors of the four castes. And whilst in the chapters where they relate the distinct formations of the castes, the Purānas assign different natural dispositions to each class, they elsewhere represent all mankind as being at the creation uniformly distinguished by the quality of passion. In one text men are said to be the offspring of Vivasat ; in another his son Manu is said to be their progenitor, whilst in a third they are said to be descended from a female of the same name. The passage which declares Manu to have been the father of the human race explicitly affirms that men of all the four castes were descended from him. In another remarkable text the Mahābhārata categorically asserts that originally there was no distinction of classes, the existing distribution having arisen out of differences of character and occupation. " In these circumstances we may fairly conclude that the separate origination of the four castes was far from being an article of belief universally received by Indian antiquity."

The first quotation is from the Purusha Sūkta, one of the latest additions to the Rig Veda. This is believed to be the " oldest extant passage which makes mention of the fourfold origin of the Hindu race," and this, as noticed above, has evidently more the character of poetry than intended to describe a literal fact. " When (the gods) divided Purusha, into how many parts did they cut him up? What was his mouth? What (his) arms? What (two objects) are said (to have been) his thighs and feet? The Brāhman was his mouth, the Rajanya (Kshatriya) was made his arms, the being (called) the Vaisya, he was his thighs; the Sūdra sprang from his feet, the moon sprang from his soul, the sun from his eye," &c. There is great interest attaching to this hymn, as it is found among the formulas referring to human sacrifice, and in all probability has been used at them. "That at the earliest period of the Vedic time human sacrifices were quite common with the Brāhmans, can be proved beyond any doubt. But the more eminent and distinguished amongst their leaders soon abandoned the practice as revolting to human feelings. The form of the sacrifice, however, seems to have been kept for a long time, for the ritual required on that occasion is actually in the Yajur Veda; but they simply tied men of different castes and classes to the sacrificial posts, and released them afterwards, sacrificing animals instead of them." *

In the Satapata Brāhmana another poetical account is given of the origin of the three castes—viz., that they sprang from the four Vedas. "This entire (universe) has been created by Brahma. Men say that the Vaishya class was produced from the Rich-Verses. They say that the Yajur Veda is the womb from which the Kshatriyas were born. The Sāma Veda is the source from which the Brāhmans sprang. This word the ancients declared to the ancients." In the same book is another poetical account. "Brahmā (in the form of Agni, and representing the Brāhman race) was formerly this (universe) one only. . . . It energetically created an excellent form, the Kshatriya, viz., those amongst the gods who are powers, viz., Indra, Varuna, &c.; hence nothing is superior to the Kshatriya. Therefore the Brāhman sits below the Kshatriya at the Rājasūga sacrifice; he confers that glory on the Kshatriya. This Brahmā is the source of

* Dr. Haug, quoted in Muir's "Old Sanskrit Texts," vol. i. p. 11.

the Kshatriya. Hence, although the king attains supremacy, he at the end resorts to the Brahmā as his source. Whoever destroys him (the Brāhman) destroys his own source. . . . He created Vis, viz., those classes of gods who are designated by troops, Vasus, Rudras, &c. . . . He created the Sūdra class, Pushan. This earth is Pushan: for she nourishes all that exists." In yet another text it is declared that Prajāpati (Brahmā) formed "animals from his breath, a man from his soul," &c.*

The Vishnu Purāna makes the distinction of castes to be the result of the character of those forming them. In answer to a question as to how these distinctions arose, the sage Parāsara replied, "When, true to his design, Brahmā became desirous to create the world, creatures in whom goodness prevailed sprang from his mouth; others, in whom passion predominated, came from his breast; others, in whom both passion and darkness were strong, proceeded from his thighs; others he created from his feet, whose chief characteristic was darkness."

The Vāyu Purāna teaches that a thousand pairs of these different castes were formed at once. "As Brahmā was desirous to create, and, fixed in his design, was meditating upon offspring, he created from his mouth a thousand couples of living beings who were born with an abundance of goodness, and full of intelligence. He then created another thousand from his breast; they all abounded in passion, and were both vigorous and destitute of vigour. After creating from his thighs another thousand pairs, in whom both passion and darkness prevailed, and who are described as active, he formed from his feet yet another thousand couples, who were all full of darkness, inglorious, and of little vigour;" and further on this Purāna declares that in the Krita age, which answers to the golden age of the Greeks, when all men were good, "there were no distinctions of castes or orders, and no mixture of castes!" "These perfect beings, who

* Muir, "Old Sanskrit Texts," vol. i. p. 20.

were described by me as existing formerly in the Krita age, the mind-born children of Brahmā, who had been produced in this world when they came from the Janaloka, who were tranquil, fiery, active, or distressed, were born again in the Treta age as Brāhmans, Kshatriyas, Vaisyas, Sudras, and injurious men governed by good and bad actions (performed in former births)." A few verses afterwards we find that Svayambhu (the self-existent) "established divisions amongst (men) according to their tendencies. Those of them who were rapacious he ordained to be Kshatriyas, protectors of the others. As many men attended on these, fearless, speaking the truth, and propounding sacred knowledge with exactness (were made) Brāhmans. Those who had previously been feeble, engaged in slaughter, and cultivators who were active with the ground, he made Vaisyas; and he designated as Sudras those who grieved, and were addicted to menial tasks, inglorious and feeble." From this it would appear that the writer believed that at first there was no distinction of caste; but that owing to the character and conduct of men, in their later births they were thus subdivided by Brahmā. These various and apparently contradictory statements of the origin of the castes are explained as referring to the commencement of things in different kalpas, or ages; for at the end of each kalpa all created things are destroyed, and with the commencement of each a new creation takes place. Professor Wilson suggests that a better reason is that they have been borrowed from different original authorities.

The Rāmāyana teaches that the four castes were the offspring of a *woman* named Manu, the wife of Kasyapa, a son of Brahmā. The Mahābhārata contains various and self-contradictory statements on this subject. In some places the prerogatives of the Brāhmans are described in the style, and almost in the identical language, found in Manu. In another place, Mahadeva, addressing his spouse, says, "A man, whether he be a Brāhman, Kshatriya, Vaisya, or Sudra, is such by nature;" and goes on to say that "if a higher caste man acts as a lower, he will be born again as the lower; whilst one who, in the lower, acts as those in the higher, he will be born into the higher, *i.e.*, that in life no real change of caste can be effected." In another passage it declares that "until a man is born into the Veda (*i.e.*, until he is initiated by the investiture of the Brāhmanical thread) he is on the level with a Sudra;" hence the removal of the thread by a Christian reduces a man at once in the estimation of the Hindus from his high position as a Brāhman. And in yet another passage the sage Bhrigu says, "There is no difference of castes: this world, having been at first created by Brahmā entirely Brāhmanic, became (afterwards) separated into castes in consequence of works." Once all were Brāhmans, but some, owing to their evil deeds, in succeeding births were reduced to the position they now occupy.

Dr. Muir,* having given a number of texts from the parts of the Rig Veda and other Sāstras, which are generally admitted to be more ancient than the Purusha Sūkta, from which a quotation has been made, draws the following conclusion: "In general the authors of the hymns of the Rig Veda regarded the whole of the Āryan people, embracing not only the priests and chiefs, but the middle classes of the population, as descended from a common father, or ancestor, whom they designate by the name of Manu. This reference to a common progenitor excludes, of course, the supposition that the writers by whom it is made could have had any belief of the myth which became afterwards current among their countrymen—that their nation consisted of four castes, differing naturally in dignity, and separately made by Brahmā. . . . It will, I think, be found on investigation that not only the older hymns, but the great bulk of the hymns, supply no distinct evidence of the existence of a well-defined and developed caste system at the time when they were composed."

* "Old Sanskrit Texts," vol. i. p. 239.

The origin and progress of the caste system is of course difficult to trace with anything approaching certainty; nevertheless a tolerably accurate idea may be formed by the careful study of the Hindu literature as far as it can be done in chronological order. The root Brahma signifies hymn or prayer; "the term Brāhman must therefore, as we conclude, have been ordinarily applied (1) to the same persons who are spoken of elsewhere in the hymns as Rishi, Kavi, &c., and have denoted devout worshippers and contemplative sages who composed prayers and hymns, which they themselves recited in praise of the gods. Afterwards, when the ceremonial gradually became more complicated, and a division of sacred functions took place, the word was more ordinarily employed (2) for a minister of public worship, and at length came to signify (3) one particular kind of priest with special duties." * Dr. Muir cites a number of texts in which the word Brāhman is employed in the three senses indicated above, and a number of others in which gifts to the Brāhmans are encouraged; whilst the niggardly are blamed in strong language for their want of liberality. It seems evident from these texts that the irreligious man was by no means a rare character amongst the Āryans of the Vedic age, and that the priests often found no little difficulty in drawing forth the liberality of their contemporaries towards themselves, and in enforcing a due regard to the ceremonials of devotion. Still, "it will remain certain that the Brāhman, whether we look upon him as a sage or poet, or as an officiating priest, or in both capacities, was regarded with respect and reverence, and even that his presence had begun to be considered as an important condition of the efficacy of the ceremonial." "While, however, there thus appears to be every reason for supposing that towards the close of the Vedic period the priesthood had become a profession, the texts quoted (excepting that from the Purusha Sūkta) do not contain anything which necessarily implies that the priests

* "Old Sanskrit Texts," p. 243.

formed an exclusive caste, or at least a caste separated from all others by insurmountable barriers, as in later times." Still further, to prove that in the Vedic age the caste system had nothing approaching to the exclusiveness it assumed later on, there are texts which show that some who were not Brāhmans were authors of Vedic hymns and exercised priestly functions. When in later ages it was found that this fact might encourage others to attempt to perform the work and obtain the emoluments of the Brāhmans, legends were invented to show that these priests had, by miraculous means, been first made Brāhmans, and then allowed to perform the duties peculiar to that privileged caste. Again, from other hymns it is evident that the Brāhmans intermarried with women of the other classes, taking the widows and, it may be, in some cases the wives, of men still living; whilst at the same time the terms in which the evils of interference with the Brāhman's rights and privileges are described show a decided tendency to growth in strength and bitterness.

Dr. Roth's opinion on the subject, as quoted by Dr. Muir, is as follows: "The religious development of India is attached through the course of three thousand years to the word brăhmă. This conception might be taken as the standard for estimating the progress of thought directed to divine things, as at every step taken by the latter it has gained a new form; while at the same time it has always embraced in itself the highest spiritual acquisition of the nation. The original signification of the word brăhmă, as we easily discover it in the Vedic hymns, is that of prayer; not praise or thanksgiving, but that invocation which, with the force of the will directed to God, seeks to draw Him to itself, and to receive satisfaction from Him. From this oldest sense and form of brahma was formed the masculine noun Brahmā, which was the designation of those who pronounced the prayers, or performed the sacred ceremonies; and in nearly all the passages of the Rig Veda, in which it was thought that this word must refer to the Brāhmanical caste, this more extended sense must be substituted for the other more limited one. From this sense of the word brahmā nothing was more natural than to convert this offerer of prayer into a particular description of the sacrificial priest: so soon as the ritual began to be fixed, the functions which before were united in a single person, who both prayed to the gods and sacrificed to them, became separated, and a priesthood interposed itself between man and God." *

"In many places of the liturgical and legal books, the promise of every blessing is attached to the maintenance of a priest by the king. Inasmuch as he supports and honours the priest, the latter ensures to him the favour of the gods. So it was that the caste of the Brāhmans arose and attained to power and consideration: first, they were only the single domestic priests of the kings; then, the dignity became hereditary in certain families; finally, a union, occasioned by similarity of interests of these families in one larger community, was effected; and all this in reciprocal action with the progress made in other respects by theological doctrine and religious worship. Still the extension of the power which fell into the hands of this priestly caste would not be perfectly comprehensible from this explanation alone. The relation of spiritual superiority in which the priests came to stand to the kings was aided by other historical movements. When at a period more recent than the majority of the hymns of the Rig Veda, as the Vedic people, driven by some political shock, advanced from their abode in the Panjāb, further and further to the south, drove the aborigines into the hills, and took possession of the broad tract of country lying between the Ganges, the Jumna, and the Vindhya range, the time had arrived when the distribution of power, the relation of king and priest, could become transformed in the most rapid and comprehensive manner. Principalities separated in such various ways, such a division into tribes as had existed in the Panjāb were no longer possible here where

* "Old Sanskrit Texts," vol. i. p. 289.

nature had created a wide and continuous tract, with scarcely any natural boundaries to dissever one part from another. Most of these petty princes who had descended from the north with their tribes must of necessity disappear, their tribes become dissolved, and contests arise for the supreme dominion. This era is perhaps portrayed to us in the principal subject of the Mahābhārata, the contest between the descendants of Pāndu and Kuru. In this stage of disturbance and complication, power naturally fell into the hands of those who did not directly possess any authority; the priestly races and their leaders, who had hitherto stood rather in the position of followers of the kings, now rose to a higher rank. It may easily be supposed that they and their families, already honoured as the confidential followers of the princes, would frequently be able to strike a decisive stroke to which the king would owe his success. If we take further into account the intellectual and moral influence which this class possessed in virtue of the prerogative conceded to or usurped by them, and the religious feelings of the people, it is not difficult to comprehend how, in such a period of transition, powerful communities should arise amongst the domestic priests of petty kings and their families, should attain to the highest importance in every department of life, and should grow into a caste, which, like the ecclesiastical orders of the middle ages of Christianity, began to look upon secular authority as an effluence from the fulness of their power to be conferred at their will; and how, on the other hand, the numerous royal families should sink down into a nobility which possessed, indeed, the sole right to the kingly dignity, but at the same time, when elected by the people, required inauguration in order to their recognition by the priesthood, and were enjoined above all things to employ only Brāhmans as their counsellors." Dr. Roth goes on to speak of the three highest castes as being altogether different from the fourth, in that the latter were not permitted to sacrifice or to know the Vedas: the supposition being well founded that the Sudras were not originally part of the Hindu system, but were engrafted into it, and were originally composed either of the descendant of a previous migration, or were the aborigines of the country.

CHAPTER IV.

STRUGGLES FOR SUPREMACY AMONGST THE CASTES.

IT is of some interest to see that the position assumed and generally held by the Brāhmans was not obtained and held without some severe struggles on their part against the Kshatriyas whom they sought to make subordinate. In Manu * is the following verse which forms the text concerning which legends are found in more recent works showing the evils that those suffered who attempted to subvert the power of the Brāhmans. "Let the king constantly reverence ancient Brāhmans skilled in the Vedas and pure in conduct; for he who always respects the aged is honoured even by Rākshasas. Let him, even though humble-minded, be continually learning submissiveness from them: for a submissive monarch never perishes. Through want of this character many kings have been destroyed with all their possessions. Vena perished through want of submissiveness, and King Nahusha, and Sūdas the son of Pijavana, and Samukha, and Nimi. But through submissiveness Prithu and Manu attained kingly power, Varuna the lordship of wealth, and the son of Gadhi Brāhmanhood." In the later books the legends of these men's doings and their results are fully told; and the time of their existence is put back hundreds of thousands of years in order that it may be believed that they are those referred to by the great legislator. I shall now give an outline of some of these stories.

Vena was the grandson of Mrithu (death), and was, like him,

* "Old Sanskrit Texts," vol. i. p. 296.

of a corrupt nature. When he was inaugurated he forbade men to sacrifice to the gods, declaring that he was the rightful lord of offerings. The Rishis came and entreated him to recall this dreadful order, promising that if he would do so he should have a share of the offerings, but that men must sacrifice to the gods. Vena, waxing more arrogant by all this, asked, "Who are the gods? They are all present in a king's person; he is composed of all the gods." As the king would not hearken, the Munis took each a blade of the sacred grass which had been consecrated with a sacred text and smote him with them. After this they rubbed his thigh and produced from it a hideous black being who became the progenitor of the Nishādas; and by this means the evil of the king was extracted. The Munis then rubbed his right hand, and a glorious son named Prithu was the result, who by his many virtues delivered his father from hell and himself showed great respect to the Brāhmans.

Nahusha is said to have been a powerful king, who, intoxicated with pride, made the Brāhmans carry him from place to place upon their shoulders. At length his arrogance becoming unbearable, a sage named Agastya was at his own request placed amongst the bearers. As the holy men were proceeding with their load, the monarch touched him with his foot, whereupon the sage cried out, "Fall, thou serpent." Immediately the proud monarch, who had raised himself to the position of Indra, or king of the gods, by his austerities, fell to the earth in the form of a serpent, and continued in that form until he was released by Yudhisthira, the righteous king. A variation of the story is that a sage named Bhrigu was concealed in Agastya's hair; this sage had the power to bring any one to submission on whom his eye fell; but Nahusha had also the power to prevent any one he saw from injuring him. Bhrigu having assumed a diminutive size, and being hidden in Agastya's hair, was able to see Nahusha without being seen by him, and in this disguise effected the arrogant king's destruction.

The King Nimi, referred to above, had requested a Brāhman Rishi to celebrate for him a sacrifice which was to last a thousand years; but the Brāhman being engaged for the next five hundred years, said he would be glad to come at the expiration of that period. Without saying anything in reply to this offer, Nimi engaged another priest to do his work. For a time all was proceeding satisfactorily, but at the expiration of the five hundred years the Brāhman to whom the king had first spoken, coming when his work elsewhere was completed, and being incensed at the slight that had been shown to him by the engaging of another priest without consulting him, said, "Let Nimi be deprived of his body." Nimi, on awaking, learned what had been done, and because the Brāhman had cursed him without any previous notice, ordered that the vigour of the Brāhman should be given to Mitra and Varuna. When Nimi's sacrifice was complete, the gods, on the intercession of the priests, were willing to restore his form to Nimi; but he, being unwilling to take it, asked that he might live in the eyes of all living creatures. It is in consequence of this that they are always opening and shutting them, "Nimisha" meaning "the twinkling of an eye."

The story of the quarrel between Visishtha, a Brāhman sage, and Visvamitra, figures very largely in Hindu legend. Briefly, it is as follows: "One day the Kshatriya king, Visvamitra, visited the hermitage of Visishtha, by whom he was entertained in a right royal manner, and was surprised to find that the wonderful provision, of which he and his followers had partaken, had been given by a wonder-working cow which belonged to the hermit. King-like, Visvamitra wished for this cow, offered a million other cows for it, or even his kingdom, but the Brāhman steadily refused to yield his treasure. The king then tried to drive her away, but she would not move. The cow, addressing her master, asked if it was his wish for her to go, otherwise no power could possibly move her. The Brāhman, intimating that he had no wish to part with her, her appearance suddenly changed, and the calm and quiet cow became the source of an immense and powerful army, which put to flight the king's troops in a moment. The king, witnessing this miracle, which he believed to have been wrought through the Brāhman's influence, immediately gave up his opposition, and betook himself to prayer, meditation, and asceticism, by virtue of which, in process of time, he obtained the coveted position of Brāhmanhood." Some marvellous stories are told of the wonderful fervour of Visvamitra's austerity. On one occasion Dharma (religion), assuming the form of Visishtha, visited the ascetic and asked him for food. The man came with it freshly cooked and hot, upon which Dharma asked him to remain as he was for a little time. At the close of a hundred years, returning to the same spot, and finding him still standing there as he had commanded, he was so pleased, that at once he said, "I am pleased with thee, O Brāhman rishi;" by which word the desired effect was accomplished, and the Kshatriya king became a Brāhman.

Visvamitra, thus raised to the position of a Brāhman, is regarded as the author of many Vedic hymns, and, chief of all, the mysterious, awe-inspiring Gāyatri. Perhaps a more correct view of the facts would be the following. In the early Vedic days the rules which prescribed the duties of each caste were not so carefully drawn as in later times. Probably at that time the Brāhman and the kingly Kshatriya alike performed priestly functions; but in after years, when the Brāhmans claimed an exclusive right to perform the duties of priest and teacher, it was found inconvenient to have one so prominent as the Kshatriya Visvamitra in their religious history, and to be acknowledged as the author of their most sacred hymns. Hence the idea was started, and numerous legends invented to substantiate it, that this man, though born in another caste, by means of protracted and intense religious fervour had gained admission into the privileged class. For in a work later than the Vedas, but older than the Purānas, it is stated that a Brāhman must officiate at sacrifices that only a Kshatriya can offer. In the Markandeya Purāna is a most interesting story of Harischandra, a king who offended a great Rishi, and of the sufferings he had to endure in consequence. The story was evidently written to show that Brāhman though he had become in spirit and in conduct, he was still inferior to the Brāhman born. It may also have been inserted with the intention of showing the great benefits that kings obtain when they bow submissively to Brāhmans, even though the demands of the spiritual man be most unreasonable. The king when hunting, hearing, as he thought, the cry of a woman in distress, and being bound as a Kshatriya, like the knight-errants of the West, to redress human wrongs, inspired by Ganesa, uttered an imprecation which aroused the anger of the sage. It appears this sage was attempting to master the sciences by his religious fervour, and they in their distress cried out, and their cry reached the ears of the king. The sage, bursting forth into a rage at this interruption of his religious occupation, destroyed the very spirits he was trying to overcome. Harischandra, grieved and terrified at what he had done, offered most costly gifts—gold, his son, his wife, his body, his life, his kingdom. The sage's first demand was the empire of the world; everything, in fact, but the king's person, his son, his wife, and his virtue. All this being freely given, the king and queen having cast off their jewels and royal robes, and having put on the ascetic dress, the sage now demanded a fee for offering the sacrifice thus presented. As the king had only his son and wife left to him, he asks for a month's delay. The king set off to Benares, hoping to find a "city of refuge" in that holy place, but is mistaken; his relentless creditor is there to meet him. There being no other course open to him, the king has to sell his wife as a slave, who takes her little boy with her to her master's house. But alas! the money he received for his wife is regarded as altogether too small a gift by the savage priest. Then Harischandra sold himself to a Chandāla (one of the most degraded and despised castes), who sent him into graveyards to steal the clothes from the dead who were buried there. For a whole year the king followed this dreadful occupation, at which time his wife came there to burn her son, who had just died. At first the husband and wife did not recognize each other; but when recognition was made, they talked over their miseries, and determined to end them by burning themselves with the corpse of their child. As they are just about to carry their purpose into effect, Dharma (religion) appears, and tells the king that he has assumed the form of the cruel Chandāla to try the faith of his servant, and that, being pleased with his readiness to suffer and die rather than fail to fulfil his vow, husband and wife ascend to heaven with a divine escort, and are richly rewarded for all their painful service.

In the legends of Parasurāma we have the story told of Vishnu becoming incarnate in that hero in order that he might destroy the Kshatriya race, and how he again and again almost succeeded in the attempt. All these legends show most clearly, as might reasonably have been expected, that the Brāhmans were not suffered to attain to almost divine superiority without a contest. In the story of Parasurāma we read of the final struggle in which the Brāhmans gained the supremacy.

The few instances just given are of men of other (twice-born, *i.e.*, the three highest castes) castes being raised into the position of Brāhmans. The following story from the Mahābhārata will show the impossibility of any of the fourth, or lowest caste, attaining this privilege. A man named Matanga, the reputed son of a Brāhman, was one day riding in a car drawn by asses. As he was urging on one of the asses by pricking its nose, the mother tried to comfort her suffering son with the remark, "Be not distressed, my son; it is a Chandāla who is in the car. There is nothing dreadful in a Brāhman; he is kind, a teacher who instructs all creatures—how can he smite any one? The wicked man shows no pity to a tender colt, and thereby indicates his origin, for it is birth which determines the character." Hearing these words of the mother-ass, Matanga descended from the car and asked what she meant by casting reflections on his birth. The ass then assured him that he was no Brāhman's son; but that his mother, when in a state of intoxication, had received the embraces of a barber, and that he was really the barber's son. Speedily returning home, he commenced a life of such severe penance as to alarm the gods, who in their fright extracted from Indra the promise of a boon for the devotee. He asked to be made a Brāhman, but this Indra refused, as he assured him that such a gift would mean his death. For a hundred years more Matanga continued his austerity, when Indra again refused to grant the gift he asked, and told him that a "Chandāla can only become a Sūdra in a thousand births, a Sūdra a Vaisya after a period thirty times as long, a Vaisya a Rājanya (Kshatriya) after a period sixty times the length, a Rājanya a Brāhman after a further period of sixty thousand lives." Dissatisfied with the answer, Matanga performed the severest penance for a thousand years, but again Indra assured him it was impossible for him to give the boon desired.

Having considered the teaching of the Hindu Scriptures respecting the Hindus, let us now see what is their teaching respecting those outside of the four castes, the people, *i.e.*, whom they found in India when they migrated there, and the people of other lands who had no connection whatever with the Hindu system. Manu is very explicit on this subject. He says: "Three castes, the Brāhman, Kshatriya, Vaisya, are twice-born; the fourth, the Sūdra, once-born; *there is no fifth.*" And in harmony with this teaching he declares them all to be outcastes, as we should now term them, such as the Chandālas, the descendants of mixed marriages of those who were included in one or other of the four castes; the descendants of such mixed marriages being regarded by him as the offscouring of the earth. And he enumerates a large number of outcaste tribes, and gives their pedigree, showing that in all cases they are the descendants of some who were once within the bounds of the Hindu castes. The common name Dasyas (slaves) is applied to all these outcaste peoples. In the same book it is taught that all these classes ought to respect the Brāhmanical institutions; and certain general moral lessons are given for their guidance. "Such duties as these, which have been ordained of old, ought to be observed by all people." In the Vishnu Purāna is a story which accounts for their origin in harmony with Manu's teaching. A child named Sāgara, who was born in a forest where his father and mother had escaped after being deprived of their kingdom, hearing his family history from his mother, when he was grown up raised an army and recovered his paternal estate. When he was about to exterminate his conquered foes, they applied to Vasishtha, his family priest, for protection. On their behalf this priest interceded with the king, saying, "You have done enough, my son, in the way of pursuing these men who are as good as dead. I have compelled them to abandon the duties of caste and all association with the twice-born." Acting on the advice of his spiritual guide, Sāgara compelled these tribes to alter their costume. He made the Yavans shave their heads, the Sakas shave half their heads, the Pāradas to wear long hair, and the Pahlavas beards. These and other Kshatriyas he deprived of the study of the Vedas, in consequence of which, and of their desertion by the Brāhmans, they became Mlechhas, or outcastes. From these and similar stories it seems clear that the writers imagined that the people inhabiting the countries bordering on their own were once part of their own nation, who through their wickedness lost their position as the members of one or other of the four great castes. Of other nations beyond the Hindu writers betray the grossest ignorance.

CHAPTER V.

CASTE AS IT NOW EXISTS.

Having considered caste as far as it is referred to in the sacred books, I shall now describe it as it is seen in the present day. It is true there are those who declare that it never actually existed in the precise form there indicated; that the whole scheme is purely imaginary. This may to some extent be true; but that there was an approximate realization of it, there can be little doubt. Nowadays it is very different from what it once was; but that we have a fairly faithful account of caste as it once existed, there seems to be no reasonable ground for doubt.

In Bengal there are virtually but two of the original four castes, viz., Brāhmans and Sūdras. The Brāhmans are subdivided into an immense number of classes, some of whom will not eat or intermarry with some others. The pure Kshatriyas are almost extinct, though there are in other parts of India many who profess to be such, as are also the Vaisyas; whilst those who are known as Sūdras, in the large majority of cases, are really the descendants of some of the mixed classes. It was a peculiarity of this system, the object of which was, as far as possible, to prevent the intermarriage of the classes, that the children of such mesalliances did not enjoy the position even of the lower-caste parent, whether father or mother, but sank into a class far below either. In civilized countries the wife, whether nobler or baser, takes the rank of her husband; but this was not the case in India. The heaviest penalties had to be paid by the children when a woman married a man of a lower caste.

But this has been changed. In the present day those who contract these forbidden marriages themselves suffer. Perhaps one fruitful cause of these mixed marriages in former times lies in the fact that in addition to the proper marriage form there were others that were recognized amongst the Hindus, the one called the *Gandharva* rite, where man and woman meeting, and being mutually willing, might live as man and wife without any rite or ceremony; the other, the *Rākshasa* rite, by which the victors in war were at perfect liberty to appropriate to themselves the women of the vanquished.

At the present time the most numerous of the well-to-do Hindus of Bengal are the Vaidya and Kāyastha castes. These are reckoned as Sūdras, though, according to Manu, the former was originally the offspring of a Brāhman father and Vaishya mother; the latter, the offspring of a Vaishya father with a Sūdra mother; whilst almost the lowest caste of all, the Chandāla, was the offspring of a Sūdra father with a Brāhman mother.

In theory the supremacy of the Brāhman remains. There can be little doubt that in many places the people generally regard the Brāhman as little less than divine. It should, however, be clearly understood that all the Brāhmans never were, nor are they now, engaged as priests. *Some* Brāhman families have for generations been acting as priests in the various temples, and others have so officiated in the palaces of the kings and in the homes of those who were able to pay them for their services; but these, styled Pujāri Brāhmans, *i.e.*, those who perform religious services for payment, are regarded by their fellow-Brāhmans with considerable contempt. It is not because of his office as priest, but by reason of his birth as a Brāhman, that he obtains the adoration of the people. The guru, who in many sects is not necessarily a Brāhman, is also reverenced as a god by his own disciples. But when the office of guru is superadded to the birthright of Brāhmanhood, no class of men on earth have greater reverence shown to them by their fellow-men. Some Brāhmans are priests: all priests are Brāhmans; it is not their employment but their birth that secures them respect. And this respect is most profound. As he walks through the streets low-caste people account it an honour to take the dust from his feet and place it upon their head; and in extreme cases to drink the water in which his feet have been washed. This is done partly through fear of the holy man's curse, partly through reverence for his imagined sanctity and power to influence the gods.

In some exceptional cases the four stages of a Brāhman's ideal life, as prescribed in the Law Books, are regarded. He passes through the student, householder, meditative, and ascetic periods; but this is by no means general. A modification of the scheme is more commonly seen. Brāhmans, when growing old and infirm, will hand over their property to their heirs, and go away to Benares, Gaya, or some other place on the banks of the sacred streams, there to await their end in peace. This is the wish of multitudes, who have not the means of its gratification. The old idea that it is derogatory to the dignity of a Brāhman to sell his services has quite given way to the pressure of circumstances, and men glorying in the *poitra* and in the possession of most honourable names are to be found engaged as clerks, schoolmasters, physicians, engineers, and shopkeepers. The old pundits admit that the proper position and work of the Brāhman does not pay in this degenerate age, as the Vishnu Purāna predicted would be the case in the Kali Yuga. In the towns, at any rate, they can with impunity violate almost every law laid down for their guidance by Manu; though in some of the country places, where superstition is stronger, it is necessary for them to be a little more careful. Each caste in a district has its *dal*, or committee, presided over by its dalapati, or president, to whose judgment the members are bound to submit; and when any violation of the rules of the caste are reported against a member, the dal considers the matter, and, if it is proved, sentence is pronounced; and this punishment must either be endured, or the delinquent is put out of caste, *i.e.*, the members "boycott" him. They will neither visit nor eat with him; nor will they allow their sons to intermarry with his family. The punishment of this social ostracism is most severe.

Some of these dals are very strict in their observance of the rules of their caste, some are just as lax. In cities like Calcutta, some of them allow their members openly to violate rules that at no distant age were most rigorously observed, and which to this hour are binding amongst sections of the Hindus who are not so much influenced by European ideas. Nowadays a man may eat beef, drink wine, wear shoes made of cowhide, sit down to table with Europeans, without losing his position in society. I know gentlemen, who are regarded as orthodox—at any rate are not expelled from their *dal*—who frequently visit houses of Europeans, eating and drinking quite freely with them. In country districts I have partaken of roast meat in Hindu gentlemen's houses where a Mahomedan cook was kept; and this quite openly; the Brāhman host sitting down with me at the table. Public dinners are given in European hotels where Hindu gentlemen of various castes publicly partake of food together. The young men who ventured to cross the sea were, on their return to India, subjected to most severe penance as a method of purifying them from contact with the despised Mlechhas; but as many resented this, the process of purification has been very considerably modified. The Hindu community found that by outcasteing those who had been bold enough to go to England to qualify for good positions in their own country, they were casting off the men who were throwing the brightest lustre upon their nation, and therefore a way was soon made by which they could be retained. With the exception of a very few of the more orthodox dals, Hindus may do almost anything they wish except receive Christian baptism. *That* still remains as a recognized separation from the community, although certain pundits in Calcutta have openly declared that they could find no word against baptism in their Scriptures. However, the feeling of the community at present is in favour of the expulsion from caste of those who thus openly assert their faith in Jesus Christ.

Dals exist in connection with all the various castes, and the members are subject to their authority, in some cases the power of the dals being superior to law; *e.g.*, it has been enacted that it is lawful for a Hindu widow to remarry; but though this law has been in existence for years, the number who have availed themselves of it is exceedingly small; the power of Hindu prejudice has proved itself so strong, that those have been excommunicated who have transgressed what they consider the Hindu sacred law on this question. Some of these communities are much more strict than others. Some years ago a Hindu gentleman, who had by his mode of living (he was a frequenter of European hotels, and freely partook of forbidden food) made himself obnoxious to the members of his own set, for a time got on very well indeed without being admitted into their strict society. He had friends like-minded with himself, who afforded him the society he needed. But as years rolled by, and his daughters were old enough to be married, he found his isolation prevented him from obtaining husbands for them. He therefore applied for admission in vain to several sets of his own caste, and was refused. At last he found one liberal enough to admit him as a member, and so he died "in the odour of sanctity," though he scarcely changed his mode of life. In addition to these smaller communities, there are what might be almost termed Hindu General Assemblies; *i.e.*, societies formed for the express purpose of explaining and enforcing Hindu law and custom, to whom important social questions are referred for decision, the members of which are mostly learned pundits, with a sprinkling of well-to-do men engaged in secular employment. As a specimen of the subjects taken before them for discussion and settlement, and also as an example of the subtlety with which they harmonize common sense with the teaching of the Scriptures, may be mentioned that connected with the introduction of the water supply into Calcutta. Hinduism forbids its followers from drinking water from a vessel that has been touched by people of another caste. The water that flows through the pipes in the city is obtained by the mass of the people from stand-posts with taps, to which low-caste Hindus, Mussulmāns, Christians, &c., have free access. At first an attempt was made to have taps set apart for the different castes, but when this was found to be impracticable, the Hindu Dharma Rākshini Sabha (*i.e.*, the Society for the Preservation of the Eternal Religion), determined that although it was contrary to the teaching of Hinduism for men of different castes to drink water which came from the same vessel, yet, as the people had to pay taxes to meet the expenses of bringing this water, this money payment should be considered a sufficient atonement for violating the ordinances of the Hindu religion. This certainly is a great concession, when it is remembered that in many places in India there are tanks set apart for the high-caste people, which the low-caste people are not permitted to approach. The idea of an indulgence being granted for an open violation of a religious ordinance is certainly a clever mode of obtaining a desired though forbidden boon. That there are degrees of strictness amongst Brāhmans, and that some esteem themselves of a very superior stamp, the following story will show. A few months ago, when travelling on the East India Railway, I met with two Brāhmans from Mysore. They were educated men; one of them was expecting to appear in the following B.A. Examination of the Madras University. When we were leaving Benares, it occurred to me to ask if they had any friends in that holy city. They said, "No, but we soon found some Brāhmans from our part of the country." I said, "Oh, then you were well received and hospitably entertained by them, of course?" I shall never forget the look of infinite disdain with which one of them replied: "Do you think we would eat with men who live in such a city as Benares, and associate with the Brāhmans of this district? No, we contented ourselves whilst there with one meal a day, which we cooked for ourselves." My question appeared to them about as reasonable as if I had asked a nobleman in England if he had dined with scavengers.

Even Christianity is not sufficiently strong in every case to obliterate this caste prejudice. In some churches in the South of India at the communion service two cups are used, one for those who have come from the higher castes, and one for those from the outcastes, and it is believed that if this custom were not permitted, many of the caste Christians would absent themselves from the Lord's table rather than drink from a cup that was used by those who were formerly outcastes. In some parts of Bengal a similar spirit was allowed to manifest itself for a time; but a few years of severe discipline was successful in restoring the people to conformity with what seems to be the Spirit of Jesus Christ in this matter. In cases of church discipline the system of caste is occasionally imitated in the Christian Church. When for any misconduct a man is put out of fellowship with his church, the members refuse to visit him, or to give him their hookah (pipe). And it is said that frequently this exclusion from the friendly offices of his brethren leads to penitence, and restoration to the fraternity follows.

The position of the mixed castes is considerably improved. Next to the Brāhmans, in Bengal, at any rate, the most respectable castes are the Vaidyas and Kāyasthas. These classes are regarded as gentlemen, and a Brāhman will associate with them on almost equal terms, though of course he will not eat, nor will his family intermarry with them. He will drink water that they may have brought as water-carriers, &c.

These classes tread hard upon the heels of the Brāhmans in the colleges and schools, and secure some of the highest honours in the universities. It is very difficult to say how this change has been effected. Certainly at one time these were despised classes; *now* their position is almost equal to that of the Brāhmans; whilst the mechanics, who probably were the Sūdras in ancient times, have sunk much below them in modern times. A good story was told me by an eye-witness of the way in which European training acts in destroying these caste prejudices. On one occasion, at the Medical College, Calcutta, a professor, in illustration of his lecture on Hygiene, brought samples of different kinds of cooked food. There was beef roast and boiled, and ham—all, of course, obnoxious to the strict Hindu. No sooner was the lecture concluded, and the lecturer's back turned, than the students rushed from their seats and boldly ate up the various kinds of food in the presence of each other—an act that a generation before would certainly have been followed by the excommunication of every member of the class.

The lines have been far more tightly drawn around the different classes with respect to intermarriage and to the taking of food together. It is evident that in Manu's time it was a most common thing for men of one caste to have a wife belonging to another; and that the punishment for such offences did not fall upon the guilty parties, but on their children. Nowadays, those who commit the fault are made to suffer; hence it very rarely occurs. To an outsider it is difficult to understand the minute distinctions that are made between the classes of the same caste. For example, the Brāhmans of Bengal are divided into several *Srenies*, or classes, as Rauries, Barenders, Vaidiks, and Saptasatis. The Srenies are again subdivided into Kulins, Srotiyas, and Vangsajas. Those belonging to the subdivisions will interchange hospitalities, but will not freely intermarry; the Srenies, however, will neither exchange hospitalities nor intermarry with each other.

Though it is a most common thing in India for a man to

follow the same profession and calling as his father—so common, in fact, that Europeans have come to speak of different trades and callings as *castes;* as, *e.g.*, they speak of a man belonging to the weaver *caste*, the blacksmith *caste*, the carpenter *caste*, &c.; yet this is a mistake; the *caste* of the people is really different from the trado or calling; though it is very common indeed, almost universal, for men of the same trade to be of the same caste. Custom rules with an iron hand throughout India, and generally a father trains his son to work at the same trade as himself. It is not at all common for a boy to be apprenticed to strangers as in England; as soon as he can be of any assistance to his father, he goes with him to his work, and continues in the same walk of life. In our schools are found, side by side with Brāhmans, boys whose fathers are mechanics or small farmers, and though they may not have the same influence to obtain employment as the Brāhmans, it is not their religion that prevents them from engaging in office or scholastic work. In the army are to be found men from all castes, and it has been used as an argument against the men of lower castes obtaining promotion, that though, when on duty, the higher caste man would be under the authority of the lower, when relief from duty came, the low-caste officer would bow before the high-caste private. The spread of education has done much to level up the masses of India, and to lessen the profound veneration for the Brāhman that he has received as his birthright for many generations.

Another interesting fact is the ease with which a man who has been excommunicated can regain admission to his caste. In most cases it is by the mere payment of a sum of money to provide a feast for the members of his dal, after which the offender is as pure in their eyes as he ever was. A man may be brought up before the tribunal, and if the penalty be promptly paid, it fully atones for his misdeeds; *e.g.*, a servant is seen to touch an egg, or food in which there are eggs; on this being reported, he must spend about a month's wages on a feast, and is then absolved! A man openly joins in a dinner with men of other castes, or goes to England to study; he has to pay a fine and go through certain purifying ceremonies more or less difficult, according to the character of his society, and all is well with him. It is certain that the great majority of educated men of the present day do not care for the benefit of being retained in caste, so far as they are concerned; but they do not like to be passed by when birth, marriage, and funeral ceremonies of their friends are held; neither do they like a father to object to allow his son to marry their daughters. Hence multitudes, purely on social grounds, continue under the restraints of caste. In former times it was the greatest disgrace that could happen to a man for a son to embrace Christianity: not only was the son lost to his family, but the whole family was shunned as contaminated. Now some fathers say to their sons, "You can become a Christian if you wish, and, were I alone to be consulted, you should remain at home as before; but for the sake of my caste connections, and the disgrace ostracism would inflict on the family, you must go elsewhere." As most of the large families now have lost at least one member of their family, through the efforts of missionaries, the disgrace that was felt on this score has largely diminished. It is perfectly true that there are many still who regard caste as a divine institution, and dread the divine penalties that follow any infringements of its rules; more especially is this the case with the vast majority of the lower orders. They would prefer death to partaking of forbidden food, or doing anything that they thought was contrary to the teaching of their peculiar sect. And there can be no doubt whatever that it was largely owing to a widespread report that the Government was about to abolish caste that led to the Indian Mutiny of 1867. Lies on this subject were circulated, and men to whom caste purity was dearer than life listened to the advice of the seditious, who cared little for caste themselves, but who hoped out of the general commotion to gain something.

Sometimes in a European household in India these caste distinction present themselves in a ludicrous light. If a Hindu servant is sent for anything, from a child to a letter, that is in the hands of a low-caste servant, the article cannot be taken direct from the hand of the one who has it; it must be laid down on the ground, or whatever is near, and taken up by the other. There must be no personal contact; nor must they touch the same article whilst the hand of the low-caste person is upon it, or they are defiled. Hindu servants will not object to assist in removing a piece of furniture with Christians, but if a sweeper or other low-caste man attempts to touch it, they will at once turn away. Of course it often happens that when a man does not wish to do anything, or is ordered to do what he regards as the work of another servant, he pleads caste difficulties where those rules do not at all apply.

There is one thing more that should be mentioned here, and that is the widespread notion that the prohibition of flesh meat for food is one of the most general restrictions of caste. As a rule it is doubtless true: Hindus are vegetarians and abstainers from intoxicating drink; but there are many who are not so, and yet are good Hindus. What is forbidden as ordinary food becomes lawful when it is eaten as part of the worship that is rendered to a deity. There are some classes who will never partake of fish even, but these are few; as a rule fish is freely eaten by Hindus of all castes, venison is generally allowed, and goat's flesh may be eaten under certain conditions. The goats that are sacrificed to Kāli in some of her many forms are by that act sanctified, and may be freely eaten. Hence, if a man wish to eat meat, he has simply to send his goat to the shrine of Kāli, pay his fee to the priest, bring home the body, and he can then partake of it. Flesh, though distinctly ordered to be eaten at the Shrădhas, or funeral feasts, is not often provided. For men too poor to purchase a whole kid or goat, there are butchers' shops in the cities in which an image of

Kāli stands, before which the goat is slain where he can purchase as much as he may require of this sanctified meat. In like manner, when a man wishes to indulge in bhang, or any other intoxicant, he has simply to engage in the worship of Siva, who, when incarnate, was particularly addicted to the use of intoxicants. In fact, though, looked at in some aspects, Hinduism is a most rigid system of rules for the guidance of men in all the relationships of life, in other aspects it is a most accommodating system, as it provides a way by which men may indulge in pleasures which by some of their Scriptures are forbidden.

It would necessitate far more space than I can spare, and be most tedious to the reader, were I to enumerate, with the briefest notice of their peculiarities, all, or nearly all, of the many castes that now exist. Dr. Wilson describes no less than twenty-five *classes* of Brāhmans alone, and these again are subdivided into numerous subdivisions. These divisions are largely geographical; but yet each class has marked peculiarities, and in many cases there is no real intercourse permitted between them. The following is a brief account of the Brahmans in Bengal. "Formerly only one order, called the Satsati Brāhmans, were found there, all of whom were equal in honour. Matters stood thus till the time of Adishura, a Bengal Rāja, who, offended with their ignorance when wishing to offer a sacrifice to obtain rain, solicited from Vira Singha, the king of Kanyakuvja, five Brāhmans to officiate at this sacrifice. The first Brāhmans sent were rejected because they wore stockings, and rode on horses; those afterwards sent were approved; they performed the sacrifice to the great satisfaction of the monarch, who gave them grants of land in what the Hindus call the province of Rārha; and from these five Brāhmans are descended almost all the Brāhmans now in the province. They still retain the family names of their original ancestors—Kasyapas from Kasyapa the sage, Bharadwajas from the sage Bharadwaja, Sandilyas from Sandilya, Savarnas from Savarna,

Bātsyas from the sage Bātsya. Some of the descendants of these Brāhmans, in consequence of removing into the province of Vārendra, are called Vārendra Brāhmans, and those who remained at Rārha are known as Rārhis. These comprise all the Brāhmans in Bengal, except the Vaidikas, and about 1,500 or 2,000 families of the Satsati, or original Bengal Brāhmans, of whom there were about 700 families in the time of Adhisura. The Vaidikas are said to have fled from Orissa from the fear of being made Vāmācharis; and because they were better students of the Vedas than the other Brāhmans they were called Vaidikas.

"From these ancestors have branched no fewer than 156 families, of which the precedence was fixed by Ballāla Sen, who reigned in the twelfth century of the Christian era. One hundred of these families settled in Vārendra, and fifty-six in Rārha, or Northern Bengal. These, though now dispersed through the province, retain the family distinctions fixed by Ballāla Sen. They are denominated from the families to which their five progenitors belonged, and are still considered Kānyakuvja Brāhmans." *

The principal classes amongst them are the following :—

1. *Rārha Kulina Brāhmans.* These form the highest class as fixed by Ballāla Sen, because of their possessing the following nine good qualities: Observance of Brāhmanical customs, meekness, learning, good report, a disposition to visit holy places, devoutness, observance of marriage amongst equals only, asceticism, and liberality. And, because possessed of these high qualities, special privileges were given to them, particulars of which will be given in another chapter.

2. *Bhanga Kulinas; i.e.*, those whose *kul*, or honour, is broken: this has resulted from their marrying beneath them. Of these there are no less than thirty-six classes.

3. The *Vanshaja* class is formed of those who are born in the fifth generation after the first act by which a Kulina of the first class fell into the second, or became a Bhanga

* Wilson, p. 205.

Kulina. The *Ghattaka*, or marriage-brokers for the Brāhmans, generally belong to this class.

4–8. The Rādiya Shrotiya Brāhmans, or *Vaidikas*. These are said to possess only eight of the nine excellent Brāhmanical qualities. These are generally the most learned in the Sāstras of the Brāhmans of Bengal; the *Vārendras* are similar to the Rādiya Srotiyas; the *Saptashatis* are the descendants of the original Brāhmans who were passed over by king Adhishāva because of their ignorance. They earn their living by attending at Shrādhas, &c. The Vaidikas were originally the priests of the five tribes of Brāhmans who came to Bengal. These are said to have been excluded by Ballāla Sen from the higher classes because of their want of learning; *they* said it was because they questioned the right of the king to make arbitrary divisions of their order.

9. The *Agradānis*. These have sunk in caste, and can only intermarry amongst their own class, because they do not scruple to take presents of gold, &c., at the Preta Shrādha; *i.e.*, the first ceremonies for the dead. 10. The *Maraiporas* are those who repeat the mantras over the dead, by which act their honour is lost, a fee of ten rupees being taken by them as compensation. 11. The *Rapalī* Brāhmans are those who perform religious ceremonies for the Rapalis who work in jute: in like manner, those who do similar acts for goldsmiths, fishermen, &c., bear the name of the class for whom their services are available. Generally the doing of duty in this manner for low-caste Hindus greatly lowers them in the esteem of their caste fellows, who will not eat with them on this account. After doing this work they have to find their associates in those who are ready to sell their services in a similar manner. 12. The *Pir Ali Brāhmans*. To this class some of the most respectable families of Calcutta belong. Years ago one of their ancestors went to the house of a Mussulmān law officer, where a trick was played upon him. The Mussulmān had heard it said to "smell food was half eating it;" and in the wish to convert some of the Brāhmans

in his neighbourhood he invited them to his house, and whilst they were seated there he ordered his dinner to be served. They smelt the food, and their caste was gone—so it was decided. Some of them became Mussulmāns; but one who preferred to remain a Hindu, though his caste was injured, became the founder of another class, called the Pir Āli, after the man who had played the trick upon him.

Though many of the Brāhmans have taken to other employment, a large number are supported by lands that were given for this purpose by kings and rich men. At the religious festivals they are well paid for their presence and work, though they complain bitterly of the evil times in which their lot is cast. Ward says, "I have been informed that in the district of Burdwan, the property applied to the support of idolatry amounts to the annual rent of fifteen to twenty lacs of rupees. It has been lately ascertained that in the Zillah of Nadiya the lands amount to above 600,000 acres. When all these things are considered it will appear that the clergy in Catholic countries devour little of national wealth compared with the Brāhmans."

CHAPTER VI.

PROPORTION OF PEOPLE IN THE CHIEF CASTES.

From the last census (1881) a few interesting facts can be gathered respecting the numbers included in several of the most important castes. The divisions adopted by the Government were as follows :—1. Brāhmans ; 2. Kshetriyas ; 3. Other Hindu castes ; 4. Aboriginal classes ; 5. Hindus not recognizing caste distinctions ; 6. Castes not stated. I shall give a general idea of the distribution of the Hindus in Bengal, which may be taken as a fair example of the condition of the people in India generally. The Hindu population of this province being reckoned at about 45½ millions, we find them classified as follows :—

I. Asiatics other than natives of the Indian Empire	7,026
II. Natives of the Indian Empire :—	
a. Aboriginal tribes	1,365,215
b. Semi-Hinduized aborigines	10,618,415
c. Hindus proper :—	
1. Superior castes (Brāhmans, Kshetriyas, &c.)	4,897,426
2. Intermediate (Vaidyas, 84,990 ; Kayasthas, 1,450,848, &c.)	2,777,124
3. Trading classes (Vaisyas, 9,320)..........	963,159
4. Pastoral classes, chiefly Gwallas	4,115,377
5. Classes engaged in preparing (cooked) food	924,984
6. Agricultural classes	6,875,197
7. Classes engaged in personal service (*i.e.*, barbers, washermen, palanquin-bearers, &c.)	2,804,003
8. Artizans	4,482,471
9. Weavers	1,619,344

10. Labourers	546,839
11. Fish and vegetable salesmen	142,417
12. Fishermen and boatmen	2,131,433
13. Dancers, musicians, beggars, and vagabond classes	43,255
d. Persons enumerated by nationality only	48,114
e. Persons of Hindu origin not recognizing caste, such as Vaishnavas, Gosains, &c.	683,227
f. Hindus, castes not stated	376,451

In this enumeration about 100 different castes are mentioned; of these the Gwalla, or cow-herds, are the most numerous, numbering nearly 4,000,000; the Brāhmans number about 2¾ millions. The proportion of the classes mentioned above are as follows:—

1. Superior castes	10.77
2. Intermediate	6.10
3. Traders	2.11
4. Pastoral classes	9.05
5. Food sellers	2.03
6. Agriculturalists	15.12
7. Servants	6.16
8. Artizans	9.86
9. Weavers	3.56
10. Labourers	1.20
11. Greengrocers	0.31
12. Boatmen and fishermen	4.68
13. Musicians, &c.	.09
14. Uncertain, and those not recognizing caste	1.50

"Thirty castes have representatives in every division of the province, and a reference to their names in the margin will show that they are all castes of general utility, whose services are indispensable to that microcosm, the Bengal village.

Brāhman,	Kandu,
Rājput,	Kayastha,
Baniya,	Kumhar,
Barhi,	Kurmi,
Barni,	Madak,

"The Brāhman has a home in every hamlet as family or temple priest, or in secular employ as teacher, orderly, or other superior service. The Rājput plays a simi-

Chamār, Māli,
Dhobi, Mallah,
Dom, Nāpit,
Gwalla, Sunri,
Hāri, Tamoli,
Jaliya, Tanti,
Jugi, Teli,
Kahar, Tevi,
Kaibartha, Bhuinya,
Karmakar, Khawar.

lar secular part. Where half a dozen huts cluster together, there the Baniya sets up his petty shop and opens his loan business. No village is complete without its oil-man (Teli), or its carpenter (Barhi), who mends its ploughs, builds its houses, and supplies the wood for the cremation of its dead. Not less necessary is the cobbler (Chamār), who skins the carcases of the village cattle, makes the cart-man's whips, and keeps in repair the shoes of the community; while his wife has the monopoly of obstretric practice. The washerman (Dhobi) and the barber (Nāpit) are as indispensable to a people hedged around by ceremonial observances as the scavengers (Dom, Hāri) are to remove unclean substances and to maintain an affectation of sanitation. The services of the blacksmith (Karmakar, or Lohar) are in daily requisition, and the potter (Kumhar) makes the earthern plates and bowls which nine-tenths of the people use for cooking and eating from. The confectioner (Madak and Kandu) is a necessity among a people whose food is almost wholly farinaceous, and who are often obliged to have it in a portable form, and to eat it under the shadow of a tree, or by the roadside, whenever they find leisure to do so. The petty luxuries of village life are provided by the Sunri, who sells wine, and the Barni and Tamoli, who grow and vend the aromatic pān-leaf and the astringent betel-nut so dear to native palates. The Tanti and the Jugi weave the coarse clothes which the village folk wear, and the Māli grows the flowers for the local shrine, or the frequent domestic festival, as well as the better kind of vegetables with which the villager mends his coarse fare. All these artizans work for a community whose main ingredients are cultivators and herdsmen. The agricultural element, from which few castes are altogether dissociated, is mainly supplied by the Kaibarthas in Bengal,

Kurmis in Behar, and Chassas in Orissa. The Gwalla (cow-keeper) is a familiar and frequent figure in every corner of the land. The cow is to the Hindu much more than the camel to the Arab, and it fills a large place in every phase of his daily life. . . . The great rivers of Bengal support a numerous race of boatmen (Mallah), and the craving for fish among a people to most of whom other animal food is interdicted, either by necessity or prejudice, employs as large a number of fishermen (Tevi). The Kahar is ubiquitous, sometimes as a carrier of palkies, and therefore indispensable at all weddings, or as a domestic servant. The Kayastha, who once shared with the Brāhman the monopoly of learning, still thrives in every hamlet, from Patna to Cuttack, as the schoolmaster, the village accountant, or the landlord's confidential secretary. Lastly, the shifting population of the community, the daily labourers and field hands, are supplied by two castes, the Bhuinyas and the Khawars; the former of whom Mr. Magrath thought were once the autochthones of Behar; while the latter name, being that of a large separate tribe, is an alternative epithet for one subdivision of the Santhals." *

There is one very important and interesting fact brought out by these returns as compared with those of the census of 1872, respecting the semi-Hinduized aboriginal tribes, as they are called, showing how very rapidly those who only nine years ago were regarded as aboriginals are now reckoned as Hindus.

	Census of 1872.	1881.
Aboriginal tribes	2,738,813	1,365,215
Semi-Hinduized tribes	9,474,243	10,618,451

The Census report says: "Looking first at the figures for 1881, the most obvious point to the observer is the large proportion of the class of semi-Hinduized aborigines. Accepting the distribution of 1872, they now appear to number nearly one-fourth of the Hindu population. They are for the most

* Bengal Census Report, vol. i. p. 138.

part hewers of wood and drawers of water, and are beyond cavil the remnants of the nations whom successive invaders, culminating with the Āryans, found in possession of the country, and absorbed more or less into their system of polity. Those of the aboriginal tribes which were most remote from the scene of the invasion, or were so situated as to be able to withstand it, have retained to this day their primeval language and customs, and their tribal faiths. Those, on the other hand, who were most exposed to the wave of conquest, who were least able to resist, or who were most ready to amalgamate with the new-comers, were absorbed into their community, but relegated to its lowest grades, and employed in its most menial offices. Such was the treatment which the inhabitants of the country received at the hands of the Hindu invaders. The question of absorption is only one of time and opportunity. Many of the castes shown as low-caste Hindus, and now universally accepted as such, have peculiarities which give rise to the suspicion that they are not pure Hindus of the Āryan type; but they are to all intents and purposes low-caste Hindus, and are treated as such without question. The class of semi-Hinduized aborigines are only a stage behind them in their progress towards Hinduism. What many of the low-caste Hindus once were, the semi-Hinduized aboriginals are now; and in the lapse of time they, too, will recruit the ranks of the Hindus, as intermarriage and social intercourse gradually obliterate more and more their distinctive characteristics."

It is interesting to see how the embracing of Hinduism in past ages has dignified their descendants in the present day. It is probable that Brāhmanism did not spread through Nepāl until the fifteenth century. Driven there by the Mussulmān invasion, the Hindu exiles readily received converts, making them, and also their own descendants by the hill women, Kshatriyas. From these two sources spring the *Khas*, originally the name of a small clan of creedless barbarians, now the proud title of the Kshatriya order of the kingdom of

Nepāl, who also bear the family names of the Brāhmanical orders. And, strange to say, the Brāhmans there who officiate in temples and at festivals not only eat goats and sheep, but also fowls, and rear pigs for their own tables. Both the strict Brāhmans and the so-called Kshatriyas may also drink water that is brought by the Kachar Bhutiyas, men who kill cows and eat beef without scruple; yet in some other respects caste is most rigorously observed. In the matter of marriage and adultery the strictest rules prevail. A Brāhman, if a soldier, and the Kshatriyas are bound in honour, if their wife prove unfaithful, themselves to slay the offender and cut off the wife's nose and drive her from their home.

The history of the conversion of the Manipuris to Hinduism is most interesting, and shows clearly how the propagation of the faith is carried on. About a hundred years ago Ghorit Nawaj, the founder of the family of the present Rāja, was converted to Hinduism by a wandering Sanyasi, who then declared that the Manipuris were all Hindus, but had forgotten their privileges and duties. He ordered the people to bathe and make expiation for their long neglect, and then declared them to be good Hindus of the Kshatriya caste. A similar story is told of the Hindus of Cachar.

CHAPTER VII.

*KULINISM AND POLYGAMY.**

I HAVE reserved all notice of Kulinism for a separate chapter, as it is one of the worst excrescences of Hinduism, and affords a notable instance of the way in which the bestowal of honour upon those originally regarded as worthy has come to carry with it a license to indulge to an almost unlimited extent the worst passions of human nature.

As a rule the Hindus are not polygamists. It is true that under special circumstances it is permitted to them to take a second wife whilst the first is still living. In cases where seven years after marriage no son is born, the Law Books authorize a man to take a second wife, because a son is regarded as necessary to perform the funeral rites of his father, and not for his father only—for three previous generations the happiness of his ancestors is imperilled by the neglect of these ceremonies. In these cases the new bride comes to her husband's home, and though the superseded wife remains the nominal head of the household, it follows that the presence of the new and favoured wife, especially when she has a son in her arms, renders the position of the older woman most painful. One has only to read the domestic life of Jacob to see what must inevitably follow where the younger and more fortunate wife resides in the same house with the older and despised one. Sometimes, it is true, the older wife receives the younger with kindness,

* See *Calcutta Review*, vol. ii., Article "Kulinism."

but if the home life as depicted in tales by native writers be correct, generally there is jealousy and misery. Many of the well-to-do men do not scruple to keep concubines, but these have a separate establishment; it is, however, not uncommon for the children of these separate homes to meet together, fully aware of their common fatherhood. But though concubinage is by no means peculiar to India, in the privileges of the Kulin Brāhman, however, who may marry as many wives as they wish, there is something peculiar to Hinduism. In order to make the origin of this system clear it will be necessary to repeat a little of the history of the Brāhmans in Bengal.

In the reign of King Adisur, himself a member of the Sen, or medical caste, the number of Brāhmans in his kingdom of Gour was considerably reduced, and those who remained were for the most part ignorant men who were unable to read the Vedas in the original Sanskrit; whilst of the Sagnic Brāhmans, *i.e.*, those versed in the ritual of certain sacrifices, not one was to be found. A drought of unusual duration threatening his country, the king, wishing to make a sacrifice at which only Sagnic priests could officiate, sent to the king of Kanouj, the capital of Hindustan proper, for a number of these learned men. When this request was read five priests who happened to be present, tempted by the liberal offers made by the king of Gour, consented to migrate to his kingdom to perform his sacrifice.

These five men were Brāhmans of the highest order, who could trace their origin to the divine sages, the sons of Brahmā himself. They belonged to the Sāndilya, Kasyapa, Bharadwāj, Sāvarna, and Batsya gotras, or tribes. Immediately on their arrival at Gour they commenced their sacrificial work, and the names of the officiants are still remembered—"Vedagarva, Sriharsa, and Chandra chanted the Rich, Yajus, and Saman Vedas, while Daksha and Nārāyan officiated at the sacrifice." Neighbouring princes who were present at this important celebration returned to their homes delighted and amazed at the superior piety and knowledge of these newly-arrived priests who had come from what they regarded as their ancestral home.

When the work for which these men had been brought was completed they settled down in their new home to enjoy the honours and emoluments the king showered upon them. But despising the native Brāhmans on account of their ignorance and mode of life, they would not associate with them in their feasts, nor would they intermarry into their families, but continued to form an entirely separate sect. After a time, however, their descendants becoming numerous, were not so scrupulous; many of them fraternized to a greater or less extent with the Brāhmans of the country. At length a king named Ballāla Sen coming to the throne, a king who in the stories of the country is said to have been a son of the river Brahmaputra, and whose doings the poets have never ceased to praise, dissatisfied with the ecclesiastical condition of his kingdom, determined to arrange the priests into classes. He saw that many of the Kanouj families were not as pure, nor were their priests as learned, as they ought to be. He selected some from their number whom he believed to be possessed of certain excellences* to whom he gave the title of *Kul*, or Honourable; whilst to others, as he conceived them proportionately less worthy, he gave less honourable titles. These men, styled *Kulins*, were intended to be the founders of a spiritual aristocracy; their children, if born as the result of marriages into families equally honourable, were to inherit all the honours and privileges granted to their fathers. In fact, the privilege of a Kulin cannot be taken away from him for any personal transgression, even though he marry a woman other than of a Kulin family; it is his children, not himself, who is called upon to suffer.

At the present time, however, we find that this Kulinism is the cause of unnumbered ills, many of those regarded as Kulins esteeming it quite beneath their dignity to work,

* These qualities are mentioned in the previous chapter.

though they do not object to be supported by the parents of those whom they have condescended to ennoble by marriage; in most of them the virtues for which the title of "honourable" was given being conspicuously absent.

"The Kulins, who were ennobled by Ballāla Sen, and afterwards enlarged by Lakshman Sen, were of divers *mels*, or orders, of which four were, and are still, considered primary. They take their designation from the places where, at their own request, they were allowed to settle, and they are to this day distinguished by the names of Fule, Khardah, Sarvānandi, and Ballāvi. In these orders were comprehended the most meritorious of the descendants of the five colonists from Kanouj; that is, the most virtuous of the Banerjeas, Mookerjeas, Chatterjeas, Ghosāls, and Ganjulies." It will of course be understood that not *all* bearing these very common names are Kulins, nor are all the immediate descendants of these regarded as honourable at the present time. Some of the Banerjeas, for instance, were never admitted into the honourable brotherhood, and some once honoured have, through intermarriage with other than Kulins, caused their descendants to pass into lower grades. It is a noticeable fact that the honours of Kulinism continue to a man through life; born a Kulin always a Kulin was the rule; and further, that a *mésalliance* is the only means of depriving their offspring of the same honour. "Of the Banerjea family two persons were raised, Maheshwar and Makarand; of the sons of Daksha, *i.e.*, the Chatterjeas, Bahurup and Arabind were honoured; Utsava was the only member of the Mookerjea family descended from Sriharsa that was distinguished; three of the Ghosāls, or sons of Chandra, viz., Jagat, Govardhan, and Kami; and two of the Ganjulies, or descendants of Vedagarva, viz., Sisho and Rodhaker, were likewise exalted. These were all the principal Kulins raised to dignity by King Ballāla, and they were designated either after one or other of the four *mels* already named, or from the family to which they were respectively attached.

"Lakshman Sen, the son and successor of Ballāla Sen, followed up and improved the heraldry instituted by his father, and enlarged the names and orders of the Kūls to an enormous length. The primary orders were left untouched; the inferior or secondary orders were spun out into nearly thirty subdivisions.

"Besides these Kulins another order of Brāhmans was honoured in Ballāla's time who were called the Srotriyas. The descendants of the five Kanouj Brāhmans, though at first they avoided all intercourse with the Saptasati or aboriginal Brāhmans of Bengal, were subsequently induced to accept their daughters as wives. The offspring of these marriages were considered inferior to their fathers, but superior to their mothers and maternal grandfathers. They had half the blood of Kanouj, and were therefore esteemed superior to the aboriginal priests, and they had half the blood of the Saptasatis, and so were held inferior to their fathers. The most meritorious of these persons the king honoured with the title of Srotriyas. They had this privilege amongst others, that the Kulins might marry their daughters without prejudice to their ranks. They have accordingly proved a connecting link between the Kulins and the Saptasatis. Their houses are the authorized nurseries for breeding wives for the exalted Brāhmans, and they take no small pride in reflecting on the importance which this honour imparts to the class. What enhances their privilege is the fact that the Kulins cannot marry women from any other families, not even from the subordinate Kulins themselves, without degrading their offspring.

"The Kulins are strictly forbidden, on pain of forfeiting their title, to receive wives from families which are inferior to themselves, with the exception of the Srotriyas just mentioned. When this rule is transgressed, although the delinquent himself does not suffer personally, his *kūl* is said to be broken. He himself dies, as he was born, in the enjoyment of his honour; but his offspring forfeit the title, and the glory of the family becomes tarnished." "Although an unequal marriage breaks a person's *kūl*, his immediate descendants are not classed with the common (Vansaj) Brāhmans; for four or five generations the recollections of their ancestral dignity secures for the sons of a broken Kulin great honour and distinction. The descendants of a Kulin, even after the disruption of his kūl, are for several generations considered superior in rank and dignity. The brightness and lustre of a noble family are supposed to be incapable of being tarnished at once and by a single act, though the days of its glory are numbered, and nothing will restore it to its primitive greatness. The immediate offspring of such a family are designated the sons of a Swakritā bhanga, or self-broken Kulin, and esteemed as a second grade, or inferior by one step only to the untainted orders. The next generation is esteemed the third in rank. This gradual deterioration continues to the fourth and fifth generations, after which the glory of the family is obscured, and it sinks to the level of the commonalty." It is said that it is now difficult to find Brāhmans of unbroken kūl. Many of the highest rank are once or twice removed from those who had this honour.

The law prohibiting under these severe penalties the marriage of Kulins with those of less honourable rank was made to secure the family purity of this high class, and in order to become united to this aristocracy it is considered desirable for a Brāhman to marry his daughter to a Kulin husband. Not the Srotriyas only, but the Brāhmans of the inferior orders, are most anxious to obtain a Kulin son-in-law. Hence these men are eagerly sought after, and immense sums of money paid to purchase their consent to wed their daughters; and hence has arisen the great evil of the system—viz., polygamy to an almost unlimited extent.

"The laws which regulate the marriage of Kulin females are cruelly stringent; these must not on any account be given to any unless they are of an equal or superior grade. Neither the Srotriyas nor any inferior order can aspire to the hand of a Kulin's daughter. An indelible disgrace would be affixed upon such a prostitution of a girl of birth and family. Thus her hereditary honour becomes her heaviest misfortune. The greatest difficulty is experienced in settling her in life. The only circles from which a husband can be selected are in request everywhere and by everybody. To outbid the Srotriyas and others in the purchase of a noble bridegroom requires larger funds than many a Kulin can command. The greatest misery and distress are accordingly occasioned. . . . No parent dares to risk his daughter's virtue by allowing her to live a single life. The institutions of Hinduism, too, denounce the fiercest anathemas against such conduct. The severest condemnation is passed on a Brāhman who neglects to get his daughter married before her tenth year. The most meritorious way of disposing of her is to present her at the hymeneal altar when she is eight years old, the next before her ninth year is terminated. At all events her wedding must not be delayed beyond her tenth year. Longer delay entails upon the delinquent the guilt and infamy of infanticide." Under these circumstances the poor Kulin father is in the greatest difficulty. He cannot allow her to marry any one belonging to a lower caste; he cannot afford to purchase a husband in his own. His only resource is to appeal to some decrepit old Kulin Brāhman, who already has a multitude of wives, to save the honour of his family by adding one more to his list. Parents have been known, when a man has evidently been at the point of death, to go through the marriage ceremony of their daughter with him rather than incur the disgrace of having her remain unmarried.

Kulinism, then, is the root cause of polygamy. Sometimes from cupidity, sometimes from pity, sometimes from mere animalism, a man is led to marry a multitude of wives. Of course he cannot live with them all, nor does he attempt to take them to his father's house as the ordinary Hindu bridegroom would do. He chooses the house of one of his fathers-in-law as his home, and pays an occasional visit to his other wives when their fathers offer inducement sufficient to lead him to honour them with his presence. It is true some Kulins are content with one wife, and work hard to maintain a comfortable home; but many are simply the husbands of their many wives, and expect to be supported by the men whom they have honoured by becoming their sons-in-law. Some well-to-do Srotriyas and other Brāhmans make the home so comfortable for their sons-in-law that they are content to be the husband of one wife only. A system more calculated to lead to immorality and misery it would hardly be possible to imagine. And this is the outcome of an arrangement that was ordained for the special purpose of doing honour to some who were considered by the king more worthy than the rest of their caste-fellows.

The kūls hitherto spoken of are those of the Rāreya Brāhmans, so called from the neighbourhood in which they settled. But the neighbouring princes, seeing the glory of the five Brāhmans who came at Adisur's invitation, wished to have their country also illumined by the presence of these wise and holy men. Birmallah, king of Barender, father-in-law to Adisur, preferred a similar request to the king of Kanouj, in answer to which five Brāhmans were sent to him also. These two classes, although they came from the same place, and might have been considered equal in their own country, now form two great classes—the Barenders and the Rāreyas—between whom intermarriage is prohibited, as are also the rites of hospitality. The patron of the Barender Brāhmans arranged their descendants into classes, as Ballāla Sen arranged those in his dominions. Of the Barenders, eight families are reckoned as Kulins: viz., the Maitras, Bhims, Rudras, Sandels, Lahurys, Sadhobs, Bhaders, and the Bhaduris; whilst the Karanjans, Nandabasis, Nauris, Atars, Bhandashalis, Kāmdebs, Champatis, and the Jhampatis, were reckoned as Srotriyas.

Ballāla Sen did not only establish kūls amongst the Brāhmans, but gave titles of honour also to the Kayasthas who came as their attendants, although, according to the strict teaching of Hinduism, they were sankers, or half-castes; viz., descendants of the Vaisya fathers and Sudra mothers. Sriharsa was attended by Makaranda Ghose, Chandra by Dasaratha Bose, Daksha by Kāli Dass Mitter, Nārāyan by Purushottama Datta, and Vedagarva by Dasaratha Guha. These five men were the progenitors of the most respectable Kayasthas in Bengal. Of these five, three only, viz., Ghose, Bose, and Mitter, acknowledged themselves to be the slaves of the Brāhmans, and were rewarded for their servility by being made Kulin Kayasthas. Datta made the same admission, though with some reserve, and was not thus honoured, though intermarriage between his family and that of the Kulins was permitted; but Guha, refusing to give up his freedom, was regarded as a Kulin only as compared with the Kayasthas he found already settled in Bengal.

Such, then, is the origin of Kulinism, a source of unmitigated evil to many families at the present time. It is, however, only fair to say that some of the more respectable Hindus, and amongst them some of the Kulins themselves, have endeavoured again and again to have an end put to this most iniquitous system: and when it is known that the authority for the institution is not to be found in the Hindu Scriptures, but was an arbitrary arrangement made by a man who was a great admirer of the Brāhmanical order, and one who wished to increase their honour and add to their wealth, it certainly seems to be one of those cases in which humanity cries aloud to the Government to step in to put an end to most cruel practices for which there is no authority in the writings regarded by the people as sacred. There would be an outcry, doubtless, from those who now benefit by the system; but the immense relief that the stoppage of the practice would give would be far greater than any such discontent.

Ward gives the following description of the evils of the system:—

"Each Kulin Brāhman marries at least two wives—one

the daughter of a Brāhman of his own order, the other of a Srotriya; the former he generally leaves at her father's, the other he takes to his own house. It is essential to the honour of a Kulin to have one daughter, but by the birth of many daughters he sinks in respect. . . . Some inferior Kulins marry many daughters. . . . Numbers procure a subsistence by excessive polygamy: at their marriages they obtain large presents, and as often as they visit their wives they receive presents from the father; and then, having married into forty or fifty families, a Kulin goes from house to house and is fed, clothed, &c. Some old men after the wedding never see the females; others visit them once in three or four years. A respectable Kulin never lives with the wife who remains in the house of her parents; he sees her occasionally as a friend rather than a husband, and dreads to have offspring by her, as he thereby sinks in honour. Children born in the houses of their fathers-in-law are never owned by the father. In consequence of this state of things both the married and unmarried daughters of the Kulins are plunged in an abyss of misery." He then goes on to speak of the natural results of this iniquitous system: immorality, public prostitution, and abortion.

The following official notice of their doings may be taken as a sober, carefully weighed statement. It appeared in the Gazette of India, Feb. 7, 1867, and is signed by C. P. Hobhouse, H. T. Prinsep, Suttshara Ghosal, Ishwar Chandra Surma, Ramanath Tagore, Joy Kissen Mookerjea, Degumber Mitter; the last three gentlemen, while subscribing to the report generally, state that the practice of polygamy among those who observe it obtains in a much more mitigated form than a few years before.

"We will now describe some of the main customs in the matter of marriage, which, on the authority of the statements made in petitions to the Legislative Council, and in some instances within the knowledge of more than one of the native gentlemen on our committee, obtain amongst the

Bhanga Kulinas; and we will state what are declared in the papers before us to be the evil results of some of those customs:—

1. In addition to the presents usually given amongst all classes of the Hindus on the occasion of marriage, a Bhanga Kulina always, except when he gives his daughter to a brother Bhanga, and takes in exchange that brother Bhanga's daughter, exacts a consideration for marriage from the family of the bride.

2. A present is often given in addition on the occasion of any visit made to the house of the father-in-law.

3. If the daughters of the first and second subdivisional classes of Bhanga Kulinas cannot be given in marriage to husbands of their own classes, they must remain unmarried.

4. The number of wives, including those of the same class, is said to be often as many as 15, 20, 40, 50, 80.*

5. Polygamy is said to be resorted to as a sole means of livelihood by many Bhanga Kulinas.

6. Marriage, it is said, is contracted quite in old age, and the husband often never sees his wife, or only, at the best, visits her once in every three or four years or so.

7. As many as three and four, even twenty-three marriages, have been known to have been contracted in one day.

8. Sometimes all a man's daughters and his unmarried sisters are given in marriage to one and the same individual.

9. It is so difficult to find husbands in the proper class for Kulina women that numbers, it is said, remain unmarried.

10. The married and unmarried daughters and wives of Kulinas are said to live in the utmost misery: and it is alleged that crimes of the most heinous nature, such as adultery, abortion, infanticide, and prostitution are the common results of Bhanga Kulina marriages generally.

11. Cases are cited of men who have married 82, 72, 65, 60, and 42 wives, and have had 18, 32, 41, 25, and 32 sons; and 26, 27, 25, 15, 16 daughters.

* Wilson mentions some cases known to pundits, with whom he had conversed on this subject, where the number was 100 and 150.

12. Lists have been adduced of families in the Burdwan and Hugli districts alone showing the existence of a plurality of wives on the above scale, and of numerous cases.

13. The principle on which Kulinism was perpetuated, viz., that of preventing intermarriages between certain classes, is violated.

14. Families, it is said, are ruined in order to provide the large sums requisite to give a consideration on the occasion of their daughters' marriages, or are unable to marry their daughters at all for want of means to procure such consideration.

15. Marriages, it is said, are contracted simply in order to [obtain] this consideration, and the husbands do not even care to inquire what becomes of their wives, and have never even had any intention of fulfilling any one of the marriage duties.

16. The crimes that are said to result from the Kulina system of marriage are said to be habitually concealed by the actors in them and by their neighbours, and this so as to baffle the efforts of the police at discovery.

17. No provision is made for the maintenance of one wife before marriage with an unlimited number of others."

Surely if these statements can be relied on, and they form the body of a report on the subject to the Legislative Council of India, and if it were possible would certainly have been controverted, no words of comment can add to their weight. These Kulinas are strict Hindus, and are accounted worthy of the respect of the community. They are the "honourable class," the aristocracy of India.

WORSHIP.

CHAPTER I.

*HINDU WORSHIP.**

In this and the following chapters, the worship, the strictly religious life of the Hindus, will be described, as distinguished from their ordinary social, or, as we might say, secular life. It is true that the whole life of the Hindu is religious. His Scriptures teach him how he must dress, eat, work, and conduct himself in all his various relationships. According to the belief of a Hindu, he is as guilty, in many respects more guilty, in the sight of God, when he violates some apparently trivial caste regulation, as when he is guilty of falsehood, dishonesty, or immorality. Still, as we make a distinction between religious acts and ordinary life, I wish to treat in this chapter of that which is known amongst us as religion proper; *i.e.*, the worship that the Hindus pay to their deities, and the time and manner of doing it.

As the Christian's aim in worship differs diametrically from that of the Hindu, it naturally follows that their methods will

* The books that are regarded as authorities for teaching the worship proper of the Hindus, and also for regulating their daily life, are the Vedas, the Epics (*i.e.*, the Mahābhārata and the Rāmāyana), the Purānas, and the Tantras. Some of the Tantras are older than some of the Purānas, though generally it may be said that they are the most modern of all the Hindu Scripturse. The Tantriks, indeed, claim respect for their books, as a fifth Veda, and regard them with reverence equal to that given to the Vedas. Thus in the Siva Tantras that deity is represented as saying, "The five seas isaued from my five mouths. These five are known as the paths to final liberation. There are many seas, but none equal to the upper one" (*i.e.*, the Tantra, which came from the uppermost head). It is said that it was owing to a curse of Gāyatri that in the Kali Yuga the Brāhmans have become Tantriks.

widely differ. In a word, the Christian's aim is to know and love God; that knowing Him he may know the character it is his duty to strive after, and loving Him, he may have an all-constraining motive impelling him to attain it. To this end he reads the Word of God, has spiritual fellowship with Him, and strives, by uniting with others like-minded, to deepen that love, until his whole nature shall become like to that of God's. With the Hindu the aim is altogether different from this. His belief is that he is part of God, but through ignorance is unable to realize this identity. He fears the objects of his worship, and tries by presents to purchase their favour, and by knowledge of his identity with the Supreme, as a drop of water falling into the sea loses its identity, to obtain re-union with Him. His books teach him that there are two ways of gaining that desired end. The one is meditation, by which a man at length ceases to think of anything, becomes idiotic, as it seems to an onlooker, so far as the appearance of those who have nearly gained this end can be relied on. The other is by the performance of works of merit; religious acts, which, though not absolutely necessary, will in the end ensure the doer of them great reward in the future life. In describing the duties of the Brāhman, I have already spoken of the holiest life man can live according to Hinduism, viz., the mendicant or ascetic life, which is regarded as the best preparation for meeting God. All Hindus hope eventually to attain, after numerous successive births, to that high position. But for those who are not Brāhmans, and who, therefore, cannot in their present birth by any possibility attain to that holy character, a system of religious works is prescribed by which they may raise themselves in the estimation of the gods, and in another birth, after enjoying years of happiness in heaven, appear on earth as Brāhmans, and then have the opportunity of living the holy and devout life which will enable them to obtain final absorption into deity. The "good works," then, the religion proper of the Hindus, such as bathing, visiting temples, shrines, worshipping the gods, are not the means by which the "highest good" is to be directly attained; by their aid a step in advance may be made; the possibility of obtaining absorption coming to them when in another life they are born as Brāhmans, which they consider the highest type of manhood. By this means, too, Brāhmans rise from the lower to the higher grades, and by a gradual process attain to the most perfect stage. I shall now describe the religious acts, *i.e.*, worship proper taught by Hinduism.

Brāhmans have assured me, and I have no reason for doubting their truthfulness in this matter, that if they perform their daily religious rites properly, at least two hours in the morning and the same time in the evening would be fully occupied with them; and an hour or so in the middle of the day should also be devoted to similar work. Many of the orthodox Hindus, there is no doubt, do spend a long time before and after business hours in this manner. Men living the ascetic life, whose whole time is at their own disposal, may not find this very trying; but for those engaged in school or office for a good many hours of the day it certainly must prove irksome. Some of the more wealthy engage a family priest to perform many of these ceremonies for them, and by occasionally looking on, hope to obtain the benefit that would come to them had they personally performed them. Men often come to their daily work weary with the efforts they have made before leaving their homes to comply with the demands of their religion. As the daily religious duties of a Brāhman are very numerous, and the instructions most minute, it will be possible to mention only the more important. The ordinary religious duties of the lower castes will be described afterwards.

There are four chief duties or sacraments to be performed daily by all good Brāhmans :—The study of the Vedas, offering of gifts to the departed, and to the gods, and the reception of guests. But first, and as a preparation for the due performance of any of these, there is—

Ablution. On rising from his couch he must clean his teeth with a twig of the pipul-tree, after which the twig must be thrown away. Then he must proceed to the Ganges, or some holy stream, or a tank, if no river is near (or to a well, and bathe by pouring water upon his body), and first sip a little water and sprinkle some before him. He must then throw water eight times over his head, and pour a little upon the ground, by which he destroys the demons who war upon the gods. Then thrice plunging into the water, and repeating each time the expiatory prayer which recites the creation, he washes his clothes and sits down to worship the rising sun. With each of these acts there are appropriate prayers to be offered, the object of which is to enable him to perform the rites properly, and to be blessed with health and general prosperity.

The sun is next worshipped. To do this properly, reciting the Gāyatri, he ties up the lock of hair which is allowed to grow long on the top of his head, by which he hopes to be lifted up to heaven. He then again sips water several times, and touches the various parts of his body with his wet hand. If during this exercise he happens to sneeze, he must wait for a moment and touch his right ear as an expiation. For fire, water, the Vedas, the sun, moon, air, all reside in the right ear of a Brāhman ; and Ganga being there too, and sacrificial fires in his nostrils, when these are touched all sin vanishes in a moment. He then closes his eyes and meditates on Brahmā, Vishnu, Siva, in their respective forms, and whilst holding his breath, his left nostril being closed with the fingers of his right hand, three times repeats the Gāyatri. This notable text is as follows: "Om (a word indicating the three great gods of Hinduism—Brahmā, Vishnu, Siva), earth, sky, heaven! We meditate on the adorable light of the resplendent generator (the sun), which governs our intellects, which is water, lustre, savour, immortal faculty of thought, Brahma, earth, sky, heaven." This text is interpreted by the commentators to mean the following: "That effulgent power which governs our intellects is the primitive element of water, the lustre of gems, and other glittering substances, the savour of trees and herbs, the thinking soul of living beings: it is the creator, preserver, destroyer; the sun and every other deity, and all which moves or which is fixed in the three worlds named earth, sky, and heaven. May he unite my soul to his true radiance." Another interpretation of the Gāyatri differs from the former mainly in the last part, in which it is said, "The power exists internally in my heart, and externally in the sun; being one and the same with that effulgent power, I myself am an irradiated manifestation of the Supreme Brahmā." From the following explanatory passage it is clear that the sun is thus really worshipped: "That which is in the sun, and thus called light or effulgent power, is adorable, and must be worshipped by them who dread successive births and deaths, and who eagerly desire beatitude." This prayer is preceded by the names of the seven worlds, signifying that this glorious light permeates them all. These seven worlds are as follows: 1. *Earth*, in which we are now living. 2. The world, in which beings who have passed from the earth are now unconsciously awaiting the end of the present age, when they will again awake to consciousness. 3. *Heaven*, the abode of the good. 4. The middle world, *i.e.*, the region between these three lower and the next three higher worlds. 5. The world of births, in which animals destroyed at the great conflagration which closes each age are born again. 6. The mansion of the blessed, which is occupied by the sons of Brahmā, who by their austerity are fitted for its blessedness. 7. The sublime abode of truth, the home of Brahmā, the Supreme. Entrance into this is attained by true knowledge, the regular discharge of duties, and veracity: once attained it is never lost. The mystic syllable Om must precede and follow this repetition of the names of the seven worlds, or the efficacy of their repetition is lost. Though all rites, oblations, sacrifices, pass away, it is declared that this awful word, as it is the symbol of God, cannot pass away.

After the three suppressions of the breath which represent the threefold utterance of the Gāyatri, the worshipper, after again sipping water, prays to the sun and the deities who preside over sacrifice to prevent him from imperfectly performing the ceremony; and asks, further, "May whatever sin I have committed by night, in thought, word, or deed, be cancelled by day. Whatever sin is in me, may it be far removed;" and, with other prayers, he offers water to the sun, throws water eight times over his head, and then upon the ground. As a means of cleansing his heart from sin, he takes up a little water in the hollow of his hand, inhales a little with one nostril, and exhales it by the other, and concludes the ceremony by again sipping a little water. The worshipper next worships the sun standing on one foot and resting the other on his ankle or heel; looking towards the east, and holding his joined hands opened before him, repeats other prayers; again and again the Gāyatri, in a slightly altered form, is repeated, and an offering is made of flowers, grains, water, &c.

A Brāhman who is living the religious life must also bathe at midday and in the evening; whilst the forms are very similar, the prayers differ slightly; but it is stated that for a householder who has other duties to attend to, the midday and evening bathing may be dispensed with, and the prayers shortened in the morning. Where bathing in water is inconvenient, other modes of ablution are prescribed—rubbing of the body with ashes, standing in the dust raised by cows treading the earth, exposure to the rain—these, under special circumstances, may be substituted for bathing in a river.

Preparatory to any religious act, or when he bathes with the express object of obtaining freedom from sin, the worshipper must bathe with certain rites, and uttering of certain prayers that do not essentially differ from the foregoing. He calls on the names of the sacred streams, and concludes with a prayer to earth, saying, after taking up a handful and scattering it, "O Earth, whatever sin has been committed by me, do thou, who art upheld by the hundred-armed Krishna, incarnate as a boar, ascend my limbs and remove every such sin." On continuing in the water and seeking deliverance by them, after addressing the water and plunging three times in the stream he says, "O consummation of solemn rites, who dost purify when performed by the most grievous offenders, thou dost invite the basest criminals to purification, thou dost expiate the most heinous crimes, and atone for sins to the gods by oblation and sacrifice; I expiate sins towards mortals by employing mortals to officiate at sacraments; defend me from the pernicious sin of offending the gods." This form of worship is also used at the ordinary midday ablution. The sun is then to be worshipped with uplifted arms, not as in the morning with joined hands.

There are also instructions given as to the prayers to be offered, and rites to be performed, before the reading of the Vedas commences; offerings have to be made of grain, &c., with various ceremonies to the gods inviting them to be present and cheerful as he reads the holy writings; then to the great progenitors of mankind, to Yāma, to his father, grandfather, and great-grandfather, mother, and other near relatives who have died; afterwards for those more remote, and lastly, for all men—the idea being that the gifts of water and grain will relieve the wants of any who may be suffering in some of the many hells, or give increase of blessedness to those in the regions of the blessed. When the Vedas are not read, the offerings of grain, water, &c., to the progenitors, spirits, deities, and ancestors are made. These ceremonies can be shortened or lengthened at the wish of the individual; but the duties are all prescribed, and in some cases literally fulfilled, and when they are performed the Brāhman prepares for his meal. Here, again, other religious rites have to be observed. He first gives a portion to the gods, progenitors, relatives who have passed away, and to all other beings, then feeds his guests, and is ready for his first meal. After washing his hands and feet, and sipping though not swallowing the water, he sits on a stool or cushion, not on a couch or bed, which must be placed in a clean place and marked off with quadrangular lines. When the food is brought in, he bows to it, raises his hands in the form of a humble salutation to his forehead, and adds, "May this be always ours." After sitting down he should lift the plate with his left hand, and say, "Thou art invigorating." As the food is given to him he says, "May heaven give thee!" and accepts it with the prayer, "May earth receive thee!" Before eating he moves his hand round the plate to insulate it and his person from the rest of the company. He then offers five lumps of it to Yama, sips the water, makes five oblations to breath, wets his eyes, and commences to eat in silence.

At night similar duties to those of the morning are gone through, and in many cases offerings of flowers, &c., are made to the gods. If a Vaishnava, the Sālgrāma, the common representation of Vishnu, is worshipped : if of some other sect, some emblem of the special deity. Thus an unceasing round of duties are discharged, though it is difficult to see how the great majority of them can have any moral or beneficial effect on the character. Repetition of the same rites and words so frequently one would think must lead to a merely mechanical performance. And as far as one can see this is the case ; though of course some of the Brāhmans are better than their creed, and better than their ritual could ever make them.

The Vishnu Purāna gives the following interesting particulars respecting part of the daily worship of the Brāhmans, and it is quite in harmony with the teaching of other Scriptures. As part of the morning worship it is the duty of a man to make a daily oblation of water for the benefit of his ancestors and relations in any former birth who may be suffering in hell. The prayer is as follows : "May the gods, demons, serpents, and trees, birds, fish, all that people the waters, earth, or air, be propitiated by the water I have presented to them. This water is given by me for the alleviation of the pains of all those who are suffering in the realms of hell. May all those who are my kindred, and who are not my kindred, and who were my relations in a former life, all who desire libations from me, receive satisfaction from this water. May this water and sesamum presented by me relieve the hunger and thirst of all who are suffering from those inflictions wheresoever they may be" (p. 303). After making an offering to the gods in general, he is then to cast a few grains of rice broadcast on a clean place, for the good of creation at large, with some such formula as that above.

Before taking his food, when all is ready, he must wait in expectation of a guest's arrival; for "he who feeds himself and neglects the poor and friendless stranger, in want of hospitality, goes to hell." And it is his duty to treat his guest well, for if he depart from one house unsatisfied and goes to another in order to obtain a sufficiency of food, he transfers his sins to the man whose house he leaves, and at the same time robs him of all his merit that he may have laid up in heaven. Brahmā himself is present in every guest, and he it is who partakes of the food that is given. Next he must see that any married woman in his house, any who are ill, aged, and very young, are fed, and then he can himself partake of his food; but the severest punishment is threatened if he eat without first bathing, praying, and consecrating his food, and before the children and the aged are supplied.

Whilst the daily duties of the Brāhman are thus numerous and lengthy, those of the mass of the people are not so by any means. Most Hindus regard it as a religious duty to bathe daily if this is at all convenient, and to raise their hands and bow towards the sun as he rises; but beyond this little or nothing is done daily. In the houses of the well-to-do there will be an image with its ministrant priest, and as the conch shell is blown or the bell rung some members of the household may look on at the ceremony, and some of the poorer neighbours run in for a few moments, as flowers, fruits, grain, and water, are offered to the image. But the mass of the people have no regular daily private worship. The shopkeepers, as a rule, have a picture or an image of Ganesa in their shops, and before commencing business in the morning a little incense is burned before it; and occasionally a devout workman will salute his tools before he commences work for the day. But except in the homes of the Brāhmans, who have rites to perform for themselves, and the homes of the rich in which there are hired priests to attend to these matters for them, there is no ordinary household religious worship. The professed ascetics are supposed to devote *all* their time to religion of course; but I am now speaking of the people who have not given up their secular life.

The worshippers of Vishnu, if they can spare the money to purchase it, have a Sālgrāma in their houses, or at any rate try to cultivate a small Tulasi plant the representative of his favourite mistress, after whom the plant, is named. Vishnu's spouse, being jealous of her husband's attentions to Tulasi, changed her into a plant; Vishnu, in order that he might still enjoy her company, transformed himself into the Sālgrāma, an ammonite that is found in some rivers in the Nepalese territory, and which is most highly valued by the Vaishnavas or worshippers of Vishnu. In the houses of the people these Sālgrāmas are most carefully kept and regarded as though they were living beings. In the hot season they are carefully bathed, and in many cases a jar of water is hung over them, from which, through a little string, the water slowly drops upon them and keeps them cool. The Tulasi plant is also most carefully tended. Before these the daily prayers are offered, or at least their deity is acknowledged by a most profound salutation many times during the day.

As another part of the private worship of the Hindu should be mentioned the repetition of the names of the gods. It is considered a meritorious act to repeat these names a great number of times during the day: some of the sects prescribing the use of the rosary so that the people may easily reckon up the number of times that they repeat these names. Stories are found in their religious books showing the immense benefit that comes from this—some even obtaining entrance into heaven, though they had lived very immoral lives, because they had uttered the sacred name in teaching it to their parrots. It is a most common thing to see Hindus sitting at their doors loudly or silently repeating these names.

When the women go to the rivers to bathe, where there is no temple of Siva present, they make an image of mud in the form of the Linga; but as the Saivite women are not taught the mantras or sacred texts, their worship consists in bowing the head or body to this little image, after which it is thrown into the river.

Though the deity worshipped differs, and to some extent the form of worship varies with the different Hindu sects, yet in the main there is great similarity in their forms of worship. In the following account of the ceremonies of the Saktas,* *i.e.*, those who worship the female deities chiefly, will be found a fair example of the religious exercises of the religious members of the Hindu community. As there are Brāhmans devoted entirely to religion and Brāhmans engaged in secular work, so there are men of other castes who devote far more time to their religious duties than do the rest of their brethren. And as it is allowable for the Brāhman to shorten his morning and evening exercises, so is it for the other castes. In fact, when circumstances are unfavourable for a lengthened period of devotion it is taught that it is sufficient for a man simply to repeat the *mul mantra* as it is called, *i.e.*, the text that he was taught by his guru when

* *Calcutta Review*, vol. xxiv. p. 41.

he was originally received into the sect to which he may belong. In fact, as mentioned previously, many of the Hindus content themselves with bowing to the sun as he rises, and with the uplifting of their hands before partaking of their food, and the repetition of the name of their deity. It will be noticed that in the daily devotions of the Brāhmans there was the distinct utterance of petitions for pardon; prosperity, long life, &c.; but in the case of those whose worship consists in attending to the Sālgrāma and Tulasi, there is no prayer, no expression of the heart's desire to God. There are twenty distinct acts in the following elaborate ritual of the Saktas:

1. *Anchmana.* The object of this is the purification of the worshipper, and consists in taking up water from a copper vessel with the left hand in a small copper spoon, and pouring a small quantity on the half-closed palm of the right hand. A little of this water is sipped three times with the lips, but it must not be swallowed. The fingers are then dipped into the spoon, and thus wetted touch the lips, eyes, ears, and other parts of the head, during which an appropriate mantra is recited.

2. *Sasthi Bachāna.* The object of this ceremony is to render the whole act of worship beneficial to him who performs it, and consists in repeating the name of the month, the age of the moon, the day of the week, and certain mantras, the recital of which are supposed to bring general prosperity to the reciter.

3. *Sankalpa.* This forms what may be termed the petition-part of the ceremony. At this time the worshipper mentions the object he has in view in this act of devotion: he then repeats again the name of the month, the age of the moon, the day of the week, his own name, and that of the great progenitor from whom he believes his family has descended. During all the time of this exercise a betel nut, or some other fruit, is held in the water that stands in the copper vessel standing near.

4. *Ghatasthāpana.* This consists in placing an earthen-jar, a brass pot, or sometimes simply a piece of mud hollowed out, in which, if it is obtainable, a little water from a sacred river is placed. A bunch of leaves, a green cocoa-nut, or a ripe plaintain is then put on the top of the vessel, and the distinctive marks of the worshipper's sect are painted in red paint upon it. This ordinarily takes the place of an image, but sometimes an image of the deity is set up and worshipped: when this is not done the jar of water is regarded as the representative of the deity.

5. *Sāmānya Argha Sthāpana.* This is the offering of prayers to the ten guardians of the earth; *i.e.*, to the beings who are supposed to rule over the eight main points of the compass, the Zenith and the Nadir. This is done by offering an argha, *i.e.*, a small quantity of soaked rice, and a few blades of durva grass which are placed in a conch shell to the left of the worshipper. If a Brāhman happen to be present, a few grains of rice must first be given to him, and then the whole is thrown upon the representative of the deity, whether it be an image or the pot of water mentioned above.

6. *Ashan Suddhi*, *i.e.*, the purification of the seat. This really means the determination of the posture of the worshipper during the ceremony. The Tantras declare that there are 80,000 postures in which the worshipper should sit or stand, the form being determined by the object he has in performing the worship. The most common position is to sit cross-legged upon the ground.

7. *Bhuta Suddhi*, *i.e.*, the purification of the body. The body is said to be composed of five elements—earth, water, fire, air, and ether. In this part of the ceremony the fire and ether, which dwell in the forehead, are supposed to work wonders owing to the force of the mantras that are here repeated. The fire consumes the whole of the old body, and the ether, mixing with the ashes, forms a new one from them.

8 and 9. *Prānāyam* and *Rishyādinyās*. These are prayers or invitations to the goddess to be present at the celebration of her worship. During the repetition of these mantras, the worshipper must close his nostrils with his fingers, and remain without breathing as long as possible. It is said that some can do this for a great length of time, owing to which their bodies become so buoyant that they float in the air. Most wonderful stories are told of the doings of some of these worshippers, but unfortunately I have never seen any who could thus set at defiance the law of gravitation.

9 and 10. *Matrikānyas* and *Barnanyas*. These consist in the repetition of the Sanskrit alphabet, first simply, and then with the strong nasal sounds peculiar to that and the cognate languages. Whilst this is being done, the worshipper touches fifty different parts of his body. If an earthen image of the goddess forms the object of worship, the corresponding parts of the idol are also touched by the ministrant.

12. *Dhyana; i.e.*, meditation. Closing his eyes, the worshipper forms a mental image of the deity; the mantra repeated at this time being a description of her.

13. *Abāhan*. When an earthen pot is regarded as the representative of the Deity, a simple invitation is given to make it her temporary dwelling-place; the words used are as follows: "O goddess, come here, come here; stay here, stay here. Take up thine abode here and receive my worship." But when an image is employed for the same purpose, two more elaborate rites are performed, viz., the Chakshrudāna, or the giving of eyes, and the Prānpratishtha, or the giving of life. These ceremonies are performed by the officiator touching the eyes, breast, and cheek of the image with the first two fingers of the right hand as he says, "Let the soul of the goddess long continue in happiness in this image."

14. *Puja* or worship. This consists in the offering of rice, fruit, flowers, incense, &c. There are two kinds of

puja—the one simple, the other more expensive. In the simpler form only five articles are required—incense, a burning lamp, sandal-wood powder, flowers, and a cone of soaked rice, adorned with fruits, grain, curds, sweetmeats, &c. In the more elaborate form of puja, sixteen articles are mentioned as necessary—an āshan, or seat, *i.e.*, a small square plate of gold, a formal reception of the deity, water to wash her feet (this ceremony is performed by lading water from one vessel to another), argha (an offering of sandal-wood paste and rice as a sign of respect), water for cleaning her mouth, a copper jar containing ghi, honey, and sugar, water to clean her mouth a second time, water for her bath, clothes, ornaments for her hands, feet, nose, ear, neck, and waist; and finally praise is given to her as the person officiating walks round and round the image. This praise is expressed in the most adulatory strains, in which her greatness and goodness are extolled, and in which she is reminded that she is the one supreme deity, of which all the others are but representatives.

15. *Lelchi mudra.* This consists in shaking of the fingers, with the palm of the right hand placed upon the back of the left.

16. *Abarana*, *i.e.*, the worship of the ghosts and demons who form the usual attendants of the goddess.

17. *Mahakāla* is the worship of Siva, the husband of the goddess, in one of his many forms. It is understood to be a most sinful thing, an act that will ensure the sufferings of hell, if a man worship Sakti and neglect at the same time to adore her lord.

18. *Balidāna.* The offering of a sacrifice; it may be a kid, sheep, or buffalo.

19. *Kabajan Path.* The reading or the reciting of the warlike deeds of the goddess.

20. *Homa.* This is a burnt-offering. For this a bed of sand about a foot square is prepared, on which a little ghi is laid, together with a few sacred leaves. This is then set on fire,

and with some of the ashes the forehead of the worshipper is marked; the rest is most carefully kept in the house.

It will of course be understood that this elaborate and expensive ritual is not gone through daily in its entirety. On ordinary days parts of it only are performed, the whole being prescribed for special occasions.

CHAPTER II.

TEMPLE WORSHIP.

Before noticing the worship as it is carried on in the Hindu temples it will not be out of place to give a sketch of an ordinary temple. Accustomed as we are to Christian churches, we are apt to imagine that heathen temples are of somewhat similar style, and used for a similar purpose. But this is an altogether erroneous view. The churches of Christendom have been built to hold great crowds of worshippers, who have come together to witness the grand processions of the officiants, to hear the solemn strains of music, and, in later times, to listen to the instructions and exhortations of the preachers. And for such a purpose they are well adapted. Further, though there are small and costly buildings that have been erected through the munificence of a few faithful and generous givers, as a rule they have risen through the united offerings of many people for their common convenience and good. But the ordinary temples of the Hindus, having a very different purpose to serve, are built in a very different style. There are in India a few large temples but as a rule they are quite small, not being more than ten or twelve feet square. No congregation gathers in them to witness an imposing ceremonial; no addresses on religion and morals are given; there are no seats for those who come. With the Hindu the object of visiting a temple is simply to walk round the building, hand over his offering to the officiating priest, and, if possible, catch a glimpse of the idol it contains, and after prostrating himself before it, to return to his home.

The Hindu temple comprises an outer court, quadrangular in form, sometimes with verandahs round, in which the pilgrims may reside for a day or two when they come there to worship, and an edifice at one end containing the shrine. This shrine is again divided into two parts—the Sabhā, or vestibule; and the Garbhagriha, or shrine in which the image is placed. This inner room is so small that it permits only of the entrance of the priest as he performs the worship. Generally a bell is suspended over the door of this shrine. When, therefore, a worshipper approaches, this bell is rung to call the attention of the god to the presence of his follower, who, having walked round the building, hands his gift to the priest, bows to the image, and then walks away. On the great festival days, when a constant stream of people pass in front of the idol to make their offerings, all appearance of devotion and reverence is wanting, as they jostle against each other in the attempt to approach the shrine. In temples such as that at Kālighat, where bloody sacrifices are offered, the courtyard has all the appearance and frightful smell of the worst shambles, for on certain days of the year the executioners are at work from dawn till dark decapitating the victims, whose blood streams over the pavement, whilst the sun is shining in all his strength; the frame-work in which the animals are placed being in the courtyard of the temple about thirty or forty feet from the shrine itself.

Many of the temples are the gifts of private individuals, who have erected them in order to obtain "merit," *i.e.*, the fruit of works of supererogation as a set-off against a certain number of sins. If a man has determined to spend a certain amount of money for this purpose, in most cases he will devote it not to the building of a grand and imposing structure, in which a number of people could unite in presenting their praises and their prayers to

God, but in erecting seven, fourteen, twenty-one, or some greater number in multiples of seven of these small shrines. When the visitors desire to make their offerings in more than one of these, worship is performed in them; but generally one or two of them may be used, whilst the others are seldom entered. This fact also suggests a reason why so many new temples are springing up, whilst others in their close neighbourhood are allowed to fall into ruin. If a man of the present generation were to spend his money in repairing a temple that was already standing, the "merit" of his deed would be reckoned to the account of the original builder, and not to himself.

There are other temples that are kept in good repair, because they are largely endowed; some of these endowments being the gifts of previous governments, some of devout worshippers now passed away. As these are largely frequented by hosts of pilgrims who by this means hope to obtain entrance into heaven, and as all who come make an offering of some kind, they are a source of considerable income to their owners or guardians. In some cases men are employed in travelling from place to place proclaiming the benefits that a visit to them will secure. In this way large revenues are obtained, and it is the interest of their owners to make them as attractive as possible. In speaking of Pilgrimage, I shall describe some of these larger temples; but it must be understood that whether the temple be large or small, the plan is much the same in all, and the part the worshippers take identical—it is a mere promenade round the shrine, the bestowal of an offering to the deity, and an attempt to catch a glimpse of the idol in whose honour and for whose worship the building has been raised. So far as I have seen, no instructive work is done in them; nor is there any gathering of a congregation for the presenting of their united prayers to the gods.

In the Hindu temples the worship proper is all performed by the priests (who must of necessity be Brāhmans), though they are regarded as of a lower order than others who do not engage in this work. There may occasionally be some people curious enough to watch the ministrant at the altar, but, as a rule, he has no lookers-on, except those who may assist. There is no attraction to the ordinary Hindu to stand by, because the texts are muttered, not distinctly whispered even; and if it were possible for the words to be heard, all being recited in the Sanskrit language, they would be unintelligible to him. Moreover, the meaning of the various parts of the service are known only to the priests; this is their proper work, and the common people would not for a moment attempt to understand, much less to practise that which belongs by birthright to the sacerdotal class. It is the priest's duty to repeat the texts, and make offerings to the gods; it is the people's duty to provide these gifts, and to fee those who condescend to be their mediators with the gods. The mass of the people have nothing more to do with the temple worship.

Looking now to the worship as it is performed by the priests, we find that they treat the images as though they were living beings; the ritual observed and the attentions paid being precisely similar in spirit to those that would be shown by a servant to his master. In the worship of different deities, of course the texts somewhat differ, as also do the offerings presented; Vishnu, *e.g*,, in all his forms being most careful of all forms of life—no bloody sacrifices are made in his temples; whilst Durgā, delighting in blood, is regaled with the blood of slaughtered victims in vast numbers. Still, a description of the daily work in one temple is very similar to that in others. I shall now give the worship that is paid in the temples in which Gopāl is worshipped. This is the name given to Krishna, one of the incarnations of Vishnu, when he was a boy living in the house as the reputed son of Nanda, a cowherd. The word Gopāl signifies the cowherd.

1. *Mangala.* About half an hour after sunrise the god is taken from the couch on which he has been supposed to sleep

during the night, is then washed and dressed, and placed upon his seat; slight refreshments are offered to him with betel-nut, pān-leaf, and spices—a mixture of which the Hindus are very fond.

2. After an interval of about an hour and a half, *Sringāra* is performed; the image is anointed with oil, camphor, and sandal-wood, and robed in gorgeous garments.

3. Next comes *Givala*, about three quarters of an hour after the preceding; he is visited as though he were now going out to do the work of a cowherd, which in his younger days was Krishna's occupation.

4. *Rājā Bhoja*. This is the midday meal, when Krishna is supposed to come in from the fields to dine. All kinds of delicacies are placed before the image in the way of food; these are prepared by the officials of the temple, and afterwards distributed to the votaries present, and sometimes even sent to the homes of well-to-do people in the neighbourhood, who are friends of the temple and of its priests.

5. *Uthāpan*, *i.e.*, the awaking of the god from his afternoon sleep, which takes place a couple of hours or so before sunset.

6. *Bhoja*. The afternoon meal; this is given about half an hour after he has been awakened from his sleep.

7. *Sandhya*. At sunset the ornaments, &c., are taken off from the image, and he is anointed and perfumed afresh.

8. *Sayan*, repose. About eight or nine o'clock in the evening the image is placed on a bed, refreshments, water, and betel-nut are left near at hand, when the priest retires, and the temple is shut until the following morning.

This goes on, with slight variation in the offerings made and texts recited from day to day, the whole year round. There is no established ritual for general use, nor any prescribed form of public adoration. At certain festival days—some account of which will be given in another chapter—other rites are performed, having reference to the chief events in the life of Krishna. When, as is sometimes the case, the images are very heavy, they are not made to lie down at night.

CHAPTER III.

RELIGIOUS FESTIVALS.

In addition to the daily worship of the deities whose images are set up in a permanent form in the temples and in the homes of the people, there are certain days of the year on which important events in the earthly life of these deities are commemorated by festivals, and there are other deities whose worship is almost entirely limited to the days that are regarded as sacred to them. Just as we have the events of the Saviour's life especially brought to memory on Christmas Day and Good Friday, so the Hindus commemorate the birth, &c., of Krishna and the other gods by special festivals; and as we have saints' days, such as St. John, St. Matthew, &c., so the Hindus have gods' days, *i.e.*, special days for the worship of certain deities, such as Lakshmi, Sarasvati, &c. On the special festival days an image is prepared for the occasion, which, as soon as the worship is completed, is destroyed. As it is considered a work of merit to observe these festivals, on these days the houses of nearly all the well-to-do Hindus are converted into temples for the time being, and crowds of people flock in to see the images there set up for worship.

Opposite to the entrance-gate to the Hindu house is a platform, which is built for the special purpose of receiving the images that are connected with the religious festivals; whilst the open courtyard in front is evidently made for the purpose of admitting a large number of spectators who may come in to witness the ceremony, or to enjoy the amusements that are generally provided for the night, when the worship proper of the idol is completed. Though ordinarily no one would enter the house uninvited, on these occasions all who wish may come, and a cordial welcome is given them. Generally—though the image itself may not be very costly, and the fees to the officiating priests may not be very large—it is an expensive affair to have one of these celebrations, because amusements for the public must be provided, and a great number of guests entertained. In places where there are not many of the large family houses, it is no uncommon thing for a number of neighbouring villages to unite in celebrating these *pujas*, each householder being expected to pay his share. In this case a temporary building of mat-work is erected, and the donations are spent in providing the idol and the requirements of a feast.

When a gentleman determines to set up an image for public worship in his house, or when in the case of a cluster of villages doing the same, the first thing is to order the image. These are made of various sizes and styles of decoration, according to the price agreed upon by the purchasers. The workman receiving the order first gets his bamboos, which are split and tied together into the shape of the desired image. On this framework he binds hay, until there is something of the human form made. Upon this mud from some sacred stream is laid and moulded into shape, and then placed in the sun to harden. As soon as it is dry it is painted, dressed, and decorated according to certain designs, the authority for which is found in the Sāstras.

When the image is completed it is taken to the house where it is to be worshipped, and at an auspicious moment the priest who has been engaged to conduct the worship goes through an interesting ceremony called the giving of life (prān pratishtha), by which he invites the deity to reside in it for one, two, or three days. Prior to this the image is regarded as ordinary mud, &c., and any one may even touch it with impunity; but the mere repetition of certain magical words is supposed to change all this; just as in the Catholic Church the repetition of the words, "This is my body," is supposed to convert the bread and wine into the body and blood of our Lord. After this it would be regarded as profanation for any one except a Hindu to approach the image, or for any one but a Brāhman to touch it. The officiating priest is occupied for a couple of hours or so in the morning, and the same time in the evening, repeating texts, offering flowers, fruit, &c., engaging in a similar round of ceremonies to those that are rendered to an image in a temple. In the case of the worship of Durgā, in any of her forms, a kid, sheep, or buffalo is sacrificed in front of the image, and a vessel of the blood from the victim is placed before her. In the courtyard of Hindu gentlemen who worship Durgā, the frame for holding the victims whilst they are sacrificed remains permanently.

After the evening worship is concluded, in the courtyard immediately in front of the image which is believed to be inhabited by the deity, amusements of varied kinds take place. Sometimes these consist of the singing of songs by professional singers, not necessarily in favour of the particular deity whose worship is then being celebrated. These songs are often of a most lascivious kind. Sometimes there will be a Nautch, in which professional dancers, who as a class are prostitutes, dance, sometimes without, sometimes with, most immoral gestures. Sometimes there are Jātras, or theatrical representations of mythological scenes, after the style of the miracle plays of Europe, in which men always perform. It will be understood that at these festivals women in large numbers are present, and these indecent representations are made, not only in their presence, but in front of the image supposed to represent the deity. In home services, as in the temples, it will be noticed that the *people* generally have no part in the worship proper of the deities; this is all done by the officiating priests, generally with merely a few curious onlookers, who are not supposed to have the remotest connection with this part of the ceremonial.

On the day following the worship of the images another interesting ceremony is performed, viz., the farewell of the deity is taken. Before her supposed departure, the priest thanks her for the favour she has bestowed on the worshipper in becoming his guest, and after asking her to regard him with special favour, an invitation is given to her to return the next year, when another image will be prepared for her habitation. After her departure, the materials that for a time were regarded as sacred are considered so no longer. Any one may now touch them. Just before sunset the image is carried to the river bank, or if there be no river near, to the side of a tank, preceded by a procession headed by a band of music, and as darkness comes on torches are lighted. With bands playing, women dancing, men shouting, and torches burning, a most weird procession is formed. On reaching the water's edge, a couple of boats are lashed together, on which the image is placed. These boats are then rowed into the middle of the stream, the lashing cut, the image falls into the water, and the whole ceremony is complete.

I shall now pass on to notice the various festivals that are held during the year. It should be noticed that although a Hindu may have his own chosen deity to whom he gives special worship daily, he is bound by the fear of evil from its neglect, and by the hope of benefit arising from its celebration, to worship the many who form the Hindu Pantheon. A few are to be found who are content with the worship of one of the many gods; but I have known men who themselves, in their private worship, are the devout followers of Vishnu, to whom all life is sacred, not only witnessing, and thus countenancing the offering of bloody sacrifice to Durgā, but themselves officiating as priests at these festivals. When this inconsistency is pointed out to them, they excuse themselves on the ground that they must live, and it is only by this means that they can gain a livelihood.

I shall follow the order of the Bengāli Festivals from the commencement to the end of the year, as marked in their almanack.

1. *Vaisākh.*

This is the first month of the year, according to the Bengāli reckoning, answering to parts of April and May. No public religious ceremonies inaugurate the New Year. On this day the tradespeople and others open new accounts, and the year's business is commenced by the painting of an image of Ganesa, the god of wisdom, on their shop doors. The Bengālis have great faith in omens, and are most anxious to transact a good amount of business on this day, in the belief that it will then prove a prosperous year. In order to have a large number of transactions to record, it is no uncommon thing for friends to pretend to purchase goods, so that their names may appear on the books, though the goods and money are returned a day or two afterwards.

Though no great ceremonies occur, it is considered a specially holy month. Generally it is the hottest month of the year, and as a work of merit the Hindus place jars of water near their houses, that the cows as they pass may quench their thirst; and vessels of water are also placed in the trees for the birds. Jars of water are suspended over the Lingam and Shālgrām, that these representatives of the great deities Siva and Vishnu may be kept cool and not suffer from thirst. In this month, too, the gods are fed with more dainty food, and the Brāhmans gladdened with more costly gifts. The worship of the river Bhāgirathi and the bathing of the images of Vishnu take place, but these are comparatively unimportant festivals. There is, however, one festival that calls for notice, viz., the worship of the Dhenki. The Dhenki is a large wooden beam working on a pivot, by which rice is husked. It is said that Nārad, the patron of the pivot, hearing a guru teaching his disciples to repeat the word Dhenki a hundred and eight times a day, was so pleased with the man's devotion that he paid him a visit riding upon a Dhenki and translated him to heaven. At several important domestic ceremonies—such as the giving rice to a child for the first time, marriage, the investiture with the sacred thread the Dhenki is worshipped; but in the first month of the year the women worship it, as it is to them one of the most useful implements of domestic use. The head of the beam is painted with vermilion, anointed with sacred oil, and presented with rice and the holy Durva grass. Dharmarāja, the lord of virtue or religion, too, is worshipped in some places; as also, in a few localities, but not at all generally, a log of wood called Devāni, *i.e.*, partaker of the Divine nature. This wood is said to have the power of visiting the sacred places of pilgrimage through subterranean roads for the benefit of its worshippers.

2. *Jaishtha.*

(1) Dasahāra;* this festival commemorates the descent of the Ganges from heaven to earth and is called Dasahāra, because bathing at this season is said to remove all the sins committed in ten births, *i.e.*, during ten different lives. This is a most interesting ceremony. Thousands upon thousands of the people bring their offerings of flowers, fruits, and grain to the river side, and then enter the sacred stream. It is a thing worthy of note that although in many places men and women bathe together, the men having on simply a cloth round their loins, and the women often having the upper part of their bodies exposed, I have never seen the slightest impropriety of gestures on these occasions. In some festivals, as previously noticed, the grossest impropriety of language and gesture are freely indulged in; but at bathing festivals I have never noticed anything indecent. It is proper to bathe in the Ganges for those who live near enough; but other rivers may take the place of the Ganges, and legends have been manufactured to show that their virtues are even

* For a fuller account of this, see chapter on Pilgrimages, Gangā Sāgar.

greater than those of the Ganges; if there is no river convenient, then a tank can be substituted.

(2) The Snān Jātra; *i.e.*, the first of the three great festivals performed in honour of Jagannātha. At Puri, the headquarters of Jagannātha's worship, this is the great festival of the year; but it is not confined to that place. At several places in Calcutta this ceremony is performed. Near Serampore, in a village called Mahesh, is a temple with cars almost as ponderous as those at Puri, that are called into requisition in the following month for the Rath Jātra, which attracts almost as many people from the neighbourhood as Puri itself, whilst most large villages has its own car for the festival. The ceremonies are much the same as those at Puri; but, being performed in a place which has no sacred enclosure to shut out the non-Hindu population, it can be witnessed by any who may wish to do so. And I certainly think that, of all the festivals of Hinduism, this is the most imposing that I have seen. On this occasion the image that has been kept in its shrine since the similar festival of the preceding year is brought outside the temple, and on a high platform, erected for the occasion, bathed, anointed with holy oil and clothed by the priests, in the sight of an immense concourse of people. From 60,000 to 80,000 people stand round this platform, with their gaze directed to the priests engaged in their holy work, and as the time for its completion approaches, there is scarcely a sound heard. Many of the people probably have gone there out of mere curiosity, some have gone simply for amusement; but multitudes, it is certain, have been brought there with the earnest desire to *see* Jagannātha, the sight of whom they believe will take away all their sins. At length the bath and the robing being completed, the god is raised up so that the people can see him; and from the vast crowd there goes forth a shout, "Jai, Jai, Jagannātha; Jai, Jai, Jagannātha," which once heard will never be forgotten. On this occasion the whole neighbourhood has the appearance of a fair, and when the religious

ceremony is over, the fair begins. There are stalls with all kinds of goods for sale, shows, and various kinds of amusements. And as the great majority of fallen women, having been outcasted when they took to a life of immorality, have become Vaishnavas, they are to be found in great numbers at this, almost the only religious festival in which they can have a share. Certainly the music, dancing, and general merry making, that prevail after the religious part of the festival is over, are altogether out of harmony with what has always appeared to me as the most impressive ceremony I have seen connected with Hinduism. Every large town and many villages have their image of Jagannātha, so that yearly there is the observance of this festival within an easy distance of almost every part of Bengal. It is my belief that this festival is more largely attended, and its lessons more widely taught, than those perhaps of any other; not excepting even the Durgā Puja. There are ceremonies, such as the sacrificing of goats in the Durgā Puja, that offend the prejudices of the more earnest followers of Vishnu; but in Jagannātha's worship, as it is practised away from Puri, there is nothing to offend the prejudices of any Hindu. At Puri caste distinctions are ignored; but this is not common at other places.*

(3) Sasthi, the goddess who rules over women and the protector of children, though regularly worshipped at six seasons of the year, and at special seasons also, has her proper festival in this month. At childbirth, and even before, her blessing is invoked; and after birth until the child attains to manhood or womanhood, it is supposed to be under her special care. In the sickness of children her aid is first invoked to effect their recovery. At this festival it is not common to set up an image of the goddess; but as the banian-tree is regarded as specially sacred to her, she is represented by it on this occasion. On the day of worship the women of the neighbourhood march with music playing

* For further account, see chapter on Pilgrimages.

to the tree; the mothers of sons with joy written upon their faces, those as yet unblessed with disappointment in their looks and fervent prayers for this blessing in their hearts and even on their lips. The mantras are recited by the priests; the honoured mothers who have sons give presents to those who have none, and the procession wends its way back to the village. After this is over sons-in-law are invited to the houses of their fathers-in-law, and after being hospitably entertained there, are sent home laden with presents. On the whole, it is one of the happiest days of the year.

"On this festive occasion, the son-in-law is invited to spend the day and night at his father-in-law's house. No pains or expense is spared to entertain him. When he comes in the morning, the first thing he has to do is to go into the female apartments, bow his head down in honour of his mother-in-law, and put on the floor a few rupees, say five or ten, sometimes more, if newly married. The food consists of all the delicacies of the season, and both the quantity and variety are often too great to be done justice to. . . . Surrounded by a galaxy of beauty, the youthful son-in-law is restrained by a sense of shame from freely partaking of the feast specially provided for him. . . . If this be his first visit as son-in-law, he finds himself bewildered in the midst of the superfluity and superabundance of preparation. Many are the tricks employed to outwit him, and in their own way the good-natured females are mistresses of jokes and jests; and nothing pleases them better than to find the youthful new-comer completely nonplussed. This forms the favourite subject of their talk long after the event. Shut up in the cage of a secluded zenāna, quite beyond the influence of the outside world, it is no wonder that their minds and thoughts do not rise above the trifles of their own narrow circle. . . . Ample presents of clothes, fruit, and sweetmeats, are sent to the house of the son-in-law, and every lane and street in Calcutta is thronged with male and female servants trudging along with their loads, in full hope of getting their share of eatables and a rupee or half a rupee each, into the bargain."*

3. *Asārha.*

The festival of this month is the Rath Jātra, or Car Festival. For fifteen days after the Snān Jātra Jagannātha remains invisible to the public. It is supposed that by the exposure on that occasion he caught cold and suffers from fever during the days that he remains hidden. At Puri, this is the time for cleaning and repainting the image, which, owing to the many offerings of his worshippers has in the course of the year become covered with dirt. The deity having recovered from his indisposition on this day is placed on a ponderous car and dragged a mile or two to the temple of some other god whom he is supposed to visit, and with whom he remains a few days. The ceremonies connected with this festival will be described when speaking of Puri, the ritual observed at the head-quarters of his worship being most scrupulously followed in the other places. In former days, these cars were, and in some out-of-the-way places are still, adorned with most obscene pictures, but the purer tastes of the people, or the watchful eyes of the magistrates, being averse to this, in most places they have disappeared. Great profits arise from the establishment of such a popular temple and car as those at Mahesh, in Bengal; and it happened a few years ago that, owing to a dispute arising between those who benefited by them, a rival car was built and a rival image set up. But after a year or so, the popularity of the old establishment proved too strong for the opposition; for whilst the old car found plenty of willing assistants to drag it to the appointed place, the other had to remain stationary, and the god had to lose the benefit of a ride and a change of residence.

The Ulta Rath, or the return of Jagannātha to his temple. About a fortnight after the Car Festival, another of a somewhat similar character is held, though it is by no means so

* "Hindoos as they are," p. 90.

popular as the former. The image of Jagannātha is brought out from the temple where it has been on a visit, placed upon the car, and then dragged back to its own proper temple. The people come in large numbers, but there is nothing like the same enthusiasm manifested as when the deity was taken out for his visit. Sometimes the people have to be rewarded by sweetmeats, &c., to induce them to give assistance in dragging the car; whilst at the Car Festival there were more volunteers than necessary. To assist in the holy work of removing the ponderous car is believed by the more superstitious to secure the favour of the god, and to improve their position in heaven. Jagannātha being a form of Vishnu, it is this great deity's favour that is obtained when honour is shown to this idol, hence the Vaishnavas, as a whole, take part in these ceremonies.

4. *Srāvana.*

The Julana Jātra. This festival is held in the temples of Krishna, and also in those houses where a regular shrine of this deity is set up. On this occasion, in a room adjoining the shrine, the god is placed in a swing, and after swinging for a time taken back to the shrine, when the feasting and merriment commence. Friends are invited to the feast, and then Jātras and other celebrations are performed. As the Jātras form an important part in most of the Hindu festivals, and as they are one of the most important agencies for teaching the people about Hinduism, a few words descriptive of them will not be inappropriate here. These Jātras come nearer to the old miracle plays of Europe than to anything else with which we are familiar. In front of the platform on which the image is placed is a space railed off for the performers. I have never seen them on a raised platform or stage; but as the front rows of people generally sit down, those standing behind can obtain a good view of the performance. The actors are men and boys, who are in great request at these seasons. There is generally a band of music, which plays between the scenes of the Jātra.

The performance takes place immediately in front of the idol, although it can hardly be regarded as part of the worship, as it commences after the worship proper is over; yet it is supposed to be as much for the delight of the god as for the amusement of the people who gather to witness it. These plays, which begin about eleven o'clock at night, and are continued until six or even seven o'clock the following morning, give representations of the important parts of the lives of the gods and goddesses of the Pantheon—the amours and amusements of Krishna, the quarrels of Siva and Parvati, the life of Rāma and Sitā, being the most common. The actors are dressed and painted in imitation of the deities they represent, and frequently the conversations are rendered attractive by sensual and obscene allusions; whilst in the interludes boys dressed in women's clothes dance with most indecent gestures. The worst dances that I have ever seen have been in front of an image, and as part of the rejoicings of a religious festival. Crowds of men, women, and children sit to watch them the whole night through, and certainly these theatrical representations of the acts and words of the deities form a most successful method of teaching the people the most memorable events of their lives. The words and dress of the actors being all according to the teaching of the Sāstras, there can be no doubt that they exert an immense influence over the people. Lessons taught by this method are not easily forgotten.

Manasā. At this time there is also the worship of Manasā,* the queen of snakes, who, though not forgotten at other seasons, has her chief celebration towards the end of this month. Sometimes an image is made, sometimes a pot of water is regarded as her representative. It occasions no surprise that in a country infested with snakes, some of which are so venomous that death follows their bite in about half an hour, some protection from their baneful influence should be sought. And as they all, large and small, are supposed to be under

* "Hindu Mythology," p. 395.

the control of Manasā, she is worshipped with Divine honours. A day or two before the festival it is no uncommon thing for mothers to prepare a dish of rice with treacle, which is placed before a pot of water under a village tree or in the homes. After it has been offered to the deity it is eaten by the mother and her children, whom she hopes to preserve from these reptiles by this simple worship. At Manasā's festival the snake-charmers are called into requisition, and receive presents for their performance. These men, seated on a platform of bamboos, expose themselves to the bite of the most venomous reptiles, pretending that by their religious mantras they are proof against the poison. It may be that they are inoculated with it, or, what is more probable, the poison glands of their snakes have been previously removed. Some of these performers are remarkably skilful, for to hear them speak and watch their actions, it would appear that there are snakes everywhere, that they have simply to call them and they appear. I have seen large snakes suddenly show themselves in most unexpected places where it had been indicated that it was the wish of the spectators that they should be found. The reason of this worship is found in stories in the Mahābhārata and elsewhere. It should be noticed that this, the chief worship of the snake deity, is held at the commencement of the rainy season, when, owing to the earth being saturated with moisture, snakes are driven from their holes, and become unusually destructive of human life.

5. *Bhādra.*

In this month is one great festival, viz., that of the birth of Krishna, and is called Nandotsaba, the joy of Nanda, the adopted father of the great cowherd. In describing this festival as it is observed at Puri,* we have said all that is necessary to be said. It is a festival that is observed all through the country where there are Vaishnavas. Away from Puri there is one form of it that is not practised there.

* See chapters on Pilgrimage.

After the strictly religious rites are over, the excited worshippers dig a hole in the yard before the image of the deity, and pour in water, curds, turmeric, &c.; and, after plunging into this filthy mess, dance and shout the praises of their god. They then walk through the streets in this state until they reach another tank where they bathe. In the afternoon processions of singers walk about singing the praises of Krishna and Rādhā. It should be noticed that in no worship does singing and music figure so largely as in that of Krishna. He was a musician himself, and there is no doubt that the rejoicing and merriment attendant on his worship have done much to attract followers from the more quiet and sometimes cruel ceremonies that constitute the worship of Siva. At this season of the year the disciples are looked up by their gurus, and receive more liberal donations than at other times.

6. *Aswin.*

In this month fall the festivals connected with Durgā and Lakshmi. As the Durgā Puja is emphatically *the* festival of the year in Bengal, I shall describe it in detail.

A Hindu who determines to have the Durgā Puja celebrated in his house on the day of the Rath Jātra takes a piece of split bamboo into the room where the family idols are kept, and the family priest, after a prayer to Vishnu, anoints it with sandal-wood paste, and invokes Durgā's blessing upon it. This bamboo remains there until the Janmasthami, *i.e.*, the birthday of Krishna, when the maker of the image removes it, that the work of constructing the idol may commence. The materials for this purpose — bamboos, grass, and Ganges mud are carefully selected, and on an auspicious moment the holes are drilled in a piece of wood on which the images are to be fixed. When this is done, and the rough skeletons made, they are covered with a preparation of mud, cow-dung, and the husks of rice. The figures that cluster around Durgā are her two sons, Kartikeya and Ganesa; and Sarasvati, the bride of Brahmā, and

Lakshmi, the wife of Vishnu. There are also representations of Mahesha, the buffalo fiend, whom Durgā came to slay. When the figures are dry, at appointed times the painters come to paint and the decorators to adorn the image. Round these figures, on what is called a roof, but which is really a circle, divided into compartments, pictures of other deities are painted, or some mythological scenes represented. These vary considerably according to the taste of the gentleman in whose house and at whose expense the worship is carried on. The central figure, Durgā, has ten hands, in which are various weapons; for, though bearing a most mild and gentle expression, it is supposed to represent her when victorious over the great Asura, the enemy of gods and men.

This worship may be performed or not, according to the religious state of the householder. On the one hand, it is a sin of omission to neglect it, whilst to perform it will ensure great good to the worshipper. One Sāstra says: "Whoever from ignorance, vanity, or jealousy, or from any other cause, does not worship Devi (Durgā), the wrath of the goddess falls on him, and destroys all his wishes." Another declares that "the gratification of Bhavāni is the assurance of happiness for the whole year, is for the destruction of spirits, goblins, and ghosts, and for the sake of festivity." Another speaks still more strongly, as it declares that "the meritorious effects of gratifying Durgā, even for half a minute, cannot be described by Mahesh (Siva), the five-faced, in a hundred years." Where circumstances prevent a man from incurring the expense of setting up an image in his own house, it is no uncommon thing to worship her as represented by a picture or a jar of water, or to send their offerings to the temporary shrine that is set up at the house of a neighbour or relative. It is declared in one of the Purānas that the offerings of even slaves and outcasts are acceptable to the goddess at these festive seasons.

The first part of the ceremony is the Bodhāna, or the

awaking of the goddess, who is supposed to have been sleeping for the past two months, a part of which ceremony is the worshipping of a twig of the bēl-tree, which is especially dear to her. The texts differ as to when this ceremony should take place. When the time arrives for the commencement of the worship, the head of the family, after certain purifying ceremonies, declares his name and expresses his purpose to perform the Durgā Puja with proper rites. He then, in due form, appoints the officiating priests, who in his name and on his behalf perform the ceremonies. The priests then go through a long and tedious list of ceremonies, worshipping other deities as well as Durgā, and sanctifying by their mantras all the various implements, &c., that are used in the celebration. Part of this worship is called Dhyan, or meditation, in which the priest thinks of Durgā according to the representation that is there before him. The most interesting part of the ceremony is that in which the goddess is invited to visit the house, and dwell in the image that has been prepared for her. The priest, in order to obtain this blessing, after several other ceremonies have been performed, places his right hand on the breast of the image and says, "Om! welcome, Devi, to my house with thy eight Śaktas. Accept my worship done according to the Sāstras, O Dispenser of blessings; O Lotus-eyed, I perform this autumnal festival. Respond to me, O great goddess; . . . Annihilator of all trangressions in this unfordable ocean of the world. Save me, blessed goddess. I salute thee, beloved. O Sankāra (Siva), protect my life, my honour, my offspring, my wives, and my wealth. As thou art the only defender of all, O goddess, the most beloved in the world, enter and stay with this sacrifice as long as I am worshipping thee." First the right eye, then the left, then the eye on the forehead are touched by the priest, and after this the other parts of the body, and an appropriate mantra recited, by which means the ceremony of Prānpratishtha, or the giving of the life to the image, is performed. After this all the various vessels and articles used in the worship are sanctified by mantras.

For three mornings and three evenings the worship is continued. In some houses, though not in all, a kid, or three, or seven, are sacrified. In some cases a buffalo is added. The victim is sanctified by certain ceremonies, Ganges water is sprinkled on its head, a little vermilion is placed on its forehead, and its head, having been made fast in a strong frame, with one blow of the sacrificial knife is severed from the body. A little of the blood and a piece of flesh is then placed before the image.

On the afternoon of the fourth day the goddess is supposed to take leave of the image. Most elaborate dismissal ceremonies are gone through, and an invitation is given to her to return at the next annual festival. When this is over the image is taken down from the platform, and the women of the household and others walk round it, and throw rice, water, and betel leaves upon it. It is then carried to the riverside, and, accompanied by music, cast into the stream amidst the shouts of the spec tators.

This festival, in Bengal at any rate, is the most popular of all. It is a universal holiday, and at this season husbands and sons, who by their business may have been absent from their homes, endeavour to rejoin their families. It is not inaptly termed the Christmas of Bengal, in the sense that it is a time of universal rejoicing and merriment. In front of the image at this festival as at others already described, when the evening worship is concluded, there is the usual singing, dancing, and theatrical representation throughout the whole night. As these images are set up in the villages as well as in the towns, the poorer people are able to attend them. And when it is remembered that the amusements are perfectly free for all, it is not surprising that immense crowds are seen at these religious festivals. In the three nights of the Puja Calcutta is awake the whole night, and any one unacquainted with the cause, as the drums are beating all over the city, might fancy that the whole city was in arms. And although these nights are given up to merriment, the police have little to do except to keep the vehicles in motion, in order to prevent a block. Occasionally a few drunken men are seen, but this is a rare exception. As a rule, the immense crowds that are afoot are most peaceably inclined and well conducted as they walk from house to house to see the jātras and nauches.

The other festival of the month is the Lakshmi Puja, which takes place on the night of the full moon following the Durgā Puja. This is the goddess of prosperity, the wife of Vishnu. Where an image is not made, her representative is kept in every house, viz., a basket for measuring corn. On this occasion the basket, filled with rice, and decorated with flowers, is covered with a piece of cloth. Some people prefer to have an image made, and then the worship is performed by priests, as in the case of other deities. As Lakshmi is supposed during the night to pass over all who may be awake, it is usual for the people to sit up playing at cards, or amusing themselves in some way, so as to keep themselves awake. Here we see a custom not unlike one that prevails in many parts of England on New Year's Eve, where the people sit up in the belief that it is a proper thing to watch the old year out and the new year in.

7. *Kartik.*

Shyāmā Puja. This is the worship of Durgā under quite another aspect. In the dreadful war with the demons, Durgā, or Kāli, or Tāra, as she is called at this time, gained a great victory over Rakta Vija, the commander-in-chief of the enemy's forces, and was so elated by her feats of prowess that she began to dance so vehemently that she shook the world, and the gods were afraid that it would fall to pieces. In their distress they cried to her husband, Siva, for help. As he saw no other means of pacifying her, he fell down prostrate amongst the slain. Directing her gaze to the ground, she observed that she was dancing upon the body of her husband, and became at once calm with shame, and thrust out her large tongue. In the images which represent her at this festival, she is black, as her name, Kāli, implies, and her husband is lying down under her feet. Her tongue protrudes from her mouth, her four arms are extended —one hand grasping a sword, another the head of a giant, and the other two signalling to her hosts. As ear-rings, she has two dead bodies of her foes; her neck is adorned with a necklace of skulls, and her only garment, a zone, is made with the hands of her vanquished foes, whilst her hair falls down in long tresses to her waist. Intoxicated with the blood of her foes, her eyes flash with rage, her eyebrows are dyed with crimson, and blood flows down her breast. Her worship is in keeping with her character. It takes place on the night of the new moon, at midnight, when numbers of animals are sacrificed to her. The darkness of the night, the bleating of the victims, the flashing of the sacrificial knife, the shrieks of the ministering priests as they cry, "Jai, jai, Tāra," the flicker of the torches, the gestures of the intoxicated worshippers, make this one of the most terrible of all the festivals in India.

Two days after the Shyāmā, or Kāli Puja, it is customary for Hindu sisters to feed their brothers. In this festival they put a little paint on their foreheads, and as they are engaged in this work, they seek this blessing: "While I put this paint on your forehead, may the path to Yama's kingdom be planted with thorns." Yama (the God of the spirit world) is then worshipped with appropriate rites. After the religious part of the festival is over, the brothers are feasted with all kinds of delicacies. In the beginning of this month a special service is performed in honour of Yama by the unmarried girls of the family, the object of which is to secure from him a husband and sons, and exemption from punishment in the next world. This ceremony is performed in the following manner:—A small pit having been dug in front of the house, the four corners of it are sown with wheat or barley, and planted with branches of the plantain-tree. The young ladies then put on new clothes, sprinkle Ganges water on their heads, and, going to the pit, present garlands of flowers to Yama. A kourie shell is put into a vessel kept there on thirty successive mornings, and on the thirtieth day these shells are given to the person who dug the pit.

Jagaddhātri. In this month, too, Jagaddhātri (the mother of the world), another of Durgā's many forms, is worshipped. This festival is almost identical with that of Durgā, but with fewer ceremonies, and extending over one day only. On the day following, as in the case of the other festivals, the images are thrown into the river.

Kartikeya. Towards the close of the month Kartikeya, the god of war, is worshipped. He is the son of Siva and Parvati. His worship is performed one evening only, and as he is unmarried, but keeps a concubine, this worship is peculiarly attractive to the immoral women of the cities. Perhaps next to the festivals in honour of Krishna, there is more of licentiousness and revelry connected with Kartikeya's festival than with any other.

Rāsa Jātra. This festival is held to commemorate the sports of Krishna with the milkmaids of Vrindāvana. It continues for three nights. A high platform is erected near the temples of Krishna, to which the image is brought, and it remains there during the bright moonlight night whilst the amusements are continued. The deity is first worshipped with due solemnity, and then the fun begins. Singing of love-songs, jātras, dancing, alternate throughout the night, and at early dawn the idol is taken back to its temple, where it remains until the next evening. This is a most popular festival, and immense crowds of people come to this annual fair with all the attendant festivities and excesses.

8. *Agrahāyana.*

The festival of this month is what may appropriately be termed the feast of first-fruits. It is held at the season when the new rice is ripe. An offering of rice, milk, and fruits, is first made to the gods, then to the great progenitors of mankind, then to the cattle, then to the scavengers, *i.e.*, crows and jackals, and then the people partake of some themselves. And when it is remembered that Bengal is pre-eminently an agricultural country, there is something very beautiful in an offering of the first-fruits to the Deity in acknowledgment of the fact that it is He who is the giver of all their good. Often fireworks and gifts to the Brāhmans and spiritual guides close the ceremony.

9. *Poush.*

In the country districts a festival more social than religious is held, which is called Poushāli. During the day a number of men go round with baskets from house to house for offerings. When their work is completed the gifts are taken to the village green, where Brāhman cooks prepare the food so that all may freely partake of it. All who have given towards the feast are welcomed, and in friendly chat a few hours are spent together, after which the feasters return to their homes.

The other festival of this month is the Feast of Cakes. This festival continues for three days, during which Lakshmi and Manasā are worshipped, and in many places Sasthi is also included in the ceremony. Cakes made with rice, treacle, and milk are prepared, and men, women, and children partake of them. On the first day of the feast the furniture of the house is bandaged with straw, the idea being that by thus tying it, it will never be removed from the house.

10. *Māgh.*

Sarasvati Puja. This is the worship of Brahmā's wife, the goddess of learning, who is worshipped alike by the followers of Siva and of Vishnu. All who have the slightest smattering of learning feel bound to reverence her; and not her image only, but pens, ink, paper, books, &c., by which knowledge can be acquired and taught. The women have no share in this worship, though it is certainly strange that the patron of learning should be a woman.

11. *Phalgun.*

In this month the Dol Jātra or Holi festival, in honour of Krishna, is held. In speaking of the Jagannātha worship at Puri, we shall have to describe this. It is a festival common throughout North India, and where there are no temples of Krishna, the people go about in excited crowds throwing red powder upon passers-by, and singing indecent songs. It is almost impossible for a woman to walk through the streets without being insulted. It commemorates Krishna's voluptuous amusements. In this month Ghentu, the god of itch, is also worshipped, for whom a dunghill is regarded as the representative, or an old broken earthen pot daubed with lime and turmeric. The mistress of the house acts as priestess: when a few doggerel verses about the god have been recited the vessel is broken into bits. At this time Shitala, the goddess of smallpox, and Olâ Bibi, the goddess of cholera, are also worshipped.

12. *Chaitra.*

In this month the Charak Puja takes place. It is said that an ancient king, by reason of his great austerities, obtained an interview with Siva, in commemoration of which this festival is held. The peculiarity of the worship consists in the fact that the devotees of Siva belonging to the lower castes assume the profession and dress of Sanyasis for a week or ten days, and march about the streets soliciting alms from people. On the first day of the festival the *pro. tem.* Sanyasis throw themselves down from a bamboo platform about eight or ten feet high upon knives that are so arranged that they fall down under the weight of the body, though occasionally an accident happens. Processions of these men parade the streets to the great temple of Kāli, some with spears in their tongues, others with pans of burning incense, where they make their offerings and return. At this season, too, there is a sort of carnival. Processions are formed and *tableaux vivants* arranged on platforms, representing different trades and professions, are carried through the streets. In former years the gestures as well as the scenes represented were of the most obscene character, but of late years these objectionable features have been largely curtailed. On the second day of the Puja the swinging which has given its name to this festival takes place. In former years, a hook was inserted in the flesh of the men, to which a rope was fixed; this rope was tied to a bamboo, which was made to rise or fall from the ground, being attached to another bamboo that was fixed in the ground, lifting the victim a great height. At the present time either a bundle of clothes is swung as the representative of the men, or a rope is tied round the body in which the hook is hung. Trevelyan, in the Competition Wallah, gives the following most graphic description of this festival as it occurred in Calcutta, in a letter dated April 17, 1863:

"One morning, at the beginning of this month, as I lay between sleeping and waking near the open window, I began to be aware of a hideous din in an adjacent street. At first the sound of discordant music, and a confused multitude of voices impressed me with the vague idea that a battalion of volunteers were passing by in marching order headed by their band. This notion was, however, soon dispelled by my bearer, who informed me that this was the festival of Kāli (the bearer was wrong; it was Kāli's husband), the goddess of destruction, and that all the Hindu people had turned out to make holiday. I immediately sallied forth in the direction of the noise, and soon found myself amidst a dense crowd in the principal thoroughfare leading to the shrine of the deity. During a few minutes I could not believe my eyes, for I seemed to have been transported in a moment over more than twenty centuries to the Athens of Cratinus and Aristophanes. If it had not been for the colour of the faces around, I should have believed myself to be on the main road to Eleusis in the full tide of one of the Dionsyiac festivals. The spirit of the scene was the same, and at each step some well-known feature reminded one irresistibly that the Bacchic orgies spring from the mysterious fanaticism of the Far East. It was no unfounded tradition that pictured Dionysus returning from conquered India, leopards and tigers chained to his triumphal car, escorted from the Hyphasis to the Asopus by bands of votaries dancing in fantastic measure to the clang of cymbals. It was no chance resemblance this, between a Hindu rite of the middle of the nineteenth century and those wild revels that stream along many a Grecian basrelief and wind round many an ancient Italian vase; for every detail portrayed in these marvellous works of art was faithfully represented here. If one of the lifelike black figures in the Etruscan chamber of the British Museum could have walked down off the background of red pottery into the midst of the road leading to Kāli Ghāt, he would not have attracted the notice of the closest observer. Every half-minute poured by a troop of worshippers. First came boys stark naked and painted from head to foot in imitation of leopards and tigers, whilst others guided them with reins of thin cord. Then followed three or four strange classic figures, wearing the head-dress which is familiar to us from the existing representations of bacchanalian processions, dancing in an attitude which recalled, spontaneously and instantly, the associations of Smith's 'Dictionary of Antiquities.' The only circumstance which was not in common between 'Tolly Nullah' and the Cephisus was the censer of live charcoal which these men carried before them, supported by wires passed through the flesh under their armpits. Into this from time to time they threw a powder, which produced a sudden flash, and a most infernal smell. Behind them, his brows crowned profusely with foliage, was led in mimic bonds the chief personage of the company, who was supposed to be under the direct influence of the god. All around him, musicians were beating tomtoms and clashing tambourines, like the satellites of Evius on the day when he leapt from his car into the arms of the forsaken Ariadne; as he still leaps on the glowing canvas of Titian. All was headlong license and drunken frenzy. After struggling through the throng for a mile and a half of dusty street, I came to a narrow slum which descended to the Ghāt, or landing-place of Kāli, which lies on the nullah [stream] of the mythical hero Tolly [Col. Tolly was a gentleman who owned a large house and grounds on the banks of the stream, a historical person who resided there in the last century, and not a mythical personage], who perhaps was the Atys of this Oriental Cybele. From this lane, a passage of a yard or two in breadth opened on to a dirty court, in which stood the sanctuary whence Calcutta derives its name, which was an object of awe and reverence to the surrounding population for ages before the first ship, laden with Feringhi wares, was warped up the neighbouring river. It seemed impossible to pierce the mob of devotees, and penetrate to the holy place; but not even religious madness, not even the inspiration of bhang and toddy, could overcome the habitual respect paid to a white face and a pith helmet. A couple of policemen cleared a passage before me to within a few feet of the sacred image. It appeared to be a rude block ornamented with huge glass beads (it is really the head only of the goddess that is visible), but I dare say the Palladium which fell from heaven was not a very elaborate device, and yet it saved the reputation of a young Roman lady, and gave a synonym to an English jury. Before I reached home, what with the jostling and hubbub and stench, I was very glad to get back to the society of clean, fragrant Christians. As I grew every moment more tired and hot the exhibition seemed to savour less of the classical and more of the diabolical. At last I came to the ill-natured conclusion that Satan was at the bottom of the whole business, and not the golden-haired Dionysus."

This completes the list of the chief religious festivals as they are held throughout the year. It is a long list, and coming as they do at short intervals the interest of the people is kept up in religious matters. No special day of the week is sacred to the Hindus, as Friday with the Mussulmāns or

Sunday with ourselves; in the native shops and fields work goes on steadily from Monday to Monday. These festivals, however, give some relief. On these days little or no work is done; the religious part of the community and those seeking pleasure merely, when set free from work, find their satisfaction in these various festivals.

CHAPTER IV.

PILGRIMAGES.

BENARES.

The next form of Hindu worship, and scarcely less important than the preceding, is the visiting of particular shrines—the undertaking of journeys to see the temples, bow down before the images, and pay their offerings to the deities to whom these places are peculiarly sacred. Pilgrimage is the peculiar work of those who have given themselves up to a life of religion. One of the virtues of the highest class of Brāhmans, which gave them the privilege of Kulinism, was their pre-eminent devotion in wandering from shrine to shrine; in fact, in the ideal life of the Brāhman one quarter of his manhood should be spent in this work. And this is the life-work of millions who by virtue of it are regarded as the most holy of men, the saints of Hinduism. But the visiting of shrines is by no means peculiar to those classes who have adopted the religious life. It is the ambition, the earnest desire of many of the ordinary people, at least once in a lifetime, to visit one, if not more, of these sacred places. And certainly if one can judge of the earnestness of the people, and of their implicit faith in the teachings of their leaders, by their joy as they come in sight of these places, their intense sufferings on the way to them, which are borne with exemplary patience, or by the look of satisfaction with which they speak of having accomplished these journeys, they are very earnest, and their faith most marvellous. I have seen the people throw themselves on the ground and kiss the very dust as soon as they have caught sight of the holy city of Benares; I have seen them take the dust from the wheels of Jagannātha's car, and place it on their head with signs of the intensest pleasure. I have heard them shout with joy as they have come in sight of the meeting of the waters of the Ganges with the sea at Saugor Island; and there can be no doubt whatever that in the minds of many there is the most implicit faith that a visit to these places will ensure them invaluable blessings in this world and the next. A few years ago as one of these pilgrims was returning from Benares by train an accident happened, and he was asked to give evidence against the railway official who caused it; but the man refused to do this, and was apparently disappointed that through the attentions of the surgeon he was restored to health; for he would have preferred to die under such circumstances rather than return to his ordinary avocations, and by a sinful life lessen the amount of merit that had been obtained by a visit to the holy city. Many by the exercise of the greatest self-denial save a little year by year for twenty or twenty-five years from their scant earnings, and are able in this manner to provide for the expenses of the journey and for the offerings they have to make at the shrines. Multitudes of poor women, when their husbands are sick, vow to go to some of these places, and though for years they cannot obtain the necessary funds, as soon as they can they start on these journeys. And when it is remembered that it is taught, *e.g.*, that once bathing in the sea at Saugor Island will wash away all past, present, and future sins, it cannot afford much surprise that they should wish to go.

Formerly the journey to these places was far more difficult and tedious than at present. Railways and steamers carry their hundreds of thousands of visitors with comparative safety and comfort. But *all* will not avail themselves of these "aids to devotion." Some persistently walk as far as it is possible, and then crowd into unseaworthy boats, so that scarcely a year passes without some of these capsizing in the wide creek which has to be crossed in order to reach the scene of the festival at Saugor. The road to Jagannātha's festival at Puri is literally strewed yearly by the corpses of those who die by the road-side on their journeys to and fro, and by over-crowding when they arrive there. Others again, in fulfilment of vows or in their desire to please the deity by their sufferings, travel for miles by measuring their length upon the ground. They lie down with their faces to the ground, and stretch their hands beyond their heads; and having marked the ground with their fingers, place their toes there and again stretch themselves upon the ground. In this manner they continue for days together, until they become completely exhausted. When a poor pilgrim starts for some of these places at a great distance from his home, it is with the expectation that he will never return. Often the death of these poor people is accelerated by the extortions of the priests extracting all their money from them for offerings, and leaving them little or nothing for the expenses of the homeward journey.

And what is the life they lead at these places? Benares, though called holy and sacred, is one of the most wicked cities in India. At Ganga Saugar quite a colony of prostitutes go there to ply their infamous traffic. In direct connection with the temples in some places, or living in close proximity to them in others, are prostitutes who regularly pay a portion of their earnings to the shrines which attract the worshippers. The pilgrims who go for religious purposes merely bathe, make offerings at the shrines, walk round the temples, suffer many inconveniences for want of proper accommodation and wholesome food; but worship in the true sense of the word there is none. Many of them know little more than the names of the many deities whose shrines they visit; nor would the contemplation of the lives of most of these deities, were the people familiar with them, conduce to make them holier in heart or purer in life. It is absolutely true that in the majority of cases the more closely a man follows the example of his gods, the more impure in heart and life will he become.

I shall now mention some of the more celebrated places of pilgrimage, and give a brief account of the particular shrines the pilgrims visit. One means of attracting visitors to these shrines is for touters to go from town to town singing their praises and extolling their virtues. I once had the opportunity of seeing the origin of one of these that may in the course of years become famous. One of the keepers of the shrine, a little less astute than the others, let me into the secrets of the place. It appears that some one professed to have seen a spirit hovering over a small and dirty tank, who declared that the tank had healing virtues. A company of some thirty men soon sought to take advantage of this. A mud temple was erected, and one half of the company travelled from town to town telling the people the benefits that would accrue from a visit, whilst the others remained to attend to the temple. The day I visited the place, some three hundred or more were gathered there; some blind, some dumb, some crippled, had made their way to this place of healing; and most wonderful stories were told of some who had been healed. So incomplete were the arrangements that an image had not been placed there; a dirty piece of rag covered a heap of bricks, the pilgrims imagining that an idol was there, though they could not see it. Another place, Tarkeswar, a Siva temple in Bengal, is visited twice a year, on festival days, by 60,000 to 70,000 people. In villages I have heard most wonderful stories of the blind receiving sight and the sick being healed by simply visiting this place. It is by means of the travelling members of the company that the excitement is kept up and the attention of the Hindus directed towards these shrines. When I ventured to express a doubt as to the efficacy of a visit to such places as a means of curing bodily diseases, the narrators simply stared at me in blank astonishment that I should for a moment question the power of the idol to heal. Faith-healing is not by any means confined to the people of England.

It is not, however, as a means of getting relief from sickness that the pilgrims chiefly visit the shrines. Sometimes it is in fulfilment of vows, because they believe that the deity has blessed them in some hour of trouble, and who will, therefore, be pleased with this act of homage; often it is to obtain the greatest of all boons, a son; but in the great majority of cases it is to obtain *merit*, an entry to be written on the credit side of their account with the gods as a set-off against the sins (debts) they have committed. As a pilgrimage is a work of supererogation, it is believed that it will counterbalance many sins. Many of these shrines have little stones or other things hung on trees near, which have been placed there as witnesses of vows; these will be redeemed by more substantial gifts when the boon asked for is granted.

*Benares.**

Of all the shrines of India, Benares is the most sacred. It is peculiarly the city of Siva, the great god of the Hindus. Being a place peculiarly dear to him, it is the earnest wish of his worshippers if possible to die within its sacred precincts; but if that be impracticable, at least once in a lifetime to visit it. Hindus who can afford it, and especially Brāhmans when growing old, give up their position in their family and move there to end their days, in the assurance that by this means they will gain easy entrance into heaven. The legend † by which this excessive sanctity of Benares is taught is as follows. On one occasion Brahmā and Siva quarrelled respecting their respective positions. As Brahmā declared that he was supreme, Siva cut off Brahmā's fifth head, and thus was guilty of the most heinous crime of

* See *Calcutta Review*, vol. xl. p. 253.

† "Hindu Mythology," p. 228.

injuring a Brāhman, Brahmā being the progenitor of the Brāhmans. After giving vent to his anger, Siva found himself in a most miserable plight; the dissevered head of his rival adhered to his hand as the blood of his slaughtered guest adhered to the hand of Macbeth. In order to get free from this dreadful sign of his revengeful spirit, Siva wandered from shrine to shrine, and practised the most arduous penances; but all was vain until he reached the sacred city of Benares. There he lost his burden; and following his example, his worshippers, weighed down with the burden of sin, go from shrine to shrine; but in Benares, of all other places, find peace of conscience and the assurance of salvation. As Siva found relief in this city that no other place could give, it is natural that his followers should wish to dwell in the place that was so beneficial to their deity, and which they believe is especially dear to him.

The sanctity of this holy shrine is not bounded by the city proper, but extends from the holy river Ganges to a road called the Panch-Kosi road, *i.e.*, a road that is not more than ten miles distant from the banks of the river. This road starts from the river bank at the south part of the city, and winds through the country until it rejoins the river. It is about fifty miles long, and contains hundreds of temples of different deities, who are supposed to act as a police force under orders of Bisheshwar, the divine king, in keeping the peace of the city. The whole of the land enclosed between this road and the stream is most sacred; and it is one of the meritorious acts of the thousands of pilgrims to Benares to traverse this sacred path. The regular inhabitants of the city are taught that at least once a year they ought to walk along it, to obtain deliverance from the sins they may have committed even in the holy city. The entire area thus enclosed is regarded as Benares, and whoever dies within it, whether Hindu, Mussulmān, or Christian, whether pure in heart and life or outcast and guilty even of murder, is sure of obtaining the blessedness of heaven. In order to secure the benefits promised to those making this journey, the pilgrims must bathe before starting and at the close of each day's journey; must walk barefooted, only very young children and sick people are allowed to be carried by others. They must not give food or water to their friends, nor take these things from others, but each must make provision for his own wants; nor must they indulge in bad language or quarrel with others, or the merit of the journey is lost. There are six regular longer or shorter stages where the pilgrim stays for the rest of the day; and on reaching the Mankarnika Ghāt whence he started, he must bathe, give his gifts to the attendant priests, and pay a visit to Sakhi-binaik, the witness *Ganesa*, where his act of penance is recorded, otherwise his labour will be lost. This fifty-mile walk is generally the final act of a successful pilgrimage to Benares.

There is no doubt that Benares is one of the most ancient cities of India; but *when* it was founded cannot now be ascertained with anything like certainty. "By some subtle, mysterious charm this city has linked itself with the religious sympathies of the Hindus through every century of its existence. For the sanctity of its inhabitants, of its temples and tombs, of its wells and streams, of the very soil that is trodden, of the air that is breathed, and of everything in and around it, Benares has been famed for thousands of years. The poor deluded sensualist, whose life has been passed in abominable practices, or the covetous usurer who has made himself rich by a long course of hard-fisted extortion, or the fanatical devotee, fool, and murderer, more simple than a babe, yet guilty of the foulest crimes, still comes, as of old, from the remotest corners of India as the sands of time are slowly ebbing away; and fearful lest the golden thread should be snapped before his long journey is ended, he makes desperate efforts to hold on his course, until, arriving at the sacred city and touching its hallowed soil, his anxious spirit becomes suddenly calm, a strange sense of relief comes over him, and he is at once cheered and comforted with the treacherous lie, that his sins are forgiven him and his soul is saved."

The form of religion in Benares is Purānic, which most probably began to exert its influence over the people as Buddhism lost its authority. There is no doubt that Vedantism more or less colours the philosophical creed of the more thoughtful and better educated, but the worship of the masses is pure and simple idolatry in its lowest and grossest forms—the worship of ugly idols, monsters, the lingam and other indecent figures. There is no city in India where the reverence paid to idols is more absolute and complete than in Benares; and though better things might be expected of the pundits and thinking men, they join in this as well as the more ignorant and superstitious. It is interesting to know that there have been more temples built and more money spent in idolatrous worship since the country came under British rule than during the same number of years when the Mussulmāns were masters. Owing to the cruel oppression of their masters the people were poor; now, as their life and property are secure, many have, under the belief that it will add to their bliss in heaven, built temples in the holy city, or lavished gifts upon those who minister to those already existing. There is one noticeable fact that there is no solidarity in Hinduism. A temple of costly material and of beautiful workmanship will be allowed to go to ruin whilst a new one is being erected by its side. The building of the one now passing away has done its work, secured the blessings of the donor; the building of the new one will in its turn benefit its builder. No one would think of giving money to restore the structure that another hand raised. To an onlooker it appears as if Hinduism were as vigorous as ever, *i.e.*, judging by the number of temples that are being built in the strongholds of that religion. But, as hinted above, these people having more money in the present day, the more superstitious are better able to gratify their religious cravings.

Some years ago the temples of Benares were counted by order of one of the magistrates, and it was found that in the city proper exclusive of the suburbs there were one thousand Hindu temples: this number has since been increased, and did not include the niches in the walls of the houses and ghāts, in which images of some of the many deities are to be found. Although most of the temples are of modern date, yet the sites of many shrines remain, where for many ages there has been a constant stream of worshippers. The pundits in Benares say that Ganesa is worshipped in 56 places, Yogani in 64, Durgā in 9, Bhairava in 8, Siva in 11, Vishnu in 1, the Sun in 12, all of which shrines date from the mythical period when Devodās, the famous Rāja of Benares, was prevailed upon to allow the gods to return to their ancient home from which he had expelled them. There are vastly more temples than this now where the people present their offerings to the gods. Owing to the fact that they profess to believe that all these deities differing in character and appearance, are but varied representatives of the *One*, they have a strange fancy for accumulating many idols in one spot. Not content with placing one deity in a temple, they make niches in the walls in which images of others are placed, or arrange them in rows in the temple enclosure. In some places there are twenty, fifty, or even a hundred of these gods congregated together; and sometimes it happens that these subordinate deities, so far as size and position indicate their importance, are equal to their chief, and they receive as much attention from the worshippers as the one in whose special honour the temple was erected.

The temple that is considered the most important in the whole city, and that to which the pilgrims hasten on their arrival there is that of Bisheshwar, *i.e.*, God of the world, a name of Siva. He is regarded as the king of all the gods in Benares itself and in the whole of the sacred territory enclosed by the Panch-kosi road mentioned before. His Kōtwal or magistrate is Bhaironāth, and the gods along the sacred path are his watchmen. The image of Bisheshwar is the Linga, similar to that which is found in all Saiva temples. All day long crowds of people of all classes pass in front of this image with their offerings of sugar, rice, ghi, grain, flowers, money, &c., which are taken by the ministering priests as their own. Over the narrow gateway leading to the shrine is an image of Ganesa on which the pilgrims sprinkle a few drops of water they have brought from the river as they pass. A bell is hung in front of the image, which is kept sounding all day long, by which the attention of the deity is supposed to be called to a worshipper as he goes to pay his respects. Sometimes the appearance of the worshipper as he approaches the image is distressing and solemn. His soul seems to be overawed, but with what sentiments cannot well be affirmed. Fear certainly seems to be the prevailing emotion; nor is this to be wondered at when the stories about this dreadful god are remembered, and the worshipper believes him to be really present in that stone which he is approaching. As soon as the image is passed and the temple precincts are left, the fear at once passes away. It seems they have a dread lest by some inadvertence they should excite the anger of this most irascible deity. Outside of the enclosure on the north side, in what is called the "Court of Mahādeva," are a number of the stone emblems of Siva and his consort: possibly these are the images that were left when some of the old temples were destroyed by the Mussulmāns.

Near the temple just described is the Gyan Kup or well of knowledge. Tradition says that once the rains were withheld for twelve years from Benares. The people being in great distress, a Rishi pierced the earth with Siva's trident, when there issued a copious stream of water. Siva hearing of this promised to reside in that well for ever after. The worshippers throw in water, flowers, &c., as sacrifice to the god inhabiting it. The stench arising from this is one peculiar to this sacred city, and one that is not readily forgotten.

The next chief attraction is a temple to Annapurna, a form of Durgā. Under the orders from Bishēshwar it is her duty to feed the inhabitants of the city. The story is that when Benares was first inhabited Annapurna found the work of feeding so many people rather difficult. Gangā came to her relief and promised that if she would give a handful of grain to every person, she would supply them with a (lotah) vessel of water. In honour of this goddess hundreds, perhaps thousands, of poor people are daily fed by grain, a handful being given to as many beggars as the donor can afford to supply. Near this temple there is always an ample supply of beggars waiting to receive the gifts of the pious.

Near the temple of Annapurna is the temple of Sakhibināik, the witness-bearing Bināik; a deity who keeps a record of the pilgrims' names who visit the holy city and march along the road which encircles it. It is generally visited by the pilgrims as they are about to return to their own homes.

About a mile to the north of the temple of Bisheshwar is that of Bhaironāth, the magistrate (Kōtwal) of Benares. It is his work to keep the peace of the city, and to prevent the entrance of evil spirits. It is through his help that the Hindus who go to Benares to end their days there obtain salvation. He is represented in this temple by a stone staff or cudgel. His vāhan or vehicle was a dog, a representative of which is placed near the image. It will be remembered that whilst many pilgrims visit Benares with the expectation of returning to their homes, many go there to die. Hindus of means whose homes are in other parts of India have a house in Benares, and whenever attacked by sickness, or old age comes on, they go there in the hope that death there is only an entrance into a higher and better life than the present.

The Mankarnika well is one of the greatest attractions of Benares, and is amongst the first places visited by the pilgrims. Its filthy water is regarded as a healing balm that will wash away all sins and make the human soul pure. Murder and all great crimes are said to be washed away by simply bathing in its foul water. The story which gives it this great attraction is as follows. Vishnu who dug this well with his discus, filled it with perspiration from his body, and called it the Chakrapushkarani, or discus-produced tank. On the north side of the tank this deity was engaged in his religious exercises when Siva arriving saw in the water of the well the glory of a hundred million suns, and was so delighted that he promised to give Vishnu any boon he might like to ask. Vishnu asked that Siva would always remain with him: on hearing such a request Mahādeva was delighted, and in the excess of pleasure his body shook so that an ear-ring called mankarnik fell from his ear into the well. From this circumstance Siva gave the well the name of Mankarnik, and endowed it with two properties—viz., the power of giving mukti or salvation to his worshippers; and secondly, the power of granting success in every good work: and commanded that it should be the chief and most efficacious of pilgrimages. A flight of stone steps leads down to the water, and an image of Vishnu is on the north side of the stairs; there are also sixteen small altars where offerings to ancestors are made. The water is only two or three feet deep and abominably foul, yet the people bathe in it in the hope of gaining the advantages promised to those who visit it.

Amongst the other many temples is one to Vridhakāli, the lengthener of time, and who, pleased with the devotion of an old man who went to Benares to die, not only restored him to health, but renewed his youth, in gratitude for which one of the grandest old temples of the city was built, in which is a representation of the sun and the planets; Kāli and Hanumān are represented too. Daksheswar temple seems to have been erected to keep in memory the story of Siva's anger at the slight his father-in-law Daksha showed by not inviting him to the great sacrifice that he made. Siva in his anger is said to have sent his awful emissaries, who cut off Daksha's head, which was replaced by that of a goat, because his own could not be found. Daksha wandered to Benares as a penance for his sin; Mahādeva meeting him there forgave him, where Daksha as a mark of his gratitude is said to have erected this temple.

CHAPTER V.

PILGRIMAGES (*continued*).

KĀLI GHAT—GANGA SĀGAR—GAYA.

Kāli Ghāt.

KĀLI GHĀT is the name of a temple situated near Calcutta, a corrupted or anglicised form of which is seen in the name Calcutta. The temple is said to have a supernatural origin. When, owing to her anger at the slight shown to her husband by her father neglecting to invite him to his great sacrifice, Parvati destroyed herself, Siva was inconsolable at her loss, and throwing her corpse over his shoulder, wandered through the earth causing the greatest consternation and trouble. Vishnu appealed to by mankind in their distress, let his wondor-working discus fly through the air, by which Parvati's body was cut into fifty parts, and wherever any part touched the ground a temple rose. It is said that at Kāli Ghāt the second toe of her left foot is preserved. It is interesting to note that excepting in the case of Krishna's bones being preserved in the image of Jagannātha at Puri, and the parts of Parvati being preserved in these temples, there is no regard for relics shown by the Hindus.

To this temple at Kāli Ghāt pilgrims come every day in the year, but on the days of any festival connected with the worship of Siva, *e.g.*, the Charak Puja, and on the days when Durgā in any of his forms is worshipped, immense crowds gather there. The great purpose of pilgrims in visiting Kāli's temple is not simply to walk round the building, and try to catch a glimpse of her black face as they pass in front of the image, but to sacrifice a kid, sheep, or buffalo. Parents desirous of sons, families in any great sorrow vow to Kāli that if a son be given, or the trouble that oppresses be removed, a kid will be sacrificed to her, and it is in a large number of cases in the fulfilment of these vows that they come. There is no promise of relief from sin, or of entrance into heaven, such as attract to the shrines at Benares; it is rather as the giver of good in this present life, and as the deliverer from pressing evils, that Kāli's temple is sought.

The image of Kāli is most hideous. She is black, as her name (The Black One) implies, and came, as did Durgā, to destroy the demons who were afflicting mankind. When her work was over as she was dancing with joy, there was fear of the earth falling to pieces, her husband threw himself down on the ground amongst the corpses. Seeing him under her feet she thrust out her tongue to express her shame, and in this posture her image is formed. At Kāli Ghāt her large golden tongue is almost the only part that is clearly visible, as the offerings that are thrown over the image make it dirty, whilst the place is exceedingly dark.

This temple is a source of considerable profit to the proprietors, as not only do the pilgrims make their offerings, but a fee of about sixpence is taken for every kid that is sacrificed there; and on some days the victims are numbered by hundreds, if not by thousands. The Haldar family is now divided into a number of branches, each of which receives the offerings for a week or ten days; but on the great festival days all the branches have their representatives present, and the receipts are divided amongst them.

The temple or shrine is not much larger, though it is considerably more lofty than the ordinary Hindu temple. In front of it is a sort of covered platform upon which the Brāhmans sit to read the Sāstras, and on which the spectators stand to witness the sacrifices. The sight of the courtyard around the place of sacrifice is most repulsive, whilst the smell is most sickening. I certainly was surprised when first I saw this place at the time of sacrifice. I looked in vain for any, the slightest, sign of reverence as the people were offering their victims to the deity. On busy days there is a noisy, bustling crowd, each one trying to get his gift first attended to. The people bring their victims, pay the fee, and the priest then puts a little vermilion on its head. When their turn comes the executioner takes the animal, fixes its head in the frame, and then beheads it. A little of the blood is placed in front of the idol, and the pilgrim takes away the headless body. Throughout the whole ceremony, there seems to me nothing expressive of sin or the desire for purity; nor is there in the ceremony itself anything at all calculated to impress the people with the idea of devotion; nothing calculated to make or keep them pure. The whole ceremony from beginning to end seems utterly unfitted, as far as one can see, in any way to benefit the worshippers.

Ganga Sāgar.

This is one of the great bathing festivals, and though it is considered a good thing to bathe in any part of the Ganges, the most sacred part is at the mouth of the river where its waters mingle with those of the sea. It is held on the southern shore of Saugor Island. Ganga Sāgar simply means the River-Ocean; and as the island of Saugor faces the sea and the waters of the river flows on either side of it, the water there is really partly sea and partly river water. The people believing that by bathing here salvation from sin is certain, they come from places hundreds of miles distant to attend the great festival which is held annually in the month of January.

In the Rāmāyana * a story is found which explains why the waters of the Ganges is so efficacious here that people

* "Hindu Mythology," p. 383.

come from all parts of India once in a lifetime at least to wash away their sins. There is a fulness in the promise to those who bathe in its flowing waters; it is that all sin—past, present, and future—is by that act at once removed. And as in the early days of the Christian Church the converts delayed their baptism until late in life lest after receiving the rite they should fall into mortal sin and have no resource by which they could be freed; so in many cases it is the aged that attend the festival at Ganga Sāgar, that there may be the less fear of their falling into sin. For few a second visit would be practicable, the trouble and expense connected with a visit being so great.

The story from the Rāmāyana is as follows:—A king named Sāgar (it is from him that the island takes its name), being childless, prayed repeatedly to the gods for a son. At last Siva, pleased with his devotion, gave him 60,000. After a time this king wished to obtain the position of Indra, or king over the gods. This could only be obtained by the performance of the Asvamedh, or sacrifice of a hundred horses. All preparation was made for this important ceremony, and had proceeded satisfactorily until ninety-nine had been offered. The hundredth horse, as was customary, the night before it was to be sacrificed was set at liberty to wander where it wished. On the following morning search was made for it in vain. The reigning Indra had stolen it in fear that if Sāgar's sacrifice were properly offered he would have to resign his throne. Great consternation was manifest as the missing horse could not be found. The sons of the king searched everywhere, but their efforts were for a long time fruitless. At last they commenced digging, and working away until they came to the middle of the earth, they found the horse tied to a tree beside a saint named Kapila, who is said to have been an incarnation of Vishnu. Angry at what they considered an act of theft, they abused this saint; and he in his turn becoming angry, cursed them, and they became a heap of ashes. Only *one* son who had remained with his father was spared. The king, in great sorrow at his loss, is told that only by one means could his sons be restored to him, and that was by inducing Ganga (the River Ganges) to come down from her abode in heaven, which was in the Himalayah mountains. Sāgar was thinking for 30,000 years how he could manage this; but seeing no way, he resigned his kingdom to his son, and went to heaven. But it was not until his great-grandson, Bhagiratha, had by a life of most severe penance obtained a boon from the gods that she could be persuaded to come. When at last she came, she was in a great rage at being disturbed; but her husband Siva, catching her in his hair, quieted her, and at length she reached this heap of ashes, and no sooner touched them than the princes all sprang up to life again, and were immediately carried in golden chariots to Indra's heaven. And because it is said that it was at this place she manifested this great power the people visit it to bathe. As here she brought to life Sāgar's sons, and gained admission for them to heaven, the people say, here, more than elsewhere, is she able to wash away sin.

At the festival held in January it is estimated that not less than 100,000 are present. During the greater part of the year the place where it is held is quite uninhabited, in fact, it is under water, as the waters of the Bay of Bengal are carried over it by the south-west winds. But a week or two before the bathing day shopkeepers and others come, and then the pilgrims crowd in with every tide. On reaching the island they generally make temporary dwelling-places for themselves on shore, as they have had a good deal of discomfort to endure on board the boats by which they have come. As a rule, they simply make enclosures with strips of calico, having no covering overhead.

Of course the great object in coming is to bathe, and it is a most interesting sight to see thousands of people rushing into the sea in the assurance that this will wash away their sins. That this is the firm conviction of multitudes there can be no doubt. For this journey many have been saving a little out of their scanty earnings for twenty years or more. For this they have been travelling for days and weeks, exposed to all kinds of danger and discomfort; and from the lips of many I have heard the assurance that they could now die in peace, because they had washed in holy Ganga's stream. As soon as it is light these crowds of pilgrims plunge into the flood with shouts of exultation; they are gratifying the desire of many long years, and doing what by many of them is regarded as the most holy act of religion.

Another important work for the pilgrim is the worship of the many deities that are there represented by their idols, and whose praises are extolled by their priests. Along the sides of the main thoroughfares images are set up with their priests sitting by to receive the gifts of the pious. And I have watched hundreds of the pilgrims going up one side and down the other, giving something to the guardians of every idol, evidently fearful lest inadvertently omitting one this neglected deity, being angry, should bring down all kinds of evil upon them. It is the extortion of these priests that greatly adds to the expense of a visit to such a place, because they each declare that the neglect of the particular deity in whom they are personally interested will bring down his curse. In addition to the deities there are hundreds of Sanyasis (saints), whom it is accounted an honour and a work of merit to feed; and these idle parasites are fed by the poor people, who in this way lavish their hard-earned money upon those who are able, but not willing, to work for their living.

The most important object of worship at this festival is an image of Kapila, the saint near whom Sāgar's horse was found, and who in his anger burnt up the sons of the king. This is a shapeless piece of stone daubed over every year with a fresh coat of red paint. During the year the image is kept carefully packed away in Calcutta, but a week or two before the festival it is entrusted to a number of priests, who agree to take charge of it during the festival on condition that they receive a percentage on the gifts of the pilgrims. This image is set up in a temporary temple, as by the encroachments of the sea the old brick temple has been destroyed. A platform of sand about four feet high is first raised; a hut is then erected on the platform, and in this the image is set up for worship. A bamboo railing is placed in front of it, and a crowd of people from daylight until dark, on the three days of the festival, is constantly hurrying past it. All give something. And when asked why they do so, the answer is: "If Kapila Muni could destroy Sāgar's sons, how mighty he must be! And if we please him with our gifts he will pray to the gods for us, and we shall be blessed through his intercession." Of course where the belief prevails that he was an incarnation of Vishnu, it is easy enough to see why the people should be ready to make their offerings to him. I have watched the poor people as they have been hurried past this block of stone giving of their poverty, aye, often all they had, and felt that these were amongst the most religious people I had ever seen. Their faith in the power of the gods to curse and to bless is almost unlimited; and it appeared to me that after bathing in the sea and, as they believed, washing away their guilt by that act, they now came with glad hearts to make a thank-offering for the great boon they had received.

Stories such as the following taken from the Rāmāyana tend to excite and sustain the faith of the people in this method of purification from sin, and to lead them to make pilgrimages to the banks of this sacred stream. A pre-eminently wicked Brāhman, who from youth had been associated with a harlot, was walking in a wood when a tiger seized him, ate his flesh and drank his blood. A crow snatching up a bone was flying with it over the Ganges, when a vulture attacked him, and in the fight the bone fell into the water. Immediately the bone touched the stream the emissaries of Vishnu seized the soul of the departed as it was being carried off to Yama. In their rage and despair these men go into the presence of their king and narrate the story of their loss. Yama in his turn, being greatly excited, immediately rushed off to Vishnu with the story of his supposed wrongs. Vishnu listens attentively to all he has to say, and then declared that Ganga had gone down to earth with the express purpose of taking away the sin of man; that her power was such that even he, the Lord of all, could not properly estimate it, and further declared that as far as the waves of the Ganges should roll Vishnu would extend his protecting arm to those whose bones should fall into her stream, and that as soon as the bones touched the water the soul of the man should immediately ascend to heaven; and that the drinking of a draught of water from this river will fully atone for all the sins of a lifetime.

The following invocation to Ganga is found in a child's reading book, and has doubtless influenced many in their religious practices:

"Oh ancient Purifier of the fallen, the drinking vessel of Brahmā was thine abode. At his side didst thou dwell, and sanctify the city of the gods. Seeing the sad state of mortals, to deliver them from fear of the future, thou, goddess of the gods, camest upon earth. . . . The most wicked sinner upon touching thy waters goes to heaven in his body. . . . The low Sudra or Sanyasi on dying goes to heaven if he has bathed there when the sun enters Capricorn. By pronouncing thy name he obtains admittance to the house of Vishnu; he is spared the sight of Yama's city. When life has fled from the corpse, the father and mother will drag it to the place of cremation, and whilst they forsake it, thou foldest it in thy bosom. The corpse fed upon by crows and jackals floats till it reaches thy banks where hundreds of heavenly courtezans with fans in their hands come to attend upon it. . . . The most wicked sinner if he but touch thy waters enjoys thy favour in the last extremity."

Carrying Water from the Ganges.—Another very common form of pilgrimage to the Ganges—if possible to Hurdwar where its waters rush from the hills, but if that be too far distant then to some nearer spot—is to bring a vessel of water thence to bathe the image of some particular deity whose aid has been sought in time of sickness or trouble, and to whom this offering of sacred water was promised if a favourable issue resulted. During the cold weather months it is a most common thing to see numbers of people travelling with an earthen vessel of this water most carefully preserved. In some cases a vow is made that the person interested will himself fetch this water and carry it to the temple of the god to whom it has been promised, and this may necessitate a journey of a thousand miles. Sometimes a servant will be sent on this errand, or it may be purchased from men who earn their living by carrying it to places remote from the river. In times of trouble large sums of money are often paid for it by those who believe that this is the most acceptable offering they can make. The water taken from Hurdwar is put in bottles which bear the seal of the officiating priests of the temple there. When this sacred water is poured over or before an image of Vishnu, or any of his incarnations, it is carefully caught and drunk by his worshippers, as it is supposed to have healing and purifying virtues; but owing to a curse of his wife's, that which is poured over Siva's image is not allowed to touch human lips. In most of these forms of worship the idea of David when King Araunah wished to *give* him cattle for a sacrifice and wood to burn is seen. He says, "Nay, but I will surely buy them from thee at a price. Shall I give to Jehovah that which costs me nothing." It is generally when some loved member of the family has recovered from sickness, or a law-suit has been decided in favour of the offerer that, in gratitude for what he believes the particular deity to whom the offering is made has done for him, these lengthy and wearisome journeys are made;

though the offering is intrinsically of little value, it is believed to be most acceptable to many of the deities.

*Gayā.**

This well-known place of pilgrimage is resorted to for the benefit not so much of the living as of the dead; for the Srādha, or funeral ceremonies for the departed, is considered to be of far greater benefit if performed here than elsewhere. Originally Gayā was the headquarters of the Buddhists, as it was there that Buddha lived during his hermit-life and attained to the highest state of purity. Here for centuries Buddhists flocked from all parts of India and the farther East, though now as a Buddhist shrine it is almost deserted. In fact, the shrine that the Buddhists regarded as perhaps the most sacred spot on the face of the earth has been under the charge of a Saiva Mahant and disciples, who enjoy the benefit of the gifts of the people who visit the sacred tree near the temple. His income from lands and offerings is reckoned at eighty thousand rupees per year; out of which he was to feed on an average about one hundred pilgrims and ascetics daily. The town in which this shrine is found is called Buddha Gayā, to distinguish it from Brahma Gayā, or simply Gayā, which is five miles distant, where the Hindus now resort. The town of Gayā has existed for 2,400 years; it was there that Buddha made his home, and it was there that he first conceived the idea of devoting himself to a life of meditation which was to secure to mankind the highest blessing. The people here were the first to believe in him and receive his doctrines, and it became for a time the headquarters of his faith. But at the beginning of the fifth century it had lost its Buddhist character and had relapsed into Hinduism. In the Gayā Māhātmya of the Vāyu Purāna is a legend to account for this change, and for the sacred character it possesses in the

* "Buddha Gayā," by Dr. Ragendra Lall Mittra.

minds of the Hindus of the present day. I give this in an abbreviated form :—

Brahmā created all things by the order of Vishnu, who from his fierce nature produced the Asuras, and from his humane nature the noble-minded Devas. Among the Asuras was one Gayā, who was endowed with great strength and vigour. This great giant measured 576 miles in height, and was 268 miles in girth, and was a most devout worshipper of Vishnu. With his breath suppressed he practised great austerities for many thousands of years until the gods became afraid, and in their distress repaired to Brahmā for aid. Brahmā, hearing their request, led them to Siva, and he in his turn led them to Hari (Vishnu), who was sleeping on the milky ocean, saying, "He will devise some means of relief." Arriving in his presence they adored him in a hymn, and being gratified, he revealed himself to them, and asking what was their need, told them to proceed to the Asura Gayā, and that he himself would accompany them.

Arriving in his presence the three deities asked him why he persevered in his austerities and assured him that they were prepared to grant him any boon he might ask. The request was this: "Make my body purer than that of Brahmā, Vishnu, Siva; purer than the Devas or Brahmans, purer than all sacrifices, and sacred pools and high mountains, purer even than the purest of the gods." "Be it so," said the gods, and repaired to heaven. The result of which blessing was that mortals who believed or touched the demon at once ascended to the heaven of Brahmā; the world became empty, and Hades, Yama's dominion, was deprived of inhabitants.

When Yama, Indra, and the other deities thus became deprived of their subjects, they repaired to Brahmā and resolved to resign their positions, as, having no subjects to govern, there was nothing for them to do. Led by Brahmā, they again repaired to Vishnu, and complained that "by the sight of the demon whom you have blessed all mortals are being translated to heavén, and the three regions (earth, sky, and hell) have become empty." Under the advice of Vishnu, the gods then repaired to Gayā, to ask him to give up his body to them that they might offer a sacrifice upon it, by which means he assured them they would escape from their present difficulties. The demon was delighted at the honour which was paid to him, and, addressing Brahmā and the gods, said: "Blesssed is my life this day, blessed is my penance; verily I have attained all my objects since Brahmā has become my guest. Say why you have come, and I will at once execute the task for you." Brahmā then told the Asura that of all holy pools that he had seen, there was none to compare with the demon's body as a place of sacrifice, and asked him to grant it for this purpose. Gayā replied: "Blessed am I since you have asked for my body; my paternal ancestors will be sanctified shouldest thou perform a sacrifice on my body. By you it was created, and it is well that it should be of use to you: it will then be of use to all."

Having thus spoken, the demon fell prostrate on the ground, leaning towards the south-west. Brahmā produced from his mind the officiating priests (Ritvijas), and collected the necessary articles, and offered the sacrifice. The priests having been fed and the bathing over, he and his companions were greatly surprised to find that the demon's body was moving on the ground. He therefore ran to Yama, and asked him to bring the stone of religion (Dharmasila) and place it upon the demon's head; but though this was done, Gayā still moved. The gods then sat upon the stone to press down Gayā's head; but all their efforts were useless, the demon continued to move. In his distress Brahmā repaired to Vishnu, and told him of the power of Gayā in moving, though all the gods were trying to keep him quiet. Vishnu then sent a fierce fiend who issued from his person; but even this was powerless too. At last Vishnu himself came, bearing his mace, called Gadādhara, and striking the demon with it, and sitting with the other gods and goddesses upon the stone, was able to keep the demon quiet. Upon this Gayā, addressing the gods, said: "Why should you treat me thus, when I have given my sinless body to Brahmā? Would I not have become motionless if Hari (Vishnu) had asked me? Why then should he torture me with his mace? And why should you all join in this torture? Now show mercy to me?" The gods, delighted, promised to grant him his desire. Gayā prayed: "As long as the earth and mountains, seas and stars shall last, may you, Brahmā, Vishnu, and Mahādeva, rest on this stone. May you, the Devas, rest on it too, and call this place after me, The Kshetra (field) of Gayā, extending over ten miles, of which two miles are covered with my head. Therein, for the good of mankind, let all the sacred tanks on earth abide, where persons by bathing and offering of oblations of water, or funeral cakes, may attain high merit for themselves, and translate their ancestors blessed with all that is desirable, and salvation, to the region of Brahmā. As long as Vishnu in his triple form shall be adored by the learned, so long let this be renowned on earth as the sacred place of Gayāsura, and may resort to it cleanse men of even the sin of killing Brāhmans." Hearing this prayer, the gods, headed by Vishnu, said: "Whatever you ask shall be accomplished. By offering the Pinda (funeral cakes) and performing Shrādhas here, persons will translate their ancestors for a hundred generations, as also themselves, to Brāhmalok (heaven), where exists no disease. By worshipping our feet they will attain to the highest reward in after life."

It is the influence of this legend which leads numbers to visit Gayā annually to perform the Shrādha of their deceased relatives. And monstrous as the story at first sight seems, Dr. Mittra suggests a very plausible, and at the same time reasonable, explanation of it. The Asuras (literally non-gods) are generally described as the enemies of the gods; but this Gayā was a devout worshipper of Vishnu, and through this worship gained such immense power. Gayā then represented Buddhism, which at one time threatened the extinction of Hinduism, and by its simple rites and the abolition of sacrifice, did away largely with the necessity of the priests, and so cut off their resources that were derived from the offerings of the people. He was regarded as a heretic, and at that time the Buddhist religion extended over as large a portion of India as is represented by the immense body of this Asura. The headquarters of Buddhism were then at Gayā; the attempt of the gods to hold down the head of the giant represents the attempt of the Brāhmans to attack the heretical system at its great stronghold; and Vishnu's mace represents the appeal to force where reasoning and the milder measures had proved of no avail. Then the gods blessed the means employed, and made what was once the head of a heretical creed the most beneficial place of pilgrimage for the faithful.

The Hindus have appropriated to themselves the chief places of this district, as well as in Orissa and elsewhere, that once were sacred to the Buddhists. The footmarks of Vishnu in the chief Buddhist temple at Buddha Gayā are most religiously worshipped by the Hindus, and the same Purāna which praises Gayā as a place of pilgrimage for Hindus teaches that, before offering the cakes for their ancestors, they must first visit and worship the sacred pipul-tree near the Buddhist temple, under which Buddha is said to have meditated, as the dwelling-place of Vishnu. And though this tree is about five miles from the Hindu Gayā, in that book the whole district, fifteen miles in length, is regarded as sacred; though some parts of it are said to be more sacred than others, especially a small well called Gayāsiras, the Head of Gayā. It is here that the town called by the people Purāna Gayā stands, which is almost exclusively occupied by the Gawāl priests, who are called into requisition for the funeral ceremonies of people in all parts of India. As many as six hundred families live there, but as they only intermarry amongst themselves, the race appears to be dying out. Other parts have special names—Rāma Gayā, Vishnu Gayā, and Buddha Gayā, which was mentioned before, which are specially sacred to the deities named here, though the whole district is holy ground.

CHAPTER VI.

PILGRIMAGES (*continued*).

THE TEMPLE OF JAGANNĀTHA * AT PURI.

AMONGST the most popular *tirthas*, or places of pilgrimage, is Puri, the town in which the temple of Jagannātha stands. The whole province of Orissa is regarded as peculiarly holy; the many temples, and particularly the one at Puri, give it this peculiar sanctity. "Its whole extent is one uninterrupted tirtha. Its happy inhabitants live secure of a reception into the world of spirits, and those who even visit it and bathe in its sacred rivers, obtain remission of their sins, though they weigh like mountains. Who shall adequately describe its sacred streams, its temples, its khetras, its fragrant flowers, and all the merits and advantages of a sojourn in such a land? What necessity, indeed, can there be for enlarging on the praise of a region which the Devatās themselves delight to inhabit? † However popular some of the other temples may have been in past times, *e.g.*, those in Bhuvaveswara, when Saivism was more common than it is at present, it is to Jagannātha-Khetra that the bulk of the pilgrims wend their way, and with "seeing" the deity there they generally remain content.

The name *Puri* signifies *the city*, it being regarded by many of the Hindus as the most holy place on the face of the earth.

* Dr. Ragendra Lall Mittra's work on Orissa.

† "Kapila Sanhitā," quoted in As. Ser. Journal, vol. xv. p. 166.

It is a town built on the sandy shore of the Bay of Bengal, and the *hill* on which the great temple is built is only about twenty feet higher than the surrounding plain. One of the strangest facts about the temple and its great inhabitant Jagannātha is this, that whilst he is regarded as the incarnation of Vishnu, the mildest and most genial of all the deities of the Hindu Pantheon, in European writings he is regarded as the Moloch of India. It is true that many have perished by throwing themselves under the wheels of his car whilst it was being drawn through the streets; but this has been not because the people imagined that blood was a pleasing offering to him: but either because those who thus sacrificed their lives felt so secure of heaven if they died within the limits of the sacred khetra or holy place, that they did not wish to return to the wicked world to incur fresh sins; or possibly some who were familiar with the cruel rites supposed to be acceptable to some of the forms of Devi, in their ignorance of Jagannātha's real character, imagined that their voluntary immolation would be acceptable to him. This is very probable, when it is remembered that many pilgrims start on a protracted course of wandering, going from shrine to shrine; and though brought up in one particular sect, and knowing what, according to its tenets, is pleasing to the deity they usually worship, they do not stop to learn what is pleasing to others. It is also possible that in a few cases it was owing to the excitement of the moment, not as a premeditated act of devotion, that they cast themselves under the wheels of the car, in the hope that such complete self-sacrifice could not fail to receive its reward. Whatever the motive, it is certain that from what is generally taught as the character of Jagannātha, and the rites that are performed in his worship, there is nothing to lead men to regard him as a cruel deity delighting in death, but the very opposite.

The town of Puri has nothing to attract save its temples and maths, or monasteries; it is composed mostly of ruined huts, with a fixed population, mostly Hindus, of about 23,000.

At the great festivals there are from 60,000 to 100,000 pilgrims present there. Its history naturally divides itself into three periods:

1. The Early Hindu Period. The authority for this are chapters in the three Purānas—the Skanda, Kurma, and Nārad. The legends are evidently written with the object of casting a halo of glory round the place, which, at the time they were written, was growing in popularity. The information is given in answer to an inquiry why Vishnu assumed the form of a log of wood, by which he is represented at the temple at Puri.

Brahmā, feeling distressed that he had not provided sufficient means for human salvation, repaired to Vishnu with the request that he would provide a simple method. This was not immediately granted, but Brahmā was reminded that those who were really in earnest in their search for salvation could easily obtain it by living in the secret abode of the divinity by the sea-shore. In praise of this place Vishnu then said: "On the north shore of the sea to the south of Mahānadi River is my favourite abode, which alone can confer all the blessings to be derived from all the other sacred places on the earth put together. Those wise sons of Manu who reside there enjoy the fruits of all the good deeds performed by them in previous births. . . . None who has little merit or is weak in faith, can live there. . . . The Blue Hill (the site of the temple) is the most secret place on earth; most difficult of access even to you (Brahmā). I dwell there in a bodily form, and that holy spot, rising above all mutability, is unassailable by creation and destruction. As you see me here, so you will see me there. On that Blue Hill to the west of the Kalpa fig-tree, there is a fountain named Rohinā; dwelling near it men may see me with their mortal eyes, and washing off their sins with its water, attain equality with me." This does not merely refer to moral, but also bodily, likeness; for on Brahmā's visiting the place, it is said that he saw a crow first dip, then plunge into the water of this fountain—the result was that the crow came forth out of the water the exact counterpart of Vishnu, and at once went to his heavenly abode. On seeing this, Brahmā was convinced of the glory of the place, and determined to extend and enhance it. Other stories are given, one of which is to show that Yama has no control over those who die there, the souls of the departed obtaining at once complete salvation. Another teaches that this place is not subject to decay and dissolution as are others, but will continue in its glory when all other places have been swept away.

This same authority gives the following account of the building of the temple, and the establishment of the worship of a wooden image there. In the earliest stage of its existence, Puri was a forest, having the Blue Hill in the centre, the Kalpa tree on its brow, the sacred fountain of Rohinā on the west, and on its side an image of Vishnu in sapphire. This stone gave its name to the image, viz., *Nila mani* (the blue jewel). Indradyumna, King of Mālava (Malwa), hearing of the glories of the place, and the benefits to be derived from worshipping there, from an ascetic, determined to visit it in person. Before setting out, however, it was thought advisable to send an officer from his court to see if this account were true. The priest's brother went, and on arriving at the spot, saw a number of Brāhmans who had been changed into Vishnu's form, having each four arms. The chief of the community at first was unwilling to allow this officer to see the sacred bower, but afterwards consented, and gave him a heavenly wreath of flowers, which was taken from the neck of the god.

On his return the king was most anxious to start on his journey, and his earnestness was increased by a visit of the sage Nārad, who told him that all other holy places, and all religious ceremonies would not yield him a thousandth part of the benefit that would come through faith in Vishnu.

When the king reached the borders of Orissa, he was met by its king, and they together worshipped Siva under the usual form of a Linga in a mango forest; the place to which Vishnu had exiled him when he drove him from Benares. He then proceeded to the secret temple, but great was his disappointment to find that the sapphire image had sunk through the sand; and the deity had left his favourite earthly abode and gone to Pātāla, the nether regions. At first the king was almost inconsolable, but at length Nārad was able to comfort him; he told him that he could form a wooden image of the departed deity, the sight of which would obtain as great comforts for mankind as though they saw the god himself, and led him to set about a great sacrifice of 1,000 horses, which would prove of the greatest benefit to himself and others. The sacrifice was commenced with great pomp and magnificence, and on the seventh night of the ceremony the king had a dream, which rewarded him for all his trouble. He saw a noble tree, within which was Vishnu, accompanied by his wife Lakshmi, and Ananta. In his hands were the usual emblems—the conch, discus, mace, and lotus; and by his side the celestial wonder-working wheel, Sudarsana. A few days after this, an immense log of wood was washed upon the shore, in which were the marks of Vishnu, and its arrival was regarded as the fulfilment of the dream. From this log were formed images of Jagannātha (Vishnu), Balarāma, Subhadra, and the Sudarsana. And when these were ready, at Indradyumna's request, Brahmā and the gods came down from heaven to assist at their consecration and the inauguration of the worship of Vishnu under the form of Jagannātha at Puri.

2. The Buddhist Period. The temple records quietly ignore the very existence of Buddhism, and invent stories of the district being overcome by Mussulmāns and others; but the truth seems to be that at one time Puri was really one of the important centres of Buddhistic teaching. When the Gayā Asura fell down in worship, whilst his head was said to be at Gayā, his navel in the same legend is said to have been at Puri, clearly indicating that Puri was one of the important

centres of that worship. There is much to be said in favour of the idea that the relic which is supposed to be enshrined in the image of Jagannātha, which is most carefully transferred from the old to a new image, and which the Hindus believe to be the bones of Krishna, or according to others the soul of the deity, is nothing else than the tooth of Buddha, which it is known was most carefully preserved, and over which a magnificent temple or Dagoba was erected at a place called Dantapura. Where Dantapura was situated is uncertain; but it is highly probable that it was at Puri, and that the building erected as a shrine for the tooth of Buddha has given place to the temple in which the image of Jagannātha is worshipped. This relic was taken to Patna, where some miracles are said to have been wrought through its power, on seeing which the Brāhmans of the place exclaimed: "There are many incarnations of Janārdana (Vishnu); this bone is part of him. If not, whence such influence as this." And a careful examination of the Vaishnavism of the present day will show how the main lessons of Buddhism have been incorporated in it, and its emblems modified or explained to be identical with those of the Vaishnava sects.

3. The Vaishnava Period. As far as can be distinctly known, it was about the close of the fifth century of the present era that a king, named Yayāti Kesāri, came from Magadha and established, or, as the Hindus say, re-established Hindu-Brāhmanical worship at Puri, where Buddhism had for centuries held sway. This same king is said also to have made preparations for the erection of the great tower at Bhuvaneshwara, where Siva-worship has its great stronghold. This may be true, for instances are known of men who show their impartiality by erecting temples or supporting the worship of the temples of several deities; or it may be that he changed the object of his worship—he who at one time was an earnest worshipper of Vishnu possibly became as earnest a follower of Siva.

This is a probable account of the king's action. Finding a

19

Buddhist temple with three mystic monograms, together with the wheel of the law set on high at one end, before which the worshippers bowed and then went on their way, these three emblems Yayāti called by Hindu names, and taught that they were representations of Vishnu and his brother and sister, and the Buddhistic wheel an image of Vishnu's wonderful discus. Placing Hindu priests there, the mantras were changed, and some slight changes in the ritual introduced also. He probably repaired the temple, and slightly changed the representatives of deity; but it is unlikely that he did more than this. There are some records which describe this king as building a new temple and setting up new images, which so delighted the people that they called him Indradyumna II.; but this, as Dr. Mittra says, is most unlikely. At first the changes introduced were as few as possible, in order that it might appear that the really new system was only a development of the one with which the people had been familiar.

The present building was completed in 1196, the account of its erection being found in the temple annals. A king of Orissa, named Kāmadeva, determining to erect a new temple in place of the one which had partly fallen into ruins, pulled down the old one, and collected materials for a new building; but after working at it for five years he died. His son, Madan Mahādeva, was at first engaged in the erection of a temple at a place eight miles from Puri; and when this was finished, he turned his attention to the work commenced by his father. But he died after reigning four years only, and his brother, Ananga Bhima, succeeded to the throne, and also took up with great energy the work of the re-building of the great temple. He took as his model the great tower of Bhuvaneshwara, but surpassed his model in beauty and grandeur. This man having been guilty of the almost unpardonable sin of killing a Brāhman, tried to make expiation by erecting temples, crossing rivers with bridges, making good roads, digging tanks, &c. To him Jagannātha appeared in a dream and told him to go to Puri and there call upon his name. And it was to the effort of the king to atone for this sin that the temple owes its completion. His descendants are the guardians of the holy shrine, and glory in the title of "the Sweepers of the sacred Temple."

It was during the reign of his successor, Pratāparudra, that Puri was visited by Chaitanya, the great reformer of Bengal; who, finding that so many pilgrims came there from all parts of the country, considered that it would be a good place to promulgate his doctrines, and remaining there for years, by his teaching greatly changed the character of the Vishnu worship. He taught that Bhakti (trust) was far more acceptable to the deity than fastings, penance of various kinds, and the performance of religious rites. Hitherto fear and veneration had been the emotions that men had thought to be most acceptable to God; he taught that the highest type of worship was the passionate love which man cherishes for woman; and though in his own teaching there was little that was objectionable, as his followers have developed it it tends to render those who embrace it most voluptuous. The Buddhist character of the place served his purpose; the name of the deity (Jagannātha, *i.e.*, the Lord of the World) was suited to his world-wide idea of brotherhood. Caste had been almost destroyed by Buddhism; and Chaitanya taught that within the temple enclosure all men were brethren, and were permitted to eat together of the food that had been made sacred by being presented to the deity. Aided by the Rāja who became one of his most devout disciples, the ritual was changed and the mystic songs of Jayadeva were sung at the morning and evening worship of the god; and the "Lord of the World" in his worship was regarded very much as a man with human sympathies such as were in his followers. "The divinity ceased; and in his place rose the being who may be looked upon at option as the master, friend, parent, or mistress of the worshippers; and his service was modelled accordingly. A human being on rising from bed must first wash his face and brush his teeth; and the first service was accordingly made to typify washing and brushing. Bathing, breakfast, recreations, dining, and sleeping all followed by symbolisms, and the service of the divinity was changed to the service of man. This anthropomorphic form of worship, first introduced by Chaitanya, still obtains, and traits of it will be seen in the accounts of the feasts and festivals" connected with the worship at this place. "The memory of the reformer is held in the highest veneration, and there are upwards of eight hundred temples devoted to his worship in Orissa."

It has been frequently stated that the worship of Jagannātha is associated with much that is licentious. Dr. Hunter and Mr. Fergusson state that it is on the Vishnu temples that the more indecent sculptures are to be found, but Dr. Mittra distinctly and emphatically denies this. He says that in the Central Provinces and Orissa, where these representations are to be found, they are at least as common on Siva temples as on those of the many incarnations of Vishnu; and concludes by saying: "As a Hindu by birth, and Vaishnava by family religion, I have had access to the innermost sanctuaries, and to the most secret of Scriptures; I have studied the subject most extensively, and have had opportunities of judging which no European can have, and I have no hesitation in saying that, the 'mystic songs' of Jayadeva and the 'Ocean of Love' notwithstanding, there is nothing in the ritual of Jagannātha which can be called licentious."

During the Mussulmān rule the images of this as well as other temples were once and again destroyed, but it is believed that before the Mussulmāns attacked the temple the relic, whatever it is, which is said to be preserved in the image, was carefully removed, and when safer times came, new images having been made, the relics were restored; so that though the perishable part of the deity has been frequently renewed, that which gives special sanctity to it continues unimpaired.

The large temple which gives such great sanctity to the whole city stands on a mound about 20 feet high. The courtyard surrounding it is 665 feet by 644 feet, and is enclosed by a thick stone wall about 22 feet high, but which is of a much later date than the temple itself. There are four gateways; the principal one being to the east, in front of which is a splendid stone pillar that was originally in front of the Sun Temple at Konāsak. The building itself is of the pyramidal form which is common in Orissa.

Besides the chief figures for whose worship the temple was erected, there are others occupying less conspicuous positions. On the staircase by which the pilgrims enter are images of Siva and Rāmachandra. On the right is the Snān-Vedi, or platform on which the god is bathed at the great festival of the Snān Jātra; near to it is a small pavilion in which the goddess Lakshmi is placed to witness this ceremony; whilst on the opposite side of the courtyard is a similar pavilion on which she sits to welcome him on his return from his annual ride on the car. There is the cook-room in which sacred food is cooked, and a covered way leading from it to the temple, so that it can be carried by the priests without fear of defilement into the presence of the god. There is also a house called Vaikuntha (the heaven of Vishnu), in which some priests reside, and which is used as a place where the rich pilgrims are taken to ratify their endowments to the temple; and a sacred place where the old images are buried when new ones are instituted in their place.

The inner enclosure, 400 feet by 278 feet, is secured by double walls, with a space of 11 feet between them, which are supposed to have been made thus in case of need, to be filled in with earth to strengthen the defence. The centre of this enclosure is occupied with the great temple, as well as a number of smaller shrines and spots regarded as especially sacred. Amongst these the most important object to the pilgrims is the sacred tree, under which it is said the messenger from Indradyumna met the keeper of the forest; but as the tree now growing is the Vata (*Ficus Indica*), and the tree mentioned in the legend is the Asvattha (*Ficus religiosa*), and as the present tree is not more than two hundred years old, it is certain that this cannot be the identical tree though it is probable that it stands where some noted tree that was sacred to the Buddhists once grew. The tree is called the Kalpa-briksha, and has the virtue of making barren women fruitful. When visited for this purpose the woman spreads her cloth on the ground, and if within a reasonable time a fruit falls on it from the tree she takes it as a sign that the god is propitious and will bestow on her the desired boon. The Kapila Sanhita declares, "whoever stands under the shadow of this tree, immediately clears himself from the sin of killing Brāhmans; and whoever walks round it and then worships it, Hari remits all his sins committed in the course of a hundred generations. At its foot is an image of Mangalā, the giver of prosperity to the gods; whoever beholds and adores her emancipates himself from all delusion." Near this is a hall open on all sides in which Pundits read and explain the Sāstras to any who may come to listen; and then comes a small lake in which it is said the crow dipped and came out in Vishnu's likeness, a representation of which is seen on a stone close by. Near by, strange to say, is a shrine sacred to Vimalā Devi, the wife of Siva, to whom once a year, in the middle of a moonless night, a kid is sacrificed within the enclosure which is sacred to Vishnu, to whom all life, that of animals as well as man, is sacred; thus affording another illustration of the idea so firmly insisted on by the Hindus that the many gods are but varied manifestations of the one Supreme Being. It should be stated, however, that the Pundits usually deny that this sacrifice is made. There is also a temple of Lakshmi, the wife of Vishnu, who, though not enshrined in the large temple with her spouse, takes a prominent part in his annual worship; and a temple of the Sun, but his image is so completely hidden by those of Rādhā and Krishna that it can only be seen even at midday by those who go behind these later additions and carry a light with them.

The temple has four chief rooms—first the Bhoga Mandapa, or Hall of Offerings, a room 58 feet by 56 feet; this leads to the Dancing Hall, 69 feet by 67 feet, in which, on certain occasions, the amusements of the temple are held. Leading out, and as a part of this, are four smaller rooms, in one of which Siva is represented by the Linga; another is devoted to Krishna; a third is called Lakshmi's dressing-room, as it is here that she is got ready to go to take part in the festival; and a fourth for the musicians of the temple, who play daily at certain portions of the service, when they are not performing in the large hall. In these rooms there are sculptures of a most obscene character. Then comes the porch or audience chamber of the temple, 80 feet by 80 feet; and finally the temple or shrine proper, also 80 feet by 80 feet. Three large niches in the shrine contain figures of three of Vishnu's incarnations, viz., the Varāha (Boar), Nrisingha (Man-lion), and the Vāmana (Dwarf). In the plinth is a small niche, in which there is a figure of a human being with his hands and feet chained. This is to represent the eleventh day of the lunar month, which Hindu widows have to observe as a strict fast, and which good Hindus of both sexes regard as specially holy. To allow *one* day in the month to be observed as a fast where feasting is the rule, and where the priests make large profits out of the food sold, would not pay, so a story has been written, of which this figure is an illustration, to the effect that Ekadasi, *i.e.*, the 11th, contended with the genius of the temple in favour of the fast being observed even here; but Jagannātha explained to him that though the rule held good elsewhere, his will was higher than the law. As, however, Ekadasi was not satisfied, he was chained, and remains enchained to this day, as a warning against those who would resist the authority of the "Lord of the World," and as an encouragement to nervous Hindus, who might otherwise wish to fast on this day when at Puri.

"All the four gates of the sacred enclosure are left open until a late hour at night, but the rule is that, except in the case of special permits, granted by the Khurdā Rāja (the custodian of the temple), pilgrims should enter by the east gate, turn to the left in the inner enclosure, circumambulate the great temple once, thrice, or even seven times, and then enter the Dancing Hall by the north door. Proceeding thence to the audience chamber (or porch), and standing in front of a log of sandal-wood, which cuts off further approach, they behold the Lord of the universe on his sanctum in front. Persons paying largely are allowed to cross the bar, and enter the sanctum. Those having special permits, which cost from Rs. 500 to Rs. 5,000, enter by the south gate, and have the right of getting into the inner enclosure, which is cleared of all other visitors for the time they remain inside. They, of course, have the right of entering the sanctum itself. This sanctum is so dark, that without the aid of a lamp nothing is visible within even at midday. Going thrice round the temple at noon with the sun glaring on the whitewashed houses, and devoting the greater part of the time in looking upwards towards the cornice and the tops of the temples and other erections, to which their attention is constantly directed by the cicerones, the eyes of the pilgrims get so dazed, that it is impossible immediately after to see anything placed in a dark corner; and under the best of circumstances the poor pilgrims, standing before the sandal-wood bar, see very little. Even those who get beyond the bar cannot see much at first, until their eyes adjust themselves to the light. The priests attribute this to the effect of sin, which renders carnal eyes unfit to behold the divinity. When that sin is destroyed by devotion, the divinity becomes visible." As the great object of the pilgrims visiting Puri is to *see* Jagannātha, many have to return without being able to gratify their desire.

Dr. Mittra tells an amusing story of a certain Rāja, who, lax in morals and of thrifty habits, visited this temple, and, being unable to see the image after walking round the temple in the glare of midday, went to his lodgings and prayed day and night, vowing to do a great number of good deeds, one of which remains to this day in the metalled road that runs from Puri to Cuttack, a distance of fifty miles. Returning to the temple the next day, and passing into the sanctum without walking round the temple, his eyes were opened, and he was able to see the god! Dr. Mittra's own experience is quite as amusing. After walking round the temple and entering the sanctum, he could see but little, so asking the attendant priest to conduct him round the throne three times, during which his eyes became accustomed to the darkness, he, on his return to the front of the image, could see distinctly. He declares that a shrewd priest with whom he afterwards conversed on the subject, declared that the priests knew well to what cause the supposed miracle was due.

Another miracle is repeatedly spoken of to the pilgrim. It is said that the roar of the sea so terrified Subhadrā, the sister of Jagannātha, whose image is next to his own, that it caused her hands and arms to shrink into her body. Whereupon her brother commanded the sea not to allow the noise of his waves breaking upon the shore to enter the sacred enclosure. And it is a fact, that though the sound of the "sad sea waves," is distinctly heard outside, owing to the very high walls which surround the temple, and the noise of the multitudes near, the sound is scarcely audible within. But no miracle is necessary to account for this.

According to the same authority, the images which are sold at Puri fairly represent those within the shrine. Those worshipped in the temple are made of iron-wood, a hard, close-grained wood, capable of taking a high polish, and so bitter that insects will not eat it. The images are each made of one solid block. They are most ugly and rude imitations of human figures, without hands or legs. They have stumps of arms on which golden hands are fixed; and it is said that Subhadrā's arms which cannot be seen, are lying by her side; those of the other two being nailed on to the body.

Jagannātha is painted black; Balarāma, his brother, white; whilst their sister is golden coloured. The figures of the male deities are six feet high; that of Subhadrā about four and a half feet. The Sudarsana is a mere stump about six feet high, on which Dr. Mithra could see no mark of the wheel, but which the priest declares has that mark on the top. Several times a day the dresses and ornaments of these images are changed, but none save the priests are allowed to see them in their native ugliness. The people admit that these are not beautiful, and the following legend has been invented to account for this.

When King Indradyumna determined to establish the worship of Vishnu under this form, he applied to Visvakarma, the architect of the gods, to assist him in the erection of the temple and the construction of the image. To this the deity consented on the understanding that he was to be allowed to work without being overlooked by the king or any of his people. The king assenting, the work was commenced forthwith, and the temple arose under the magic touch of Visvakarma. But the image occupied a much longer time. When the king had restrained his impatience for about a fortnight, being very anxious to see how the work was progressing, he ascended a ladder and was peeping over the wall, when Visvakarma, noticing him, at once left his work unfinished and returned to his heavenly home. The king, seeing the unfinished ugly images, was greatly distressed at first, but Brahmā and the other deities consoled him with the promise that they would be present at the installation of the image, and that, ugly though the images were, the worship that he inaugurated should be most popular amongst the whole kingdom. This prediction has certainly been fulfilled as far as Puri is concerned, and the people generally who worship Jagannātha at other places, too, do not appear to see any incongruity in worshipping Vishnu as represented by these ugly deformities.

Other stories are told to account for these strange figures

being worshipped, *e.g.*, it is said that as God is great no figure can fairly represent Him, hence these ugly ones are made to drive people through fear to propitiate Him with gifts. The true explanation, as I believe, being that they are modifications of the old Buddhist worship, the Sudarsana being nothing else than the wheel of the Law—the only object placed in the Buddhist halls before images of Buddha became common; whilst the three figures are modified forms of a monogram composed of the initial letters of the five elements—air, fire, water, earth, and ether—which in Pali characters arrayed in a peculiar manner, placed over the wheel, do not look unlike the representatives of Jagannātha and his companions. This certainly appears to be a natural and reasonable explanation of what otherwise is inexplicable.

The images are renewed from time to time, as the old ones become unfit for further duty. It is said that the best time for doing this work is when the month of Āsādha becomes an intercallary one; but as it is believed that the king in whose reign it is done dies soon after, there is not much inducement for any one to renew them. When the renewal takes place, the relic is taken from the old ones, which are then solemnly buried; whilst the relic is put into the body of the new ones. A great mystery attaches to this relic. The priests refused to tell Dr. Mithra what it was; and, as before stated, there is every reason to believe that it is a Buddhist remain. When hard pressed by rich pilgrims, the priests with their natural kindness do not like positively to refuse to say what it is, so give one story to one, and another to another, as they think likely to quiet the importunity of the questioner. Some say it is a part of the original image, the wood of which came floating in from the sea; others that it is a bone of Krishna; a Hindu clerk at Cuttack, in writing a history of Puri, declares that "a boy from a potter's family is selected to take out from the breast of the old idol a small box of quicksilver, said to be the spirit, which he conveys inside the new." The boy who renders this service is always removed from the world before the end of the year.

These three images are placed on a platform, four feet high and sixteen feet long. In front of them is a gold image of Lakshmi, and a silver one of the earth (Bhudevi); and several smaller ones. The principal images are never moved except at the time of the great festivals. Their dresses are changed frequently, and the transformation caused by this is so great that they look like quite different objects at different times of the day. Amongst these varied dresses is one called Buddhavesa, the garb of Buddha, another incidental proof of the rise of this worship from Buddhism. At times the image is dressed in boys' clothes to represent incidents in the life of Krishna. At such times, a rope is tied round his waist and fastened to a post to represent the way in which Krishna was tied by his foster-mother to prevent him from stealing the curds: and again he is dressed in the dress peculiar to Ganesa, and, to make the resemblance complete, he has a trunk attached to his face, such as that of the elephant-headed god of wisdom.

The daily service of the temple is very similar to that of other deities as described fully in the account of Bhuvaneshwara. The work of the day begins by ringing a bell to awake the sleeping deities; offerings and the repetition of mantras go on until about eleven p.m., when a bedstead is presented to them, and they are invited to retire for the night. Small quantities of food are brought into the sanctuary itself, which belongs to the priests alone; but at the four principal meals of the day, large quantities of cooked food are taken into the refectory, and consecrated by being placed in front of the idol. Excepting the offering of the Rāja of Khurda, those made by pilgrims are not taken into the sanctuary, but into the dining-room; and one class of sweetmeats are prepared specially at the Rāja's palace, and sent daily to the temple, the proceeds of which are given to him; the money received from the sale of the other sacred food being taken by the priests. When it is remembered that on some days food for 100,000 people is prepared in the temple, and sold, it will be seen that the yearly profits must be something enormous.

The food is cooked by low caste men, who profess to be the descendants of the woodman who conducted Indradyumna to the original shrine; but such is supposed to be the sanctifying effect of this holy place, that it is cheerfully eaten by people of all castes; it is even carried away to their homes by the pilgrims, and regarded as the most sacred treasure. A single grain of this consecrated food, placed upon the cakes offered at the funeral ceremonies of the dead, is believed by the Vaishnavas to be more effectual in saving the departed from misery than anything and everything else that could be offered. It is called Mahaprasād, and the gods even are said to be delighted if they can obtain a portion. The greatest sins are removed the moment a grain of this rice touches the tongue. Legends such as the following are given to strengthen the faith of the people. A man proud of his high caste came to see Jagannātha, but would not touch what he regarded as unclean food that had been cooked by outcastes. But, after leaving the city, on his way home his arms and legs fell off, and in that state he remained, until a dog happened to come near who dropped a few grains of this holy food from his mouth. The man in his distress managed to crawl to the spot, and licking up this rice, Jagannātha forgave his pride, and caused his limbs to grow again, and he returned home a firm believer in the wisdom of following the teaching of the Lord of the World.

In connection with the worship of Jagannātha, a number of festivals are held, at which religion and amusements are blended, and which tend largely to increase the popularity of the idol, and to bring pilgrims in greater numbers to its shrine. Some of these have an astronomical origin, *i.e.*, they are to celebrate some particular season of the year; some are held with the view of calling to memory events in the life of the deity during his temporary sojourn on earth. A brief account of these will not be without interest. There is a calendar peculiar to Orissa, which we shall follow; and according to this, the year begins with the month Agrahāyana (Nov.-Dec.).

1. *Ghornāgi* is held on the sixth of the waning moon of the first month of the year, and at this time the images are clad in shawls, and other warm and costly garments. This is the day some women in Bengal set apart as a day of fasting for the benefit of their sons.

2. *Abhisheka, i.e.*, the coronation, when the images are arrayed in royal robes. (This is the same as the Pusha Jātra of Bhuvaneshwara).

3. *Markara, i.e.*, the day Sun enters the sign of Capricornus on his return to the north. It is a day of feasting with cakes, &c., and one of general rejoicing.

4. *The Dol Jātra or Holi.* This, next to the Snān and Rath Jātras, is the most popular festival at Puri. It is the continuation of a festival, with modern innovations, that was held in Vedic times to celebrate the arrival of spring. In all countries that has been a season of unusual merriment, and the people of India to-day, with the exception that the youths do not run about naked, follow in the same lines as those which prevailed in Rome and Germany, and which may be seen to-day in the Carnival, as it is observed in continental towns. Drinking, buffoonery, licentious talk and gestures prevail; and the throwing of red powder. It is called the Dole, or Swing Festival, because on this day the images of Krishna, or his representatives, are placed on a swing; swinging being the most common form of amusement, especially for women, in the North-west Provinces of India. It is a most common festival, celebrated with greater or less expense in most of the Vaishnava temples, and fun and frolic form the chief part of the ceremonies. At Puri, owing to the great weight of the idols, and to the fact that some years ago an accident happened to Jagannātha, they are not

swung; but two other images, those of Madanamohana and Lakshmi, are substituted for them. Another reason for relieving Jagannātha and his companions from this swinging was that the red powder or Holi, which was freely thrown on them, injured the paint. It is said that this festival is to commemorate a deed of heroisn of Krishna's when he slew a demon called Holi. All through Upper India this is a season of great licentiousness. The red powder is thrown, or red water squirted on passers-by. The ceremony at Puri lasts for one day only; but the merriment generally continues in the streets for about four days.

5. *Rāma navami, i.e.*, the ninth of the waxing moon of Chaitra, the day regarded as the birthday of Rāma. As Jagannātha is said to be a later incarnation of the same deity as Rāma, on this day he is dressed and worshipped as Rāma.

6. *Dasnā Chori;* on this day the proxy of Jagannātha is worshipped; it is a festival to celebrate the stealing of some thyme by the great deity himself.

8. *Chandana Jātra,* or Flower Festival. The proxies Madanamohana and four Lingas are carried to a small temple, on an island in the Norendra tank, where they remain twenty-one days. Every evening they are taken for a row on the lake, flowers, sandal-wood, &c., are presented, and the worshippers entertained with singing and dancing.

8. *Rukmini harana.* This is to celebrate Krishna's carrying off his wife Rukmini, who was originally betrothed to Sisupāla; but, loving Krishna, she ran away with him. At Puri, Madanamohana, because of the difficulty in transporting the great image, takes Jagannātha's place, and, being carried to a neighbouring garden, is supposed to steal his bride, and when he has brought her home, they are married at night under a sacred tree in the enclosure of the temple.

9. *Snān Jātra* is held on the fifteenth of the waxing moon of the Jaishtha. This festival is held to commemorate the day when the first image was commenced by Indradyumna. The

images are brought out from the sanctum and bathed at mid-day on a platform kept specially for the purpose, with water taken from a well near the sacred tree, after which they are dressed in beautiful robes. When the ceremonies of the bath are concluded, the images are taken to one of the smaller rooms in the porch called the Sick Chamber, where they remain for a fortnight, it being understood that fever resulted from their unusual exposure on the day of bathing. During this time the outer doors of the temple are closed; there is no cooking of food, no regular worship. The real reason of this is that during this time the images are being re-painted, and it would lessen the respect of the people for their deities if they saw them in this state. When it is remembered that water, flowers, and other offerings are thrown upon them daily, it will easily be understood that annually a fresh coat of paint is quite necessary.

10. The *Rath Jātra*. After the painting is complete, the gods are exposed to the public gaze as they are taken for a ride upon their raths or chariots. These immense cars are made according to fixed rules as to size, &c. The height of Jagannātha's car is 45 feet, that of Balarāma 44 feet, that of Subhadrā, 43 feet. The first car has sixteeen wheels with sixteen spokes each; the second, fourteen wheels with fourteen spokes; the third, twelve wheels with twelve spokes. These cars are most strongly and clumsily built, are of immense weight, and can with great difficulty be moved. When the time comes for the ride, the lady is carried on the shoulders of men; the other two, having a silken cord round the waist, are dragged to the car, and then drawn up an inclined plane to their seat, by people of the same caste as those who cook the food in the temple, whose ancestors have done this work for generations, the priests holding the idols in an upright position. When placed upon their seats, the images are dressed in gorgeous robes, and golden hands and arms attached to them.

When all is ready, the Rāja of Khurda, the "Sweeper of the Temple," descends from his elephant about one hundred yards from the cars, and sweeps the road until he reaches them; he then worships each of the idols, and after making his offerings, just touches the ropes of each car as though he dragged them, when hundreds of coolies, who for this work hold their land rent free, aided by the voluntary effort of hundreds or thousands of pilgrims, set the ponderous cars in motion.

These cars are dragged to a suite of temples about two miles distant. The journey occupies four days; and on their arrival the image of Lakshmi is taken from the Puri templ to see her lord. After remaining here four or five days, the cars are brought back much in the same way as they went, and on their arrival at the temple, Lakshmi, as a faithful wife, is waiting in a pavilion to welcome home her husband.

Much speculation has arisen as to the origin of this Car Festival. There seems, however, to be little reason to doubt that it is a continuation of a Buddhist festival to celebrate the birth of that saint. There is evidence to show that it was common for images of Buddha to be dragged through the streets in this manner; and there is nothing in the older Hindu books, nor is there any tradition of this practice being commonly practised by the Hindus, except in connection with Buddhistic worship. The reasons for believing that this practice is of Buddhistic origin, are the following: There is no doubt that Puri at one time was one of the chief centres of Buddhism; the images of Jagannātha and his companions have been shown to be modifications of Buddhist emblems; the possession of a relic in the idol is almost peculiar to this temple; caste differences are obliterated at Puri; in the representations of the ten incarnations of Vishnu, Jagannātha takes the place of Buddha, who, according to the Vishnu Purāna, was an incarnation of Vishnu for the purpose of deceiving mankind; and at this season of the year a car festival was common amongst the Buddhists in honour of the birthday of Buddha.

11. *Sayana Ekadasi;* this day is observed with feasting and

rejoicing, and at night the three images, represented by small gold idols, are put to bed for four months. Some say it is to represent Vishnu's descent to Pātāla; others that it is to commemorate his sleep upon the ocean. The probable reason is that this being the rainy season, travelling is most difficult, and the professional pilgrims remain in the monasteries instead of wandering about. The more pious Hindus regard it as a season when they should be unusually abstemious, much as in some Christian homes the season of Lent is observed. During these months weddings are not celebrated; nor as a rule are the temples of the gods visited.

12. The next festival is the *Julana Jātra*, or Swinging Festival. Madanamohana has again to do duty for his lord, and, profusely adorned, is put into a swing, and every evening regaled with music, feasting, and dancing.

13. *Janmāshtami*, *i.e.*, the birthday of Krishna at Mathura. This festival, common throughout the whole of North India, is here celebrated with great *éclat*, and eye-witnesses declare that in the presence of a crowd a dancing girl plays the part of the mother, and a priest that of the father, and the "ceremony of his nativity is performed to the life." The story is as follows: Krishna's mother fell asleep as soon as he was born, and to save him from the cruel hands of his uncle his father took him to the home of a cowkeeper's wife, and changed him for her newly-born girl, whom he placed by the side of his sleeping wife. Dr. Mittra denies that there is any obscenity in the representation. Certainly it is a delicate subject for representation, and as I have heard it described by Hindus it is not represented in the most delicate manner. Attached to this temple are girls, some as dancers, and some as singers, who are said to be married to the deity, of whom the most that Dr. Mittra can say in favour of their purity of life is that they are not more unchaste than the actresses and ballet girls of Europe. These are professional vestal virgins, and it may be, of course, that some of them remain pure; but certainly the common belief amongst the Hindus them-

selves is that this is a very rare exception, and it is admitted that the one selected for taking the part of Krishna's mother is no better than the rest.

14. *Pārsva parivartana* is a festival held to celebrate the turning of the images on to their right side, they having been laid on their backs when first they were placed in position for their long sleep.

15. *Kāliya damana;* the slaying of the serpent Kāliya in the river Yamuna by Krishna. Jagannātha's image is wrapped round with an imitation serpent, made of cloth, whilst his proxy is carried to a tank close by, with music and singing, where he is supposed to slay the demon.

16. *Vāmanjanam.* On this day Jagannātha is dressed to represent Vishnu when he appeared on earth as a dwarf: in the Hindu calendar it is the day when Vishnu, in his sleep before the re-creation of the world, turned over from his right to his left side.

17. *Utthāpana Edadasi* is the day when Vishnu awakes from his sleep. The metal images are aroused, bathed, dressed, and worshipped in due form.

It should be noticed that besides these there are several other less important festivals.

The garden-house to which Jagannātha is taken in his car is said to be the place where Indradyumna pitched his tent when he first came there to worship: it was here that he performed his great horse sacrifice; and it was near here that the log of wood is said to have been washed ashore which was used in making the first image.

There are a number of smaller temples of no great importance, but are interesting chiefly because they furnish an illustration of the way in which the supremacy of one god is asserted over others. At Bhuvaneshwara, where Siva is worshipped as supreme, Vishnu and his consort are made *guardians of the city;* here, as *Vishnu* is the chief deity, Siva and his wife, in eight different forms, have the duty of wardens of the city assigned to them. There are also tanks here as in

Benares, the waters of which are declared to have the power immediately to cleanse the soul from impurity, and to give emancipation from future evil; but in connection with them there are conditions of a similar nature to that which permits only the pure to see Jagannātha in his temple.

CHAPTER VII.

PILGRIMAGES (continued).

BHUVANESHWARA.

THIS place was in former years far more attractive as a place of pilgrimage than it is at the present day. It may have been commenced as a rival shrine to Benares; or it may have arisen during the time that Buddhism prevailed there before its influence was felt in Orissa.* Some pilgrims call here on their way to or from Puri, and thus pay their respects to the two great deities whose worship is carried on at these two important places; the majority, however, pass by Bhuvaneshwara, content with the expense and labour incurred in the journey, and the offerings made, to Jagannātha.

The image of Siva, the Linga, being an upright stone pillar, and remaining fixed in its place, does not admit of the same variety of ceremonies as are possible with movable images such as those at Puri; but the ceremonies, though somewhat differing in form, are much the same in spirit. The following account describes the daily worship in the temple, and the special festivals that are held there.

The image is bathed daily with a great quantity of water, milk, and bhang, and large quantities of food are placed

* The full name, Tribhuvaneshwara—meaning the Lord of the three worlds, heaven, earth, and hell; Jagannātha, signifying Lord of the world only—suggests a third cause of its origin, viz., as a rival shrine to that of Jagannātha at Puri.

before it. Flowers, sandal-wood, and clothes, too, are presented. The daily service begins at dawn with the ringing of a bell to wake up the idol; then a lamp is moved about in front to light him to get up. Then comes the cleaning of his teeth; this is done by moving about a stick bruised at the one end, similar to those used by the Brāhmans for this purpose; a bowl of water and towel are next brought, to wash his face. Then comes his bath: this consists of water, ghi, and milk thrown over the stone, which is then washed and dried. Next comes the dressing; the clothes worn on the previous day having been washed are put round the lower part of the stone. After this a light breakfast of sweetmeats is given, which is followed a couple of hours later, at ten o'clock, with the regular breakfast. At eleven o'clock another breakfast is prepared, the difference consisting in the kinds of food that are presented. Incense is burned, the doors of the temple are closed, and the deity enjoys his midday repose. At four o'clock the doors are again opened, and pretty much the same ceremonies are repeated in the evening until bed-time comes, when the deity is invited to repose, with the phrase that "Parvati awaits her lord." Twenty-two ceremonies are performed on ordinary days; on special festival days others are added, for each of which there are the proper mantras or texts to be employed. The festivals generally refer to some events connected with the history of Siva, of which appropriate legends are told; though it is evident that several of these have been written to make these festival days attractive to the people, at the time when there are special festivals held in connection with deities worshipped in other temples.

The chief festivals of Siva are the following:—

1. *Prathamāstimi*, literally the first (feast) of the eighth day of the moon of the first month of the year, according to the sacred calendar used in Orissa. On this occasion a small image called Chandrasekhara is taken from its shrine as a substitute for Bhuvaneshwara, and placed upon a car

with much pomp and music, and is taken to a tank which, as its name, Pāpāsini, implies, has the power to wash away sin, and there bathed; it is then dressed in new clothes, worshipped, and brought back amidst a crowd sometimes numbering as many as ten thousand people.

2. *Pravaranotsava* is a festival held when the cold season is considered to have fairly set in. The flat stone forming the base of the image has warm clothes placed upon it; from its shapeless form it cannot of course be properly robed.

3. *Pushya Jātra.* On this occasion 108 pitchers of water brought from the Vindu Sāgara Lake are poured over the image, after which it is dressed in new clothes, and presented with a garland of mustard flowers, and regaled with music and singing.

4. *Markara.* This is held on the day when the sun commences his return to the north. On this occasion, too, 108 pitchers of water are thrown over the idol, and offerings of new rice, fruits, &c., are made. This is a sort of harvest festival.

5. *Māgha Saptami, i.e.*, the seventh day of the new moon in the month of Māgh. The image mentioned before as Siva's substitute is taken to a temple of Bhaskareshwara (Lord of the Sun) a mile distant, and then adorned with new clothes, feasted and worshipped. The reason why a substitute is carried about instead of the image itself is this: It is taught that when once an image of Siva has been fixed in any place it is a great sin to move it. Hence we find many images of this deity standing amid ruined temples because it is believed sinful to remove one that has once been set up for worship.

6. *Sivarātri* is held on the fourteenth night of the wane of the moon in Phalgum. The origin of this festival is given in the following legend: A fowler having lost his way in a wood took refuge in a bêl-tree, and, weeping, his tears fell on a decayed leaf and carried it to a Linga of Siva that happened to be near. The deity was delighted with this un-

intentional offering, and so the pious Saivites regard the day as a fast, and worship Siva at the four watches of the night. At Bhuvaneshwara 100,000 bêl leaves are offered at the four watches to an image representing half Vishnu and half Siva.

7. *Asokāshtami.* This day is sacred because Sitā when confined by Rāvana offered some asoka leaves to Siva in order to induce him to assist her to rejoin her lord. On this day at Bhuvaneshwara Siva's substitute is carried to a temple of Rāma with great pomp, where it remains for a few days. This is the rival ceremony to the Car Festival at Puri, and the practices of that ceremony are most closely followed in the worship of Siva.

8. *Daman-bhangika Jātra.* This festival is peculiar to Orissa. As on this day Jagannātha is supposed to go to steal thyme from a neighbouring garden, Siva's representative is taken to a plātform where he receives presents of ornaments made of thyme.

9. *Chandana Jātra.* On this occasion the proxy is taken to a temple on an island in the Vindu Sāgara Lake, where he remains for twenty-two days. Each evening he is carried about in a boat, and amused with music and dancing. During this time Bhuvaneshwara himself receives an extra smearing of sandal-wood paste daily.

10. *Parasurāmāshtama.* On this occasion Chandrasekhara is carried in a sort of chair on men's shoulders to a temple of Parasurāma, where he is entertained with flowers, music, and dancing. It will be noticed that all these visits of the god to other temples are an acknowledgment of their equality with the great deity himself.

11. *Sayana Chaturdasi.* This is the time when Siva and Parvati, represented by small images, are put to bed for their long sleep of four months. The day is spent in rejoicing. In the address to these deities it is said that by their sleep their worshippers will have rest.

12. *Pavitrapani Jātra* is the day when a new portia or sacred thread is presented to the god.

13. *Yamadevitrya.* Yama, the Lord of Hades, on this day was worshipped by his sister Yami, who by this act obtained longevity. Hence it is common on this day for sisters to feed their brothers, and present them with new clothes. At Bhuvaneshwara this festival is observed by Siva's proxy being carried to a temple of Yama, and is supposed by this act to obtain long life for his lord, the immortal Siva.

14. *Utthān.* This is the festival of awakening the deity after the four months' sleep. The idol is bathed, dressed, and worshipped. At all these and other festivals there are peculiar mantras and slightly differing forms of worship; but the variation is very slight.

A noticeable feature of the worship of Siva at this place is that, as at Puri, large quantities of rice and other articles of food are cooked and presented to the deity, and then Hindus of all castes purchase and eat it because of its supposed sanctifying power. This custom is peculiar to these two shrines. It is the more remarkable that in Siva-worship, the teaching of which is generally in favour of the caste system, this custom should prevail; but it is evidently copied from the practice prevailing at the great rival establishment at Puri. Though many pilgrims travelling to Puri pass within a few miles of this temple on their way to see Jagannātha, they are too excited to remain here, whilst on their return journey they are generally too poor to pay it a visit, the gifts made at Puri having quite exhausted their resources. There is, however, no lack of legends to prove that of all places this is the most sacred, and its deities and tanks most beneficial to the worshippers. As a means of extracting money and offerings from the pilgrims before they approach the image of the great god, they must first present themselves before a colossal figure of a bull Nandi, which represents Siva's vehicle; then they must worship Bhāgavati, Khartikeya, and Ganesa, who are regarded as guardians of the shrine. In addition to this they must on their entrance into the town worship Vishnu as represented in a temple called Ananta; it was by his permission Siva was able to make this his secret abode. Each pilgrim must also ask from Vishnu permission to bathe in the sacred tank and enter the holy temple. He must next visit the temple of a goddess called Ardhapāpāharini, or "the one who removes half of a man's sins," and then he is free to bathe in the water of the sin-destroying tank. Great evil is threatened if any of these temples be passed by without worship being offered.

The lake referred to, the Vindu Sāgara, has this name because it is said that water from all the sacred tanks in heaven, earth, and the lower regions are constantly falling into it. It is taught, in the common language of panegyric, that once bathing in it will give more real merit to the bather than ten visits to the source of tho Ganges, Allahabad, Prayāga, or Ganga Sāgar. It is difficult to estimate what this virtue can be, as a *single* visit to any one of these places is said to wash away all sins of the past, present, and future. In the tank the crocodiles are well behaved, for though numerous it is declared that they never seize the pilgrims. Bathing in this tank is considered an indispensable part of the pilgrim's duty who visits this shrine.

CHAPTER VIII.

HINDU WORSHIP.

HOW SUSTAINED, AND OBJECTS SOUGHT THROUGH IT.

The people of India, as a rule, are uneducated. Of the total population in Bengal, as appears from the last census, 1 in 17 of the males are able to read and write; whilst of the females, 1 in 566 only possess this knowledge. When this fact is taken into account, a reason will at once be seen for the methods of instruction in religion that prevail in India.

1. There is Home Instruction. Knowing the inability of the masses of the people to read, though of course one cannot fail to be struck with their ignorance of Hinduism as a whole, at the same time the accuracy of the knowledge of the people of what belongs to their own particular sect is equally remarkable. I have no hesitation at all in saying that the illiterate Hindu knows far better what, according to the teaching of his sect, he ought to do and leave undone, than multitudes know of the simplest truths of Christianity in our Christian country. In India every man is, more or less, religious; and even when his moral life may be bad, his observance of caste rules and religious rites and ceremonies is generally most strict. Men who can scarcely count beyond twenty, and know not the letters of the alphabet, would die rather than eat food which had been prepared by men of lower caste, unless it had been sanctified by being offered to an idol; and would kill their daughters rather than endure

the disgrace of having unmarried girls at home beyond twelve or thirteen years of age. Every year thousands perish of disease that might recover if they would take proper nourishment, and drink the medicine that science prescribes, but which they imagine their religion forbids them to touch.

Whence is all this knowledge obtained? Largely through the teaching in the homes. In India, as elsewhere, the women are by far the most religious and superstitious; and here, as elsewhere, where people cannot read, it is found that the memory is unusually retentive. Stories heard when a child, and implicitly believed, are repeated, with embellishments often, to their children, and thus there is a constant religious education of the masses going on by the mothers chiefly, and by the fathers also, to some extent. I have often been struck with the correct notions that the children have, when very young, of the peculiar practices of the caste to which they belong. Just as in England there is an unconscious teaching by example, and a conscious, direct teaching by word; and in very young children it is easy to tell the character of the home in which they have lived: so it is in India, with this difference—that in England the social customs and life in the home are not universally regarded as under the law of religion; in India everything that has to be done, even to the choice of food, mode of dress, &c., has been settled by religious authority. As far as my observation has gone, I am decidedly of opinion that the Hindus are by far the most religious people I have met with. If a question is asked in England, "Why do you do this or that?" the answer would be, "I don't know; others do it, and we do as they do." In India it would be, "It is our dharma, our religion, that ordains it." Here and there, it is true, you find infidels, men who do not care for the gods, but these are most rare; and though they may not give anything to the gods as offerings, they must respect the rules of their caste, or they must either give up their old companions and unite themselves to some sect in which caste rules are disregarded, or live a solitary life. In the temples, mothers teach their children to present their offerings, and to bow down before the idols; in the rivers they teach them to bathe with becoming reverence; in their journeys to the sacred spots they tell them of the great benefits to be derived from all this painful effort; and in the homes they tell them the names and doings of some of the many gods that are commonly worshipped by the people. And as a result of their earnestness in religion in our mission work we find that the greatest obstacles to our progress are those that the mothers and wives place in our way.

2. The Teaching in the Schools. The efforts of the educational department of the Government to induce the indigenous schools of the lowest grades to place themselves under Government control and inspection, and the fixing of text-books for study, in order that the children may appear in the periodical examinations, has done a great deal towards removing this method of religious instruction. Before the Governmental system came into operation, and in some places now where the Pātshālas (primary schools) are not included in the Government schemes and the teachers are free to select their own text-books, books are read which have had a large influence in the education of the people in Hinduism. As the Hindus are a religious people, it is only natural that they would wish their children to read religious books; and religious books for them, of course, mean books in which the religion of the Hindus is taught. In these books there are stories from the Purānas of some of the various deities worshipped, and the time devoted to the reading of these stories gives an opportunity for the teacher to enlarge upon the benefits that come from the proper adoration of their idols, very much as an earnest Christian would seek to explain and enforce the lessons of the Christian Scriptures. But this method of teaching is fast passing away, as the books selected for the examinations are generally free from distinctively religious instruction.

3. Next to the teaching of the mothers, perhaps in some

respects even more influential than that, is the teaching of the guru, or spiritual guide. When a child is about nine or ten years of age, if a Brāhman, Kshatriya, or Vaishya, he is invested with the sacred thread, and thus initiated into the Hindu religion; or if of the lower castes, he is initiated by the receiving of the mantra only from his guru. The father chooses a guru for his child, and the guru, either from the name the child bears or from some other causes, decides which of the many deities is to be the Ishta Deva of the child. This term means, "chosen deity"; and it is supposed that though all the gods of the Pantheon are his guardians, this one will be particularly propitious to him, and it is this deity that he must worship above all others. The initiation is performed by the guru whispering in the candidate's ear a mantra or text, which on no pretence whatever must be repeated to another person, or the most dreadful results are threatened. I have heard several of these mantras from those who, having embraced Christianity, have no superstitious fears respecting them, but can make no meaning out of them, nor could those who received them. It is, perhaps, more reasonable to suppose that the words were formed with some skill, expressing some truth, if the key to their interpretation were only known. But so far as I have been able to learn, the words only are given without any clue to their meaning. One word in the mantra is, of course, the name of the chosen deity. This mantra it is the duty of the person receiving it to repeat at least once daily on rising from sleep, and once before retiring to rest; but as there is believed to be great virtue in its mere repetition, by many it is done 108 times during the day. When the initiation is completed, the guru receives a fee from the father varying according to his circumstances, and the one initiated is reckoned ever after as a disciple of this guru, and the bond thus formed is indissoluble except by death. As is noticed in the chapter on sects, in some cases the guru is taught to be worthy of respect equal to that given to the god; in others he is said to be superior even to deity. Hence it is no uncommon thing when a disciple meets his guru for him to prostrate himself before him, and take the very dust from his feet and place it on his head.

The guru, being the spiritual guide of his disciples, visits them from time to time. Some visit their disciples monthly, some quarterly, some yearly, and some at even longer intervals. Whenever they go they expect to be paid for their visit; and as some of these have no home of their own they spend their time in the homes of their disciples, moving from one to another, and staying a day or more with each. All these gurus acknowledge some central authority, to whom they are expected to pay a portion of the fees they receive. When they go to see a disciple they generally give some instruction in religious matters. The most common plan is to read a few passages from some of the many sacred writings, and translate and expound them. As the gurus are generally illiterate, ignorant men, they often learn by rote a few sentences of Sanskrit, which they interpret to their disciples; and when the time comes for them to pay another visit, they prepare for it by learning more. In travelling about the country this fact strikes one when in conversation with the people, that a good number of them appear to be familiar with one set of stories about one or other of the deities, and employ the same religious phraseology, a few miles only away quite a new set of religious ideas and words prevail, those of the other district being almost unknown. The explanation of this fact, I think, is this—that the gurus of the one district have taught one part of the Hindu Scriptures, the gurus of the other district being better acquainted with some other parts.

For the women who receive the mantras there are female gurus, usually of the Vaishnava sects; in some houses, however, the male gurus enter freely, and it would be regarded as a great sin, and productive of immense evil, were the doors closed against one of these saintly men who might wish to enter. The gurus in their periodic visits seem to discharge the duties of the minister who visits his people in their homes to supplement the lessons given from the pulpit, and has even more influence over his disciples than the confessor in the confessional. There is no doubt, therefore, that by this means the doctrines of Hinduism are taught, and the religious enthusiasm of the people excited. For when it is remembered that there are shrines connected with all the various sects of which the gurus are the main advertisers, and that the advice of the guru is taken as the voice of God, it is his duty, as it is his interest, to recommend a pilgrimage to these holy places, in which he, as well as others, will participate in the offerings made there. The great reformers of Hinduism have shown their appreciation of the great influence these men and women exert by the fact that they have generally settled down for years at Benares, Puri, and other holy places, that they might teach their doctrines to the gurus and professed religious ascetics who assemble there.

4. The next important method of instruction is the religious festivals, as we have already shown. Each month has some day or days that are especially sacred to some one or other of the deities; and though each has his own peculiar guardian deity, he is also bound by fear of the evil of neglect, or by the hope of gaining some good, to show his respect to each and all of the rest. Some of these deities, whose images are enshrined in temples, have special days on which some event of their lives is brought into special prominence by the ritual observances which have been already noticed; whilst those who have no permanent images are brought before the people, and the events of their lives taught by means of images that are made for the occasion, worshipped for a longer or shorter period, and then cast away. In a few cases, deities whose images are to be seen in the temples are also worshipped in the houses. In speaking of the places of pilgrimage sacred to Siva and

Vishnu, I have already described some of their festivals, and it will be easily seen that as Good Friday and Christmas Day bring to the remembrance of the Christian community the fact of Christ's birth and death, and as the Passover preserves amongst the Jews the memory of the deliverance of the first-born in Egypt; so these festivals in the temples, and in the houses of the people, which are attended by thousands of people, are immensely powerful as a means of instruction to the ignorant, and tend to stimulate the faith and devotion of others.

With this round of festivals, with the change of image month by month and all the attendant ceremonies, with the descriptive song and mythological representations, it is not at all surprising that the people know a great deal about the most popular deities. It would be almost impossible to find in all India a man as grossly ignorant of the names and doings of the chief deities of the Pantheon as some in England are ignorant of Jesus Christ and His apostles. The processions meet the gaze of all, the sound of music and singing reach every ear, and the natural inquisitiveness of human nature prompts men to ask what it all means. The quiet and respectable services in Christian churches are all that could be desired for those who, by other agencies, are taught the truths that are embodied in these services; but for the mass of the ignorant who cannot read, there can be no doubt whatever that the attractive festivals of heathenism as an instructing agency are far superior. Teaching by the eye is more easily understood, and more easily retained in the memory, than that which comes through the ear only. One has only to see how people laugh or weep as they witness ludicrous or pathetic plays and long remember them, and compare this with the comparative inattention to discourses from the pulpit; whilst it is true, as O. W. Holmes says, that though men listen to, say, one hundred theological lectures in the course of the year, comparatively few can express the doctrines taught in an intelligible manner.

5. Reading of the Rāmāyana or Mahābhārat and the Purānas. There is yet another method of instruction. A man in fulfilment of a vow made in time of trouble, or from some other motive, will engage readers to read the Mahābhārat or Rāmāyana to the people.

Sometimes the readers will sit in the courtyard of the house, or if the weather be favourable, under the shade of a tree, and hundreds, sometimes thousands, will gather round him and sit for two or three hours in the morning and again in the evening to listen to them, some of whom are most entertaining with their comments. These sacred books are not lacking in promises of good to those who read or hear them read. Almost every chapter closes with the assurance that those who read or hear it will by that simple act obtain freedom from all their sins. It is a meritorious act for a man to have them read; it is a meritorious act for the paid reader to read their sacred words; and it is a meritorious act to sit and listen to them. At the Ghāts in the North-west there are men whose work it is to read these or other books during the greater part of the year, and a more orderly and attentive audience one could scarcely wish to have. The reader often stops to explain the meaning of the more difficult passages; whilst, as a relief from the monotony of his voice, and to give him breathing time, at a sign from him, the audience breaks forth into a sort of response; generally taking the form of praise to some one or other of the deities. It is a most interesting sight to see hundreds of faces directed towards the reader, intent on hearing the life-giving, saving words; and then as he looks up or raises his hand, to hear from the multitude the cry, "Jai, Jai, Rāma" (Glory, glory to Rāma). When it is remembered that, whilst the Vedas are not to be read to the common people, the two great epics are said to contain the essence of the Vedas, it occasions no surprise that when these oracles are read aloud, large numbers of low-caste people, both men and women, should gather together and try to hear what they believe to be the words of God to man. At times, though not very frequently, if a man does not quite understand what is read, he will ask for an explanation. This is the kind of promise given to those who hear these books; it is the encouragement to hear the Vishnu Purāna. Listening to the first book of this Pūrāna "expiates all offences. The man who hears this Purāna obtains the fruit of bathing in the Pushkara lake (bathing but once in this lake is said to remove all sin) for twelve years, in the month of Kartik. The gods bestow upon him who hears this work the dignity of a divine sage, of a patriarch, or of a spirit of heaven."

I have now described the many methods by which the Hindus are instructed in their religion, and the means by which their faith is strengthened and their zeal is fired. And though it is true of most of the educated Hindus that the entrance of the light of truth, scientific, historic, as well as religious, has revealed the errors and evils of Hinduism, one cannot move about amongst the uneducated people or the more ignorant of the Brāhmans without being impressed with the fact that Hinduism has a firm hold of the minds and hearts of the people. It is said with truth, that the gifts in the temples are not as numerous or as costly as they were, that the numbers of pilgrims visiting the shrines are lessening year by year, that the Brāhmans are compelled to seek for employment, or they would starve, who once were richly supported by the offerings of the people. But, notwithstanding all this, Hinduism is a mighty power in the land, and has an immense hold upon the people, as a visit to Jagannātha's festivals, or to any of the great shrines, will easily demonstrate. The most absurd stories are easily believed by the people; and the miracles of the New Testament are commonplace beside those that the people hear of as having been wrought by some of their many deities when they were incarnate amongst men.

I shall now try to show what is the object or end of all this worship; what is the main good the people expect to obtain by this long and costly round of duties.

In studying the religions of the people of India one cannot fail to be struck with the great variety of methods by which it is taught that the greatest good men desire can be attained, and, at the same time, the failure to find the rest that the performance of the work prescribed promised. It is stated, *e.g.*, in the plainest language, that bathing in the waters of the holy Ganges will cleanse the soul from all sins of the past, present, and future; nevertheless, those who live on her banks and daily wash in her holy purifying streams, at the proper season of the year will visit some particular part of the river, it may be hundreds of miles away from their home, where her waters are said to have greater purifying power. It is declared in the Mahābhārat and Rāmāyana that the mere hearing of the words of a single chapter of these books will have the like effect upon the human soul. It is declared that an offering made at some particular shrine, or bathing in some particular well, such as the Mankarnika well at Benares, will bring about the successful accomplishment of any desired work, and give to the believer the much desired mukti (final deliverance) from future births. Then again, we read that a visit to the holy city, and walking round the sacred enclosure will ensure entrance into heaven. Then a visit to some shrine, such as that of Jagannātha at Puri and others, promise similar boons. And yet when any or many of these good works have been done, the Hindu, as a rule, fails to find the peace he sought. I can account for this hurrying from one means of salvation to another partly by the gross ignorance and morbid fear of the people, excited by the fact that, though one act of merit may have satisfied one deity, others who have not been pacified may wreak their vengeance upon them. At great *mêlas* I have seen how the fears of the people are aroused. Some poor women who had bathed in the holy stream, paid their respects to the great deity that was worshipped there, were walking along with a crowd to see the sights of the place. A number of itinerant shrines having been set up, as is commonly the case at such places, as the people were not liberal enough with their gifts to these subordinate deities, the priests shouting loudly with angry looks assured the people that unless they gave something to them, the anger of these gods being excited, suffering here and hereafter would come upon them, notwithstanding the merit that had been attained by the visit to the festival. In fear the poor people give out of their poverty. There are so many creditors amongst the heathen deities that it seems to be more than a life's work to get out of their debt. Incited by the declarations of the priests, shrine after shrine is visited and work after work is done; still in the minds of the many there is a fear that some deity has been neglected who may at any moment demand his rights, and punish them for neglecting him.

Another noticeable feature of Hindu worship is the way in which each deity, in its turn, according to the particular faith of its worshipper, or object of the writer of the scripture which authorizes its worship, is regarded as superior to all the rest. Brahmā, Vishnu, Siva, Krishna, Sakti, each, in their turn, is regarded as supreme over all; it being declared that the others have received their being from the one who is being adored; and, in like manner, bathing, giving, hearing the Scriptures, penance, pilgrimage, is regarded for the moment as *the* way of salvation. The mind becomes bewildered. But as there are so many deities, and so great a variety of character in these deities, and such various kinds of work are pleasing to them, it is a fact that almost any habit can be indulged in, almost any vice committed, under the impression that it is pleasing to some deity or other. Is a man inclined to drink spirits, bhang, or use opium? He can do this as an act pleasing to Siva. Does he wish to eat flesh? This can be done as part of the worship of Kāli. Is he lustful? He has an example in Krishna. Is he fond of travel? He can go on pilgrimage.

An eminent Bengali Christian expresses himself on this subject as follows: "So grossly have the pernicious practices, ceremoniously observed in the country, blunted the sentiments of piety in her people, and corrupted their notions of the very fundamentals of divine worship, that a native [Hindu] scarcely ever thinks of worshipping his god except by means of unintelligible sounds which he has been taught to articulate without understanding their meaning, and to which he attributes a more than magical efficacy in propitiating the gods. . . . The Hindu ritual, of which the largest portion is carefully concealed from the vast majority of the inhabitants [*i.e.*, in Sanskrit], and no portion whereof can be used by the servile classes but in the presence and under the superintendence of the twice-born, has entirely disregarded the duty of rendering a rational and spiritual service to God. . . . It is the voice, no less of reason than of revelation, that hymns are uttered by means of words which the understanding does not comprehend, and can never expect a hearing or acceptance from Him . . . who, though a God that heareth prayer, cannot be expected to take pleasure in the mere acoustic of a religious ceremony." * As an illustration of the foregoing remarks is the following story from one of the Purānas. A man, in the hour of death being thirsty, called to his son, named Nārāyana, to bring him a little water. Vishnu, hearing the man repeating one of his names, though the idea of the god was not in the mind of the dying man, was so pleased that he sent his messengers to convey him safely to heaven, and save him from Yama, the king of Hades and the judge of men.

As some shrines promise special blessings—*e.g.*, Jagannātha promises pardon, Benares certain entrance into heaven, &c.—many visit them in the hope of obtaining the particular benefit promised there; but what is the desire and aim of the Hindu in his ordinary acts of worship? The following extract from the Vishnu Purāna puts in a clear and definite

* *Calcutta Review*, vol. iii. p. 142.

form the benefits the worshipper may obtain from worshipping him:

"He who pleases Vishnu obtains all terrestrial enjoyments, heaven, final liberation, and, in a word, all his wishes find gratification with whom Vishnu is pleased. How is he to be rendered complaisant? The supreme Vishnu is propitiated by a man who observes the institution of caste, order, and purificatory practices; no other path is the way to please him. He who offers sacrifice, sacrifices to him; he who murmurs prayers, prays to him; he who injures living creatures, injures him; for Hari is all beings. He is propitiated by him who follows the duties prescribed for his caste; who does good to others, never utters abuse, calumny, or untruth; who covets not another's wife or wealth; who never beats or slays any animate or inanimate thing; and who is diligent in the service of the gods, Brāhmans, and religious preceptors."

1. Worldly prosperity, or deliverance from some present or threatened evil.

With the great bulk of the people who visit the temples on ordinary occasions, it is with the definite hope of obtaining some desired object that the journey is undertaken. In times of sickness or trouble of any kind, the superstitious will make a vow that if deliverance is obtained a goat or goats will be sacrificed to Kāli, or a pilgrimage to Puri undertaken, or sacred water will be brought from the holy river and poured forth on, or in front of, some particular image. The idea of being able to purchase the favour of a special deity by their act of worship is a most common one. Bribery is one of the most common vices of the people. When a trial was pending, it used to be the common practice to bribe all connected with the court, from the judge to the lowest officer; and it was pretty well understood that the possessor of the longest purse would win the case. Now the European officers are known to be above suspicion in this respect, but it is believed by the people, and by their superior officers too, that the native officials of the lower courts are frequently bought in this manner. The same idea seems to prevail amongst the people respecting their gods—a costly offering being made, or a wearisome and dangerous journey being undertaken, in the belief that this act of homage will render the god propitious. That this is the case is further evident from the fulsome language which is addressed to these deities in turn. Whoever the god addressed may be, as the deliverer from threatened danger, or the giver of some desired boon, he or she is *the supreme being*. It is nothing more nor less with many of the people than an attempt to bribe the deity into compliance with their wishes; the idea of a God of love and goodness, who is ready without solicitation to do good to all His creatures, is unknown in Hinduism. God is regarded rather as an enemy whose favour must be purchased, a judge whose decisions can be influenced by gifts and service; this is by far the commonest notion that prevails throughout the country. Of the multitudes who flock to the festivals, it is not love that attracts, but fear that drives them there. "If we do not go," they say, "our crops will fail, our children or our husbands will die, our enemies will trample over us." If there is no special boon to be asked, there is this general evil to be averted.

2. Religious merit.

It is a most common and widespread notion that a man by doing any extraordinary deed (supererogation), such as the setting up of an image in his house, visiting the shrine of any deity, bathing, pilgrimage, incurring bodily suffering, can have a certain number of good deeds written down to his credit, which will be an equivalent for a certain amount of sins, caused by neglects of duty or by the committal of actual offences. A balance will be struck when he leaves the world, and his future condition depend upon the preponderance of good or evil. If good outweighs the evil, his next birth will be higher; if the evil preponderate, he will sink in the scale of creation. A low-caste man may, by his meritorious acts, become a Brāhman in a succeeding birth; and, in like manner, a Brāhman through sin may sink into a lower caste. Hence the religious are ever trying to lay up a stock of *punya* (merit), which will stand on the credit side of their account in the day of judgment. And though there are manifold ways prescribed for getting rid of sin, it seems to be a settled conviction, as it is explicitly declared in their Sāstras, that pardon of sin is impossible. As a man's works so will be his reward. But if there is no pardon, no forgiveness on God's part, there is the payment or the giving of an equivalent on theirs. And this is what is meant by their works of *merit*; it is an attempt, by means of religious acts, over and above what is absolutely necessary, to make a sort of set-off against their sins.

As far as I can gather from observation and conversation with the people, by their acts of worship there is no attempt after real purity of heart, the conquering of an evil nature, and a desire to please God in return for His goodness. Men sin at the shrines as they do in their homes, and on their return as before their visit. Nor is it thought anything remarkable that this should be so, excepting perhaps in the case of those who have left their homes, and gone to some sacred place in the hope of ending their days there. In cases of this kind I have heard of a higher, purer life being attempted, and of the expectation of this by those who know them. But certainly there is neither the attempt nor expectation of this in the minds of the large majority of the people who go on pilgrimage. It is not that they may be made pure, but that, by an act of penance, they may give an equivalent to the gods for their sins. Sin and punishment are indissolubly joined together; the penance of a pilgrimage is believed to be the punishment of sins committed, though in another form; if this were not self-inflicted, the gods would bring upon them the natural penalty that by unalterable decrees have been attached to the offences committed.

The Hindu Scriptures contain many stories to show how

men and demons (Asuras) even have, by their religious fervour and protracted penance, forced the gods to grant them the boon desired. Sometimes to their own hurt, often to the injury of the other deities, boons have been extracted from the gods by the pious acts of their worshippers; and it will be easily seen how the people's faith in their religious acts can be excited by the narration of such stories. Even in the present day will be found those who in great distress approach the gods, in the belief that they can by persistent suffering compel them to do their bidding.

The following is a typical story of the power of penance. A demon king of Tripura by the force of his austerities extracted a boon from Brahmā, much against his will, that he should be invulnerable save by a son of Siva. As that deity had no son it seemed likely that he would remain for ever free from injury; he therefore became so tyrannical that he even took by force treasures from the other gods, who in their distress repaired to Brahmā for advice and help. As a boon once granted could not be withdrawn, it was arranged that Siva should have a son, through whom the common enemy of the gods was destroyed. In a similar manner a worshipper of Siva, named Hiranyakasipu, obtained a boon that he should not be slain by man or beast, by day or night, in heaven, earth, or hell, presuming on which he made himself obnoxious to Vishnu, who exercised great ingenuity in getting rid of his foe without violating the letter of the promise Siva had given him. He came as a man-lion, *i.e.*, neither man or beast, slew his enemy at twilight, which was neither day or night, under the eaves of a house, which is proverbialy declared not to be in heaven, earth, or hell. In a chapter on the future life the benefits expected from worship will be further considered.

CHAPTER IX.

RELIGIOUS NOTIONS COMMON TO THE HINDUS GENERALLY.

1. *Unity of the Godhead.* This will seem strange to those who hear of the vast number of deities worshipped by the Hindus; yet it is a fact that there is scarcely any truth, as an article of faith, on which they are more agreed than this. "God is one without a Second," is a phrase that is on the lips of every one who speaks about the deity. They freely confess that this One God made the heavens and the earth; that He is the Creator of all men, whatever their race, colour, and creed; and that it is He who has made the distinctions between Hindus and those of other faiths. They explain their position in this manner: God is great and cannot be fully expressed by any one being; all the gods, differing as they do in form and character, represent a part, but only a small part, of His immensity. And they have no difficulty whatever in admitting that it is possible that Jesus Christ is another of the many partial manifestations of this Great Being, and Christianity another form of religion equally good in itself as Hinduism, though not for them. It is the claim of Christians for the supremacy of Jesus that offends them; were the Christian teacher willing to speak of Him as one of the Avataras, all that he advances in proof of this claim would be freely admitted by most of the Hindus. As an illustration of the belief in the unity of the Godhead, as has been noticed, each deity in his turn is extolled as supreme,

all the others being regarded as emanations from him. The same worshipper will use the same epithets in addressing any one of the gods, and so long as a general respect is shown to the other gods the Hindu has no objection to raise against any one employing the most laudatory epithets to any of the deities in turn. At times, owing to the many manifestations of this one God, the followers of Hinduism are puzzled to know which is the cause of any calamity; and hence it is not at all an uncommon thing for them to make vows to one after another in the hope that they may discover and so be able to appease the one whom they imagine has been offended.

2. *Belief in the holiness of God, and at the same time belief in the immoral character of His incarnations.* When asked the character of God the Hindus will repeat most glibly a string of attributes, most of which the devout Christian would admit as being truly descriptive of God. They will say He is without beginning or end; truthful, holy in nature, righteous in act, pure, merciful, almighty, all-wise, everywhere present; and yet they as firmly believe that this same God, when incarnate amongst men, was a "man of like passions with ourselves;" using His greater wisdom and power for the doing of greater evil. The stories of Siva's infidelity towards his wife and their consequent quarrels; Krishna's unbounded licentiousness (he is generally represented and worshipped not with his own wife but with the wife of another man); Rāma's ignorance of his wife's whereabouts when she was carried off by Rāvana, and his inability then to rescue her, and, when found, his inability to say whether she had continued true to him during her enforced residence in Ceylon, are as fully believed as the moral attributes of God just mentioned. And further, though God is declared to be almighty, we read of demons or men by the power of their religious fervour making even the deities to tremble with fear lest they should lose their thrones and divine honours. Hindus have admitted to me that they should be very sorry

for the gods to live near them and their families; and it has passed into a proverb, that whilst the teaching the gods have given is good and worthy to be followed, the example they have set is bad and unfit to be copied. In the present day there are philosophizing men who try to explain away a good deal of the worst teaching of the Purānas in this respect, and to give a poetical interpretation to the stories of the varied immoralities of the gods; but the mass of the people believe these accounts in their most literal form, and merely say that acts permitted to the gods are forbidden to men. The most disgusting stories are to be found in the sacred writings, with which the common people are made familiar; stories that explain the reason why certain emblems are worshipped as the representatives of certain gods; and in front of the images, as soon as the strictly religious part of the ceremonies are over, most "fleshly" voluptuous songs are sung, not merely for the delectation of the people, but for the amusement of the deity too. Generally speaking, the Hindus profess to believe in a Supreme Deity, who is holy, pure, and good; but the manifestations of that Deity in every case are opposed in character to this ideal Being. And yet it is most difficult to enable them to see the incongruity of this faith.

3. *Belief in innumerable incarnations.*

The Hindu who professes to believe in millions of incarnations of deity, finds no difficulty in adding to this number at any time; hence we see that when any great teacher or reformer arises he is either deified during his lifetime or by his followers after his death. Buddha, although a most stern and successful opponent of the popular Hinduism, was seen to be far too influential to be regarded as an ordinary mortal, and so he is declared to have been an incarnation of Vishnu, who appeared for the special purpose of deceiving men and leading the devout worshippers of the gods into heresy, that by this means their power might be diminished. Chaitanya, who three centuries ago was an ordinary teacher of a new sect, became exalted to divinity, and is now worshipped with as great veneration as Krishna, whose devoted servant he professed to be. So earnest was the devotion of some of Keshub Chunder Sen's followers a few years ago, that they addressed him in terms differing but little from those employed in the worship of God; and there can be little doubt that, but for fear of public opinion, that same tendency would have led his followers to place him amongst the gods. Even now, no one is allowed to sit upon the platform in the mandir (church) where he sat to teach, as though *he* were still the minister or teacher, present in spirit though absent in body. The addition of another incarnation is a comparatively easy matter with the Hindu. But the clumsiest of all is certainly that of Buddha, mentioned above, where the deity is said to have come down to earth simply to lead devout men into error, because of the immense merit they gained through their earnest devotion.

4. *The belief in Māyā.*

This term, meaning illusion, plays a very important part in the philosophy of the Hindus, but I wish to speak of it here only as it influences the religious life of the people. The common notion of the mass of the people is, that the world and all that is are an emanation from God; that as the snail comes out from the shell and can withdraw itself at will from sight, so the universe has come out from God, and He can withdraw all into Himself. And yet, though all things are God in other forms, men think of themselves as something different from Him! This is all Māyā, or illusion. True wisdom consists in realizing the oneness of all things with God; and when this is done the man's separate existence ends, and he gains true blessedness in reunion with the Divine Spirit. The common phrase the people use is that creation is the play or sport of God. He was tired of being alone, and for His own amusement formed the world from Himself; all the pains and miseries and vexations of life come from the influence of Māyā, from the individual imagining himself to be something distinct from God. There are several ways by which this illusion can be overcome. Some seek to overcome it by the observance of the rites of religion, by obtaining merit that shall greatly overbalance the sins of life; but when it is gained in this way, by some it is taught that it is only a partial, temporary blessedness that is secured. The best way of all is by meditating on the identity of the soul with God, until the mind becomes conscious of nothing else. In other words, as it seems to an outsider, supreme bliss consists in having no knowledge and no desires; indifference to heat and cold, hunger and thirst, day and night, self and the world. A life of inaction is the noblest man can live; and a life without thought is better than an active, self-denying one. Certainly most of those who are thus seeking bliss appear almost idiotic. Their life is perfectly useless to themselves and to others, and their chief virtue consists in indifference to the comforts and conveniences, or the pains and disappointments of life. It always appeared to me that the ideal of human life, as illustrated by these men, gives the most complete condemnation of Hinduism next to that of the character of the incarnations of deity.

5. *Pantheism.*

Connected with, in a sense, as an outcome from it, is the general belief in Pantheism: God is everything; everything is God. I have heard men exclaim repeatedly, "I am part of God;" and it is a most common reply, when it is attempted to show the evil of sin, that sin is not sin, *i.e.*, not violation of God's law; that man's acts, whether good or evil, are not his own; he does simply what God compels him to do. Nothing tends more to blight a man's moral sense than this loss of the sense of freedom and moral responsibility; and yet it is the common belief of the large majority of the Hindus. They will laugh at illustrations such as that of the Judge and the Prisoner;—"I was impelled by God to strike that man, I am therefore not responsible; but I am also impelled by God to punish you"—and yet go away quite comfortable in the assurance of their own immunity from punishment for similar deeds. It is most generally believed and most freely admitted, that God induces men to sin, as He induces them at other times to do right; and that the blame in the one case and the merit in the other is God's, not man's. The idea is rejected that we are conscious of freedom of choice, and that upon this alone rests the possibility of a just judgment of mankind by God. It is argued that since "God is everywhere, He must be in me; and if He is in me, He, being mightier than I, must induce me to act as He wishes." When it is remembered that the gods themselves were not over-scrupulous in their conduct, it need occasion less surprise that it can be believed that He would induce men to sin also.

6. *Fate.*

No doctrine is more commonly and implicitly believed than this, that all man's life is arranged by the deity, and that it is useless for him to attempt to go against the Divine decrees; all that man can do is to submit. During the first few days of a child's life the deity is believed to write a sketch of his career on the forehead, and what is written is said to be inevitable. Hence when trouble comes it is regarded as a sufficient explanation to say, "It is written." There is only one way, so far as I know, of gaining an alteration of this destiny, viz., by bathing in a tank at Benares, where it is promised to the bathers that they can obtain a successful issue for their plans, although the opposite has been written by the gods. No doctrine seems to be more necessary to India than this—that it is not enough to say, "God mend all," but that man must help Him to mend what needs attention. This bowing to Fate paralyzes effort, and multitudes die year by year through its baneful influence. In times of sickness remedial measures will not be tried, because if it is written that the patient must die he will die, whatever trouble be taken or expense incurred.

From what has already been said on the subject of Hindu worship, it will be noticed that there is nothing in the example of the gods to lead to purity of heart and life, and the ritual observed in the public and private worship has no tendency in this direction, whilst many of the attendant ceremonies have just the opposite tendency, it occasions no surprise that a man who strictly observes the rules of his particular caste, and repeats the mantras of his guru, and is liberal in his offerings to the temples or gurus, is accounted a good Hindu, whatever his moral character may be. The practical side of religion, as seen in the renunciation of sin and the obtaining of a pure nature, is almost forgotten in Hinduism. That there are some truthful, pure-hearted men there can be no doubt, but it is not the result of their strict adherence to their religion that has made them so. The Sālgrāma, the ammonite used as a representation of Vishnu —which is accounted by the Vaishnavas as the most holy thing on earth—is a form into which he is said to have changed himself when his wife metamorphosed one of his mistresses into the Tulsi plant, in order that he might continue near to her. The associations of Hinduism have a demoralizing, polluting influence. And it is freely admitted by the more thoughtful that nowadays it does not matter what a man believes or does so long as he attends to the restrictions and duties of his caste, whilst caste itself is losing much of its influence over the educated and thoughtful of the people. Love to God and love to man are certainly not the natural outcome of the close observance of caste regulations, and of the most scrupulous performance of the rites of the Hindu religion.

WOMAN.

CHAPTER I.

*THE POSITION OF WOMAN, AS TAUGHT IN THE SĀSTRAS.**

At first sight it may appear strange in a work on the Hindu Religion to devote a book to the position of woman. In Christian countries, where woman is regarded as the equal and companion of man, if writing of those brought up in the Christian religion, where the highest privileges are obtainable by all who seek them, of course this would not be necessary. But as in India the position of woman is so inferior to that of man, and as this inferiority has the sanction of the Hindu sacred writings, it is necessary to a complete view of the Hindu religion that this should be most clearly stated.

It is commonly asserted by the Hindus, when their attention is called to the prevalent custom amongst the middle and upper classes of society of immuring their wives in the prison-like rooms known as the Zenāna Khanah, or women's apartments, and of preventing them from visiting other houses, excepting their own fathers, that this custom arose either in imitation or through fear of the Mussulmān conquerors. Under the rule of the Mahommedan princes, their wives' and daughters' persons not being safe, the system that prevails in the present day came into fashion. They admit that the liberty enjoyed by ladies in England may not have been given to the ladies of India, but at the same time they were not kept in anything like the same seclusion as that which

* *Calcutta Review*, vol. xxxvi. p. 315.

prevails amongst them to-day. This may be to a large extent true, but it certainly cannot be accepted as a full statement of the case. For, as we shall see directly, it is to the teaching of Manu, whose work was compiled about 900 B.C., that we must look for the origin of this system. In his work we find teaching so evil, and laws so cruel concerning woman, that no Mussulmān invasion was necessary to account for the want of confidence in woman's honour and virtue that is almost universal. It may be that when the conquerors came, some fifteen centuries after these laws had been in force, they put the crown upon the arch which was already waiting for them. Their unscrupulous conduct may have tightened the chains by which woman was already enslaved. There is, however, no doubt that the lessons of this old lawgiver were quite sufficient of themselves to account for all we see around us in India to-day. The Mussulmāns conquered other countries besides India, but it is only in that country, where Manu's book was already in authority, that we find women regarded as altogether unworthy of the respect and trust of their husbands.

In some respects the women of Greece and Rome were treated as they are at the present time in India. In a speech delivered by an Athenian on his trial for the murder of his wife's seducer, we gain an insight into the customs that then prevailed in Athens. He assures the judge that whilst he treated her kindly, he did not allow her to be master of his fortune, nor of her own actions. After she became a mother, he says, he placed more confidence in her, and allowed her to go out of his house unattended by himself, to be present at the funeral ceremonies of her mother-in-law. And it was whilst away from home on that occasion that she was seen by her seducer, and by means of her servant induced to listen to his evil proposals. Browne, in his work on their Civil Law, says of the Romans that "wives were dismissed not only for want of chastity, or for being of intolerable temper, but for the slightest causes," and further, that "they were never considered to have attained the age of reason and experience, but were condemned to the perpetual tutelage of parents, husband, and guardians." This last passage is almost identical with one of the lessons given by Manu.

We shall now examine the teaching of the Hindu Law Books on the position of woman.

She must ever be in a state of dependence upon and of obedience to others. "By a girl, or by a young woman, or by a woman advanced in years, nothing must be done, even in her own dwelling-place, according to her mere pleasure. In childhood must a female be dependent on her father, in youth on her husband, her lord being dead, on her sons. A woman must never seek independence." * The commentators add a few words to provide for all contingencies: "If she have no sons she must be dependent on and subject to the near kinsmen of her husband; if he have left no kinsmen, on those of her father; or, if she have no paternal kinsmen, on the sovereign."

This legislation is perfectly one-sided. Though the husband be altogether bad, though he be cruel and untrue to his wife, this does not at all free her from her obligation to him, as the following passage clearly teaches: "Though unobservant of approved usages, or enamoured of another woman, or devoid of good qualities, yet a husband must constantly be revered as a god by a virtuous wife." † The result of this law is that when a husband, as frequently is the case, is unfaithful to his wife, and it is known that he has other women in his keeping, there is no redress for the injured wife. She cannot obtain a divorce from him; and, were such a course possible, she would be treated in her own family as a widow; *i.e.*, as we shall presently show, her life would be made as wretched as man's ingenuity could conceive.

The wife, according to the same authority, has no separate independent existence apart from her husband. She is for-

* "Dharma Sāstra," chap. v. pp. 162, 163.

† Chap. v. p. 154.

bidden the comfort even of approaching the gods in her own name and on her own behalf. "No sacrifice is allowed to women apart from their husbands, no religious rite, no fasting. As far only as a wife honours her husband, so far she is exalted in heaven. A faithful wife who wishes to attain in heaven the mansion of her husband must do nothing unkind to him, be he living or dead." * This seems to be about the most cruel of all these laws: a woman is denied free access to the gods in her own name. Of course women are to be found in large numbers at the shrines, at the sacred bathing-places, &c.; but it is only as an appendage of their lords: only in his name can they reach the ear of heaven. It is further declared that "women have no concern with the text of the Vedas. This is lawfully settled. Having, therefore, no evidence of law, and no knowledge of expiatory texts, sinful women must be as foul as falsehood itself. And this is a fixed rule." In perfect accord with this is the teaching of some of the sects that women cannot obtain final emancipation, the highest bliss of heaven. They must be re-born into the world as men: thus, and thus only, is the highest blessedness available for them. Of the religious acts that may be performed by women in their own name we shall speak later on.

The bond uniting a woman to her husband is indissoluble even by death. Widow-remarriage is said, on good authority, to be not contrary to the general teaching of the Hindu Scriptures, and consequently a law permitting it has been passed by the Government of India; but Manu certainly teaches that a widow must continue her widowhood until her death, and the general sentiment of the community is so strongly opposed to widow-remarriage, that those who have availed themselves of this act have been outcasted by their fellows. Manu's teaching is as follows: "Let her (the widow) emaciate her body by living voluntarily on pure flowers, roots, and fruit; but let her not, when her lord is

* Chap. v. pp. 155, 156.

deceased, even pronounce the name of another man. Let her continue until death, forgiving all injuries, performing harsh duties, avoiding every sensual pleasure, and cheerfully practising the incomparable rules of virtue which have been followed by such women as were devoted to one only husband." "A widow who, from a wish to bear children, slights her deceased husband by marrying again, brings disgrace on herself here below, and shall be excluded from the seat of her lord. Issue begotten on a woman by any other than her husband [*i.e.*, of course, her first husband] is here declared to be no progeny of hers, . . . nor is a second husband allowed in any part of this code to a virtuous woman. She who neglects her former husband, though of a lower class, and takes another of a higher, becomes despicable in this world." But how different is the case with man! A few verses on we read: "A twice-born man, versed in the sacred ordinances, must burn with hallowed fire and fit implements of sacrifice, his wife dying before him, if she was of his own class and lived by these rules, *i.e.*, virtuously; having thus kindled sacred fires and performed funeral rites for his wife who died before him, he may marry again, and again light the nuptial fire." * A man may marry as often as he may wish, but the widow must remain unmarried until her death. And it is no uncommon thing for a widower, who has performed the funeral rites for his wife, to go through the marriage ceremony with a new wife, after an interval of only a few weeks. There is, however, this fact to be remembered, that his new wife being but a child, it may be necessary for him to live alone for years ere she is old enough to join him.

During her life the position assigned to the wife by Manu is one of entire subjection to her husband, and in order to ensure obedience he ordains that it is quite within a husband's rights to inflict corporal punishment upon her if she prove disobedient. "A *wife*, a son, a servant, a pupil, and a younger brother, may be corrected, when they commit

* Bk. v. p. 157, ff.

faults, with a rope or a small shoot of a cane." This seems to be generally admitted as a perfectly right position by the women. A servant in my employ had married a second wife, and expected the elder woman not only to earn her own living, but to give up her wages to him, that he might indulge his own passion for strong drink, and be able to maintain his new wife in comparative idleness at home. Occasionally the woman resented this, and was thrashed most severely for her contumacy. On one occasion, when her husband was more violent than usual, and threatened to murder her, she came to me for advice, and agreed to go the next day before a magistrate, to obtain legal protection against her husband. On the following day, when I suggested that we should attend court, she affected surprise at my suggestion, and gave what appeared to her a sufficient reason for continuing to endure his cruel treatment, as she said, "He is my husband, cannot he do as he likes with me?"

Concerning the moral nature of woman, Manu speaks in no measured terms, and his opinion is quite endorsed by other writers on morals, as we shall see. "It is the nature of women in this world to cause men to sin." "A female, indeed, is able to draw from the right path in this life, not a fool only, but even a sage, and can lead him in subjection to desire or to wrath." There can be no doubt whatever that it is this low opinion of woman that is the ultimate cause of the greater part of his legislation concerning her.

Although the wife must honour her husband as her god, and must remain a widow after his death, the husband, on the other hand, may, after seven years of marriage, if there be no son born, supersede her by another wife: nay, it is taught by Manu that "a wife who speaks unkindly may be put aside without delay. . . . If a wife drinks, shows hatred to her lord, is mischievous, or wastes his property, she may at all times be superseded by another wife."

Hitherto, in giving the laws respecting woman's position, I have quoted only from Manu's "Dharma Sāstra," a work that is regarded as of the highest authority by the Hindus. The following extracts will show the position he occupies as a religious lawgiver amongst the Hindus of all classes.

"Of Manu's antiquity and reality there can be no doubt. . . . It is clear that the code was compiled by a Brāhman well versed in the lore of the Vedas, and to a certain extent in the ways of the world, thus combining secular and book knowledge at once. Nor, again, is there any doubt as to Manu's being the main fountain whence the religious observances of a country where every custom is based on religion, the hopes and the fears of the Hindu in this life and in the next, the various regulations of society and intercourse, marriage and inheritance, birthrights and funeral pyres, spring and are perpetuated. This is indeed the Sāstra to which learned and unlearned alike appeal. The well-read Pundit, when we ask of him the reason for this or that custom, will base his answer on a text from Manu. The secular Hindu, nay, the unlettered ryot, while pleading in extenuation of some grave folly sanctioned by the transmission of ages, unconsciously repeats the substance of some time-honoured sloke. But most Hindus, if asked the age and date of their great legislator, would answer in a breath that he was the son of the 'self existent,' that he was taught his laws by Brahmā in one hundred thousand verses, and that finally he gave them in an abridged form to his son Bhrigu, who gave them currency to the world." "It is not a system of uncompromising ambition or unmingled priestcraft *suddenly* erected by some enterprising Brāhman for those whom his arms had vanquished in the field." "It covers nearly all varieties of human life. It gives laws to kings and councils, to pleaders and clients, to the husbandman in the field and the mahājan on the ship; and it lays down the law which is to regulate man in every relationship of life into which he can enter. And in many respects its laws are as thoroughly acknowledged by the mass of the Hindus to-day as when the code was originally drawn up. And not only does the system deal with overt acts, but is as careful to regulate and to dilate upon the thoughts and desires of men which could hardly be referred to in the secrets of the confessional. It is a strange mixture, for there, in startling relief, contrasting as the vivid lightning on the black thunder cloud, will be seen in perhaps one and the same page puerilities of thought joined with masculine vigour of mind; Baconian profundity and bold truisms; the manners of Confucius or of Socrates with those of the most Jesuitical dishonesty; Draco's sternness and the simplicity of patriarchal simplicity; the politeness of Chesterfield and the rampant pride of Brāhmanical domination; wise saws straight as a sunbeam, and casuistry tortuous and at variance with itself; sensible views of natural history, and vague and childish solutions of the most common phenomena; truth and falsehood; darkness and light; and much that is noble and admirable in morals, with all that is vile and degraded of superstitions." Evidently he wrote at times as though men were good; at other times, seeing certain evils prevailing, he gives a sort of sanction to them, as though he saw that at present there was no reasonable hope of their being prevented; *e.g.*, "he legalizes abduction, and makes it one of the eight *forms* of marriage."

Before passing on to notice the present position of woman, I shall add a few words from a code of Hindu laws drawn up at the close of the last century by order of the Government of the day for the guidance of the judicial officers. The Hindus were to be judged according to their own time-honoured laws and customs—hence the necessity for some authority. It will be seen from the few extracts given that the spirit, and almost the words of Manu, reappear in this more modern code.

"A man both day and night must keep his wife so much in subjection that she by no means be mistress of her own actions. If the wife have her own free will, notwithstanding she be sprung from a superior caste, she will yet behave amiss." This passage is followed by another almost identical with the one quoted from Manu, declaring that her father husband, sons, &c., must have her under their care. "A woman is not to be relied on."

"A woman who always abuses her husband shall be treated with good advice for a year; if she does not amend with one year's advice, and does not leave off abusing her husband, he shall no longer hold any communication with her, nor keep her any longer near him, but shall provide her with food and clothes. A woman who dissipates or spoils her own property, . . . or who has an intention to murder her husband, and is always quarrelling with everybody, or who eats before her husband eats, such woman shall be turned out of the house."

"A woman shall never go out of the house without the consent of her husband; . . . shall never hold discourse with a strange man; . . . shall not laugh without drawing her veil over her face; shall pay a proper respect to the Deity, her husband's father, her spiritual guide, and the guests, and shall not eat until she has served them with victuals. A woman shall never go to a stranger's house, shall not stand at the door, and must never look out of a window."

"If a man goes on a journey, his wife shall not divert herself by play, nor see any public show, nor laugh, nor dress herself in jewels and fine clothes, nor see dancing, nor hear music, nor sit at the window, nor ride out, nor behold anything choice and rare; but shall fasten well the house door, and remain private. She shall not eat any dainty victuals, blacken her eyes with eye-powder, or view her face in a mirror. She shall never exercise herself in any such agreeable employment during the absence of her husband."

"It is proper for a woman, after her husband's death, to burn herself in the fire with his corpse; every woman who thus burns herself shall remain in Paradise with her husband 35,000,000 years by destiny." The text does not say how it will be if the husband is unworthy of attaining all these years of blessedness. If his deeds demand the punishment of hell, is it the duty of a faithful wife, as a reward for her self-immolation, to go there with him? "If she cannot burn, she must in that case preserve an inviolable chastity; if she remains chaste, she goes to Paradise; and if she does not, she goes to hell." *

"Confidence must not be placed in woman." "If one trust a woman, without doubt he must wander about the streets as a beggar."

Founded upon and in harmony with the spirit of these laws are proverbs commonly known and accepted by the people. "Blind sons support their parents, but a prince's daughters extract money from them;" *i.e.*, sons, however weak and helpless naturally, will nevertheless prove helpful to their parents, whilst daughters will simply prove a source of constant expense and trouble. "Unless a daughter dies, she cannot be praised for her virtue;" *i.e.*, that women are so frail, that however good and pure their lives may have been, there is no certainty that they will continue so.

It is true that in one passage Manu speaks a little more kindly of woman than he did in the texts quoted above. In one place he says that "good women, eminently fortunate and worthy of reverence, irradiate the houses of their lords, and between them and Lakshmi, the goddess of abundance, there is no diversity whatever." In another passage he says: "Where females are honoured the deities are pleased, and when they are dishonoured religion becomes useless." But as this is so utterly opposed to his general teaching, a writer in the *Calcutta Review* says truly, that "as Manu's 'Institutes' were evidently a compilation, had there been new and revised editions of his work, these gallant expressions would have been eliminated."

I have gone rather fully into the legal position of woman as taught in the Hindu writings, because it will be seen, when we come to consider their condition at the present

* "Code of Hindu Laws," 1776, pp. 285, 286.

day, that Manu legislation of 2000 years ago is still substantially the law of the Hindu community.

It must not be overlooked, however, that before Manu's day a very different state of affairs existed. In the Vedic times it is evident that woman was regarded more as her husband's companion, was treated with more confidence and respect, and was permitted to join her husband in the public religious festivals. "The original normal Vedic idea of religious worship appears to have been that it should be performed by a married couple, the husband officiating and his wife assisting. The normal household had one husband and one wife on a level of equality at the hearth, which was the altar of sacrifice. The wife had charge of the sacred vessels, prepared the sacrifice, and even sometimes composed the hymn." But even in the Vedic hymns, whilst sons are prayed for, and blessings implored on their behalf, daughters are not asked for, nor is intercession made for them. In one passage the inferiority of woman is implied as "the highest praise which the Rishi Syavaswa could give to a queen, his greatest benefactor, who had not only treated him with reverence, but had given him a herd of cattle, and costly ornaments, and put him in the way of obtaining the woman on whom he had set his heart. 'Sasiyasi, *though a female*, is more excellent than a man who reverences not the gods, nor bestows wealth,' on the principle that a living dog is better than a dead lion."* Several of the hymns show, further, that the old Aryans had not the highest opinion of woman's purity and virtue.

In the Epic Poems, scenes are described which are quite at variance with the prevailing custom of secluding women. The Mahābhārata has stories of Swayambaras, *i.e.*, festivals held at which princesses selected their husbands from a host of admirers, reminding one of the jousts and tournaments of the Western world. Meetings were held at which neighbouring princes were invited, and the prize for excellence in archery was the hand of the fair princess, who was permitted in those

* "The Vedic Religion," p. 165.

days to see and be seen by others. In one of these the skill displayed was far in excess of anything that is heard of in the present age. The target was a fish suspended from the top of a high pole, the competitors not being allowed to look directly at the object, but to shoot as they saw its reflection only in a vessel of water. Several competitors tried and failed. At length came Arjuna, the friend of Krishna, who was treated with the laughter and ridicule of several as he approached the place of trial; but hitting the mark, he carried off the prize, much to the chagrin and envy of those who had ridiculed him.

From the various forms of marriage, as they are termed by Manu, it is evident that women enjoyed far more freedom than is permitted now, or some of these would have been impossible, except amongst the lowest orders of the people, who are unable, owing to their poverty, to immure their wives and daughters; but, as mentioned previously, Manu evidently wished to give a sort of sanction to the customs he found prevailing which he was unable to suppress.

CHAPTER II.

THE PRESENT POSITION OF WOMAN.

It should be understood that this account refers more especially to the women of the middle and upper classes in North India. The poorer people would, if it were possible, seclude their wives as do those in more favoured circumstances. But when we consider the style of house, or rather hut, in which the mass of the people live, and the fact that it is necessary for the wife to go to the markets, draw water, and attend to all the duties of the house, seclusion for them is impossible. But the desire to act in the same manner is almost universal. I have known household servants as scrupulous in keeping their wives hidden from the public gaze as men of large incomes. It is not, therefore, that the husbands of the poorer classes are more kind and trustful than the rich; but simply that circumstances are against their carrying out their wishes in this respect.

The degradation of women commences from the very hour of their birth. Whilst the story of Hannah, as written in the Book of Samuel, is true of every Hindu wife who has not been blessed with a son, daughters are seldom prayed for, nor is their advent in a family welcomed. Though other reasons of a secular nature may be given for the universal desire for sons, it is doubtless the religious one, that a son is able to perform successfully the funeral rites of his parents and ancestors, that has the greatest influence. Unless these rites are properly performed, all a father's good works go for nothing; he must suffer in hell until some one performs them. A story is told in the Mahābhārata which enforces this duty. A man before he had entered the marriage state determined to live an ascetic life. In process of time he came into the spirit world, and there saw four men in the greatest distress, hanging by their feet from the bough of a tree overhanging a deep precipice. Rats were gnawing at the ropes which held their feet, so that they were in momentary expectation of being dashed to pieces. Entering into conversation with them, he found they were his father, grandfather, great-grandfather, and great-great-grandfather, doomed thus to suffer because their descendant had refused to marry and provide one who could, by his performance of the Shrādha, deliver them from their pains. Manu teaches, in the extravagant way common to Hindu writers, the immense benefits sons can confer on their families. A son born in a family where husband and wife, Brāhmans, were married according to the Brahmā form of marriage (*i.e.*, where the wife was given and accepted without gifts on behalf of either party), "redeems from sin, if he performs virtuous acts, ten ancestors, ten descendants, and himself the twenty-first person." A son born after marriage, according to the Daivya rite (*i.e.*, where a daughter, gaily dressed and laden with ornaments, is bestowed upon an officiating priest), can in like manner "redeem seven and seven in higher and lower degrees. Sons of marriages, according to the Prājāpatya rite, six; and those according to the Arsha rite, three ancestors and three descendants." It is interesting to see how the Roman Catholic doctrine of Purgatory, which makes the rescue of the souls of the departed depend upon the offerings of their living friends, has its counterpart, perhaps its origin, in Hinduism. I once heard a priest in a Catholic Church exhorting his people to arrange for masses for the souls of their friends based upon arguments that Hindus might well have used.

Hindu wives not blessed with sons give costly presents to the deities, undertake journeys to particular shrines, where the boon of sons is promised to visitors, endure long and severe fasts, and incur expense and fatigue to obtain this blessing. The trees near to the shrines are laden with stones, rags, &c., that superstitious women have tied there in commemoration of a vow, that if a son be given to them within a certain time, they will again visit the shrine with an offering of a certain value. Nor is this to be wondered at when it is taught by Manu that "a barren wife may be superseded by another in the eighth year (after marriage), she whose children are all dead in the tenth, she who brings forth only daughters in the eleventh." In addition, then, to the negative pain of having no son to prove a comfort and support, there is also the positive evil arising from the thought that she may have to give up her position of wife to another and more fortunate woman. And sometimes it happens that they are called upon to take a second wife to the home, because of the dreaded consequences of having no son in the house to perform the funeral rites. In the names of many of the Hindus, a history is suggested as in that of Samuel—"asked of the Lord." The names Kāli Prasanna, Durgā Prasanna, &c., indicate that in the belief of the parents it was "by the favour" of the deities after whom the child is named that they were given; and probably a vow had been previously made, that on the birth of the son an offering would be given at their shrine.

But whilst there is this great desire to obtain sons, daughters are seldom prayed for. When a son is born there is great rejoicing in the family, and friends come with their congratulations; but on the birth of a daughter there are no sounds indicative of gladness in the house; whilst, if friends call to see the father, it is with the offer of consolation. "The Bengali Kulin Brāhman sees in a daughter a bitter well-spring of anxiety, expense, and possible humiliation; for she must probably marry a man who already has many wives, most of whom he seldom sees; she must live as a burden in her father's house, and be exposed to manifold trials and temptations through the absence of her husband." And what is true of the Kulin Brāhman is true of the ordinary Hindu family, only in a less degree. The girl must be married before she is twelve or thirteen years of age; and to provide a husband will necessitate the expenditure of the savings of years; or, if there be no money in hand, debts will be contracted which it will take years to pay off.

In the religious ceremonies pertaining to the births of children there is a marked difference in the treatment of boys and girls. In order that the boy may be protected during the days of infancy and childhood, Sasthi, the special protectress of mothers and children, must be invoked on his behalf. She is propitiated with gifts that she may take the child under her care and save him from dangers incident to infancy. And on the fifth night after the boy's birth the father is most careful to place in the room, where the mother and her helpless babe are lying, pen and ink, flowers and fruits, so that Vidhāta, who is supposed to come down from heaven to write upon the infant's forehead all the main events of his life, being pleased with the offerings, may write a favourable and prosperous history. But in the case of girls all this religious work is omitted. Girls seem to be regarded as unworthy of attention, and from their very advent into the world are regarded as far inferior to men. It is this which accounts largely for the practice of infanticide which has prevailed so commonly in many parts of India.

We shall now pass on to notice the *girlhood* of Hindu women. Whilst the boys are early sent to school, as a rule the girls remain at home spending their time in play; and, further, whilst the boys are initiated at the age of seven or eight into the Hindu system by the guru appointed for them by their father by whom they are taught the mantra, and are then free to worship the gods, the Hindu girl's whole religious training has to do with certain ceremonies performed with the simple object of obtaining a husband, and that he may live long.* When it is remembered that these religious

* "The Hindus as they are," p. 35.

rites are first performed when the girl is but five years of age, it will be evident that the children must be taught a great deal that it would be far better for them not to know at so tender an age.

The following are the religious acts permitted to girls:—

1. Siva Puja, *i.e.*, the worship of Siva. The object sought by this ceremony is that she may obtain a husband as Siva. The origin of this rite appears to be the following:—When Siva's wife, Parvati, was angry with her father because he failed to invite her husband to his great sacrifice, she destroyed herself, and hence, among other names, is known as Sati, or the faithful wife. When she was born again into the world as Durgā, she was most anxious to be re-united to her husband; but as he had just commenced a life of severe penance, there seemed to be little chance of obtaining her heart's desire. However, she commenced to worship the ordinary image of her husband immediately in front of Siva, who was engaged in meditation, whilst Kāmadeva (the Indian cupid) promised to shoot an arrow at him whenever he raised his head. After a time, the opportunity coming, Kāma let fly his arrow; and Siva, seeing Durga engaged in his worship again became enamoured of her, and she obtained the blessing she sought. But Kāma suffered for his part in the transaction. A fierce fire issued from the third eye of Siva, which consumed the god of love to ashes. Little girls are taught to worship the image of Siva, that they, in like manner, may obtain a husband such as he was. But why they can desire one like him it is difficult to say; he is considered a model husband in this ceremony; but the Purānas teach that he was anything but true to his wife, and the quarrels of Siva and Durgā are anything but edifying reading. The ceremony is as follows:—"On the 30th of Chaitra, the last day of the Bengali year, the Hindu girl is required to make two little earthen images of this god; and, placing them on the rind of a bel-fruit (wood apple) with leaves, she begins to perform his worship. Before doing so, she is en-

joined to wash herself and change her clothes, a requirement which enforces upon her thus early—cleanliness, and purity in habits and manners, if not exactly in thought and feeling. The mind being filled with young susceptibilities, she imbibes almost instinctively an increasing predilection for the performance of religious ceremonies. Sprinkling a few drops of holy water (*i.e.*, water from some of the sacred streams), she repeats the following words: 'All homage to Siva. . . . All homage to Hara (another name of Siva). All homage to Bajjara' (meaning by this two small earthen balls like peas, which are stuck on the body of the images). She is then to become absorbed in meditation about the form and attributes of the god, and afterwards she says her prayers three times in connection with Siva's several names. Offerings of flowers and bel leaves are then presented to the god with an incantation (mantra). Being pleased, Siva is supposed to ask from heaven what Brata or religious ceremony Gauri (Durgā) is performing. Gauri replies that she is worshipping Siva that she may get him for a husband, because Siva is a model husband." *

2. Krishna Puja, or the worship of Krishna. This is performed with the object of obtaining a good husband and sons. "The two feet of the god being painted in white sandal-wood paste on a brass plate, the girl worships him with flowers and sandal-wood paste. The god, seeing this, is supposed to ask what girl worships his feet, and what boon she wants. She replies, 'May the prince of the kingdom be my husband; may I be beautiful and virtuous, and be the mother of seven wise and virtuous sons and two handsome daughters.' She also asks that her daughters-in-law may be industrious and obedient; that her sons-in-law may shine in the world by their good qualities; that her granary and farm-yard may be always full; . . . that when she dies, all those who are near and dear to her may enjoy long life and prosperity; and that she may eventually, through the blessing of Krishna, die

* "The Hindus as they are," p. 36.

on the banks of the sacred Ganges, and thereby procure entrance into heaven.

"It is worthy of remark here that even young Hindu girls, in the exercise of their immature discretion, make a distinction between the gods in the choice of a husband. In the Siva Puja a tender girl of five years of age is taught, almost unconsciously, as it were, to prefer that god to Krishna for her husband, because the latter, according to the Hindu Sāstras, is reputed to have borne a questionable character. I once asked a girl why she would not have Krishna for her husband. She promptly answered that that god disported himself with thousands of gopinis (milkmaids), and was therefore not a *good* god, whilst Siva was devotedly attached to his one wife Durgā." It will be noticed that in the Siva Puja the girl asks that Siva may be her husband, whilst in the Krishna Puja she asks the deity to provide her with one. It is not easy to see why both these gods should be worshipped with the same object; and certainly it is not easy to see how women can desire for a husband any one at all like Siva.

3. The worship of heroes. "This requires that the girl should paint on the floor ten pictures of deified men, as well as of gods, with rice paste (pitali). Offering them flowers and sandal-wood paste, she asks that she may have a father-in-law like Dasaratha, the father of Rāmachandra (one of the ten chief incarnations of Vishnu, the second person of the Hindu Triad), a mother-in-law like Kausalya, his mother, a husband like Rāma himself, a husband's brother like Lakshmana, Rāma's younger brother; that she be a mother like Sasthi, whose children are all living; like Kunti, whose sons were renowned for their justice, piety, courage, and heroism; like the Ganges, which allays the thirst of all; like Mother Earth, whose patience is inexhaustible. And, to crown the whole, she prays that she may, like Durgā, be blessed with an affectionate and devoted husband; that, like Draupadi (the wife of the five Pandavas), she may be re-

markable for her industry, devotion, and skill in the culinary art; and that she may be like Sita (Rāma's wife), whose chastity and attachment to her husband were worthy of all praise." It will be noticed that all these prayers and worship are expressive of the desire for a husband and for the obtaining of those virtues which will enable them to retain his affections. The second and third of these ceremonies are performed in the month Vaisakh (April and May), which is considered by the Hindus as the holiest of the twelve.

There are two other forms of worship which Hindu girls are taught to offer. The first is called the Sanjuti Vrata, and "is intended to ward off the thousand evils of polygamy. . . . To get rid of the consequences of this monstrous evil, a girl of five years is taught to offer her invocation to God, and in the outburst of her juvenile feeling is almost involuntarily led to indulge in all manner of curses and imprecations against the possible rival of her lord. Nor can we find fault with her conduct because 'an overmastering and brooding sense' of some great future calamity thus early haunts her mind. In performing this ceremony the girl paints on the floor with rice flour a variety of objects, such as the bough of a flower tree, a palanquin containing a man and a woman, with the sun and moon over it, the Ganges and Jumna with boats on them, a temple of Siva, &c. Having done this, she invokes Siva and asks for his blessing. An elderly lady, more experienced in domestic matters, then begins to dictate, and the girl repeats after her a volley of abuse and curses against her *satin*, or rival wife. The following are a specimen of the curses:

"'May my *satin* become a slave; may she be exposed to infamy; may I devour her head; may she have spleen; may she die, and may I see her from the top of my house; may I never have a *satin*.'" *

The other rite is the worship of Yama, the god of the spirit world, who is supposed to be always wandering on the

* "The Hindus as they are," p. 38.

earth with a noose to seize his victims, and a club to slay them, that his kingdom may not lack subjects. The object of this worship is that a husband in due time being given to her, his life may be long spared, and she be saved from the miseries of widowhood.

This, so far as I know, is the whole of religious worship that is taught and permitted to Hindu girls. When they marry they can make offerings to and approach the gods in the name of and through their husbands. Whilst girls at home, they see the worship of the various deities as it is performed by priests in their own homes or in their neighbours' houses, and learn from their mothers the stories connected with the various deities; but they have no personal share in this worship; they are taught that the one object before them is to obtain a husband, and towards the realization of this their devotion to the gods is directed. And further, at this early age their attention is directed, by the worship they are taught to offer, to the two great evils that may be in store for them: the possibility of having a rival wife to supersede them; and secondly, the loss of the husband whom they have been taught to regard as *the one blessing* of their existence.

But not only are the girls at this tender age taught to think about marriage, and some of the possible evils connected with it, but a year or two later they are actually married. We shall now pass on to notice the laws and customs connected with this event.

Marriage and the attendant ceremonies.

The authority for the early marriage of Hindu girls is to be found in the writings of Manu, and the spirit of his legislation is seen in all its force at the present time. The prevailing idea of the Hindus to-day is this: "The marriage of a girl is to be celebrated after she is seven years old, otherwise it becomes contrary to the dictates of religion. At the age of eight she becomes a Gauri (*i.e.*, Siva's consort, who in many respects is regarded as the ideal Hindu wife). At the age of nine a Rohini (the wife of Chandra, the moon), at the age of ten a mere ordinary girl." In other words, the sooner a girl is married the better, after she is seven years of age. Manu says: "Reprehensible is the father who gives not his daughter in marriage at the proper time," and declares that if before she is eleven her father has not provided her with a husband, she is justified in seeking one for herself. In teaching the duties of the two lowest of the four great castes, speaking on the question of marriage, he declares that "a man aged thirty may marry a girl of twelve, if he find one dear to his heart; or a man of twenty-four years a damsel of eight." In his regulations respecting Brāhmans he is most particular in his description of those whom he regards as suitable for their wives. Amongst other things, a Brāhman must avoid marrying a girl whose family "has omitted the prescribed forms of religion, that has produced no sons, that which has thick hair on the body, or is afflicted with hereditary diseases. Let him not marry a girl with reddish hair, one with too much or too little hair. Let him choose for his wife a girl whose form has no defect, who has an agreeable manner, who walks gracefully like a phenicopteros or like a young elephant, and whose body has exquisite softness."

When a widower seeks another wife, as widow remarriage is repugnant to Hindu custom, and as all the girls are married before or at the age of twelve, it follows that he, however old, must take one of these children to wife. And when, owing to his poverty, a father has failed to obtain a bridegroom somewhat near the same age as his daughter, he is only too glad to allow any one, though he be an old man, to relieve him of the disgrace attaching to a family in which there is an unmarried girl of twelve living in it.

It will be remembered that these children do not forsake their fathers' house immediately after their marriage. When the first marriage ceremony is performed an iron bracelet is put upon her wrist and a little red paint on her forehead at the parting of her hair, to show that she is married; after which she remains as a child at home until she is about twelve or thirteen, when she goes away for good to her father-in-law's house, and becomes ever after a member of her husband's family. In the interval she may see her husband at her father's house, or go on a visit to her father-in-law's, and thus become, to some extent, familiar with him and his family before she goes to his home for good. It sometimes happens that, owing to distance and the exposure of travelling, she never sees her husband's home until she goes permanently to reside there.

The worst feature of the marriage system of the Hindus, resulting from the necessity of having their daughters married whilst they are children, is seen in the case of the Kulin Brāhmans, the highest caste of all. As these girls must not marry beneath them, *i.e.*, Brāhmans other than Kulins, and as the supply of these is limited, fathers, who are not in a position to induce by costly presents a young man to take their daughters, and to remain content with her as his one wife, are compelled to give their daughters to those who make a living by being husbands. A child of twelve, under these circumstances, being given as, perhaps, the fortieth or fiftieth wife of some old man; sometimes two or more sisters being given to the same man; and sometimes to one who evidently has not long to live. Though it is certain that the girl must soon be a widow—even this is considered preferable to allowing her to remain unmarried. It can therefore occasion no surprise that from this class many forsake their homes to live in immorality.

As the ordinary bridegroom is about twelve or fourteen, and the bride from seven to ten, it follows that on their side there can be no choice; in fact, it often happens that they meet for the first time on the wedding-day. The choice of a partner for life is made not by the parties most intimately concerned in it, but by their parents on their behalf. There are men and women called Ghataks, whose work in life is to arrange for marriages; they are virtually marriage-brokers, who, having received a commission from a father who has a daughter or daughters to settle in life, go from family to family to find a suitable match, and when they have found one or more who wish to have their sons married, they bring the two parents together, who then enter upon negotiations respecting dowry, wedding expenses, &c. Sometimes, of course, the assistance of these middlemen is unnecessary; the fathers of the bride and bridegroom being old friends may arrange for the marriage of their children as a means of cementing their friendship; but generally marriages are arranged for through the assistance of the professional Ghataks.

As the Ghataks play so important a part in Hindu society, it may be well to say a little more about them. The Rev. L. B. Day thus describes them.* The Ghatak "is the professional match-maker, and therefore an under-servant of Kāmadeva, the Indian Cupid. As in India, young men and women do not themselves choose their partners in life, they have to depend on the good offices of this happy functionary, who, however, bears his commission not from the parties themselves, but from their parents and guardians. . . . This worthy functionary's character is as amiable as his occupation is pleasant. He possesses the highest Christian virtue in perfection, as he possesses an unlimited measure of that charity which covers a multitude of sins. He has never been known to find fault with any young man or young woman of marriageable age. The spinster may be as ugly as one of Shakespeare's witches, and the young man may be as deformed as deformity itself, the Ghatak sees no defect in either. The one in his eye, or at any rate in his mouth, is as beautiful and gentle as Lakshmi (the wife of Vishnu, the Venus of India), and the other as handsome and accomplished as Kartikeya (the Indian Mars). . . . A Ghatak, properly speaking, is a Brāhman of a very high order, and confines his services only to the priestly class. A Brāhman Ghatak is often a man of learning, and invariably a man of

* "Bengal Peasant Life," p. 81.

persuasive eloquence, and he has the whole of the Indian 'Burke's Peerage' and 'Baronetage' at his fingers' ends. But every caste has its own Ghataks," who are acquainted with the family history for generations of the families in their neighbourhood.

Another Bengali gentleman writes much in the same strain.* "When an unmarried boy attains his seventeenth or eighteenth year, numbers of professional men, called Ghataks, or match-makers, come to the parents with overtures of marriage. These men are destitute of principle, but know how to pander to the frailties of human nature; most of them are great flatterers, and endeavour to impose on the parents in the most barefaced manner. When the qualities of a girl are to be commended, they indulge in a strain of exaggeration, and unblushingly declare that 'she is beautiful as a full moon, the symmetry of her person is exact, her teeth are like the seeds of a pomegranate, her voice is sweet as that of the cuckoo, her gait is graceful, she speaks like Lakshmi, and will bring fortune to any family she may be connected with.' . . . If the qualities of a youth are to be appraised, they describe him thus: 'He is beautiful as Kartikeya, his deportment is that of a nobleman, he is free from all vices, he studies day and night—in short, he is a precious gem and an ornament of the neighbourhood.'" This same writer goes on to state that, as in these matrimonial alliances the leaders of the household have a great deal to say, of late years women have largely supplanted the men in this work of marriage brokerage, because they can gain access to the women's apartments, and by their influence lead to the rejection of overtures made by the men, and recommend others in their place. As payment goes to the successful Ghatak, it is not to be wondered at that when women undertake this work they should drive men out of the field. They are generally widows or low-caste women who engage in this work.

* "The Hindus as they are," p. 40.

I shall now try to give, as briefly as possible, the formalities connected with a Hindu marriage. The first thing to be done when the overtures of the Ghatak have been favourably entertained, and the amount of presents fixed that will be given by both families to the bride and bridegroom, is for a representative of the boy's family, generally his father or guardian, to call to see the intended bride. The little girl, gaily dressed and elaborately adorned with jewels, is introduced to this gentleman, who, after a little talk, if satisfied, puts a gold mohur (£1 12s.) into her hand, the mother remaining in the inner apartments, anxious to know the result. If the visit take place in the morning, no feast is made; but if in the evening, the guests partake of a grand dinner before they return. A similar visit of inspection is next paid by the girl's father to the boy's house, and in like manner, if he be thought suitable, a gold mohur is placed in his hand as the expression of the bride's father's approval. When both parties are satisfied, an agreement is drawn up by which the boy's father promises to marry his son to the girl, her father also agreeing to give his daughter; this document is then signed by the respective fathers and a number of witnesses. When this is done the contracting parties consult an almanac, and by the aid of the priests select a favourable day for the preliminary rite called the Gātraharidra, or anointing with turmeric.

This ceremony takes place a few days before the wedding-day. "After bathing and putting on a red-bordered cloth, the bridegroom is made to stand on a grindstone surrounded by four plantain trees, while four women (one of whom must be a Brāhmani), whose husbands are living, go round him five or seven times, anoint his body with turmeric, and touch his forehead at one and the same time with sacred water, betel leaf, &c. From this time until his marriage the boy must carry about with him a pair of silver nutcrackers, and the girl a case containing the black dye used in beautifying the eyelids, until the solemnization of the nuptials, for the purpose of repelling evil spirits. A little of the turmeric paste with which the body of the bridegroom has been anointed is sent by the family barber to the bride in a silver cup, with which she anoints her body, together with other presents." Two or three days after this ceremony a great feast is made by the father of the bridegroom to his male relatives; on the same day the father of the girl feasts his own female relatives.

After these preliminary arrangements comes the marriage ceremony proper, in which there are many unimportant parts which it is unnecessary to narrate. On the wedding-day the bride and bridegroom must only partake of a little milk and fruit before the wedding takes place; the bride's father and officiating priests must also be equally abstemious. During the day presents are sent to the bridegroom's family, and the fathers perform a ceremony for the benefit of their respective ancestors. The mother of the bridegroom, however, eats at least seven times during the day, the reason assigned for this being the fact that when Durgā's son, Kartikeya, went back home for a moment after he had started for his bride's house, he found her eating, using all her ten hands. When asked why she was thus engaged, she declared that she was making a good meal, because she was afraid that when her daughter-in-law came she might not have food enough.

Before the bridegroom leaves the house he is superbly dressed in coloured embroidered clothes, with necklace, armlets, &c.; he then worships Durgā, and as he is about to start his mother asks where he is going, to which he replies that he is going to bring home her maidservant. She then counsels him how to conduct himself in the house of his father-in-law; and just as he starts a plate of rice and a pot of vermilion are thrown over his head by his father and caught by his mother in her clothes.

The procession now starts, headed by a band of music, with torch-bearers, &c.; the youth riding either in a gaily painted palanquin or a carriage. As soon as he arrives he is conducted to his seat of red satin in the courtyard of the house under an awning which has been placed there for the occasion. When the guests are all seated, the genealogies of the two families are loudly proclaimed. After this the bridegroom lays aside his gay dress, and, having put on a simple robe of red silk, is conducted into the place of worship where the religious ceremony takes place. As soon as he is seated there, the bride, with her face still closely veiled, is carried on a sort of stool and placed on his left side. The priest then gives the bridegroom a few blades of Kusa grass which he winds round his fingers; he next pours a little Ganges water into his hand, which he holds there whilst his father-in-law repeats a mantra. Rice, flowers, &c., are next given to him, which he places near the vessel containing the holy water. The bridegroom having placed his hand in the vessel, and the bride hers upon it, the priest ties them together with a garland of flowers. As soon as this is done the father of the girl says: "I, ———, give ——— to thee, ———." The bridegroom replying: "I have received her." The father-in-law having united their hands, pours a little holy water on their heads and blesses them. Before the water is given, a form something like the following is generally used. The bride's priest, addressing the bridegroom, says: "The bride says to you, 'If you live happy, keep me happy also; if you be in trouble, I will be in trouble also: you must support me, and must not leave me when I suffer; you must always keep with me, and pardon all my faults, and your pujas, pilgrimages, fastings, incense, and all other religious duties you must not perform without me; you must not defraud me regarding conjugal love; you must have nothing to do with another woman while I live; you must consult me in all that you do, and you must always tell me the truth. Vishnu, fire, and the Brāhmans are witnesses between you and me.' The bridegroom replies: 'I will all my life-time do just as the bride requires of me, but she must also make me some promises: she must go with me through suffering and trouble, and must always be obedient to me; she must never go to her father's house unless she is asked by him; and when she sees another man in better circumstances, or more beautiful than I am, she must not despise or slight me." To this the bride replies: "I will all my life do just as you require of me; Vishnu, fire, and the Brāhmans are witnesses between us." After this the bridegroom takes a little water in his hand and sprinkles it on the bride's head as the Pundit repeats some texts. Bride and bridegroom then bow before the sun in worship. After this the bridegroom raises his hand over the right shoulder of the bride, touches her heart, places a little vermilion on the parting of her hair, puts his shoes on her feet, and then quickly removes them. This being completed, a piece of silk cloth is thrown over the heads of the newly-married couple, the bridegroom draws her veil aside, and in many cases sees the face of the bride for the first time. As soon as this is done the boy and girl are conducted into the women's apartments, where the greatest merriment commences. And here, again, he goes through the ceremony of tying garments, and takes another peep at his wife's face. When this is over he returns to the place of worship, when the religious rites are concluded by the Hom, *i.e.*, the burning a little ghi to the deities. No sooner is this concluded than presents are made to priests, servants, friends, &c.

Next comes the feasting: the bridegroom dining with the gentlemen, the bride, of course, remaining with the women in the inner apartments of the house. As soon as the feast is concluded the bridegroom repairs to the Bāsaghar, or dwelling-house, where he and his new wife remain in company with a crowd of female relatives, who are playing, laughing, and joking during nearly the whole of the night. As soon as day dawns the little girl goes away. After breakfast the happy pair, with a grand procession, go to the house of the bridegroom's father, where a similar scene awaits them. Here, amidst other ceremonies, the mother-in-law puts on the iron wire bracelet, and the vermilion on the forehead at the parting of the hair, which are the signs of marriage.

After feasting, the newly married folk again retire to their room, and have to pass the night surrounded by their friends, who, not having shared in the games of the previous night, are quite able to continue their good-natured fun until near the dawn. During the greater part of the day the bride remains at her new home, and then returns to her father's, heartily glad, as a rule, that the long and wearisome ceremony is at an end, and that she is once again a child at home. Here she remains for a year or two, with an occasional sight of her husband, either at his or her father's house, until the time comes for her to go permanently to reside with him.

The ceremonies that precede the final departure of a girl to her husband's home are much simpler than at the first wedding. The priests are again in requisition. They recite the mantras, the bridegroom repeating them; the hands of the two are joined by him, and several deities are worshipped with the object of obtaining a blessing upon the happy pair. The parting from the home is often very sad, as meetings afterwards are not very common; whilst frequently the condition of a young wife in her husband's family is anything but enviable. Being but a child, she is under the authority of the older ladies; where they are kind, all is well; but where the opposite, it is easy to see that they frequently wish themselves back again at their old home. And having gone to reside with her husband, his home is afterwards her permanent dwelling-place; for should he die, the widow remains an inmate of his family; they, and not her own father, being hereafter responsible for her support.

We now pass on to notice the position of the Hindu married woman. As soon as the hour arrives for the wife to join her husband she enters the women's apartments of his family house and becomes one of his family. At once her freedom of movement is at an end. As a girl, though married, she could move about the house, go freely into the outer or more public apartments, was allowed, under the care of a servant, to attend school, and was as unfettered in her movements as an English girl of the same age. But when her husband conducts her to his home the scene changes entirely. She is at once subjected to all the restrictions of the Hindu home. She must live in the women's apartments, keep her face veiled when her brothers-in-law are present, and never be seen speaking even to her husband in the day-time. It would be esteemed wrong even to pronounce her husband's name, or to touch his elder brothers. And seldom can she cross the threshold of her new home except it be to pay a visit to her own father's. Manu has taught that she is "unworthy of confidence, and the slave of passion," and the lesson has been learned only too well.

If the family into which she is brought be large and wealthy, there will not be much for her to do, as all the housework will be done either by the older ladies, widows of the family, or by servants. She will never, of course, take her meals with her husband; he will eat with the other gentlemen of the family, whilst she will join the ladies at their meals. When the employment of the husband permits him to continue to live at home, she has the prospect of his company in the evening; but when, as very frequently happens, his work is at a distance, she may not see him for months at a time. Under these circumstances it is only natural that she should find her new mode of life wearisome and monotonous. In the normal condition of society she would be unable to read, sew, or engage in the many forms of employment that so well engage the minds and fingers of the fair in England, her time being occupied in gossip, personal decoration, &c.

In the case of the poorer people there is an entirely different state of affairs. There the girls, as soon as they are married, having been taught to be useful, find work in their new home, and generally, the companionship of a mother-in-law, widowed sister-in-law, or some older person, who acts as guardian of the young wife in the absence of her husband. Hard though in some respects the lot of the poor in India may be, to an outsider, the condition of the women in the poorer ranks, considering the greater freedom they enjoy, and the employment they are free to engage in, seems far to be preferred to that of their richer sisters, who are immured in their prison-like homes. In order, however, that the actual condition of women may be known, and not merely the suppositions of one who has never seen the interior of a Hindu house, I shall avail myself rather fully of an account of them given by a Bengali gentleman, who, though now a Christian, was once, as a Hindu, familiar with the home life of Hindu families. Mr. Bose writes as follows:*

"The system of early marriage that prevails here has been justly condemned by all civilized nations, and it is really a marvel that parties so capriciously affianced in early age can live happily together afterwards to the end of their lives. The young bride, between ten and eleven years of age, generally simple, artless, and unlettered, even in the case of a respectable family, is brought up almost from her cradle to look upon her future lord with feelings of extreme submissiveness." I once met with rather an amusing case corroborative of this. A Christian convert of about thirty years of age wishing to get married, and coming to me for counsel, I advised him to marry a lady somewhere near his own age; but this idea was quite repugnant to his notions, as he said that if he took any one as old as that she would not be brought into subjection so easily as a young girl! "She is a perfect stranger to freedom of action, if not actually to freedom of thought. When her reasoning faculties are somewhat developed, and she grows tired of a monotonous slavish existence, she naturally struggles to be free; but fate has otherwise ordained. The apartment in which she lives, the atmosphere she breathes, the mode of life she is enjoined to follow, the society she moves in, and the surroundings by which she is

* "The Hindus as they are," 287.

fenced—all attest the very abnormal restraints to which she is, at all hours of her life, subjected after her marriage. But she cannot altogether suppress human nature. With the development of her passions and desires the fetters of servitude gradually relax, she pants for a little freedom, because absolute freedom is denied her by the peculiar conventional rules by which she is governed, and, as a necessary consequence of this, she is permitted to move about half unveiled within the precincts of her secluded domicile. And when she becomes the mother of two or three children, through the blessing of the goddess Sasthi, the conventional restraints by degrees give way, until through her age she becomes the *grihini*, or mistress of the house—a position which gives a great extension to her privileges. She then in her turn assumes the duties and discipline of the house, and seeks to correct any little impropriety she sees in its inmates.

"An Englishman, who is but superficially acquainted with the inner life of Hindu society, is apt to conclude from what is stated above that a native woman, hampered by so many restrictions, can seldom be happy in the proper sense of the word; but however paradoxical this may appear, the reverse is true. She feels quite happy and contented when Providence gives her what she values over every other worldly consideration—a good husband and dutiful sons and daughters. Brought up in a state of perfect isolation, and practically confined to restricted thought and action, her happiness is necessarily identified with that of a few beings who are near and dear to her. Although married when she is scarcely capable of thinking and judging for herself, yet, through the kind dispensation of an overruling Providence, she is destined in most cases to enjoy the blessings of a married life. The rites and ceremonies by which she is early united in the bonds of wedlock exert little or no influence on her in her maturer years. She becomes happy in spite of the domestic and social restrictions imposed on her by what Shakespeare calls the 'Monster Custom.' The gravity of the marriage compact is due to the religious incantations used on the occasion. Though their precise meaning is scarcely understood by the boy-husband or the girl-wife, the influence of conventionalism is so powerful that a few words pronounced by the officiating priest prove absolutely binding on both to the end of their days. Nor can it be otherwise. As they advance in years, their mutual love and affection cement the bond of union that was so casually and capriciously formed. And even where the individual tempers, dispositions, habits, and ideas are irreconcilable, as is sometimes the case, open rupture between the parties is very rare, if not altogether impossible. In respectable families, in which a husband is educated, and a wife not educated, and moreover ill-tempered, a sense of honour and propriety, which is shocked at the slightest whisper of scandal, restrains the former from having recourse to a separation from the latter, even if he were so disposed. Thus we see the very difference in their characters and dispositions gradually overcome. The law of divorce was not known in the country before the English came into it. The fear of scandal, even where there is sufficient justification for it, suppresses everything at its incipient stage."

The following extract from a book written by a Hindu lady on the duty of wives to their husbands is quite in accordance with the teaching of the Hindu Scriptures, and may be taken as a fair representation of the position of the typical Hindu wife: "The husband is the wife's religion, the wife's sole business, the wife's all-in-all. The wife should meditate on her husband as Brahmā. For her, all pilgrimages should be concentrated on her husband's foot. The command of a husband is as obligatory as a precept of the Vedas. To a chaste wife her husband is her god. When the husband is pleased Brahmā is pleased. The merit of waiting on the feet of the husband is equivalent to the merit of performing all the pilgrimages in the world. To obey the husband is to obey the Vedas. To worship the husband is to worship the gods. The husband is the wife's spiritual guide (guru), her honour, the giver of her happiness, the bestower of fortune, righteousness, and heaven, her deliverer from sorrow and from sin." *

In perfect harmony with this is the following extract from the Vishnu Purāna, where a very curious question is under discussion, viz., at what season in the world's history the least amount of merit gained by good works obtained the highest heavenly reward. The learned men, unable to settle this question themselves, repaired to Veda Vyāsa, whom, when they visited, they found bathing. As his head rose above the water the first time he said, "Excellent is the Kali Yuga;" the second time, "Well done, Sudra; thou art happy;" and the third time, "Well done, women; they are happy. Who are more fortunate than they?" On being asked for an explanation of these utterances, the sage solved the problem they brought for solution. It was as follows: He declared the Kali Yuga (the fourth and worst of the four ages of the world) excellent, because a single day and night's devotion in that age obtained, as a reward, as much blessedness as the devotion of a month in the Dwāpara, or a year in the Treta, or as ten years in the Krita. And, further, the same blessedness that in the other ages is gained by abstract meditation, sacrifice, or adoration, is in the Kali Yuga gained by the mere repetition of the name of Keshava (Vishnu). In a similar manner he explained that whilst the Brāhmans had most laborious duties assigned to them, the Sudra had simply to wait upon them, and had far fewer restrictions laid upon his actions and food. And woman for a similar reason he declared to be happy, because by simply loving and honouring her husband she is able to attain the position, however exalted that may be, which he has attained as the result of immense exertion.

It is difficult for Europeans to realize what the position of the well-to-do women in India really is. Accustomed as they

* *Calcutta Review*, vol. xlix. p. 39.

are to go out from their homes to transact business or see friends, and to receive guests in their houses, to enjoy the companionship of their husbands as their equals in intelligence and education, and to feel that the love of their husbands is based upon confidence in their love and trustworthiness, it seems almost impossible to imagine a state of society where all this is reversed. A Hindu lady sees in the character of the apartments she occupies, and the fact that she cannot go outside her home without the consent of her husband, and elaborate arrangements being made to secure her privacy on a journey, that her husband has been taught to regard her as one who will easily be led into sin. Shut out by her ignorance from the world of literature and from the pleasure of profitably employing her mind and hands in work, she can only waste her days in frivolous occupations. Prohibited by custom from conversation with her husband except in her own chamber, and by her want of education from sharing in his thoughts and from being his companion in the true sense of the word, she feels that she is little more to him than a ministrant of his pleasures. As the gentlemen of the family sit and talk and amuse themselves in various ways, they are independent to a large extent of the pleasure that the company and conversation of a wife would afford. Hindu gentlemen are simply astonished as they see Englishmen entrust their wives to the protection of a friend on a railway journey or on board a steamer. To no one except her own father would they consider it prudent to leave their wives under similar circumstances. And it seems to an outsider that it must be degrading after marriage to lose their own name, and when their first son is born to be known and addressed by their relatives as "the mother of Priya," or by whatever name he may be called.

Of course it would be unwise to say that under such circumstances there can be no happiness; but that the educated husbands feel the great disparity between themselves and their wives, there can be no doubt. A graduate of the University, whose mind for years has been strained with the highest subjects of Western thought, cannot possibly have much in common with a girl who cannot read. A Hindu gentleman, speaking to me on the subject, put it rather strangely, though forcibly, as he said, "Educated Hindu gentlemen are doomed to perpetual widowhood," *i.e.*, to a life of solitude, so far as true companionship in their wives is concerned. And there is no doubt whatever that the great progress that has been made of late in female education, which was so vehemently opposed at first by the leaders of Hindu society, is largely owing to the fact that the educated Hindu desires some sort of companionship in his wife; and this has led many to devote their leisure time to their instruction. Happiness in the women there may be, as, if all one hears be true, there was happiness enjoyed by the slaves before their emancipation. Few human beings are so placed that they cannot smile sometimes. But happiness cannot be the habitual condition of women under such circumstances, nor can the highest of all happiness which comes from the perfect companionship of man and wife be known by those who are little better than the slaves of their husbands.

Further; it would be foolish to deny that women, ignorant and enslaved though they may be, exert great influence on their husbands and children. Some of the rich and highly respected members of Hindu society have confessed that they owed their success in life to the sympathy, encouragement, and carefulness of their wives. And as the women are most religious, their influence over their sons and husbands in religious matters is very great indeed. Many of the educated Hindus who have themselves lost all faith in the religion of their fathers maintain an outward conformity to its practices, largely owing to their desire not to give offence to the ladies of their household. But where there is equality in natural intelligence and culture, of course that influence is vastly increased.

In his account of Bengal village life, Rev. B. L. Day gives

a picture of the young wife's persecution at the hands of her mother-in-law, which, if all one hears on this subject be true, is far from uncommon. The wife came to her husband's house, which was small, and in these cases she would be left almost entirely to the tender mercies of the husband's mother; there was only her sister-in-law as a companion besides this old lady. "This nectar-mouthed lady was a source of great trial to poor Mālati. For some time she seemed to be very kind to her, but the infirmities of temper soon discovered themselves and made Mālati quite wretched. Whatever she did seemed to displease her mother-in-law. She did not sweep the floor well; her cowdung cakes (for fuel) are badly made; the curries which she cooks are execrable; she is very ill-bred; she walks more like a boy than a girl; her voice is scarcely audible—it is like the hissing of a serpent; she has a nasty, sneering, sarcastic smile on her lips whenever anything is said to her. Such were the criticisms pronounced by Sudhāmukhi on Mālati." This goes on from bad to worse after the father-in-law's death, until in her anger Mālati receives a slap on the face. This was more than she could stand. It is astonishing how much verbal abuse a Bengali will stand; but a blow is never forgotten or forgiven. So, on her husband's return from his work, the wife, with sobs and groans, tells him what has happened, and entreats him to send his mother away and maintain her. The husband listens to his wife's story; but when he spoke of it to his mother he is received with a shower of abuse that drives him from the house for a time, whilst the anger of the mother-in-law is allowed to cool down of itself. Scenes like this we might naturally expect to take place, and they are generally borne as patiently as possible, as it is accounted disgraceful for a son to ask his mother to leave the family house, however painful she may make his and his wife's existence. In India the people know by experience, though they have not as yet found out a remedy, that "relations are best separated," and when unpleasantness arises a woman cannot leave the house for a time; her only resource is go into a room and hide away from the family until the storm passes over.

In harmony with the spirit of the preceding paragraph are the following proverbs: "If a mother-in-law breaks a pan, it is earthen; if the daughter-in-law, it is golden." And again: "Tears come into the eyes of a daughter-in-law *six months after the death* of a mother-in-law."

Keshub Chundra Sen, in one of his addresses in England, teaches in a humorous way that women have immense influence in the homes of India as in other countries. He says, "Woman has been defined as an adjective, agreeing with the noun man. I should rather say that man is a noun in the objective case, governed by the verb woman."

CHAPTER III.

HINDU WIDOWS.

The last part of this subject is the most painful, viz., the condition of the Hindu widow; and any more distressing subject than this it is scarcely possible to conceive. It seems as if the old legislators had studied to make the widow's life as miserable as possible. As was indicated before, Manu teaches that it is unlawful for a widow to mention the name of another man; and that only by living as a virtuous widow can she rejoin her husband after death; whilst he further teaches that by re-marriage "she brings disgrace on herself here below, and shall be excluded from the seat of her lord." These penalties being pronounced on the widow who may remarry is as real a prohibition as if he had in so many words forbidden it. And further, though Manu did not order the Hindus to render her life miserable, he declared that it was her own duty to do so.

Custom now teaches the following duties for a widow, and in the majority of cases it is strictly followed in the hope that by this means she may rejoin her husband. She must take but one meal a day, and twice in a month fast for a day, *i.e.*, go without food or water for forty-eight hours. At a meeting of the highest religious court, the Sanātan Dharma Rākshini Sabha, in Calcutta, a few years ago, it was decreed that if, acting on medical advice, a widow on these fast days drank a little water, the offence should be condoned. She must wear white clothes only, not even a coloured border being allowed. She must give up all jewels, take off the iron wire bracelet, and remove the spot of red paint from her forehead, and generally deny herself of the comforts of life. Frequently she is made the drudge of the family. But lest it should be thought that an European would give an exaggerated account, I here give a statement by a Hindu widow, and anything stronger than this I have never seen written nor heard from the lips of a European. When the position of the widow is seen as it is here depicted, it need occasion no surprise that many of them, seeing no possible hope of improvement in this life, forsake their homes, and go to swell the ranks of the immoral women in the cities.

"There are four principal castes amongst Hindus, and of them all, I think the third caste, the Kayasthas, to which I belong, make their widows suffer most.

"All are treated badly enough, but our customs are much worse than those of some others. In the Punjab they are not always strict in enforcing their customs with widows; but though we live in the Punjab, our family comes from the North-West, and as we are rich and well-to-do, our customs are kept up scrupulously.

"When a husband dies, his wife suffers as much as if the death-angel had come for her also. She must not be approached by any of her relations, but several women, from three to six (wives of bärbers, a class who are kept up for this object), are in waiting, and as soon as the husband's last breath is drawn, they rush at the new-made widow, and tear off her ornaments. Ear and nose rings are dragged off, often tearing the cartilage, ornaments plaited in with the hair are torn away, and if the arms are covered with gold and silver bracelets, they do not take the time to draw them off one by one, but holding her arm on the ground, they hammer with a stone, until the metal, often solid and heavy, breaks in two; it matters not to them how many wounds they inflict, they have no pity, not even if the widow is but a child of six or seven, who does not know what a husband means.*

* In Bengal a widow may continue to wear some of her ornaments until she is twelve years of age.

"At that time two sorrows come upon every widow—one from God and one from her own people, who should cherish and support her, but who desert and execrate her. If the husband dies away from home, then, on the arrival of the fatal news, all this is done. At the funeral, the relatives, men as well as women, have to accompany the corpse to the burning ghat. If they are rich and have carriages, they must not use them, but all go on foot. The men follow the corpse, the women (all the ladies well covered from sight) come after, and last the widow, led along by the barbers' wives. They take care that at least 200 feet intervene between her and any other woman, for it is supposed that if her shadow fell on any (her tormentors excepted) she also would become a widow; therefore no relative, however much sympathy she may feel in secret, dare look on her face. One of the rough women goes in front, and shouts aloud to any passer-by to get out of the way of the accursed thing, as if the poor widow were a wild beast; the others drag her along.

"Arrived at the river, tank, or well, where the body is to be burned, they push her into the water, and as she falls, so she must lie, with her clothes on, until the body has been burned, all the company have bathed, washed their clothes, and dried them. When they are all ready to start for home, but not before, they drag her out, and in her wet things she must trudge home. It matters not what the weather is, in a burning sun, or with icy wind blowing from the Himalayas. They care not if she dies. Oh, I would rather choose the Suttee!

"Many are happy enough to die in consequence of these sorrows, for however ill they may become, no care is taken of them, or medicine given.

"I once went to a funeral (before I was myself a widow), where the burning ghat was three ghos (about six miles) from the city. It was the hottest month of the year, and though we started at sunrise, we did not reach the house again till 3 p.m. I shall never forget how much we women suffered from the hot blasting wind that blew on us like fire, and the blazing sun. We were almost worn out with heat and thirst, though we had stopped often to rest and drink. The poor widow dared not ask for a drink, or she would have lost her character; the women with her might have given her water if they had liked, but they would not.

"At last she fell, but they pulled her up again and dragged her on, told her not to give way, she was not the only widow, and taunted her, when she wept, with wanting a husband. When she had no strength left even to crawl, they dragged her along like a bundle of clothes.

"On arrival at the house she was flung on to the floor in a little room; still, though they knew she was almost dead with thirst, they did not give her a drop of water, and she dared not ask for any. She was a relative of mine, but none of us dared go near her, for it would have brought down maledictions on the head of any one who tried it. At last one young woman, after watching a long while, saw her opportunity, and slipped in with a vessel of water. The widow ran at her like a wild creature. I cannot describe how she behaved; at first she did not recognize her friend — she drank, and drank, till life and sense came back to her. Then she fell down at the feet of her who had brought the water, and embracing them, said: 'Oh, sister! I will never forget what you have done for me! You are my God—my second creator! But go away quickly, I pray, that no one may ever find out what you have done, or we shall both suffer. I promise I will never tell of you.'

"For fifteen days after a funeral the relatives must eat and drink only once in the day (twenty-four hours); but the widow must keep up this for a year, with frequent fasts. When she returns from the funeral she must sit or lie in a corner on the ground in the same clothes she had on when her husband died, whether still wet or by this time dry. Now and then one of the barbers' wives comes and looks after her, or if she is poor and not able to pay for their further *kind* attentions, she must sit alone. Oh, cruel place! Each widow knows you well, and remembers you with bitterness! Separated from her husband, though she lives she is not alive! Not only is she deprived of comforts, but her friends add to her misery. Though she is in her corner alone, and must not speak to any one, they are near and talk at her in this way: her mother says, 'Unhappy creature! I can't bear the thought of any one so vile—I wish she had never been born.' Her mother-in-law says, 'The horrid viper! she has bitten my son and killed him; now *he* is dead, and *she*, useless creature, is left behind.' And this, even though the speakers may themselves be widows. Every indignity that the tongue can speak is heaped upon her, lest the standers-by, or perchance the gods, should think they had sympathy with her.

"O God! I pray Thee, let no more women be born in this land!

"The sister-in-law says, 'I will not look at her or speak to such a thing!' They comfort the dead man's mother, and say, 'It is your daughter-in-law, vile thing! who has destroyed your house; curse her! For her sake you have to mourn for the rest of your life.'

"To the widow they say, 'What good are you? Why are you still living in the world?' If she cry, and shows her grief, they all say, 'How immodest, how abandoned—see, she is crying for a husband!' They have no pity. Only those who have been through this know what it is. You must feel this grief to prove it. Whose foot has the chilblain feels the pain. For thirteen days the widow must sit and bear this.

"On the eleventh day comes a Brāhman, like a policeman who comes for a culprit, orders money, and oil, and other things to be given. However poor the widow may be, money, or the promise of it, must be given; from the very poorest at least Rs. 13. Other Brāhmans make other demands, and if the family is rich their demands are very high. A poor widow has often to labour hard for months at grinding, or some other work, to earn money to satisfy their claims.

"O Lord! why hast Thou created us to make us suffer thus? From birth to death sorrow is our portion. While our husbands live we are their slaves; when they die we are still worse off. But they have all they wish here, and promises for the life to come.

"The thirteenth day is a bad day, though then the widow may take off the clothes she has worn ever since her husband died, and may bathe. The relatives all gather and lay rupees before the widow, which are supposed to be a provision for her for life. They do not spare their reproaches. If the rupees given amount to any large sum, it is taken charge of by some relative, who doles it out.

"Now again the Brāhmans come for more money. The widow's head is shaved, and there is another Brāhmanical tax. Then the barbers' wives have to be paid. Six weeks after the husband's death the widow must once again put on the hated clothes she wore for those thirteen days—abhorred garments! If a widow by chance catches sight of them she shudders as if a fresh widowhood were hers, and then, if possible, she must go on a pilgrimage to the Ganges, and, after bathing there, the clothes may be thrown away in the river.

"After a year has passed away, a widow who is living with her father and mother may wear ornaments again.* But why is this? If you ask the parents, they say, 'Poor girl! she has not seen much of life; if she cannot wear jewels now while we are with her, she can never wear them, and how can she pass a long life without jewels? We can't bear to see her naked; how could we wear jewels and she sit before us bare?'

"But I say, if they cannot bear to see her pass her life without jewels, how can they bear to see her pass her life without a husband or any of the pleasures of life? A veil of

* This custom does not prevail in Bengal.

ignorance has fallen upon them, so that they cannot see things in their right light. If they cannot bear to see her sorrow, they should let her marry again. What medicine for a wounded spirit will she find in jewels? Let them first take some care for her heart. As our homes are managed, how can they expect that a widow will remain pure? She has never been taught, any more than her brothers or cousins, to restrain her passions. Let those who can marry wear jewels, but not those who have no hope of marrying; and let not little children take the name and place of widows. Jewels are, for widows, a great help on the downward road. I write of what I know and have seen. All men and women love to adorn themselves, but especially women love to do so, that they may be seen and look fine. If widows wear jewels they will be sought after. I do not say that all widows who wear jewels are bad, but I do say they have taken one step on the bad road. Alas! that it is the parents who open the way for beloved daughters to go wrong. Then when consequences follow they are ready to kill them.

"The widows who have no parents are still more to be pitied; they have to serve as servants to their brothers' or sons' wives. Every one knows that if there are widows in a house servants need not be hired. A sister-in-law rules over a widow, and they quarrel night and day. If a widow remains in her husband's house, it is the same; she is hated by mother and sister-in-law, and beaten from place to place. If, for the sake of peace, she would like to live alone, she loses her character. If she has children she works for them while they are young; when her sons marry she becomes their wives' servant. If a widow is childless and rich (by the money given her after her husband's death), her relatives choose some boy to be her heir, and to be provided for by her. She may bring him up with love and care, but when he gets big he takes her property, and only allows her food and clothes while she waits on his wife. A widow has no power over property supposed to be her own. It is happier for a widow to be poor, and earn her living by grinding corn!

"Amongst us, women can inherit no cowrie of their father's wealth, it all goes to their brothers. Neither do they inherit what their husbands leave. They have only what may be given them, and if it is a lump sum, perhaps they are silly, and spend it foolishly; they are not taught to take care of it properly. If a wife die she is burned in her best clothes and jewels, but a widow's corpse is wrapped in white cloth. It is supposed that if she came to her husband in the next life without the show of mourning, he would not receive her.

"Why do the widows of India suffer so? Not for religion or piety. It is not written in our ancient books. In none of the Shastras or in the Mahabharat is there any sign of this suffering. What Pandit has brought it on us? Alas! that all hope is taken from us. We have not sinned, then why are thorns instead of flowers given us?

"Thousands of us die, but more live. I saw a widow die, one of my cousins. She had been ill before her husband's death. When he died she was too weak to be dragged to the river. She was in a burning fever; her mother-in-law called a water-carrier, and had four large skins of water poured over her as she lay on the ground, where she had been thrown from her bed when her husband died. The chill of death came upon her, and after lying alone and untended for eight hours, her breath ceased. Every one praised her, and said she had died for love of her husband.

"I knew another woman who did not love her husband, for all their friends knew that they quarrelled so much that they could not live together. The husband died suddenly away from home, and when the widow heard the news she threw herself off the roof and was taken up dead. She could not bear the thought of the degradation before her. She was praised by all. A book full of such instances might be written. The only difference for us since Suttee was abolished is, that we then died quickly, if cruelly, but now we die all our lives in lingering pain.

"We are aghast at the great number of widows; how is it there are so many? The answer is, that if an article is constantly supplied and never used up, it must accumulate. So it is with widows; nearly every man or boy who dies leave one, often more; so though thousands die, more live on.

"The English have abolished Suttee; but, alas! neither the English nor the angels know what goes on in our homes. And Hindus not only don't care, but think it good! What! do not Hindus fear what such oppression may lead to? If the widow's shadow is to be dreaded, why do they darken and overshadow the whole land with it?

"I am told that in England they comfort widows' hearts; but there is no comfort for us."

Anything more pathetic and heart-rending than the foregoing statement of the condition of myriads of widows in India it would be hard to imagine. But lest it should seem to possess too black a colouring, I add a passage from Mr. Dey's book on Hindu village life, which to some extent corroborates, and to some extent modifies it; probably both are equally true, though not of the same families. "English people have somehow or other got the idea that a Hindu widow receives harsh and cruel treatment from the relations of her husband. This is not true. There are, no doubt, exceptional cases, but, as a general rule, Hindu widows are not only not ill-treated, but they meet with a vast deal of sympathy. Old widows, in a Bengali Hindu family, are often the guides and counsellors of those who style themselves the lords of creation. . . Old widows, provided they have intelligence and good character, assert, on account of their experience in life, their superiority over men younger than they. As to the privations of life, a little too much is made of them. Besides the one supreme privation of having the fountain of their affections sealed up, the others, of which foreign writers make so much, are not worth speaking about. The most considerable of these minor privations is that only one meal is permitted them in twenty-four hours. But this restraint will cease to be regarded as a privation when it is considered that a widow's meal is usually larger in quantity and heavier in weight than that of a married woman; that the meal is taken in the afternoon, not many hours before sleep; that most widows are sleek and stout, and that many of the strong and able-bodied peasants of the North-Western Provinces, and the Hindu sepoys of the Bengal army, take only one meal in twenty-four hours." This certainly is rather a strong way of putting it; but it overlooks the fact that those who partake of one meal a day only can eat if they feel hungry, and drink when thirsty; but with the widow none of these resources are available. Moreover, it is quite a different thing to continue in habits that have been formed from infancy; and quite another thing suddenly to give up habits that have become parts of one's nature. And again, in the case of the widow, she has this additional cause of anguish: she is taught that it is owing to some sin in a previous birth that she is now called to suffer all the pains incident to her position as a widow. From what I have heard of the sadness and sorrow of the Hindu window, and from the great blessings that are promised to the Sati, or faithful wife, who ascended the funeral pile with her husband, I certainly am not at all surprised that as long as the law permitted it, many preferred the few moments of physical agony, with the hope of gaining a heavenly mansion with their lord, rather than continue in the misery which is the normal condition of the widows of Hindus to this day.

Before passing on to notice the institution and practice of Sati, it will not be out of place here to indicate briefly the improvements that are visible in the position of women in India.

First, education is rapidly spreading amongst the middle classes. When missionaries first attempted to commence work amongst the girls, it was with the greatest difficulty that they could induce parents to allow them to learn. Before this time, girls who were intended for a life of prostitution had received some instruction in order that they might prove more attractive to their visitors; hence education in women was associated with immorality. In order to overcome their prejudice, parents had to be paid to allow their daughters to attend school. Then the conservatism of the older members of the family most strongly opposed it, on the ground that the gods would be angry and show their displeasure by removing the husbands of girls who had been taught. Were the history of the progress of female education in India written, it would contain many stories of schools almost deprived of scholars owing to one of them becoming a widow, and the old women pointing to her case as a certain instance of the displeasure of the gods falling upon her and her family for departing from their time-honoured customs. But gradually this prejudice was destroyed by the quiet and persistent efforts of the ladies of various missionary societies, until nowadays in a very great number of the houses of the middle and upper classes are to be found those who have been regularly sent to school, and are able to read and write fairly well.

The Zenana work in India, which of late has so greatly excited the interest of ladies in Europe and America, grew out of the school work. When her pupils had grown too old to attend school, they asked Mrs. Mullens, in Calcutta, if she could not continue her work with them in their homes. She did so; and from this small beginning the great work that is now going on in India has grown. As education spread amongst the boys and young men they naturally wished to have educated wives; and within the last few years some Hindu girls have obtained the B.A. degree in the Calcutta University. Within a little more than a single generation the education of girls and women in India has so rapidly developed: the minds of the women forty years ago were regarded as unfit for cultivation; now some of the brightest productions of culture are to be found. Few nations can point to greater changes in so short a time.

In some classes of the community, especially the progressive Brāhmos, decided improvements have been seen in the position of women. In their mandir, or church, seats are appropriated for ladies, and week after week are to be seen at public worship, ladies who in the normal state of Hindu society would have remained immured in the dark recesses of the Hindu home. And in the houses of Europeans I have myself had the pleasure of meeting Brahmo gentlemen and their wives. By friendly intercourse of this kind the way is being prepared for the ladies to be led from slavery to freedom.

During the Calcutta Exhibition a great mark of progress was to be seen in the thousands of Hindu ladies who were permitted to come forth from their homes to witness the great show. Ladies in bands of four to twenty were to be seen under the guidance of their young brothers-in-law, or the Zenāna teachers of the various missions, most busily engaged in examining all the wonders that were there collected together. The prospect and retrospect of this visit to the outside world must have given immense delight to multitudes who for years had not been permitted to see or be seen by the outside world. Some Hindu gentlemen went so far as to say that in their opinion, had the Exhibition continued open for a year, the doors of the Zenāna Khanahs would not have been again closed; that the ladies, having once tasted the sweets of liberty, would not have been content to remain immured. A great deal of talk is indulged in against the Zenāna system by the educated Hindus; and in time the present state of affairs, so far as woman is concerned, will pass away. Ignorance and slavery can co-exist; education and slavery never. To educate is to enfranchise; and such must eventually be its result in India.

Having noticed the position of woman from birth to death, it is necessary, in giving an account of the Hindu religion, to show to what it led when English law and power did not interfere. In the case of widows, it taught that it was a proper thing for them to burn with the body of their husbands, and the name Sati, *the faithful*, is given to those who were brave and devoted enough to pass through this ordeal. In British territory this religious act has been forbidden, and those assisting, or permitting it even, are liable to an action for murder; but within the last few years it has been practised in some of the independent native States, so that it is not absolutely a thing of the past.

CHAPTER IV.

SATI, OR THE BURNING OF A HINDU WIDOW WITH THE BODY OF HER HUSBAND.

It is impossible to say when this rite first came into favour. The name Sati is given to Parvati, when, angry with her father for omitting to invite her husband to his feast, she destroyed herself by fire; but in this case, though she proved herself "a faithful wife," she did not burn herself with her husband's body. Still, as she manifested faithfulness, even to death, in the interests of her husband, the name has been given to those widows who, by their self-immolation, have manifested a similar devotion.

In Vedic times it seems certain that this rite was not practised, nor is there a single text authorizing it. There is a text, however, which, by a wilful mis-translation, has been taught by the priests to be an authority for the practice, concerning which Max Müller says: "This is perhaps the most flagrant instance of what can be done by an unscrupulous priesthood." This text, which is the one that is repeated by the officiating priest as the widow walks round the pyre on which her husband's corpse is placed, before ascending it herself, is as follows: "Om! Let those women, not to be widowed, good wives adorned with collyrium, holding clarified butter, consign themselves to the fire. Immortal, not childless, not husbandless, well adorned with gems, let them pass into the fire, whose original element was water." The correct translation is the following: "May these women, *who are* *not widows*, draw near with oil and butter. Let those who are mothers go first to the *altar*, without sorrow, but decked with fine jewels." * The passage evidently refers to ordinary sacrifices, and not to the immolation of widows.

The plan to be adopted at this ceremony, carefully taught in more modern works, is as follows: "Having first bathed, the widow, dressed in her clean garments, and holding some cusa grass, sips water from the palm of her hand. Bearing cusa and tila on her head, she looks towards the east or north, whilst the Brāhman utters the mystic word Om. Bowing to Nārāyana, she next declares: 'On this month, on this day, I' [naming herself and her family], 'that I may meet Arundhati (the wife of Vasistha, the guru of the gods), and reside in Swarga, that the years of my stay may be numerous as the hairs of the human body, that I may enjoy with my husband the felicity of heaven, and sanctify my paternal and maternal progenitors, and the ancestry of my husband's father; that, lauded by the Apsarases (celestial nymphs), I may be happy with my lord through the reign of fourteen Indras (kings of the gods); that expiation be made for my husband's offences, whether he has killed a Brāhman, broken the ties of gratitude, or murdered his friend—thus I ascend my husband's burning pile. I call on you, ye guardians of the eight regions of the world—Sun and Moon, Air, Fire, Ether, Earth and Water, my own soul, Yama (the god of the spirit world), Day, Night and Twilight, and thou Conscience—bear witness I follow my husband's corpse on the funeral pile.' " †

It is the duty of the son, or nearest relative, to apply the first torch when the widow has repeated this mantra. The texts on which it is founded are the following:—

"The wife who commits herself to the flames with her husband's corpse shall equal Arundhati, and reside in Swarga."

* "Vedic Religion," p. 32.

† Colebrooke's "Essays," p. 71.

"Accompanying her husband, she shall reside so long in Swarga as are the 35,000,000 of hairs on the human body."

"As the snake-catcher forcibly drags the serpent from his earth, so bearing her husband [from hell] with him shall she enjoy heavenly bliss."

"Dying with her husband, she sanctifies her maternal and paternal ancestors, and the ancestors of him to whom she gave her virginity."

"Such a wife, adoring her husband, in celestial felicity with him, greatest and most admired, shall enjoy the delights of heaven while fourteen Indras reign."

"Though a husband had killed a Brāhman, broken the ties of gratitude, or murdered a friend, she expiates the crime."

It should be noticed that whilst promising these blessings to the widow who performs the rites of Sati, the Brahmā Purāna, which teaches the mantras employed at the ceremony, also teaches that it is optional with a widow thus to burn, or to adopt a life of austerity such as has already been described; but having once decided to be burned, she must proceed with the ceremony, or incur defilement. It is further taught that though the widow of a Brāhman who died at a distance ought not to perform Sati, the widows of other castes might do so under these circumstances.

"The bystanders throw on butter and wood: for this they are taught that they acquire merit exceeding ten million-fold the merit of an Asvamedh (or horse sacrifice), or other great sacrifice. Even those who join the procession from the house of the deceased to the funeral pile, for every step are rewarded as for an asvamedh. Such indulgences are promised by grave authors."

In the code of Hindu laws drawn up towards the close of the last century, for the guidance of the judges, it is said: "It is proper for a woman, after her husband's death, to burn herself in the fire with his corpse. Every woman who thus burns herself shall remain in Paradise with her husband 350,000,000 of years by destiny."

The first authentic account of a Sati from the Hindu writings, so far as I can discover, is that of one which occurred about the year 1176. The lady's name was Sanjogata, daughter of Jadchand, the last Hindu king of Kanouj, and wife of Prithivirāja, the last Hindu king of Dehli. At that time princesses at least were allowed to select their own husbands at Swayambaras, or tournaments, held for this purpose. When her father inaugurated the festival, owing to an old and bitter feud between the parties, Prithivirāja was not invited; but an effigy of him being placed as a doorkeeper, the princess, passing by all the princes present, placed the garland upon the neck of the effigy, as she had heard so much of the martial exploits of him whom it represented. Soon after this the prince, hearing of the favour that had been shown him by the princess, came with an armed band and carried her away by force. She completely captivated her capturer by the force of her love and beauty. About a year after this, as the Mussulmān conquerors were at their gates, urged by his wife, Prithivirāja went out to fight them. During his absence she lived most simply, having a presentiment that she should never see his face again. This proved only too true. The enemy prevailed, her beloved husband was slain; and as soon as the news reached her, she ordered a funeral pyre to be prepared, and of her own accord entered it.

From the reports of eye-witnesses of the performance of the Sati rite, it is evident that some widows went, in the spirit of true devotion to their husbands, and with the hope of obtaining the blessedness promised, to perform this dreadful rite; whilst others, owing to the disgrace which attached to one who vowed, but had not courage to perform her vow, were drugged, so as to be unconscious of what was before them; whilst the precaution was usually taken of tying down the wood upon the victim, so that escape was impossible. I shall now give an account of the performance of this ceremony from eye-witnesses.

The first description is from Colonel Sleeman's "Rambles and Recollections." The Colonel, some years after the occurrence, was passing a temple that had been erected on the banks of the Nerbudda river, on the spot where, in 1829, the Sati rite was performed in his presence. He goes on to say that as Sati was prohibited at the time of this visit, he would record what he saw in 1829, and declares that the description being copied from his note-book written at the time, the reader may rely upon the truthfulness of the account. Colonel Sleeman forbade the erection of a temple on the site of a Sati, lest the desire for posthumous fame might lead some widows to immolate themselves.

"On November 29, 1829, this old woman, then about sixty-five years of age, here mixed her ashes with those of her husband, who had been burned alone four days before. On receiving civil charge of the district, I issued a proclamation prohibiting any one from aiding or abetting in Sati; and distinctly stating, that to bring one ounce of wood for the purpose would be considered as so doing. If the woman burned herself with the body of her husband, any one who brought wood for the purpose of burning him would become liable to punishment; consequently the body of the husband must be first consumed, and the widow must bring a fresh supply for herself.

"On Tuesday, November 24, 1829, I had an application from the heads of the most respectable and most extensive family of Brāhmans in the district, to suffer this old widow to burn herself with the remains of her husband, Omed Sing Opuddea, who had that morning died on the banks of the Nerbudda. I threatened to enforce my order, and punish severely any man who assisted, and placed a police-guard for the purpose of seeing that no one did so. She remained sitting by the edge of the water without eating or drinking. The next day the body of her husband was burned to ashes in a small pit of about eight feet square, and three or four deep, before several thousand spectators, who had assembled to see the Sati. All strangers dispersed before evening, as there seemed to be no prospect of my yielding to the urgent solicitations of her family, who dared not touch food till she had burned herself, or declared herself willing to return to them. Her sons, grandsons, and some other relations remained with her, while the rest surrounded my house, the one urging me to allow her to burn, and the other urging her to desist. She remained sitting on a bare rock in the bed of the Nerbudda, refusing every kind of sustenance, and exposed to the intense heat of the sun by day, and the severe cold of the night, with only a thin sheet thrown over her shoulders. On Thursday, to cut off all hope of her being moved from her purpose, she put on the *Dhujja*, or coarse red turban, and broke her bracelets in pieces, by which she became dead in law, and for ever excluded from caste. Should she choose to live after this, she could never return to her family. She had resolved to die. 'I have,' said she, 'tasted largely of the bounty of the Government, having been maintained by it with all my large family in ease and comfort upon our rent-free lands; and I feel assured my children will not be suffered to want; but with them I have nothing more to do; our intercourse and communion end here. My soul is with *Omed Sing Opuddea*, and my ashes must here mix with his.' Again looking to the sun—'I see them together,' said she, with a tone and countenance that affected me a great deal, 'under the bridal canopy,' alluding to the ceremonies of marriage; and I am satisfied that she at that moment really believed that she saw her own spirit and that of her husband under the bridal canopy in Paradise.

"I tried to work upon her pride and fears. I told her that it was probable that the rent-free lands by which her family had been so long supported might be resumed by Government as a mark of its displeasure against the children for not dissuading her from the sacrifice; that the temples over her ancestors might be levelled with the ground, in order to prevent their operating to induce others to make similar sacrifices; and lastly, that not one brick or stone should ever mark the place where she died, if she persisted in her resolution. But if she consented to live, a splendid habitation should be built for her amongst these temples—a handsome provision assigned for her support out of these rent-free lands—her children should come daily to visit her, and I should frequently do the same. She smiled, but held out her arm and said, 'My pulse has long ceased to beat, my spirit has departed, and I have nothing left but a little *earth* that I wish to mix with the ashes of my husband. I shall suffer nothing in burning, and if you wish proof, order some fire, and you shall see this arm consumed without giving me any pain.' I did not attempt to feel her pulse, but some of my people did, and declared that it had ceased to be perceptible. At this time every native present believed that she was incapable of suffering pain; and her end confirmed them in that opinion.

"Satisfied myself that it would be unavailing to attempt to save her life, I sent for all the principal members of her family, and consented that she should be suffered to burn herself if they would enter into engagements that no other member of their family should ever do the same. This they all agreed to, and the papers having been drawn out in due form about midday, I sent down notice to the old lady, who seemed extremely pleased and thankful. The ceremonies of bathing were gone through before three, while the wood and other combustible materials for a strong fire were collected, and put into the pit. After bathing, she called for a pān (betel-leaf), and ate it, then rose up, and with one arm on the shoulder of her eldest son, and the other on that of her nephew, approached the fire. I had sentries placed all round, and no other person was allowed to approach within five paces. As she rose up, fire was set to the pile, and it was instantly in a blaze. The distance was about 150 yards:

she came on with a calm and cheerful countenance, stopped once, and casting her eyes upward, said, 'Why have they kept me five days from thee, my husband?' On coming to the sentries her supporters stopped: she walked once round the pit, paused a moment, and, whilst muttering a prayer, threw some flowers into the fire. She then walked up deliberately and calmly to the brink, stepped into the centre of the flame, sat down, and leaning back in the midst as if reposing upon a couch, was consumed without uttering a shriek or betraying one sign of agony. A few instruments of music had been provided, and they played as usual as she approached the fire; not, as is commonly supposed, in order to drown screams, but to prevent the last words of the victim from being heard, as these are supposed to be prophetic, and might become sources of pain or strife to the living. It was not expected that I should yield, and but few people had assembled to witness the sacrifice, so that there was little or nothing to stimulate her to any extraordinary exertions; and I am persuaded that it was the desire of again being united to her husband in the next world, and the entire confidence that she would be so if she now burned herself, that alone sustained her. From the morning of the day he died, Tuesday, till Wednesday evening, she ate pān, or betel-leaves, but nothing else; and from Wednesday evening she ceased eating them. She drank no water from Tuesday. She went into the fire with the same cloth about her that she had worn in the bed of the river; but it was made wet, from a persuasion that even the shadow of any impure thing falling upon her when going to the pile contaminates the woman, unless counteracted by the sheet moistened in the holy stream. I must do the family the justice to say, that they all exerted themselves to dissuade the widow from her purpose; and had she lived, she would assuredly have been cherished and honoured as the first female member of the whole house." It appears that thirteen years before this woman had firmly resolved, if left a widow, to die the death of a Sati.

Colonel Sleeman in the same book gives an account of another Sati of which he was not an eye-witness, but of the truthfulness of which there can be no doubt. In this case it was not the wife of the deceased man who voluntarily burned herself, but the wife of a man then living, she believing that in three previous births she had been his wife, and that in her present birth she was separated from him as a punishment for a sin committed in her last previous birth. It is of course easy for us to laugh at such superstitions, and difficult to understand how people can be enslaved by them; but there is no doubt they have had, and still have, a firm grasp of the minds of millions. "All that a man hath will he give for his life," and when we see a woman choosing a painful death in the full assurance that she is doing an act that is pleasing to the gods, it shows the force of her faith in the religious teaching she has received. The story given by a relative of the deceased man to Colonel Sleeman is as follows:

"When my eldest brother, who was so long a native collector under you in this district, died about twenty years ago at Sehora, a Lodhee woman, who resided two miles distant, in the village of Khittolee, which has been held by our family for several generations, declared that she would burn herself with him on the funeral pile; that she had been his wife in three previous births, had already burnt herself with him three times, and had to burn with him four times more. She was then sixty years of age, and had a husband living about the same age. We were all astounded when she came forward with this story, and told her it must be a mistake, as we were Brāhmans, while she was a Lodhee. She said there was no mistake in the matter; that she in her last birth residing with my brother in the sacred city of Benares, one day gave a holy man, who asked for charity, salt by mistake for sugar with his food; that, in consequence, he told her she should, in her next birth, be separated from her husband, and be of inferior caste; but that, if she did her duty well in that state, she should be reunited to him in the following birth. We told her that all this must be a dream; and the widow of my brother insisted that if she were not allowed to burn herself, the other should not be allowed to take her place. We prevented the widow from ascending the pile, and she died at a good old age, only two years ago, at Sehora. My brother's body was burnt at Sehora, and the poor Lodhee woman came and stole a handful of the ashes which she placed in her bosom, and took back with her to Khittolee. There she prevailed upon her husband and brother to assist her in her return to her former husband and caste as a Brāhman. No soul else would assist them, as we got the native chief to prevent it; and these three persons brought on their own heads the pile on which she seated herself with the ashes in her bosom. The husband and his brother set fire to the pile and she was burned." After this the members of the family firmly believed the woman's story; the father of the man whose wife she declared she had been in previous births bore all her funeral expenses, *i.e.*, for funeral ceremonies after death; and a tomb is still in existence which had been erected on the site where the Sati took place.

There is quite another side to this question. That all widows who have gone through this ceremony were not anxious to suffer in this manner, the following narrative of an eye-witness will clearly prove. A rich Bania died near her house, and there was great excitement in the bazaar as it was made known that his widow, a woman about twenty-six years of age, intended to perform Sati. The magistrate tried in vain to dissuade her from the course she had chosen, but in reply she simply beat her head upon the ground, declaring that if she was not allowed to burn with her husband she would hang herself in court, for the Sāstras declare "that the prayers and imprecations of a Sati are never uttered in vain: the great gods cannot listen to them unmoved."

If a widow touch food or water after her husband's death, according to Hindu law she cannot be burned with his body.

In the hope that this woman might be forced by hunger to give up her design, the magistrate ordered the corpse to be kept for forty-eight hours unburned; but during all this time she never touched anything. At length, when consent was reluctantly given, the woman went to the banks of the Ganges, where about 5,000 people were assembled to witness the ceremony. The pile was raised, the dead body of the husband laid upon it, when the widow, after bathing in the sacred stream, lighted a brand, walked round the pile, set it on fire, and then mounted cheerfully. The flames blazed up instantly. She sat down, placing the head of the corpse upon her lap, and repeated several times, "Rām, Rām, Sati; Rām, Rām, Sati" ("God, God, I am chaste").

As the wind drove the fierce flames towards her, she shook her arms and limbs as if in agony. At length she started up and approached the side to escape. A Hindu policeman, who had been placed there with the express object of seeing that she had fair play, and was not burned by force, raised his sword to strike her. Upon his being seized by the magistrate, the woman again approached the side, sprang out of the fire, and rushed into the Ganges. When the crowd, amongst whom were standing the brothers of the dead man, saw this, they cried out, "Cut her down; knock her down with a bamboo; tie her hands and feet, and throw her in again!" and they would have done this had not the police interfered to prevent it.

The woman drank some water, and, having extinguished the fire in her dress, expressed her willingness to enter the fire again; but this the magistrate forbade, on the ground that, according to Hindu law, a Sati who once forsook the pile could not re-enter it. He then placed her in a palanquin and sent her to the hospital for treatment, at the same time assuring her that though she was now an outcaste from Hindu society, the Government would provide for her and see that she never came to want. The woman declared that in six previous births she had performed Sati, and so was most anxious to perform it for the seventh time, though when the time came human nature protested against the pain. It would have been far better for her not to have expressed her determination to perform Sati. Not having fulfilled her vow, she was not allowed to re-enter her home, and became a stranger to her family.

The Rev. G. Pearce, in an address given in Calcutta in 1869, on "Reminiscences of Life in India," gives the following description of a Sati in that city. It occurred about 1826, "One of the first intimations which I received, shortly after my arrival, of the cruel and debasing character of Hinduism, was a Sati scene that I witnessed in the northern suburbs of Calcutta. It took place on the bank of the river a little beyond Bāgh Bazaar Bridge. I can never forget it. It was about 5 p.m. when I arrived. The crowd was very great—about 1,000 in number. In the centre was a pile of wood. The corpse of the husband lay upon it. On the north side of it was a palanquin, containing the young widow to be immolated. Brāhmans stood round. I got permission to speak to her, but in attempting to do so I found her so under the influence of drugs as to render the effort useless. The Brāhmans made short work of it. On my leaving the palanquin, they took her out of it, and endeavoured to lead her round the pile; but she was unable to stand. She was then taken up into their arms and carried round once only (they ought to have gone round seven times), when they laid the poor woman on her wooden bed beside the corpse of her husband. At this moment she seemed conscious of what was before her, for she immediately drew her arms round its neck, and embraced the corpse with great affection. The Brāhmans, however, lost no time in finishing their dreadful work. Immediately they began to heap upon the bodies the remainder of the pile, until they covered them at least two feet—a weight of wood sufficient to crush the very bones themselves; and to make all the more sure, they bound down the whole pile with bamboos crossed over, lest the poor victim, in her struggles in feeling the fire, should toss it off and escape. All being duly secured, a boy of about twelve years of age came forth with a lighted torch and set fire to the pile close to the head of the victim. At this moment gongs and drums struck up their deafening sounds, whilst the vast multitude of spectators joined in shouts of 'Hari Bol! Hari Bol!' thus effectually drowning the shrieks of the poor dying creature."

According to Mr. Pearce, at this time the annual number of Satis in Bengal was about 1,200; and when Lord William Bentinck passed an Act forbidding it, a petition was sent in to the Privy Council signed by 18,000 people, many of whom represented the best families of Calcutta, asking that this practice might be allowed to continue.

Prior to this Act forbidding Sati, magistrates occasionally interfered on their own authority to prevent children of twelve years of age from performing the rite; but in the case of older women they had no power to prevent them from destroying themselves. At first the Government's efforts were in the direction of regulating, not suppressing, the custom. In 1812 the following instructions were issued to the magistrates: "The Government, after considering the replies of the Pundits, premised that the practice, generally speaking, being recognized and encouraged by the Hindu religion, it appears evident that the course which the British Government should follow, according to the principle of religious toleration already noticed, is to allow the practice in those cases in which it is countenanced by their religion, and to prevent it in others in which it is by the same authority prohibited." Accordingly the magistrates were ordered to confine their interposition to the following cases: (1) To preclude, as far as possible, the employment of all compulsory means on the part of their relatives, of Brāhmans, and of others, in order to cause them to burn themselves; (2) to prevent the criminal use of intoxicating drugs or liquors for the accomplishment of that object; (3) to ascertain whether the women have attained the age as fixed by the Hindu law at which they are permitted to burn themselves; (4) to inquire whether they are pregnant; and (5) to prevent the ceremony from proceeding in cases in which, on any of the above grounds, it may be repugnant to the principles of Hindu law. In harmony with these rules the police were instructed to obtain as early information as possible of an intended Sati, to inquire as to the age of the woman, and to see if she was acting of her own free will; and they were empowered to prevent the ceremony if the widow were pregnant, or unwilling to burn.

In 1817 these orders were further modified. A woman not in good health was to be prevented from burning, also one who had an infant at the breast under four years of age; and also a woman who had a child or children under seven for whom she was unable to provide a suitable guardian. Brāhman widows were permitted to burn *only* with their husband's corpse; not, as had formerly been the case, days or weeks afterwards with some relic of his body. And further, that it was the duty of the family to whom the intending Sati belonged to inform the police of her intention, and not leave the police to make the discovery.

During the years following the enactment of 1812, the following number of Satis were burnt in Bengal:—1815, 378; 1816, 442; 1817, 707; 1819, 839. The ages of these women varied from twenty to seventy. It will be noticed that the interference of the Government appeared rather to increase than to lessen the practice. It is possible that this increase is apparent rather than real; that the cases were more carefully reported, and not that more actually occurred.

It was reserved for Lord William Bentinck to put a stop to this cruel practice. Some of his advisers in India, fearing that an interference with Hindu custom might imperil the empire, advised delay, and urged that in time the Hindu community would themselves give it up; but the majority of his counsellors being of opinion that it ought not under any circumstances to be sanctioned, an Act was passed rendering Sati a case of culpable homicide, and threatening with severe penalties all who encouraged or in any way assisted at the ceremony. The result was that this abominable and cruel custom was put an end to in 1830 in the territories directly under British rule; but since that time, in some of the native States, Sati has been performed. The last case I heard of in India was about 1880.

MORALS.

CHAPTER I.

MORALS—THE HINDUS GENERALLY.

Of all questions connected with the Hindus, the question of morality is perhaps the most difficult to write about with anything approaching confidence, because of the opposing opinions that are held by different people, for which more or less plausible reasons can be given.

Arrian, in his "History of India," written in the second century of the Christian era, gives a most glowing account of the morals of the Hindus. Either his knowledge of them must have been of the most superficial character, or certainly as a whole they have greatly deteriorated since his day. It is certain that his words could only now be employed as the purest sarcasm. It is just possible that he wrote only of some tribes, and not of the community at large; the excellences that he ascribes to them being those in which the people as a whole are lamentably deficient. His words are as follows: "They are remarkably brave; superior in war to all Asiatics. They are remarkable for simplicity and integrity; so reasonable as never to have recourse to a lawsuit, and so honest as neither to require locks to their doors, nor writings to bind their agreements. No Indian was ever known to tell an untruth." We may say truly, if this be a trustworthy account, "How are the mighty fallen, and the bright gold become dull!"

Writing in Madras at the close of last century, the Abbé Dubois, after a lengthened experience and careful observation, gives perhaps a picture as excessively dark as Arrian's is bright. His words are:

"In my opinion the Hindus will remain after another thousand years as they were a thousand years ago. Their reserved and distant intercourse with Europeans will always continue the same, and their abhorrence of the religion, education, and manners of the latter, as well as their other leading prejudices, will continue undiminished. . . . Let Bibles, as many as you please, in every shape and in every style, be translated and circulated among the Hindus; let them, if you wish, be spread in every village, in every cottage, and every family; let the Christian religion be presented to these people under every possible light—I repeat it, with deep sorrow, in my humble opinion (an opinion grounded on twenty-five years of experience) the time of conversion has passed away, and under existing circumstances there remains no human possibility to bring it back. . . . Are we not warranted, on beholding the unnatural and odious worship which prevails all over India, in thinking that these unhappy people are lying under an everlasting anathema; that by obstinately refusing to listen to the voice of the heavens which declare the glory of God, they have for ever rendered themselves unworthy of the Divine favour; that by obstinately rejecting the word of God, which has been in vain announced to them during these last three or four centuries, they have 'filled up the measure of their fathers,' have been entirely forsaken of God, and (what is the worst of Divine vengeance) given over for ever to a reprobate mind on account of the peculiar wickedness of their worship, which supposes in those amongst whom it prevails a degree of perversity far beyond that of old pagan nations?"

In trying to describe the general moral condition of the Hindus, I shall certainly strive earnestly to give a fair and impartial description. I have lived for many years in close intimacy with the people, many of whom I love; have conversed with all classes of the community; have spent many happy years in working, as I believe, for their benefit, and, intentionally, at any rate, shall not write down aught in malice. My wonder is, considering their religious faiths, and the character of the deities they worship, that they are not far worse than they are. When I consider the state of Europe, with the example and teaching of Jesus more or less generally known, it does not surprise me at all to find the Hindus morally what they are, as I remember that whilst their books contain some of the highest and noblest moral precepts, their deities, when incarnate, are described as ignoring these beautiful lessons; and still further, when I see that religion and morality are quite separate in their view; for a man may be a most exemplary Hindu, and at the same time guilty of the grossest immorality. I shall strive to give a fair statement of their general character as far as an outsider is able to estimate it. Of course it will be understood that *all* Hindus have not all the vices, neither have all Hindus all the virtues, that I shall mention as belonging to the community. I shall first give the darker, and then the brighter side of the picture.

Ingratitude.

When one of the missionaries was engaged in the translation of the Scriptures into Bengali, he wanted a word to express the idea of gratitude. After several attempts to explain the idea for which an expression was required, after a few moments' pause, his pundit said, "How can you expect to find a word to express an idea that does not exist in a country?" And as it proved to be true that there was no common Bengali word suitable, a term had to be introduced from the Sanskrit—a standing proof of the absence up to that time of the need of an expression for this virtue. In like manner an Englishman, on going to India, is astonished to find that there is no term expressive of "Thank you" for any little acts of attention that may be shown to him by servants and others. It is an instance of the way in which "when in Rome we act as the Romans do," that up to this hour the foreigners, who are most careful to recognize kindnesses shown to them by those of their own nation, have not forced an expression into general use equivalent to those found in their own languages. Of course there are expressions which can be, and are, employed to signify pleasure received from the attentions shown; but as a rule those who in their own country would be most particular in showing their appreciation of kindness, fall into the way, common in India, of taking these courtesies as a matter of course.

That gratitude, or at any rate the expression of it, cannot be universal, the following statement of a gentleman, who for many years was the principal of a large missionary college, will show. This gentleman had laboured most devotedly for the good of the young men in India, had given hours daily to the private instruction of many who were wishful to obtain further teaching than they could obtain in the college classes, for which extra work he, of course, did not receive a single penny. After twenty-five years of such work, he said that the only expression of gratitude he ever received was from one of his old students, who at the time of the occurrence was a station-master on the East India Railway. Stopping at the station, and being anxious to obtain a time-table, the station-master offered to get one, and when he offered payment it was politely refused, as the young man said he had received many acts of kindness from his professor, and would not take the money.

The truthfulness of this story I do not for a moment doubt; but I think the experience of this gentleman was exceptional. I have met on many occasions with old students of our colleges who have expressed their thankfulness for the assistance they have received from our missionaries engaged in educational work, and also for the kindness of the Christian public in England in sending out Christian ladies to teach their wives and daughters. Then the faithfulness of the soldiers to their salt, as it is termed, *i.e.*, their gratitude to those from whom through many years they obtained their support, has kept, in troublous times, those faithful to British rule who otherwise would have taken part with comrades in rebellion. Still I fear it is a fact that as a rule gratitude is not a common virtue in India. Look, *e.g.*, at the class of Zemindars, who, by the prodigality of the British Government, were raised at once from the mere collectors of the revenue into practically the landholders of Bengal. When any attempt is made to raise the revenue, however necessary the cause, if their income be affected, how they cry out as if an injustice were being done to them! Look at the educated classes, who, through the unfair assistance that is given to them as compared with the mere trifle that is spent in mass-education, write and speak against the same Government, because, having provided most costly establishments for their instruction, it does not also provide ample employment with proportionate incomes also. Brahmā, the creator, is scarcely worshipped by the masses of India in the present day, because, his work of creation being finished, the people say, "We can obtain nothing more from him if we worship him." Gratitude, in the sense of thankfulness for past favours, is not commonly expressed by the people; though in the sense of thankfulness for favours to come it is not so uncommon.

Untruthfulness.

That this is a very general vice of the mass of the Hindus in Bengal, there can be no doubt whatever in the minds of those who come into personal contact with the people. Among the village people in other parts of India, where there is a stronger physique and greater personal bravery, and also amongst the aborigines who inhabit the hills, this general statement would not apply; but of the Bengali it is absolutely true. A gentleman who has been brought into the closest intimacy with all classes, and knows their language and habits as well, perhaps, as almost any one I have met, declares that when a question is asked, the full bearing of which on themselves or those connected with them they cannot see, you may rely upon it that the first answer you receive is false; but that when they see that the truth cannot injure themselves or any one they care for, they will speak the truth. One of the best educated of our native Christians once said to me, "You who have been born in Christian families and have been trained from infancy to speak the truth and to hate lying can have no idea of the difficulty we Bengalis have in overcoming the natural tendency in us to lying and deceit. You are taught that it is dishonourable and evil to lie; we are taught that the dishonour is not in lying, but in being discovered." And so far as my experience and observation goes, when an order is disregarded in house or office, or any theft committed, it is almost impossible for the culprit to be discovered. Those who know the truth of the affair will not inculpate others, but rather deny "with oaths and cursing" all knowledge of the affair. When a tale of wrong-doing of any *employé* is brought to us by other natives it may be taken as certain that this information is given not from the simple wish to boldly speak out the truth, but as simply the outcome of petty spite—a mean manner of revenge for injury done. In business transactions their word is never taken; the simplest contracts that are made must be written, for if any profit will arise to the promiser by repudiating the transaction it is certain advantage will be taken of the fact that there is no written evidence. I am thankful to be able to say that I have met with some exceptions to this rule, men whose word I could rely on as on that of an honest Englishman; but these exceptions are not numerous. The real secret of this untruthfulness I take to be the natural cowardice of the people, and the fact that when it served their purpose the gods themselves—notably Brahmā respecting Siva, and Krishna respecting Rādhā—are represented as resorting to this practice. If lying was lawful for a deity, where can be the harm of a poor weak mortal resorting to the same practice?

A notable instance of strict truthfulness is seen in the life of the late Bābu Rām Gopāl Ghose. This gentleman had lived in open violation of caste regulation for some time, but afterwards, for family reasons, wished to be recognized again as a Hindu. His father suggested that he should deny that he had eaten beef, &c.; but he replied, "I would do anything for you, yea, give up my life, but cannot lie."

In corroboration of the opinion expressed above as to the general untruthfulness of the Hindus, we might quote the statements of many who have written on the subject: one will suffice. In the "Competition Wallah" Mr. G. O. Trevelyan writes: "The want of truthfulness leavens the whole being of the Bengali;" and again, "It is not too much to assert that the mass of Bengalis have no notion of truth and falsehood."

Dishonesty.

Akin to lying is theft. Here, again, what is said of the mass of the people of course is not true of every individual. Amongst the lower orders, which form the servant class in the cities and stations, pilfering is almost universal, and, strange to say, those who, so far as was known, have been honest for many years, when a favourable opportunity occurs cannot resist the temptation. It is certain that prices are usually asked from their employers for goods of daily consumption higher than were paid, and when discovery is made there is but little sense of shame, as it is considered a right thing for the servant to obtain a percentage on all the money of his master that passes through his hands. So clever and so persistent are the people in their efforts to rob that it is simply impossible to prevent it unless one's whole time is given to watch. A lady may sit in the verandah of her house to see her horse fed; whilst she turns her head for a moment only, a handful of corn is stolen and secreted in the servant's clothes. A man will quietly steal into the cow-shed before others are stirring in the morning and extract a good supply of milk from your cow. A servant will accompany you to the bazaar and note the money spent with different shopkeepers, and force them, after your back is turned, to give them a percentage. "Every agent employed to make a purchase, great or small, pockets a commission unknown to his principals; this commission is called 'dustoori,' or 'the customary sum,' the amount being regulated by the impudence of the buyer and the anxiety of the seller to dispose of his goods." Trevelyan tells a story of a servant, ignorant of the fact that stamps belong to the Government, being sent to a stamp vendor to purchase stamps, knocking down the functionary of the Government with his ruler and carrying off his ledger to the Treasury in triumph because the man refused to give him his dustoori. Contractors will tender for goods to Government at a lower rate than the Europeans who manufacture them, and from whom the contractor must purchase them, their profit being made by giving short weight or measure; and to enable them to do this their profits must be shared with the officer who has to receive and pass their goods. A man will contract to purchase salt at a certain price as it is being discharged from the ship; the price falls; the Bengali will go into hiding until the shipping agents find that the least inconvenience and loss is to cancel the sale and seek other purchasers. It is seldom we hear of pickpockets and thieves who by their dexterity rob others; the common forms of theft are those where children are decoyed into secret places and there robbed of their ornaments, or where a number of men (dacoits) make a combined attack upon a house or a village, and either by setting fire to the house or by their shouts driving out the people from their homes, and then make off with all they can lay their hands on.

The use of abusive language.

The people, though cowardly, and for the most part peaceably disposed, are nevertheless easily provoked to quarrel, but not easily moved to fight. Where an excited Englishman would freely use his fists, and try by physical force to subdue an opponent, the Bengali is content to use his tongue. And certainly passion, anger, hatred, contempt, were never exhibited on any stage with greater force than may be seen almost daily in the middle of a village, or a public street in a city, when two women are engaged in a dispute. The tone of voice and action of the whole body is at times quite tragic. At such times the language, attitudes, and grimaces are of the vilest. A man or woman when quarrelling seems to lose all self-respect, and, in order to annoy the person with whom they are disputing, have no hesitation in boasting of crimes they have never committed. A man of pure morals will not scruple to say that he has committed the grossest immorality with the wife or mother of his opponent; and a woman will make a similar boast respecting her conduct with the husband of the woman with whom she is quarrelling. The commonest abuse when the people quarrel is that in which the female relatives of his enemy are declared to be all that is bad. In the police courts it is almost a daily occurrence for this to be adduced as an excuse for blows which have caused the injury or the death of their antagonists.

Perjury.

The Hindus generally, and more especially the Bengalis, are a very litigious race. Certainly either Arrian did not know the people, or they have sadly changed since his day. Often it seems as if they could scarcely be happy without having a lawsuit pending. To many Bengali gentlemen a lawsuit is an amusement, as hunting and shooting are the recreations of the British. "The natives regard a court of law not as the bulwark of the innocent and the refuge of the wronged, but as a prize-ring which affords a fair field and no favour; a stock exchange where fortunes are to be made by cleverness and industry, and lost by carelessness and stupidity; where all men have an equal chance, and no one must rely on the justness of his cause, or the blamelessness of his life, or any such natural advantage which he may possess over his fellows. The wealthiest and most respected man of a district will often be one who dates his prosperity from a suit which, as every one is well aware, was brought to a successful termination by unlimited perjury, and a document discovered at the bottom of a chest in the zenana just in time to be produced in court. His neighbours speak of him as the society of an English provincial town speak of a man who began life behind a counter, and ends it in the parlour of a county bank, whither he had pushed his way by dint of prudence and frugality." *

To lose a suit in court is not only annoying and expensive, it is also regarded as disgraceful; hence we find that all means of damaging an opponent are freely resorted to. "A planter confessed to a friend of mine that he had been reduced to the verge of ruin by a Rāja, who trumped up three actions in succession, and gained them all. The Englishman, however, won back the ground which he had lost in a suit, the facts of which had been invented and arranged by his agent and Zemindar." †

A friend of my own told me that, when living in Cachar, a man came and complained to him that a Sirdar on the estate had burned some of his charcoal. On asking how he knew this, the reply was, "Bholonātha saw him do it." Going directly to Bholonātha, and asking if he had seen this transaction, he denied all knowledge of it; but when the aggrieved party came upon the scene, the witness said, "Why did you not tell me that you wished me to give evidence?"

The most common way in which a suit is commenced is for a charge to be brought against a man altogether out of proportion to the offence given. If a blow is struck, it is magnified into an attempt at murder; if a debt is incurred, the amount is made double or treble what is legally owing; whilst the defendant will, in his turn, not be content with giving a fair statement of the case, but will try to prove that he is not indebted, or that he never struck the complainant;

* "The Competition Wallah," p. 227. † Ibid. p. 227.

it is also certain that often where no legal offence has been committed—but revenge impels a man to injure another—a charge, for which there is not the slightest foundation in fact, will be made. Men have been known to inflict severe wounds upon themselves, in order that they could lay a charge of assault against an enemy; and corpses have been hacked, in order that a charge of murder might be laid against one they wished to injure; people have been killed, and their dead bodies placed in such a position as to lead the police authorities to believe that the person against whom the conspiracy was formed had been guilty of their death. The police reports state plainly that there is reason to fear that a very large majority of witnesses in our courts perjure themselves. Magistrates declare that they scarcely ever think of deciding cases according to the evidence as it is given in court, because they know that both sides have their trained witnesses; they simply judge according to probability. Judges of the highest courts of India have declared that they did not believe a single case had come before them, in which the natives of India were concerned, which was not supported by perjury. Barristers, at times, seeing the way in which the evidence of the different witnesses is so beautifully dovetailed, to make the story of their client appear absolutely true, have sometimes to throw discredit on some of their own witnesses, lest the *art* of their solicitors in training the witnesses should be too apparent. The litigant goes into court expecting the judge largely to discount the charges made, and therefore makes them sufficiently large to allow, when the discount is taken off, to secure all he really ought to get; whilst the defendant, not content with simply disproving the charges, secures witnesses to prove a great deal more than the truth. It is a notorious fact that there are many in the neighbourhood of our law courts who are ready to give evidence on any subject, and on either side, for a mere trifle. Certainly the task of hearing the false evidence in our courts, and of judging which side is the more likely to be in the right, must be one of the most painful and irksome tasks that can be undertaken. Added to this is the belief that judges are open to bribery. Men who have any excuse for going into the presence of a magistrate or judge privately will not scruple to take money from litigants who are foolish enough to believe that they are aiding their cause by this waste of money.

As illustrations of what has been said, the following may be given. "A shopkeeper complained in court that as he was walking across the street, one of his neighbours knocked him down with a cudgel, and, as he lay insensible, robbed him of thirteen rupees. He produced seven witnesses who confirmed substantially the whole statement. It eventually turned out that the prisoner struck the prosecutor on the back with a slight switch, and that the rupees and the insensibility were an episode which had no foundation in fact." *

"A young man bought a village from a Zemindar, who sold it cheap because the inhabitants had for some time refused to pay a pice of rent. As the new proprietor was well aware that his tenants were likely to prove unruly, he went with a strong force to compel them. At that time cholera was rife in the village, and during the night the headman came, with several of his companions, and declared that if the landlord did not clear off, he would bring a corpse, cut its throat, throw it in the Englishman's camp, and lay a charge of murder against him before the magistrate."

On another occasion this same planter happened to be visiting a brother planter. After dinner a jackal began to scream, when the host and another friend took up their rifles, and went to shoot it. Not finding the jackal, one of them fired at a sheep at a little distance, and when he fired he saw a man suddenly jump up from behind the sheep, and then fall down. On going to the spot it was discovered that the

* "The Competition Wallah," p. 229.

man was shot through the heart, and was quite dead. The relations of the deceased prosecuted the planter for murder, and swore that he had tied the deceased to a tree, beaten him cruelly, outraged him in a most foul manner, and finally put him out of his misery by deliberately firing at him from the distance of a few yards." *

In Agra a Thakur, having a quarrel with a shopkeeper, a servant of the great man suggested that his master should kill him, and then charge the shopkeeper with the murder. The wife of the willing victim hearing of this, prevented her husband from sacrificing himself, so an idiot boy was murdered, and his body deposited in the premises of the shopkeeper. But unfortunately this ingenuity was not successful; the trick was discovered, and the penalty fell on the guilty parties.

Forgery.

Between perjury and forgery there is often but a single step. In order to make valid a claim or to resist oppression, in order to substantiate or disprove a charge, documentary evidence is sometimes necessary. And where this has never existed, or been destroyed, or lost, it is necessary to supply its place. As a result, it is no uncommon thing for revenue officers and judges, before whom those documents are placed, to reject them as palpable forgeries. Though forgery is not so common as perjury, because of the greater chances of detection, yet it is the opinion of those whose experience of our courts is greatest, that it is very frequently resorted to. In cases where leases are required to prove the claim of the landlord for rent it is an easy thing to manufacture them when, in the great majority of cases, the tenant is too ignorant to read or write, and so detect the fraud. And it sometimes happens with forged documents as with the trained witnesses, that the manufacture is too palpable, and thus a doubt is raised in the judge's mind which leads him to reject it. It is said that were all those prosecuted for perjury and

* "The Competition Wallah," p. 231.

forgery who are certainly guilty of these crimes, our judges would have little else to do than to try them.

Want of confidence in their fellow-men.

As a result of the natural tendency to lying—which in special cases leads to perjury and forgery—is the want of confidence that the Hindus repose in each other, and in Englishmen with whom business may bring them into contact. If a workman agrees to execute any work, he will not commence it until he has received money in advance—professedly to purchase material, really as a safeguard against his employer, who, if he did not require the article he had ordered when it was completed, might refuse to take it, and the workman would have it thrown upon his hands. In almost all business transactions of the smallest kind a written agreement must be made on both sides, and this must be stamped and registered, because it is believed that a man's word is not binding. In connection with this may be mentioned the almost universal practice of bargaining. A man who has anything to sell, or a workman who may be called to undertake any work, never dreams of asking the proper price for his work; nor does any one who has had any experience think of giving what is asked. As in Solomon's time—"It is nought, nought," says the buyer, as goods are offered him for sale; whilst the seller in his turn will not scruple to speak falsely about the value of his articles, and the prices for the same goods that others have given him. It is my firm conviction, speaking generally of the lower orders of the people, if not the middle and upper classes, that a man goes away better pleased if he has by dint of a long chaffering obtained a mere trifle over the proper price of his work or goods, than if he had taken a much higher price at first without the excitement of bargaining. In the one case he imagines that his eloquence has prevailed to induce his customer to give more than he intended; but in the other he imagines that the man has paid exorbitantly simply owing to his ignorance. There is always this feeling on the part of the purchaser—that he might have driven a better bargain; whilst the seller imagines that had he asked more, he might have got a proportionately higher price. Occasionally one meets with a man who asks a fair price, and sticks to it whether he sells or not, but such are most rare exceptions.

Oppression.

It would be difficult to find a country where the people are subjected to greater oppression from those above them than prevails amongst the Hindus. The poor are passionately attached to the soil which has been cultivated by their forefathers; are unable, owing to their great poverty, to lay aside any money to enable them to make a fresh start in another part of the country; and are naturally conservative in their habits, and would with very great difficulty be able to adapt themselves to the kind of food and the new methods of cultivation that would be necessary in other parts of the country. The poor of Bengal being in a damp rice-producing country, would be scarcely able to exist in the dryer regions where wheat is grown; nor would they know how to turn the soil to the best advantage: hence we find them submitting in many cases to oppression that we should imagine sufficient to drive them away. Bad as was the condition of the slave in the Southern States of America, there can be no doubt that the condition of multitudes of the poor in Bengal is in some respects worse. The slave was sure of food, and of a decent house in which to live, because it was the interest of his owner to feed and house him well, that he might be in a condition to work; but it is far otherwise with the poor of India. He has to pay as heavy a rent as his land will stand in fruitful seasons, when the rains fall in plenty, and his crops are good; but when the rainfall is low, or sickness may interrupt his labours, he has to accept loans at exorbitant interest from his landlord; and when once he becomes indebted it is almost impossible for him ever to free himself from the chains. The interest often absorbs more than the excess of the profits of the year over what is absolutely necessary to support the life of himself and family. In addition to the normal fixed rent which his lease gives his landlord a legal right to demand, other exactions are made which reduce the poor tenants to abject poverty. It is a known fact that the rich, well-educated landlords of India, when an income tax was levied, did not scruple to force this, that should have come out of their own pockets, from their miserable tenants; and even in many cases, after that tax was abolished, the tenants had to continue to pay it to their landlords. A marriage in his family, or a death, or any extraordinary expense that he may have to incur, is considered a sufficient reason for demanding an extra sum from his tenant. The result of this is, that the tenant is bound to continue to live and work hard on his land without the possibility of removal, as much as if a serf law were in force; and if he speak of his grievances to a sympathizing ear, and a word is spoken in his defence, his cattle, his ploughs, his all may be seized; for he has literally nothing but what is pawned to his landlord, or to some money-lending go-between. There is a widespread oppression throughout the whole country of Bengal; and the grinding poverty of the people makes one very sad as it is brought to notice in travelling through the country. Bengal, one of the richest soils on the face of the earth, which is able in many parts to support a larger population than it has, is in such a condition, that if a single season's raius are withheld, unless the Government at immense cost steps in to prevent it, it would be decimated by famine. The country produces sufficient in the years of plenty to provide for the wants of its people in the years of scarcity; but owing to the fact that they live from hand to mouth, and cannot possibly save anything for such contingencies, they are entirely dependent upon the care and generosity of the Government.

Revenge.

Hindus as a rule are unforgiving. They do not quarrel, fight, shake hands, and become good friends again. Concerning what they term their honour they are very sensitive, and will wait long for an opportunity to avenge themselves on those who have tarnished it. And as they are naturally cowardly, their methods of revenge are subtle and secret. To strike a blow in the dark is far more in the way of a Hindu than boldly to accuse a man of wrong-doing and try to punish him for it. And where the offender himself is beyond the reach of direct attack, it is not beneath a Bengali's view to try to wound him through his children or other members of his family. Even though the offence may be apparently forgotten, if months or even years after the quarrel a favourable opportunity occurs, it is seized as a means of wreaking vengeance. I have known charges to be unspoken for sixteen or eighteen years, and then brought up against one whom at last time has brought into their power; and I have known many cases where, because of some wretched family squabble, means have been used with the object of robbing the offender of his means of livelihood. When a Hindu's anger is excited, truth, honour, trust—all are forgotten, and no means are left unemployed that can injure an enemy in character, purse, and position. The term "mild Hindu" certainly is the purest sarcasm; they submit to oppression and cruelty because they are physically incapable of resistance, and not from any inherent mildness and readiness to forgive. Only give them the opportunity to avenge themselves, and to oppress others, and certainly they are as vindictive in their way as any race of men on earth. They do not use the knife or the dagger, it is true, but they resort to poison, and, what is sometimes even worse, the poison of their own untruthful tongues. A single day's journey in the country or in the streets of Calcutta, with one's eyes open, as the cartmen are seen cruelly illtreating their bullocks, or a schoolmaster punishing his pupils, will quite dispel the notion of the Hindu's natural mildness. He is mild where he cannot help it; he can cruelly oppress where he has the power.

Immorality.

There are those who say that there is no such thing as real morality amongst the Hindus; this I believe to be a most exaggerated statement. That there is a great amount of immorality, there can be no doubt; but that many are pure amongst the millions in India, is certain. A Brāhman gentleman, writing in the *Calcutta Review*, says, "Sexual impurity is, it is true, scarcely considered a sin in the males." * As far as my observation has gone, and as far as I can gather from conversation with those who know village life, I should say that in the villages of India purity of morals generally prevails. Men and women have to work hard in the fields or in the home; returning at dusk, they seldom go out again until the following day. There are no idlers to lead others astray, nor are there many opportunities of evil. Occasionally cases of infidelity even here come to light, and when discovered they often lead to the murder of one or both the guilty parties; but speaking generally, I should say that the morals of the poor and ignorant villagers of Bengal would compare favourably with the same class elsewhere. Of course in the villages there are many left as widows: these, if unchaste, generally migrate into the towns, because they would not be allowed to live near the families they have disgraced; but if they do not openly commit themselves they may continue in their homes. As a matter of fact abortion and infanticide are not by any means confined to the larger towns, but are as rife in the villages as elsewhere. Still I should say, speaking generally, the life of the villagers is pure.

But of the morality of the towns little can be said. London is spoken of as an immoral city; but Calcutta, with a population of one-sixth of that of London, has nearly double the number of prostitutes. The Zenana system has very much to do with the immorality of the Hindus. A man marries, and is called by his employment to live at a distance from

* Vol. ii. p. 23.

his family home. He deems it unsafe to take his wife; she is, therefore, left at his father's house, whilst he is absent for months or years at a time. In the majority of cases men thus separated from their families form other ties. Nearly the whole of the servants in Calcutta are away from their families for two or three years at a time. These and other causes account for the dreadful immorality of the towns and cities. The custom of compelling widows to remain unmarried drives many of them to a life of immorality.

Made a drudge in the house of her father-in-law, and having no prospect of improvement, it can occasion little surprise that they should swell the number of kept women and public prostitutes. Concubinage is so common in Bengal that no one seems surprised at it. And yet those who do not see it to be a crime to be guilty of immorality themselves, are most careful to prevent, if possible, the same looseness of morals in their wives. It is often boastfully said by Bengali gentlemen that they do not have recourse to the Divorce Court as the English do. It is not because of the purer lives of the gentlemen, certainly; nor is it because of the purer morals of many of the widows, though it may be because of the seclusion in which their wives are kept; in which case their non-sinning is not the result of a purer morality, but because of the want of opportunity. It may be that means are employed to keep secret any misconduct, lest dishonour should come to the family. Certainly, little can be said of the morality of a community in which concubinage is openly practised, prostitution common everywhere, and where abortion is carried on as a distinct profession. The reason of this I see in the fact that continence is not taught. As soon as it is possible for boys and girls to marry they are brought together. Nor must the influence of character of the gods, as taught in the later religious books of the Hindus, be overlooked. On the cars in which Jagannātha is drawn, and on the temples, are pictures and sculptures so disgusting and filthy that they cannot be described. At the religious festivals jātras are performed, in which the sayings and doings of these deities are represented by the actors; and as interludes, there is dancing of a most lascivious character, and songs of a most amorous description. Here young and old see and hear things which are calculated to inflame the passions in the very presence of the images of the gods.

Now let us turn to the brighter side of the Hindu character. And first of all virtues should be noticed their

Industry.

I am aware that residents in the cities who have to do only with the lower orders, and perhaps the worst class of these, regard the Hindus as an idle, lazy race; but there can be little doubt that this is a wrong estimate of their general character. In the country districts the men start out as soon as it is light enough to see, and continue in the fields ploughing, sowing, weeding, transplanting, reaping, according to the season, until about eleven o'clock, when they return, feed their cattle, bathe, take their first meal, and lie down to rest. About two o'clock they return to their work, at which they continue until dusk. On one or two days a week they trudge to the nearest village, where a hât, or market, is held, carrying their produce for sale, and returning with a load of necessaries for the week, which they have purchased in exchange. And this hard life continues the whole year round, with little to vary its monotony. Perhaps three or four times in the year there may be some religious festival held near, to which they go to listen to the music, to see the performances, and to purchase commodities, which are brought there from the cities, as the English peasantry used to frequent the fairs of the neighbourhood. When, therefore, it is remembered that the people have no regular day of rest, as the labourers in Christian lands have Sunday, it is certain that of the mass of the common people idleness certainly cannot be said to be a characteristic. Look, again, at the workmen in towns, where the men are paid by piece work,

From early dawn until near midnight they will be found at work—the blacksmiths before their blazing fires, the tin-men, the braziers, the carpenters, and all the varied trades are in full swing. There are idlers to be found here and there, but, taken as a whole, when it is to their interest to do it, they work as hard and for longer hours than the British workman would care to labour. Indoors the women are not less industrious. They have their children to care for, the house to keep clean, fuel to collect, food to cook, and all the ordinary duties of the home. The middle and upper classes have the household duties attended to by servants as in England, but a great deal is done by the ladies of the house. Those who have had to do with schools and colleges seldom need to complain of the idleness of the students. When it is remembered that in these colleges the students have to receive nearly the whole of their instruction in English, which is to them a foreign language, the high position taken by natives in University lists show conclusively that they must work far harder than their English competitors. A visit to a Hindu home or lodging-house for young students, late at night, or in the early morning, would at once dispel all notions of the idleness of the young Bengali.

Patience.

Though passionately fond of children, a man will see his child die and perform the funeral ceremonies with a calm and stolid countenance. He will suffer intense agony of body, as is evident from the muscular contractions, or submit without shrinking to most painful operations, and never a sound will escape his lips. He will make long, wearisome, and dangerous journeys, suffering immense discomforts from want of food and proper accommodation, &c., and never murmur. The patience of the Hindu is most praiseworthy. The secret of it lies, perhaps, in the firm conviction that his life is but the working out of a Divine plan that was formed at or soon after his birth, and that it is useless, as it is wrong, for him to resist the inevitable. Still, whatever be the cause, the fact remains that for patient endurance of physical pain, of mental distress, and of the ordinary sorrows of life, there are few if any race of people on the face of the earth to equal, none to surpass them. It is not that they do not feel, but they believe that whatever comes is their fate, and must be patiently endured by them.

A characteristic story is told of two brothers who were caught stealing horses from a regiment on the march. Before sentence was passed one of the men suggested that his brother should be sent to bring back the missing horses, and he would answer for his return with his life. As the horses were urgently needed, the plan was adopted; but as neither man nor horses returned within the appointed time, the brother who remained as a hostage was rather surprised that any one expected to see them. For saving his brother from punishment, and for enriching his friends with the money for which the horses were sold, he was quite prepared to suffer death.

Filial respect.

The word of the father or elder brother, who at the father's death becomes the head of the family, the wish of the mother or grandmother, is law. There are many of the educated young men in Bengal at this moment who would have embraced Christianity if it were not for the profound respect they have for father and mother, and the intense grief such a step as the open avowal of their faith in Christ would cause them. Long after a man is of age, and when, according to Western notions, he might be allowed to think and act for himself, the force of his filial ties is such as to hold him back from a course that may appear to him right and desirable. The fact that the son does not have a separate home, but continues to dwell in the family house after his marriage, fosters this filial respect; but even where he forms a home for himself it is seen to be almost as great as in other cases.

Charity.

The charity of the Hindus is great; by this word I mean

bestowal of gifts on the poor, whether relatives or strangers. There is no poor law in India, no guardians of the poor, no workhouses, excepting for the Europeans in the Presidency towns. The poor of a family, the halt, the lame, the blind, the weak, the insane, are provided for by their family, if it is at all able to do it; in cases where there are few or no relatives, then the burden is taken up by others. It is a "work of merit;" just as making a tank, planting trees by the road-side, or constructing a bathing-place on the banks of a sacred stream. It is no uncommon thing for a man who is at all wealthy to have a number of poor pensioners almost if not entirely dependent upon him for their support. And in a large family there are some less clever, less fortunate, and less industrious than others; the more clever, fortunate, and industrious work the harder, and putting their earnings in a common purse, all share in the results of the industry of the more successful members. Occasionally it will happen that an idle, spendthrift son will wear out the patience and strain the generosity of a brother until he is told to leave the home or work; but as a rule, with exemplary kindness, the poor and the helpless are provided for by the other members of the family. There are millions of professional beggars in India; there are many shrines whose offerings support thousands in comparative idleness. This course could not continue unless the hearts of the people were charitably disposed. At great festivals, where the people assemble in crowds, beggars abound. It has often astonished me to see poor women and men going from one to another, giving a pice here and a handful of rice there. Of course it may be said that this is a form of barter; the people give to these saints in order to gain credit for their gifts in heaven. Were the same tests applied to the gifts of Christians, would all the apparent charity be found real—*i.e.*, gifts bestowed simply because of love to the Saviour and to those for whom He has taught His people to care?

Parental love.

Another most pleasing trait is the love of parents to their children, and the long-continued and immense self-sacrifice they make to further their advancement in life. The Bengalis have a proverb referring to the way in which a man should dispose of his income. He should divide it into four parts: one part goes to pay off old debts; one part to God; one part for present expenses; one part is put into the bank. The interpretation of this is as follows: one part should be given to parents in return for all their kindness and self-denial in the past; one part should be given to God for the support of religion and for the help of the needy and suffering; a third part should be devoted to the ordinary expenses of the family; whilst a fourth part should be spent on the education of the children, which will yield interest in old age in the form of assistance from them. This certainly is a more pleasing and natural proverb than the Lancashire one, which teaches that the "old hen may scratch for her chickens; but the chickens never scratch for the old hen;" and, so far as my observation has gone, I think the spirit of this proverb is seen in the ordinary life of the Bengalis. Parents are not suffered to want as long as sons can aid them. It would certainly be regarded as a most disgraceful thing were a man who could do anything for the support of an aged father or mother to allow the burden of their maintenance to fall on strangers. I have heard of the parents of people in England who could well provide for them being allowed to derive assistance from the parish. In gifts to the poor and needy, certainly the Hindu is not lacking; and the people of Bengal do not come behind those of any country in toiling and denying themselves the comforts of life in order that their sons may obtain a good education and rise to a higher position than that attained by their fathers. Many of the educated young men of Bengal would not occupy their present position were it not for the self-denial of their fathers and mothers. Taken as a whole, whilst the Hindu has many evil traits in his character, he has many good ones too.

CHAPTER II.

THE CRIMINAL CLASSES.

Having considered the question of the morals of the ordinary people, we naturally pass on to consider the peculiarities of the crimes of those who sink below the level of the community and make themselves obnoxious to its penal laws. It must be distinctly borne in mind that the description of this class is no more true of the Hindus generally than would an account of the English people drawn exclusively from the Newgate Calendar and Police News. But it is most painful to see how in many cases those who up to a certain moment have been respectable members of society, in a fit of passion aroused by abuse, or of jealousy caused by the infidelity of a wife, or from the fear of a rival usurping their place in the affections of a husband, resort to measures which at once force them into the criminal class, and bring upon them the penalties of the law. Most of the facts here recorded are taken from a most painfully interesting work on Medical Jurisprudence, by Dr. Norman Chevers.

At the commencement of that work Dr. Chevers says: "It would probably be impossible to point to any races of men whose great crimes more distinctly emanate from their national character than is the case with those various classes of nations who inhabit the British possessions in India." In support of this statement the following quotations are made from two writers well qualified to speak concerning two classes most opposed in national characteristics: Mackintosh, describing the warlike Rājputs of the North-West Provinces; and Macaulay writing of the Bengalis. Mackintosh says:

"The Rājputs are the representatives of India. In them are seen all the qualities of the Hindu race unmitigated by foreign mixture, exerted with their original energy, and displayed in the strongest light. They exhibit the genuine form of a Hindu community formed of the most discordant materials, and combining the most extraordinary contrasts of moral nature; unconquerable adherence to native opinions and usages with servile submission to a foreign yoke; an unbelieving priesthood, ready to suffer martyrdom for the most petty observance of their professed faith; a superstition which inspires the resolution to inflict or to suffer the most atrocious barbarities without cultivating any natural sentiment or enforcing any social duty; . . . attachment to kindred and to home, with no friendship and no love of country; good temper and gentle disposition, little active cruelty except when stimulated by superstition; but little sensibility, little compassion, and scarcely any disposition to relieve suffering or relieve wrong done to themselves or others; timidity, with its natural attendants, falsehood and meanness, in the ordinary relations of human life, joined with a capability of becoming excited, to courage in the field, to military enthusiasm, to heroic self-devotion; abstemiousness in some respects more rigorous than that of a Western hermit, in others a life of intoxication; austerities and self-tortures almost incredible, practised by those who otherwise wallow in gross sensuality, childish levity, barefaced falsehood, no faith, no constancy, no shame, no belief in the existence of justice."

Of the Bengalis, Macaulay, in his Essay on Warren Hastings, writes: "The physical organization of the Bengali is feeble even to effeminacy. . . . His pursuits are sedentary, his limbs delicate, his movements languid. During many ages he has been trampled on by men of bolder and more hardy breeds. Courage, independence, veracity, are qualities to which his constitution and his situation are equally unfavourable. . . . All those arts which are the natural defence of the weak are more familiar to this subtle race than to the Roman of the time of Juvenal, or to the Jew of the dark ages. What the horns are to the buffalo, what the paw is to the tiger, what the sting is to the bee, what beauty, according to the old Greek song, is to woman, deceit is to the Bengali. Large promises, smooth excuses, elaborate tissues of circumstantial falsehood, chicanery, perjury, forgery, are the weapons, offensive and defensive, of the people of the Lower Ganges. All these millions do not furnish one Sepoy to the armies of the Company. But as usurers, money-changers, as sharp legal practitioners, no class of human beings can bear a comparison with them. With all his softness, the Bengali is by no means placable in his enmities, or prone to pity. The pertinacity with which he adheres to his purposes yields only to the immediate pressure of fear. Nor does he lack a certain kind of courage which is often wanting in his masters. To inevitable evils he is sometimes found to oppose a passive fortitude such as the Stoics attributed to their ideal sage. An European warrior, who rushes on a battery of cannon with a loud hurrah, will sometimes shriek under the surgeon's knife, and fall into an agony of despair at the sentence of death. But the Bengali, who would see his country overrun, his house laid in ashes, his children murdered or dishonoured, without having the spirit to strike one blow, has yet been known to endure torture with the firmness of Mucius, and to mount the scaffold with the steady step and even pulse of Algernon Sidney."

From these extracts describing two distinct races of Hindus, it will be seen how marked are the national characteristics; and as their natures differ, so do their crimes. A skilful detective, when a murder or any other great crime has been committed, is generally able, from the manner of its committal, to form a correct opinion concerning the nationality of the criminal. We shall first treat of—

Murder.

Of the trials in our Courts of Justice, those for murder bulk largely; and of all the means resorted to by which obnoxious persons can be got rid of, perhaps poison is the commonest—*i.e.*, where the act is premeditated, and not the result of a sudden outburst of rage. There is far less likelihood of detection in the use of poison than of any other method. In India many poisonous plants grow wild, and the people are acquainted with their nature; whilst other drugs, such as arsenic, which produce symptoms very similar to those of cholera—a disease endemic in Bengal—are easily procurable in the bazaars, as there are no strict regulations in force prohibiting their sale as in England. Preparations of opium and hemp, too, are in common use amongst the people, and are employed as means of committing suicide, or are given to those whom they wish, from covetousness or revenge, to put out of their way. The burning of the bodies of deceased persons almost as soon as life is extinct, which prevents the examination that would follow a sudden or suspicious death in other countries, rather encourages this form of crime.

A common incentive to the use of poisonous drugs, where the object is the very opposite to that of murder, but which often causes it, is found in the superstitious character of the people, which leads them to believe that by administering certain potions they can gain or retain the affections of a husband or lover. In years not far back parents who feared their sons were favourably inclined towards Christianity, rather than suffer the disgrace of having one of their family an apostate from the religion of their fathers, have administered poisons which have permanently destroyed their sons' mental powers.

It is said that the custom of burning Indian widows was introduced as a check to the women's practice of poisoning their husbands. Captain Hamilton, who traded in India between 1688 and 1723, reports this legend, apparently from oral tradition: "In Canara there are several customs peculiar to itself, and many of them are spread abroad to remote countries. Here it was that the custom of wives burning on the same pile with their deceased husbands had its beginning. It is reported that before the Brāhmans invented this law poison was so well known and practised that the least quarrel that happened between a married couple cost the husband his life, and this law put a great stop to it; and now custom so far prevails that if any faint-hearted lady has not courage enough to accompany her spouse to the other world, she is forthwith shaved and degraded, and obliged to serve all her husband's family in all kinds of drudgery."* It is highly probable, to say the least, that some such causes may have led to the custom of Sati, or of the alternative life of drudgery and degradation. Dr. Chevers also quotes from an article on Witchcraft in the Central Provinces, in which the writer speaks of poisoning for the purpose of winning the affections of man or woman, as commonly practised there as late as 1866: "It is most practised here, as everywhere else, by jealous women, or desperate lovers of either sex, for the purpose of captivating affection, of infatuating and enthralling the object of desire. But it is also used for baneful purposes—to cause disease, death, or some strange aberration." And he cites a case where a husband had died from the effects of poison administered to him by his wife as a love-potion, in which this was set up as the defence by the man who had sold the drug.

The most common use of poison was made by the Thugs, the professional murderers of India—men who regarded themselves as most religious in their deadly trade, inasmuch as they presented themselves before an image of Kāli before setting out on an expedition, and paid a certain proportion of their ill-gotten gains to her temple on their return, and who further imagined that, as human sacrifices were once common in India in the worship of this deity, they were doing what must be pleasing to her in taking away the lives of their victims. These men generally went out in gangs of not less

* "Medical Jurisprudence," p. 104.

than three. They destroyed their victims by means of a cloth drawn tightly round the neck, and pressed with the hands at the back of the neck, not unlike the practice of garotting which was common in England a few years back. The bodies were often cut into pieces and buried in loose sand near the roadside, cast into wells, or, with stones tied round their necks, thrown into the rivers. These men carried on their dreadful work on the roadside on the wayfaring people, or very commonly in the boats and ferries by which the rivers were crossed or traversed. To this day in the Sunderbans, near Calcutta, which is a network of rivers by which a large part of the produce of the countries to the East reach that city, there are legends of murders being committed by these men, who there used long boats which were exceedingly fleet. This was a kind of piracy of which we do not hear in history. Thousands of quiet, inoffensive people have thus been murdered and robbed on the highways and streams of India.

The following characteristic case of Thuggee, told by Colonel Sleeman * (though in this case strangling, not poison, was resorted to) may be of interest to show how these professional murderers carried on their vile trade. Happily the race is now extinct, owing to the Colonel's persistent efforts. "A stout Mogul officer of noble bearing, on his way from the Punjab to Oude, crossed the Ganges at Gurmuktesa Ghāt. He was mounted on a fine Turkee horse, and attended by his khitmutgar (butler) and groom. Soon after crossing the river he fell in with a small party of well-dressed and modest-looking men going the same road. They accosted him in a respectful manner, and attempted to enter into conversation with him. He had heard of Thugs, and told them to be off. They smiled at his idle suspicions, and tried to remove them; but all in vain. The Mogul was determined; they saw his nostrils swelling with indignation, took their leave, and followed slowly. The next morning he overtook the same

* "Rambles and Recollections," vol. i. p. 106.

number of men, but of different appearance, apparently all being Mussulmāns. They accosted him in the same respectful manner, talked of the danger of the road, and the necessity of their keeping together, and taking advantage of the protection of any mounted gentleman that happened to be going the same way. The Mogul officer said not a word in reply, as he was resolved to have no companions on the road. They persisted; his nostrils again began to swell, and, putting his hand to his sword, he bid them all be off, or he would have their heads from their shoulders. He had a bow and a quiver-full of arrows over his shoulders, a brace of loaded pistols at his waist, a sword by his side, and was altogether a formidable-looking cavalier. In the evening another party that lodged in the same serai became very intimate with the butler and groom. They were going the same road, and as the Mogul overtook them in the morning, they made their bows respectfully, and began to enter into conversation with their two friends, the butler and groom, who were coming up behind. The Mogul's nostrils again began to swell, and he bid the strangers be off. The groom and butler interceded, for their master was a grave and sedate man, and they wanted companions. All would not do, and the strangers fell in the rear. The next day, when they had got to the middle of an extensive and uninhabited plain, the Mogul in advance, and his servants a few hundred yards behind, he came up to a party of six poor Mussulmāns sitting weeping by the side of a dead companion. They were soldiers from Lahore, worn down by fatigue in their anxiety to see their wives and children once more, after a long and painful service. Their companion, the hope and prop of his family, had sunk under the fatigue, and they had made a grave for him; but they were poor, unlettered men, and unable to repeat the funeral service from the holy Korān; would his highness but perform this last office for them, he would no doubt find his reward in this world and the next. The Mogul dismounted —the body had been placed in its proper position, with its head towards Mecca. A carpet was spread: the Mogul took off his bow and quiver, then his pistols and sword, and placed them on the ground near the body, called for water and washed his feet, hands, and face, that he might not pronounce the holy words in an unclean state. He then knelt down and began to repeat the funeral service in a clear, loud voice. Two of the poor soldiers knelt by him, one on each side, in silence. The other four went off a few paces to beg the butler and groom would not come so near as to interrupt the good Samaritan at his devotions. All being ready, one of the four, in a low undertone, gave the signal, the handkerchiefs were thrown over their necks, and in a few minutes all three—the Mogul and his servants—were dead, and lying in the grave in the usual manner—the head of one at the feet of the one below him. All the parties they had met with on the road who accosted them belonged to a gang of Jumaldehee Thugs of the kingdom of Oude. In despair of being able to win the Mogul's confidence in the usual way, and determined to have the money and jewels which they knew he carried with him, they had adopted this mode of disarming him—dug a grave by the side of the road in the open plain, and made one represent a dead soldier."

Colonel Sleeman in the same work gives a story, a single instance out of many of a similar nature that reached his ears, which shows how difficult it was to trace these murderers, owing to the very great reluctance of the people to appear in court to give evidence against them. The narrative, which was taken down verbatim by a clerk, is as follows; the father of the poisoned boy is the narrator: "I reside in my hut by the side of the road, a mile and a half from the town, and live upon the bounty of travellers, and people of the surrounding villages. About six weeks ago I was sitting by the side of my shrine, after saying prayers, with my only son, about ten years of age, when a man came up with his wife, son, and daughter, the one a little older, the other a little younger than my son. They baked and ate their bread near my shrine, and gave me flour enough to make two cakes. This I prepared and baked. My boy was hungry and ate a cake and a half; I ate only half a one, as I was not hungry. I had a few days before purchased a new blanket for my boy, and it was hanging on a branch of a tree that shaded the shrine when these people came. My son and I soon became stupefied; I saw him fall asleep and soon followed. When I awoke, in the evening, I found myself in a pool of water. I had sense enough to crawl towards my boy; I found him still breathing; I sat by him with his head in my lap, where he soon died. I was not yet quite sensible. During the night the wolves ate my poor boy—I heard this from travellers. I did not quite recover till the third day, when I found that some washerwomen had put me into the tank and left me there with my head out of the water, in the hope that this would revive me; but they had no hopes of my son. I was then taken to the police of the town; but the landlord had begged me to say nothing about the poisoners, lest it might get them and their village community into trouble." The reason the man gave when questioned as to why he had hidden the fact of the poison being given to his son, was this: "The landholders told me that the police could never bring back my boy to life, and the whole village would be worried to death by them if I made any mention of the poison;" and so, rather than excite the anger of the villagers and be driven from the spot, he simply informed the police that his son had been devoured by wolves.

Here is another case illustrating the method by which these men tried to secure their victims:—

At Midnapore, in 1853, a man meeting three travellers on the way from Calcutta to Cuttack, accosted them, and stating that he was of the same caste, offered to share expenses with them on the road. Arriving at a shop where they were to rest, this man offered to cook for the party. When they began to eat, some of the party found some seeds in the rice, which they said were dhatura: the man denied this, but excused himself from eating any on the ground that warm rice did not agree with him. *One* of the others refrained from eating too, and when he saw his friends growing insensible he gave the alarm, and the culprit was seized, and on his person a number of the dhatura seeds were found. He was proved to be an old offender. It is by means of this dhatura poison that we often read of the immoral women being drugged and robbed by their visitors. Nor is the use of poisonous drugs confined to human victims. It is an ascertained fact that in certain districts the Chumars poison the cattle in order that they may purchase the skins. And it was a very common practice in the time when the troops marched from station to station, for their valuable horses to be poisoned so that these classes might obtain the skins, which would only be worth about one rupee each.

Though nowadays there is not a regular organization of Thug poisoners as in former times, when they were able at once to distinguish and by secret signs and language to converse with those from other parts of India, yet it seems certain that there are numbers of people known more or less to each other, and acting under orders from some central authority, who earn their living by robbery; and poison is one of their chief auxiliaries. A man was detected and sentenced to be hung, and when the rope was round his neck obstinately refused to betray his accomplices, and rather hurried the operation, lest the temptation should prove too strong. And another man confessed to having poisoned no less than seventeen persons within a space of eighteen months, and, rather than express regret, he spoke of his victims as game, just as a sportsman might boast of the results of his prowess. The victims in these cases are not by any means confined to the rich; often poor cartmen and pilgrims are the prey of these professional murderers.*

In cases of murder by non-professional murderers there is

* "Confessions of a Thug."

generally evidence to show, in the way the victim is hacked to pieces, that the murder resulted from some sudden provocation. Verbal abuse of the most gross and offensive kind is most common, and this often leads to blows; and when the naturally timid and cowardly nature is aroused, the murderer, for the time being, is simply a maniac. It may be the discovery of a wife's infidelity, or abuse of the most irritating nature, that is the cause of the fatal blows being struck. In such cases it is clear that it was not a cool, premeditated act, but the result of a temporary excitement. Often, when he finds that the blows have proved fatal, the offender will either attempt to take his own life or voluntarily surrender himself to the police. Amongst the mass of the people murder is rare.

Hanging is a common method resorted to by those who wish to commit suicide; and it is surprising in some cases how determined the person was to complete the deed. Sometimes their heels rest on the ground, and the body is bent to allow their weight to fall on the neck. Sometimes their heads are not more than six inches from the ground, as when they tie the rope to the leg of a bedstead. And because it is so common a mode of committing suicide, hanging is often resorted to as a method of committing murder; or after the person has been otherwise killed, the corpse is suspended by the neck, to lead to the impression that the victim died by his own hands.

Abortion.

The crime of procuring abortion is one of the commonest in India. On this delicate subject Dr. Chevers says: "In a country like India, where true morality is almost unknown, but where the laws of society exercise the most rigorous and vigilant control imaginable over the conduct of females, and where six-sevenths of the widows, whatever their age or position in life may be, are absolutely debarred from re-marriage, and are compelled to rely upon the uncertain support of relatives, it is scarcely surprising that great crimes should frequently be practised to conceal the results of immorality, and that the procuring of criminal abortion should be an act of almost daily commission, and should have become a trade among certain of the lower midwives.

"Ward described the crime of destroying illegitimate children in the womb as prevalent to a shocking degree in Bengal. In the family of a single Kulin Brāhman, whose daughters never lived with their husbands, it was common for each daughter to destroy a child in the womb annually; this crime he found to be very prevalent among widows. The Pundit who gave him this information supposed that 10,000 children were thus murdered in the province of Bengal every month. When Mr. Ward expressed his doubts of this extraordinary and shocking circumstance, the Pundit appealed to the fact of the many females being tried for this offence in the Courts of Justice in every zillah of Bengal. He said the fact was so notorious that every child in the country knew of it, and that the crime had acquired an appropriate name. It was a fact too, he was assured, that many women died after taking drugs intended to destroy the child. A Kulin Brāhman assured him that he had heard more than fifty women, daughters of Kulins, confess these murders. . . . On making further inquiry into this subject, a friend, upon whose authority he could implicitly rely, assured him that a very respectable and learned Brāhman, who certainly was not willing to charge his countrymen with more vices than they possessed, told him it was supposed that a thousand of these abortions took place in Calcutta every month. . . . Mr. Ward was a very careful inquirer, and if, as is most probable, much of the depravity described above existed in Bengal forty years ago, there can scarcely be a doubt that it prevails without any abatement at the present moment."

In the Police Reports are found numerous cases where death has resulted to the mother from the use of drugs and other means for effecting this purpose, so that there can be no doubt whatever about the crime being a most common one. It is also certain that in many cases it would be considered a far less evil for the mother to die than for it to be known that she had been guilty of immorality. The guilty persons in the large majority of cases are widows, though it is believed—and that not without some authority—that in districts where infanticide was common, as in Rajpootana, and strenuous efforts were made to put a stop to it, astrologers are sought who profess to be able to say whether the child *in utero* is a male or female; if a female, measures are resorted to to procure abortion.

Infanticide.

"The murder of female children, whether by the direct employment of homicidal means, or by the more inhuman and not less certain measures of exposure to privation and neglect, has for ages been the chief and most characteristic crime of six-sevenths of the inhabitants of British India. Throughout Central India, and especially in Rajpootana, in Cutch Bhooj, in the province of Agra, and in Khurdisthan, the destruction of female children has prevailed in historic times. Bengal Proper, or the Delta of the Ganges, appears now to be comparatively free from this scourge, but the Bengalis were only prevented by a stringent law from thinning their surplus population by throwing their children to the alligators at the mouths of the Ganges. It has lately been suggested in a native paper, that in Kulin families female children are systematically neglected, and that few grow up. Polyandry still obtains among the Kasias—hill people near Sylbet. Wherever this custom prevails, as among the Khurds and in the Neilgherry Hills, it points demonstratively to the practice of female infanticide. Beyond all this, the wilful neglect of female children operates destructively in every town and village throughout the length and breadth of India. By the Hindu, the advent of a female child is superstitiously regarded as a curse, and is practically regarded as a misfortune. The daughter—so welcome in the English peasant's homestead, so fondly greeted as the crowning honour and presiding grace of every European family of gentle blood—is viewed by the Hindusthani Rayat and the Rajpoot Thakur as a certain presage either of poverty or of shame hereafter. The daughter of a Hindu must always be dependent upon others for her support. She must be suitably married, and a crime will be involved in the postponement of her nuptials beyond the age of childhood. At her husband's death she must trust wholly to the support of others, and her conduct must be watched with unceasing vigilance, lest shame, with all its direst accompaniments—feud, revenge, and murder—should be entailed upon her house." * Manu's *law* on this subject is this: "He who takes to wife a damsel of full age shall not give a nuptial present to her father, since the father lost his dominion over her by detaining her at a time when she might have been a parent." Numerous cases might be cited where fathers have murdered their daughters, and brothers have destroyed their sisters who have yielded to temptation, when it has happened that, owing to poverty and other causes, a husband could not be found for them, or they have been left widows.

To what extent the practice of female infanticide is practised may be inferred from the following facts: "It is clearly established that in every country in Europe there is an excess of females. The census of 1851 showed that throughout Great Britain and Ireland the number of males then amounted to only 48·2 of the inhabitants. The first census of the North-West Provinces of India, in 1863, gave 53·4 as the percentage of males in a population of 30,271,885; whilst the official census of Mysore, for 1852, showed that in a population of 3,410,382, the number of adult males exceeded that of females by nearly 10 per cent, while the excess of female infants was 16 per cent!" † From the Report on the above census it appears that "in the Thakur caste, 52,763 strong, there was a total of 10,695 male, and of only 5,865 female children. . . . Out of every thousand of the

* "Medical Jurisprudence," p. 750. † Ibid. p. 752.

Thakoor population, there are at least forty-two girls below the age of twelve missing." *

In 1856 an officer was appointed to investigate the facts of this wicked custom in Northern India. He personally visited the district, and states that of the villages visited by him, in 26 out of 308 not a single girl under six years of age existed. In another batch of 38 villages he did not find a single girl; marriages were very rare there, and in some places were not known to have taken place within the recollection of the present generation. In another instance there was not a girl over six, and no marriage had taken place there for over eighty years. In many parts of the Benares division he also found that marriages had not taken place within the memory of the present generation. Other officers in other districts had a similar experience.

"Among the Rājputs it appears to be customary to destroy the infant immediately upon its birth; the mothers of the Rājkumar infants simply starved them to death." In other cases they are poisoned with the juice of the mudar plant, tobacco, or dhatura; or the child was strangled immediately it was born. In Benares it was a common practice to drown them in milk after a prayer had been offered that they might come again in the form of sons; whilst in other places, again, the newly-born infant was buried alive, or left exposed in the jungle.

Strong measures have been resorted to by Government with some measure of success; but there is every reason to believe that in many places the practice still prevails. The plan relied on to check the evil was to reduce the expenditure at weddings, and thus save the unfortunate father of a girl from being compelled to spend immense sums of money in feasting and making presents at the marriage. That these people do not differ much from those of other lands in the proportion of the sexes, may be shown from the following fact: "The village of Raipoor, in the Umritsur district, had

* "Medical Jurisprudence," p. 752.

become so notorious for the commission of this crime, that in September, 1867, there were only eight girls to one hundred boys. A police force was quartered upon them for two years, and in the next year thirteen girls, of whom ten are alive, were born to nine boys." *

In addition to the above-mentioned crime may be added the custom which at one time prevailed, if it does not now, viz., the unnatural exposure of children who are supposed to be possessed by a demon; and in other cases, where an illegitimate child is placed at the door of its reputed father in order that he may be induced to provide for it and its mother. If a child refused the breast, it was supposed to be possessed by a devil, and exposed in a basket tied to the branches of a tree for three days. At the expiration of this time it was taken down; if it survived the test, which was a most rare occurrence, it was taken back to its mother; but generally it was dead, and this was taken as a confirmation of the suspicion about its possession. It is said that the great Hindu reformer Chaitanya was thus exposed, and would most probably have shared the fate which others have suffered had not a Brāhman happened to pass at the time, who asserted that the infant was an incarnation of Vishnu, and for this reason he was restored to his home.

An account of crime in India would hardly be complete without mentioning one that is almost peculiar to the country, viz., the employment of professional beaters, or latials, as they are called. Two schoolboys quarrel, call each other the foulest names, and when we should expect to see them fight and then become friends, one of them will sneak away and engage a number of stalwart men, who, armed with sticks, will waylay the offender and give him a severe thrashing. In the villages it is a most common practice if a small Rayat refuse to pay his rent, or in any way offend his landlord; or if a quarrel arise between him and some neighbour, for a number of these ruffians to be hired, who

* "Medical Jurisprudence," p. 759.

may possibly set fire to his house in order to drive him out, and then fulfil their instructions of beating him. This method of firing a house and, under cover of the excitement, robbing its inmates, is a most common occurrence, and a name has been found for it—dacoity. As burglary is characteristic of a braver and more courageous people, dacoity is eminently characteristic of the weaker races of India.

For centuries torture was commonly resorted to by the representatives of Government in order to extort money from those thought to be rich, and obtain confession from those suspected of crime; and though for many years this has been strictly forbidden by our Government, there is no doubt whatever that it is frequently resorted to by masters, parents, landlords, and others, to compel those in any way dependent upon them to do their bidding. The following forms of torture were common in native village schools; through the efforts of the Rev. J. Long, photographs of them were obtained.

A boy is made to bend forward with his face toward the ground; a heavy brick is then placed on his back, and another on his neck; and should he let either of them fall within the prescribed period of half an hour or so, he is punished with the cane.

A boy is made to stand for half an hour on one foot, and should he shake or quiver, or let down the uplifted leg before the time, he is severely punished.

A boy is made to sit on the floor with one leg turned up behind his neck.

He is made to sit with his feet resting on two bricks, and his head bent down between his legs, with his hands twisted around each leg so as to hold his ears.

A boy is made to hang for a few moments with his head downwards.

His hands and feet are bound with cords; to these members so bound, a rope is fastened, and the boy is then hoisted up by means of a pulley attached to the bearers or rafters of the school.

Nettles dipped in water are applied to the body, which becomes irritated and swollen; the pain is excruciating, and often lasts a whole day; but however great the itching and the pain, the sufferer is not allowed to rub or touch the skin for relief under the dread of a flagellation in addition.

The boy is put in a sack with some nettles, or a cat, or some noisome creature, and then rolled along the ground.

The fingers of both hands are inserted across each other with a stick between, and two sticks without, drawn close together and tied.*

Among the many methods of torture that are now resorted to, the following may be mentioned; evidence of these being still used is found in the reports of trials in recent years. The burning of various parts of the body by means of a heated chillum, in which tobacco is smoked; or by the application of a lighted torch; or by a hot iron. This appears to be a common method employed by some husbands to punish a wife for disobedience. Another method of torture is by dipping the hands or feet in boiling water or oil; and a variation of this is made by pouring boiling water or oil on different parts of the body. This means of torture has some sort of authority. Manu ordered that "should one (*i.e.*, a low-caste man) through pride give instruction to priests concerning their duty, let the king order some hot oil to be dropped into his mouth and ears." And again, "If a Sudra listens to the Vedas, then the oil, heated as before, shall be poured into his ears; and arzeez and wax shall be melted together, and the orifice of the ears shall be stopped up therewith." In the cold weather, cold water is thrown upon the body of the victim; and at other times, wretched criminals, or those suspected of crime, have been thrust into a nest of ants or other insects, and driven almost mad by the torture.

The police authorities, as the Reports show, are sometimes guilty of these malpractices, which evidently at one time had the authority of the rulers of the country.

* "Medical Jurisprudence," p. 530.

DEATH, SHRĀDHA, AND THE FUTURE LIFE.

CHAPTER I.

DEATH AND ITS ATTENDANT CEREMONIES.

I THINK that perhaps in the treatment of Hindus in the approach of death the cruelty of the system is more clearly seen than in anything else; I say the cruelty of the *system*, for nothing could be farther from the thoughts and wishes of Hindu sons, husbands, and fathers than to behave cruelly to those whom in life and health they had most tenderly loved and fondly cherished. And yet this very affection which during life has led to the performance of most kindly acts prompts them to try to secure happiness in heaven for the objects of their affection by means that seem to us cruel in the extreme. Accustomed as we are to see everything done to try to alleviate the sufferings of our friends in their dying moments, it seems almost incredible that any civilized people could be such slaves to superstition as to adopt measures which cannot fail largely to increase those sufferings.

In the teaching of Hinduism on this subject we have another instance of the superlative method of instruction; *i.e.*, of the way in which each duty that is under consideration is made to appear all-important. As each deity addressed is regarded for the moment, and actually addressed as, the chief of all, so each religious rite is said to be necessary to salvation. One wonders that the people do not ask in despair, "Who, then, can be saved?" and determine that they will let the future care for itself. According to the Hindu Scriptures, whatever a man's life may have been, if he do not die near some holy stream, if his body is not burned on its banks, or at any rate near some water as a representative of the stream; or where this is impracticable, if some portion of his body be not thrown into it—his spirit must wander in misery, unable to obtain the bliss for which he has done and suffered so much in life. Or as such immense benefits are promised to those who fulfil this part of the system, it is hoped that the omission of much that should have been done will be fully compensated. Hence it is that the friends of those about to die are brought to act towards them, whom they have dearly loved, in a way that to many at least must seem most unkind. When it is taught that incalculable good will come to the dying person who dies near a holy river, and that indelible disgrace will attach to their friends who do not take means to secure this object, it is easily seen how some of the most kind-hearted of the Hindus come to assist in these cruelties.

As some of the statements about to be made may seem almost incredible to those in Christian lands, I may state that most of them are from the writings of Hindus themselves. In an article on the subject of Ghāt minders, as they are termed in the *Calcutta Review*,* the writer had before him several prize essays that were written by Hindu students, from which he obtained the greater part of the facts he gives: from this and other equally reliable sources I have collected the information that follows.

The writer referred to, in speaking of the strange contradiction we find in Hindu life, where we see those who are most scrupulous not to destroy even the life of an insect, and who regard the killing of a cow as a most heinous offence, yet taking part in the burning alive of a mother, and of the inferences being drawn that they are both humane and inhuman at the same time, says, "Inhumanity had little or nothing to do with the Sati rite, humanity has as little to do with the vegetable diet of the Hindu. It was not from

* Vol. x. p. 404.

any natural or acquired bloodthirstiness that the Hindus slew their widows; it is not from any natural or acquired blood-abhorrence that they refrain from slaying their cows. . . . The truth is that the Hindu religion overbears nature and feeling and principle altogether. . . . It takes no account of the feelings and affections of the soul. Its demands are fully satisfied when a certain round of external observance is complied with. The good or bad state of the heart can add nothing to, and take nothing from, the imagined merits of these bodily exercises. From this fact we derive the inference that from the actions required by the system, and habitually performed by its votaries, we are not necessarily to infer so depraved a state of the heart as would be implied in the performance of the actions by those whose deeds were the spontaneous effusions of their hearts." And he goes on to say that though the practice of Sati and other cruel rites cannot fail to have an injurious effect upon the soul, yet it would not be just to infer that "none but a very depraved man would burn his widowed mother, . . . though we should certainly be right were we to assert that the act of burning her would leave the man worse than it found him."

When this custom of exposing the dying on the banks of the rivers first came into practice it is impossible to say; but from the fact that the older religious books are silent respecting it, whilst the more modern abound with allusions to it, and statements respecting the benefits that the dying will obtain by its means, it is natural to infer that it is of comparatively modern origin. One of the essay writers mentioned this to prove that it commenced only about three hundred years ago; but it probably originated earlier than that.

The primary reason for the practice is found in the belief that the Ganges, or Ganga, as she is called, is a divine being, wife of Siva, the great god of Hinduism. Of her descent from her heavenly home in order to restore to life the sons of Sāgar we have already spoken, in giving an account of the great bathing festival at Saugor Island.* As the people, fully believing in the efficacy of this stream to wash away the sin of the living, visit her banks and bathe in her waters, it is but a step further to believe that at the last moments of a man's life it must be beneficial to be near her, or some other water as her representative. Hence we find that whilst the older writings tell the story of her descent from heaven, and descant upon the benefits of bathing in her, the more modern ones develop this teaching, and not only dwell upon the benefits of dying on her banks, but speak of this as an absolute necessity for a speedy entrance into heaven. It should be noticed that in the older accounts of this wonderful effect of Ganga's advent it is said that the sons of Sāgar at once ascended to heaven in golden chariots. This probably is the germ thought which has been so largely expanded in the more modern writings. As examples of the popular teaching of the benefits Ganga can confer on mortals are the following extracts; the first is a translation of a prayer to Bhāgirathi, another name of Ganga, because it was through his intercession that she came down from heaven.

"Oh, Mother Ganges! I now bow down at thy feet, have mercy on thy servant. Oh, who can describe thy virtues, since they are past the comprehension of the powers of man? The supreme divinity Brahmā can alone describe some of thy qualities. Were the greatest of sinners, the perpetrator of endless sins, to pronounce the word Ganga, he, being delivered from all his sins, shall be translated to the blissful abode of the celestials. Thou alone art properly called the 'Source of Happiness' and the 'Saviour of Men.' Infinite sources of salvation are at thy command. In whatever state a man may die, he is saved, as is proved in the case of the sons of Sāgar, who had been reduced to ashes by the curse of a sage. It is only children that say that it is necessary to be in a state of consciousness. He who performs ablutions

* See p. 256.

on thy banks not only saves himself, but also his ancestors, the ancestors of his mother, and the ancestors of his wife. Thou art material, thou art immaterial! Thou art simple, thou art compound! Thou art the eternal source of all!"

In another work, written especially to teach the virtues of Ganga, called the Ganga Bākyabali, is the following: "He who thinks upon Ganga, though he be 800 miles distant from the river at the time, is delivered from all sin, and is entitled to heaven. At the hour of death, if a person think upon Ganga, he will obtain a place in the heaven of Siva. If a person, according to the regulations of the Sāstras, be going to bathe in Ganga, and die on the road, he shall obtain the same benefits as though he had actually bathed. If a person who has been guilty of killing cows, Brāhmans, his guru, or of drinking spirits, &c., touch the waters of Ganga, desiring in his mind the remission of these sins, they will be forgiven." The Skanda Purāna says, "that by dying in the Ganges, a person will obtain absorption into Brahma." The same work contains a promise from Siva, that "whoever dies in Ganga shall obtain a place in his heaven." The Bhavishya Purāna affirms that "if a worm, an insect, or a grasshopper, or any tree growing by the side of Ganga, die in the river, it will obtain absorption into Brahma." The Brahmā Purāna says, "that whether a person renounce life in Ganga, praying for any particular benefit, or die by accident, or whether he possesses his senses or not, he will be happy. If he purposely renounce life, he will enjoy absorption or the highest happiness; if he die by accident, he will still obtain heaven." The Kurma Purāna says, "Those that consciously die on the banks of the Ganges shall be absorbed into the essence of Brahma; whilst those who die there unconsciously shall go to the heaven of Brahmā." The Agni Purāna declares that "those who die when half their body is immersed in Ganga water, shall be happy thousands of thousands of ages and resemble Brahmā."

With passages such as these, in what they believe to be divinely inspired Scriptures, who can wonder that, in their desire to obtain for their dying friends the unspeakable blessedness promised, the Hindus should act in a manner that at first sight seems to indicate the absence of all human feeling? Where these statements are believed it is the greatest charity to a sick friend to place him in such favourable circumstances, even though they may increase his present pain and materially shorten his present earthly life. In addition, however, to these authoritative texts are stories commonly told, and as implicitly believed, all tending in the same direction. On the banks of the Bhāgirathi there grew a stately banyan tree, in whose ample foliage a paddy-bird had made her nest. On a certain day the tree was torn up by the roots by the violence of a storm. The bird was destroyed, and its bones buried in the deep channel of the Ganges. The paddy-bird in its next transmigration was taken up to heaven, simply because its bones had been accidentally deposited in the river, and there became one of Indra's queens. But her residence there was not perpetual. Her visit was extended in proportion to the time taken in the decomposition of her bones. The time approaching for her return to earth, Indra offered to her the choice of assuming whatever shape she wished. She selected the form of an elephant, because its bones being of such an immense size, they would occupy a longer time in decomposing than those of any other animal. She was accordingly born as an elephant, lived on the banks of the Ganges, and when she died her body was cast into its waters, and consequently she enjoyed the company of Indra in his heaven for a countless number of years.

Having considered the authorities for the practice of the Hindus in exposing the sick and dying, we shall now consider the way they usually act in order that their friends may obtain the inestimable benefits promised. The account I give is that of a Hindu gentleman in one of the essays referred to before.

"Whenever the disease of a native patient arrives at such a stage as, according to the judgment of the native doctors, renders any further attempt for his recovery fruitless, the first thing that is suggested to his friends and relatives, as a matter of duty, is to carry him to the banks of the river, or, to use the homely phrase of the natives, 'to give him to Ganga.' Here we must observe that in the minds of the orthodox Hindus the carrying of their sick to the river is at all times and under all circumstances reckoned as a higher and a stronger duty than the seeking of means for their recovery. Their reasoning on this head is very simple. 'Life and death,' say they, 'are in the hands of the gods; but the carrying of the sick to the river lies entirely in our hands; therefore we must first do our duty, let the doom of the sick be as the gods may determine.' Such being the state of the minds of the natives, the scene which next follows is highly affecting. No sooner do the practitioners pronounce the case of a Hindu patient to be hopeless, than all the members of his family, assisted by their neighbours, begin with all haste and precaution to make preparations for taking him to the river. These preparations consist in bringing in that wretched imitation of a couch, called a khat, for the dead, and, if it be night, a number of torches, in sending for the old and experienced persons, and in giving a general notice throughout the neighbourhood. In the meantime the friends of the sick watch with great diligence and anxiety over the progress of the disease; but, alas! not because they care so much for his death, as for his dying at home. When the necessary preparations are made, a piece of cloth, the worst and dirtiest on the patient's bed, is spread over the couch on which he is to be carried, and then he himself is placed upon it. Now is presented the most moving part of the scene. All the relatives of the sick man, the females in particular, who, of course, are not allowed to go out of doors, gather round his couch, beat their breasts and foreheads; some go to clasp their dying friend with their arms;

others, in the height of grief, fall flat on the ground; whilst all raise a noise, the shrillest that can be imagined. From the midst of this most distressing scene the sick man is brought out, not without much exertion, and carried to the river, the bearers and attendants throughout the way repeating loudly the names of the gods and goddesses arranged for the purpose in a certain order.

"When they arrive at the banks of the river, they step down the ghât, and lay their burden close to the waters of the Ganges; then they ask him to cast a look at her wide expanse, and cause him to say that he has come to see the Mother Ganges. He is then brought upon the ghât, where either a low, damp, and miserable hut, or, as in some places, a decent building, but crowded with a multitude of dying people, and filled with all kinds of dirt and nuisance, receives him. Here he is taken from the khat and laid on a miserable bed on the floor, surrounded by beings like himself, whose shrieks and groanings disturb his repose at every moment. A few minutes before his death he is again brought down to the brink of the river, where, half immersed in water, he gives up the ghost."

So far as this account refers to the circumstances of the sick when they reach the river-side, I can bear testimony to its absolute truthfulness. I have frequently seen men, women, and children, lying under trees, exposed to the heat of the sun by day, and to the cold at night, waiting for their death. In some places, as stated above, are houses built for the reception of the dying; but they are open to all who come, and instead of the quiet and comfort of their home, in the hour of nature's trial, they have added to their own pains and anxieties the sight of others similarly situated. At one place I saw two sick people who had lain on the river banks for over three weeks, unwilling then to return home, as their friends would be unwilling to take them. Sometimes it happens that a sick man or woman, weary of their pains and weakness, thinking that death is near, and hopeful that heavenly rewards will follow their passing away in a sacred place, accept at once the suggestion that they shall leave their home; but in far greater numbers, when they see the preparations for their removal, entreat to be allowed to remain in the peace and quietness of home. And as might be expected, when once they hear that their friends consider that the time for their removal has come, though hitherto they have had hopes of their recovery, hope is turned to despair, and they give themselves up to death.

Once only I saw what seemed to me nothing less than murder, though it was, and still is, a common occurrence. Returning to my boat late at night, I heard a great shout, and, going to inquire about the cause, found that a poor old woman was being hurried into eternity by her friends. She had been brought to the banks of the river, and when I saw her was up to her waist in the cold water, whilst some other women were filling her mouth with the mud. She died as I stood there, and I confess it was hard to believe that these people felt that they were acting kindly towards this poor sick woman. Who knows whether in her case, as in thousands of others, proper care and attention might not have prolonged her days? It is morally certain that the treatment she received shortened her life.

I shall now pass on to another consideration; this treatment of the sick is not only cruel, but destructive to human life. In one of the essays before referred to the writer dwells on this part of the subject, and having spoken of the evil effect on the spirits of the sick, when by the actions of their friends in removing them to the river they are told that all hope of their recovery is given up; of the painful effects of the jolting in being carried on the ill-made khat, and of the shouting on the way; of the great injury they receive from exposure to the sun, rain, or cold as they are being carried in their weak state from their home to the ghât, and of the certain evil effect of inhaling the vitiated air from the proximity of these ghâts to the places where the dead bodies are burned, parts being frequently left unconsumed, which, during decomposition, give off most hurtful gases; he says, "causes which singly would make any one sick, and combined would kill him, what is there to prevent the conclusion being drawn that several at least out of many cases of the sick would not prove fatal, if they were not brought out of their homes and subjected to the above insalutary influences? Many a sick man, we may safely say, dies solely on account of being exposed to the insalubrious influence of the above destructive agents—a fate which they would not meet, were they suffered to lie at home. May we not, then, reckon the natives who forcibly drag the sick to the river perpetrators of a crime which amounts to nothing less than a species of murder?"

Here is an account of an actual case: "Some years ago we had formed an acquaintance with a native youth. Among a large class of boys, Romonāth was by far the fairest and handsomest. On further acquaintance we found him intelligent and amiable. Our acquaintance with him continued for several years. One morning we were told that Romonāth was sick—so sick that he had been taken to the ghât. At the time the tidings were brought us we were conversing with several friends, amongst whom was a medical gentleman. We at once resolved to set off to see our young friend. The day was one of extreme sultriness; and after driving under the conduct of a native guide through a perfect network of narrow and filthy lanes, we reached the place, in a state of greater exhaustion from heat than we remember ever to have felt on any other occasion during a long residence in India. We found the poor patient in a high fever, laid on the ground in a little hut of mats erected for the occasion. He was under the care of his father, who seemed almost stupefied at the prospect of losing his darling, beautiful boy. Our medical friend declared that the symptoms were scarcely more severe than might have been expected to be produced in a healthy patient by the treatment to which he was being subjected. Although this treatment had greatly aggravated the disease, which must originally have been very slight, else the patient must have died long before, his opinion was that if it were possible to have the sufferer removed to a place where he should have sufficient shelter, and to have him under proper medical treatment, there was very little doubt of a favourable issue.

"We willingly offered to convey him to our own house, and to give him an apartment which he could occupy without prejudice to his caste, and our medical friend as willingly offered to attend him there; but to this the father would not consent. The next best proposal was to have him removed to his own house, where also medical attendance was freely proffered; but all would not do. A consultation with some Brāhmans who were in attendance, completely turned the scale in the father's judgment. On the one side were the yearnings of a father's love; on the other was the dread of the disgrace that would be incurred were the son after all to die at a distance from the holy stream. After spending a long time in ineffectual attempts to gain over the father, seconded, as we thought, by the supplicating looks of the suffering son, who, although he was unable to give more than monosyllabic answers to the questions whether he would not like to go to our house or his own, seemed evidently, by the earnest gaze of his fine eyes, to be deeply anxious for the success of our suit, we had no resource but to withdraw, having only gained thus much, that the father consented, if we sent European medicine, that he would permit his son to take it. This we soon procured, and returned with it as speedily as possible; but on our return we found the hut demolished, and on inquiring what had become of the sufferer, there was pointed out to us a funeral pile, on which the lately beautiful body of our young friend was already reduced to little more than a small heap of ashes. This is a single case, and one marked by no features of singular atrocity; but it is a fair and unexceptionable example of the way in which this truly murderous custom daily acts in killing scores of our fellow-creatures who might otherwise survive, and in hastening the deaths of hundreds, and in rendering miserable the last hours of thousands."

That it is a common practice for Hindus to get rid of parents or other persons from whose death they may receive some pecuniary advantage, I do not for a moment believe; but this custom of hurrying the sick from their home, and immediately after death of burning the body, renders the administration of poison a very easy matter; and the legitimate practices on these occasions may certainly be employed with success by those who wish to become possessed of the property or position of their victim. That advantage is certainly taken of the practice under consideration the following account will show; this is a case where it happened that there was an unlooked-for obstacle in the way. "A rich native, who had been attended in various illnesses by a European practitioner of eminence in Calcutta, was taken to the ghât to die. Intimation of this fact having been in some way made to the doctor, he hastened to the spot, and found him only slightly indisposed. Observing that he was attended by one only of the sections into which he knew the family was divided, he immediately suspected there was foul play in the case. On asking if the patient had made a will, and being answered in the affirmative, he requested permission to read the document. This being granted, he found, as he had expected, that the testamentary disposition was entirely in favour of that portion of the testator's family who were now in attendance on him. With most praiseworthy imprudence he tore the will into shreds, and immediately the attendants consented that the sufferer should be removed, it being now their interest that he should recover and make a will, similar to the former one, as it was formerly their interest that he should die." From what has been said it is certain that the custom "produces death in many cases, and probably hastens it in all, while it opens up a way whereby the unnatural and murderously disposed may execute their foul purposes without the possibility of detection."

In some diseases, such as cholera, there is a stage when the pulse is scarcely perceptible, and the patient has all the appearance of death; and cases are on record where, in this condition, the sick have been revived by the heat of the fire that was kindled under them for the purpose of burning their body; and eye-witnesses have declared that the response to this sign of returning life has been a murderous blow from a bamboo, in the hands of some of the attendants. When it is understood that it is accounted a disgraceful thing in the case of a person once taken to the ghât to die for him to return home, that it is taken as a sign that Ganga has rejected him, it is easy to see how even this additional aid to death should be given under the superstitious belief that they were acting kindly rather than otherwise to their friend.

In former years a patient who recovered from his sickness after being taken to the riverside was not permitted to rejoin his family, but being "rejected by Ganga," was also disowned by his family. A large village near Calcutta is occupied by the descendants of these outcastes, who have intermarried with each other, unmindful of their former caste distinctions, because they were now equally regarded as outcastes. But this practice has now ceased, the few who survive this unnatural treatment being permitted to rejoin their families.

The following extract from another and more recent Hindu writer* fully corroborates what has previously been said. After giving a description of the ghâts, where the sick are brought to die, he says: "Can imagination conceive a more dismal, ghastly scene? Yet religion has crowned the practice with the weight of national sanction, and thus deadened the finer susceptibilities of our nature. Sad as this picture is, the most staunch advocate of Liberalism can hardly expect to escape such a fate. To a person accustomed to such scenes

* "The Hindus as they are," p. 258.

death and its concomitant agony loses half its terrors. Instances are not wanting to corroborate the truth of this painful fact. Persons entrusted with the care and nursing of a dying man at the burning ghât soon get tired of their charge, and, rather than minister to his comforts, are known to resort to artificial means, whereby death is actually accelerated. They unscrupulously pour the unwholesome, muddy water of the river down his already choked throat, and in some cases suffocate him. 'These are not the ebullient flashes from the glowing caldron of a kindled imagination,' but undeniable facts founded on the realities of life.

"The process of antajali, or immersion, is another name for suffocation. Life is so tenacious in what the Hindus call *old bones*, or aged persons, that I have seen some persons brought back home after having undergone this murderous process nine or ten times in as many days. The patient, perhaps an uncared-for widow cast adrift in the world, retaining the faculty of consciousness unimpaired, is willing to die rather than continue to drag on a loathsome existence, but nature will not readily yield up the vital spark. . . . In the case of an aged man, the return home after *immersion* is infamously scandalous; but in that of an aged widow the disgrace is more poignant than death itself. I have known of an instance in which an old widow was brought back after fifteen *immersions*, but, being overpowered by a sense of shame, she drowned herself in the river, after having lived a disgraceful life for more than a year. No expression is more frequent in the mouth of an aged widow than this: 'Shall I ever die?' Scarcely any effort has been made to suppress, or even to ameliorate, this barbarous practice, simply because religion has consecrated it with its holy sanction."

The influence of this superstition is seen in other ways. I have heard from most credible witnesses that they have seen pilgrims on the way to Saugor Island, and in other parts of the Ganges, when they have fallen into the river, or their boat has capsized, being allowed to drown without the slightest effort being made to save them by other Hindus near at hand, under the impression that they would be doing an injury to the drowning persons in taking them from the sacred water. The writer of the article in the *Calcutta Review*, before referred to, gives an account of his own experience. When walking on the deck of a small boat his foot slipped and he fell headlong into the river. His Hindu boatmen never attempted to rescue him; but fortunately another boat being near, he was dragged out of the water. When, however, his boat reached the shore, his boatmen, who had carried him over the muddy banks down to the boat, refused to carry him up to the solid ground when he was leaving the boat. Their excuse was this: "Was it not enough that we carried you yesterday, *mlecha* though you be, must we carry you now when Ganga refused to have you?"

Having described the treatment of the dying, I shall now pass on to notice the ceremonies connected with the burning of the corpse.

"The sick man dies after a stay (say) of four days at the ghât, suffering, perhaps, the most excruciating pangs and agony frequently attendant on a deathbed. During these days the names of the gods are repeatedly whispered in his ears, and the consolations of religion are offered him with no unsparing hand, in order to mitigate his sufferings, and, if possible, to brighten his last hours. The corpse is removed from its resting-place to the burning ghât, a distance of a few hundred yards, and preparations for a funeral pile are speedily made. The body is then covered with a piece of new cloth and laid upon the pyre, the upper and lower parts of which are composed of firewood, faggots, and a little sandal-wood, and ghî to neutralize the smell. The Manipora Brāhman, an outcaste, reads the formula, and the son, or nearest of kin, changing his old garments for new white clothes, at one end of which is fastened an iron key to keep off evil spirits, sets fire to the pile. The body is consumed to ashes, but the navel remaining unburnt is taken out and thrown into the river. Thus ends the ceremony of cremation. The son, after pouring a few jars of holy water on the pile, bathes in the stream and returns home with his friends." * On reaching home they all touch fire, and enter the house with the cry, "Hāri Bol!" on their lips. This tells the inmates that the last rites of their sick relative have been performed, and is the signal for renewed expressions of grief. Those who have once heard the cry of Hindu women at the loss of husband or child will not easily forget it.

When a Hindu dies at a distance from the river, if his friends can arrange to do so, the corpse is carried to its banks, and there burned. I have seen bodies carefully wrapped in sacking that have been carried over thirty miles for this purpose. Where the distance is too great, or the expense too heavy for the family, after the body has been burned nearer home, a part will be taken from the ashes and thrown into the river.

Until recent years, the police regulations having now removed the scandal, the scenes at the burning ghât, caused by the outcaste Brāhmans who have to repeat the mantras before the body is burned, were most disgraceful. These men, by reason of their office being regarded as unworthy of respect by their fellow-Brāhmans, have lost their self-respect, and act like harpies in their efforts to extract money from the friends of the deceased. The mantras must necessarily be read, and the monopoly of this duty being in their hands, disgraceful scenes of chaffering took place before they would proceed with their work. Now, the legal price has been fixed, and their unseemly squabbling at such a time and place is at an end.

"From the time of his father's death to the conclusion of the funeral ceremony the son is religiously forbidden to shave, wear shoes, shirts, or any garment other than the long piece of white cloth; and his food is confined to a single

* "The Hindus as they are," p. 259.

meal, consisting only of rice, dhall, milk, ghî, and sugar, which must be cooked either by his wife or mother, but it is preferable if he can cook for himself; at night he takes a little milk, sugar, and fruit. This regimen continues ten days if the deceased be a Brāhman, and thirty-one if a Sudra. A married daughter, when her father or mother dies, mourns for three days only. On the morning of the fourth day she is enjoined to cut her nails and perform the funeral ceremony for her departed parent."

In a hot and densely populated country like India there is much to be said in favour of cremation, but in the manner in which it is usually performed there certainly is not much to commend it to Europeans. When the friends can afford to purchase a sufficiency of wood to consume the body thoroughly there is much that is repulsive. The body is washed in a public place open to the gaze of bystanders. Only a cotton garment is used to wrap round the body, and when, as it frequently happens, the flames run along this, the limbs are left exposed. But the poorer people cannot provide wood sufficient to consume the body, and parts of it are left for the jackals and vultures to complete the work. The vicinity of a burning ghât is strewed with human skulls and other bones that have simply passed through the fire. The whole scene is most painful and disgusting to any who have not been brought up in Hinduism, and by familiarity come to regard these things with indifference.

In the account of the treatment of the dying and dead I have simply introduced accounts by Hindu gentlemen of what actually takes place under such circumstances amongst their own caste, I shall now add a few sentences from Colebrooke's account of the religious ceremonies of the Hindus,* more especially of Brāhmans, as taught in the Scriptures; the ceremonies, though varying a little in manner, are identical in spirit and aim.

"A dying man, when no hopes of his surviving remain,

* "Essays," p. 97 ff.

should be laid upon a bed of cusa grass, either in the house or out of it if he be a Sudra, but in the open air if he belong to another tribe. When he is at the point of death donations of cattle, land, gold, silver, or other things, according to his ability, should be made by him, or, if he be too weak, by another person in his name. His head should be sprinkled with water drawn from the Ganges, and smeared with clay brought from that river. A sālgrama ought to be placed near the dying man, holy strains from the Veda or from sacred poems should be repeated aloud in his ears, and leaves of holy basil must be scattered over his head." Instructions then follow respecting the washing of the corpse, the spreading of a perfumed cloth over it, the carrying it to the place of burning, and the preparation of the pile. When all is ready, if it be the body of a priest who has kept a sacred fire perpetually burning in his house, the fire to ignite the pile must be brought from it; but if not, then "it is only necessary to avoid taking fire from another funeral pile, or from the abode of an outcaste, of a man belonging to a tribe of executioners, of a woman who has lately borne a child, or of any person who is unclean."

When all its preparation is complete "a relative of the deceased, taking up a lighted brand, must invoke by name the holy places on the earth, and say, 'May the gods with flaming mouths burn this corpse!' He then walks thrice round the pile, with his right hand towards it, and (if he be a Brāhman) shifts the sacrificial cord to his right shoulder. Then looking towards the south, and dropping his left knee to the ground, he applies the fire to the pile near the head of the corpse, saying, 'Namo! Namah!' whilst the attendant priests recite the following prayer: 'Fire! thou wert lighted by him, may he therefore be reproduced from thee that he may attain the region of celestial bliss. May this offering be auspicious!'"

The burning must be so arranged that a few bones are left unconsumed for the subsequent ceremony of gathering the ashes. The other friends also throw into the fire a few bits of wood, as an offering to Agni, as they say, "Salutation to thee who dost consume flesh." Instructions are given for the burning of the body of a Hindu by proxy when he may have died far away from home or his body cannot be found. In this case three hundred and sixty leaves of the butea tree, or as many woollen threads are taken as his representative and burnt in place of the corpse.

When the body is reduced to ashes all the friends who have taken any part in the ceremony must walk round the ashes, bathe in the river, and change their clothes, and going again into the water, after taking up a little in the hollow of their joined hands, and naming the deceased and his family, say, "May this be acceptable to thee!" When this is done, as a consolation to them the following or other texts are recited:

"Foolish is he who seeks permanence in the human state; unsolid, like the stem of the plantain tree; transient, like the foam of the sea."

"When a body formed of five elements to receive the rewards of deeds done in its own former person reverts to its five original elements, what room is there for regret?"

"The earth is perishable; the ocean, the gods themselves, pass away; how should not that bubble, mortal man, meet destruction?"

"All that is low must finally perish, all that is high must ultimately fall, all compound bodies must end in dissolution, and life is concluded with death."

"Unwillingly do the manes of the deceased taste the tears shed by their kinsmen; then do not wail, but diligently perform the obsequies of the dead."

After a time the friends return home, the nearest relation going first with a new earthen jar full of sacred water. At or near the house the first part of the religious ceremony for the deceased takes place. A suitable spot being prepared, a ball of tila seed, boiled rice, honey, &c., is made and offered to the spirit of the departed with these words: "May this first funeral cake, which shall restore thy head, be acceptable to thee!" Again purifying the place and addressing the departed spirit with the formula, "May this apparel be acceptable to thee," a woollen yarn is laid upon the cake. The next offers with the same formula a pot of water and tila seeds. Some food is then laid upon a leaf for the crows.

Before entering the house the friends each bite three leaves of nim, sip water, and touch a branch of Sāmi with their right hands as the priest says, "May the Sāmi tree atone for sins!" Each mourner then touches fire whilst the priest says, "May fire grant us happiness!" In the evening of the same day water and milk are suspended in vessels before the doors of the house, and the words, "Such a one, now deceased, bathe here, drink this."

CHAPTER II.

THE SHRĀDHA, OR RELIGIOUS CEREMONIES FOR THE BENEFIT OF THE DEAD.

In the previous chapter we have described the treatment of the dying and the burning of the corpse; we shall now consider the religious ceremonies that are ordained for the benefit of the dead to be performed by their relatives.

In the case of old persons, or those who have been ill for a long time, one ceremony called the Vaitarārni rite is performed before their death. This is called after the name of a river which it is supposed the dead must cross ere they enter heaven. Before the day arrives for carrying the sick man to the river, money is given to a number of Brāhmans in lieu of a cow, rice, &c., that they may guide and assist him in crossing the river. When this is not performed before death, it forms part of the ceremonies at the Shrādha.

Of all the ceremonies connected with the Hindu religion the Shrādha is the most important, and in some cases quite equal in expense to a marriage. It takes place on the thirtieth day after the death of the person on whose behalf it is celebrated. Its main features are the feeding of large numbers of Brāhmans and Hindus of other castes, and in the presentation of offerings of food, sweetmeats, &c., to the spirit of the person recently deceased, and his or her ancestors. I shall give the particulars of these ceremonies first, as they are taught in the Scriptures, and then add an account of their ordinary observance in the present day.

"During ten days funeral cakes, together with libations of water and tila, must be offered as on the first day, augmenting, however, the number each time, so that ten cakes and as many libations of water and tila be offered on the tenth day; and with this further difference, that the address varies each time." "If the mourning last three days only, ten funeral cakes must, nevertheless, be offered—three on the first and last, and four on the second; if it lasts no more than one day, the ten oblations must be made at once. The difference in the address consists in the mention of the part of the body that is supposed to be restored by the cake. The first is for the head; the second is for the restoration of the ears, eyes, and nose; the third is for the throat, arms, and breast, &c. During this time a pebble wrapped in a part of a sheet that was laid over the deceased is worn by the heir, or nearest of kin, suspended on his neck. To this pebble, as a type of the deceased, the funeral cakes are offered. The same vessel in which the first oblation was made must be used for all the others; if it be broken, or the pebble lost, the rites must all be gone through a second time."

The relatives to the sixth degree ought to fast three days and nights, or at least one day; the near relatives must observe a partial fast as long as the days of mourning continue, *i.e.*, until the thirtieth day after the death occurred. In some cases the funeral obsequies are hastened; they *may* be performed on the third day after the body has been buried.

The first important duty after a Shrādha, *i.e.*, the offering of a cake for the deceased, is the collecting of the bones. With many rites that it would be tedious to describe, a few ashes or part of the corpse are collected and burned on the banks of the river, whilst a bone is cast into the stream itself. Before going to the river, however, there is the feeding of Brāhmans, who have been invited to honour the family by their presence. When these have eaten, the person performing the ceremony places some cusa grass on the ground, and then strews uncooked rice, tila, and ghî on it as the priest repeats for him this prayer, "May those in my family who have been burnt with fire, or who are alive, who are yet unburnt, be satisfied with this food, presented on the ground, and proceed contented towards the supreme path [of eternal bliss]. May those who have no father nor mother, nor kinsman, nor food, nor supply of nourishment, be contented with this food offered on the ground, and attain like it a happy abode!" After this he again sanctifies the place of sacrifice and offers a cake to his ancestors, asking them each to take a share. And again naming the deceased person, he offers food, thread, &c., for clothing; and then, having paid his fee to the priest, he lights a lamp in honour of the dead person, and casts the food into the fire, by which means it is supposed to reach those for whom it was given. On his arrival at the burning place he prays the gods to "convey the deceased to pleasing and eternal abodes, and grant to him long life, health, and perfect ease.

"On the last day of mourning the nearest relation puts on neat apparel, and causes his house and furniture to be cleaned; then, after offering the tenth funeral cake in the manner described, he makes ten libations of water from the palms of his hands, is shaved, his nails are cut, and the clothes worn at the funeral, and other remuneration, are given to the barber. He anoints his head and body with sesamum oil, . . . sips water, touches auspicious things, as stones, nim leaves, a cow, coral, &c., and a bamboo staff, and returns to his home purified.

"The next day a second series of obsequies are commenced, the interesting part of which is the setting free of a bullock which is regarded as sacred. According to the circumstances of the family, one, three, or more bullocks having been branded with a trident, the mark of Siva, are turned adrift—a custom reminding us of the scapegoat. These bulls are deemed sacred, and allowed to go into the fields and eat the grain. In some places, where the people are not quite so superstitious, these are caught and sold. In Calcutta many of these sacred animals are put to the ignoble duty of drawing carts. The common idea is that as the bull was especially dear to Siva, the person on whose behalf it is devoted will be raised by its assistance to Siva's heaven. Presents are given largely at these ceremonies to Brāhmans and others; and, though not absolutely necessary to salvation, are believed by the superstitious to be largely beneficial to those in whose name or on whose behalf they are given.

"The first set of funeral ceremonies is adapted to effect, by means of oblations, the re-embodying of the soul of the deceased, after burning his corpse. The apparent scope of the second set is to raise his shade from this world (where it would else, according to the notions of the Hindus, continue to roam among demons and evil spirits) up to heaven, and there deify him, as it were, among the manes of departed ancestors. For this end a Shrādha should be offered to the deceased on the day after the mourning expires; twelve other Shrādhas singly, in twelve successive months, similar obsequies at the end of the third fortnight, and also on the sixth and twelfth months; and the oblation called sapindana on the first anniversary of his decease. At the sapindana this prayer is offered, 'May the mansion of those progenitors who have reached a common abode, and who have accordant minds, foster him; may the blessed sacrifice, sacred to the gods, be his,' and by their intercession may prosperity be mine for a hundred years in this world. In most provinces the whole of these ceremonies are completed on the second or third day; after which the others are performed at the proper times, but in honour of the whole set of progenitors, instead of the deceased singly. Afterwards a Shrādha is annually offered to him on the anniversary of his decease."

Not only in connection with funerals, but on joyous occasions, especially at weddings, offerings are made to the deceased. By means of these the dead are supposed to share in the festivities of the living members of their family. With such benefits promised to those whose funeral rites are properly performed, it cannot at all surprise any to hear of the great anxiety of the Hindus for sons. Who but a faithful son would take all the trouble and incur all the expense that the proper performance of a Shrādha involves?

At the sapindana ceremony the worshipper generally offers eight cakes: *i.e.*, three for his paternal, and three for his maternal, ancestors, and two for the Viswadevas, *i.e.*, the gods. Grasping his hand with the cusa grass on which they are laid, a share is supposed to be given to his remoter ancestors. On specially sacred days, when Shrādhas are performed, such as Mahālayā, cakes are also offered separately to any deceased relation or friend in whom the offerer is specially interested.

At Shrādhas, Manu and other writers distinctly enjoin the eating of flesh; but many of the Hindus who object to this declare that those laws are now obsolete; or they make a vow to abstain and regard the obligation of a vow as superior to a command of the Scriptures. As a rule this order is disregarded.

It will have been noticed that the laws given above speak of *ten* days' mourning, and of the ceremonial defilements of those who have had any part in a funeral for the same time; in the case of Sudras this time of mourning and defilement extends to thirty days.

The teaching of the Vishnu Purāna, similar in spirit to the above for Brāhmans, and which is the rule followed by those of other castes, is as follows:—

When the dead body has been washed, adorned with flowers, and burned at the river-side, his kinsmen are to bathe with their clothes on; and looking towards the south, to make offerings to the deceased as they say, "May this reach thee wherever thou mayest be!" For ten days the mourning is continued, during which the friends are regarded as ceremonially unclean; on the first day one cake of cooked rice and spices is made and offered to the deceased, on the second day, two, and so on, each day increasing the number of cakes until the tenth day is reached, when Brāhmans are feasted and the impurity of the mourners is ended, a ball of rice being placed near the food that was prepared for the Brāhmans as an offering for the benefit of the deceased. This ceremony, with the exception of feeding the Brāhmans, is repeated monthly for a whole year on the day of the month on which the person died. At the end of the year the ceremony called sapindana is performed. Here again cakes of food are prepared for the deceased, and an interesting ceremony is performed, by which it is supposed that the spirit of the departed becomes admitted into the great company of ancestors who are duly nourished by the offerings made by the devout who are living on the earth. On this occasion four vessels of water are provided, one of which represents the person on whose behalf the ceremony is performed. The water is poured from this vessel into the other three, and thus the spirit of the person recently deceased passes into the great crowd of ancestors, to be worshipped and nourished by the offerings made by the living. The persons qualified to perform these ceremonies are a son, grandson, great-grandson, nephews, or any male relative; but if these fail, then females, or whoever is the inheritor of the property of the deceased. And it is this qualification to perform the funeral rites of any one that gives a title to the property of which he may die possessed. But if these rites are neglected, the soul of the departed cannot enter into the company, nor enjoy the blessedness of the Pitris, or ancestors, who are made happy by the offerings of their descendants.

In addition to the ordinary times specified above, it is always allowable for a man to perform a Shrādha, by which the departed will be greatly benefited, and at some special seasons a single offering of water and sesamum seeds will content the Pitris for 1,000 years, yea, in some cases for 10,000 years. And he who duly performs these ceremonies, and then bathes in some sacred stream, at once expiates all his own sins; whilst offerings made at a sacred shrine are peculiarly acceptable to the progenitors. In one place it is taught that even the uplifting of the hands by those who are too poor to give grain will prove a benefit to the friends who have passed away. "He who grudges not his wealth, but presents us with cakes, shall be born in a distinguished family. Prosperous and affluent shall that man ever be who in honour of us gives to the Brāhmans—if he is wealthy, jewels, clothes, land, &c., or who with faith and humility entertains them with food, according to his means, at proper seasons. If he cannot afford to give them cooked food, he must give them uncooked; or, in fact, such gifts as he can give, however trifling they may be. Should he be unable to do this, he can at least bow before a Brāhman and give him a few seeds, and pour out a little water upon the ground; or he can gather fodder for a single day and give it to a cow; or even if this be impossible for him, he can go into the forest and lift up his arms to the sun, and say: "I have no money, or grain, nor anything fit for an ancestral offering. Bowing, therefore, before my ancestors, I trust they will be satisfied with these arms thrown up in the air in devotion." In the following song, said to have been heard sung by one of the Pitris (patriarchs), Gāya is mentioned as the place where these offerings to the ancestors can be most acceptably made: "Those of our descendants follow a righteous path who shall reverently present us with cakes at Gāya. May he be born in our race who shall give us on the 13th of Bhādra and Māgha, milk, honey, and ghî; or when he marries, or liberates a black bull (shār), or performs any domestic ceremony agreeable to rule, accompanied by donations to the Brāhmans." In giving an account of Gāya we mentioned that cakes offered there for deceased friends and relatives are supposed to prove more beneficial than those offered at home.

I shall now give a brief account of the Shrādha ceremonies as they are performed in the present day amongst other than Brāhman castes, from Mr. Bose's work "The Hindus as they are." *

* P. 262, ff.

About a fortnight after his father's decease, the son goes into a calculation of the amount he ought to spend in the proper performance of the funeral rites. Some of the richer families are said to have expended as much as £20,000 over a funeral in gifts to Brāhmans, schools, charitable institutions, and the poor; but as it is stated, in the Sāstras, that Rāmachandra, one of the incarnations of Vishnu, satisfied his ancestors by offering to them balls of sand for funeral cakes, it is taught that the poor can obtain equal benefit to themselves and ancestors without going to any very great expense. A poor man in these days is held to have performed a proper Shrādha by making an offering of rice, tila seed, and a little fruit, and by feeding one Brāhman only—a ceremony that costs him only about four rupees.

When twenty days have passed, the son, accompanied by a Brāhman, walks barefooted to invite his friends and others whom he wishes to be present at the ceremony. On the thirtieth day he and the near relatives who have been regarded as ceremonially unclean, owing to the death of the deceased, now are shaved, have their nails cut, and put on clean clothes. On the thirty-first day he goes to the river to bathe, and as religious mendicants are ever on the watch for such people, they clamour for presents, declaring that unless their demands are satisfied, the departed cannot enter heaven. In a well-conducted Shrādha the son has to provide silver plates and drinking vessels, also a bed and clothing to be given away as presents to the Brāhmans who may honour him with their presence.

When the guests have assembled, amongst the Brāhmans will be a number of men who possess some knowledge of Sanskrit. A Shrādha is one of the field-days for these gentlemen, who beguile the weary hours before the feast takes place with argumentation on some knotty point in Sanskrit grammar or Hindu philosophy.

"From eight o'clock in the morning to two in the afternoon, the house where a Shrādha is going on is crammed to suffocation. A large awning covers the open courtyard, preventing the free access of air; carpets are spread on the ground for the Kāyasthas and other castes, whilst the Brāhmans, by way of precedence, take their seats on the raised Thākurdālan, or place of worship (*i.e.*, the place where the images made for special religious festivals are set up). The presents, with a salver of silver, are arranged in front of the audience, leaving a little space for the musicians, male and female, which form the necessary accompaniment of a Shrādha, for the purpose of imparting solemnity to the scene. . . . The guests begin to come in at eight o'clock, and are courteously asked to take their appropriate seats—Brāhmans with Brāhmans, Kāyasthas with Kāyasthas, &c.; the servants supplying them with hukhas (pipe) and tobacco. . . . The current topics of the day form the subject of conversation, while the hukha goes round the assembly with great precision and peculiarity." For each caste a special hukha is preserved, all of the same caste using the same. "The female relatives are brought in covered palanquins by a separate entrance shut out from the gaze of the males."

About ten o'clock the ceremony commences, the priest reading the texts, the son repeating them after him. This occupies about an hour, after which many take their leave, whilst others remain for a share in the gifts to be distributed. And often most unseemly disputes arise amongst these learned men in the division of the spoil. As some of the Brāhmans, though present at the Shrādha, will not eat in the house of a Sudra, they carry home with them uncooked food and other presents.

On the following day the Brāhmans and others are fed. It is this feast that is supposed to restore the son and other relatives of the dead person to ceremonial purity. Besides those specially invited, it is no uncommon thing for as many more to come uninvited to partake of the good things. The food that is provided for these feasts is composed of what is regarded as sweetmeats, and not rice, the ordinary food of the people. To eat *rice* with a man is to acknowledge equality of caste; but these sweetmeats may be eaten without the ordinary caste restrictions being broken.

On the next day the Kāyasthas and other castes are fed, and, if possible, on this day there is a greater crush and confusion than on the Brāhmans' day. On the morning of the next day the mourning for the deceased is considered over. After some hours of music in the house by professional singers, the son and nearest relatives having anointed their bodies with oil and turmeric, remove from the house what is called a brisakāt, and fix it on the ground near the house. The brisakāt is a painted log of wood about six feet long, on which a figure of an ox is rudely cut. This is a sort of monument to the memory of the deceased. After this they bathe, return home, put on their ordinary dress, and sit down to an ordinary meal.

I shall close this description of the funeral ceremonies with an account form the *Statesman* of Calcutta, of a Shrādha performed there September 20, 1882, as this was one of the most celebrated of modern times, and gave rise to a most interesting discussion on the subject of Hinduism in the daily papers of Calcutta.

"The Shrādha ceremony or requiem service of the Dowager Maharāni, widow of the late Maharājah Kāli Krishna Bahadur, and grandmother of the Maharājah Harendra Krishna Bahadur, was held last Sunday morning.

"It was performed in the spacious quadrangle of the Rājbāri (palace), one of the largest in Calcutta. The quadrangle was very tastefully and elaborately decorated, . . . and presented the unusual spectacle of a stately *dānsāgar* (ocean of gift), consisting of sixteen sets of beds, sixteen sets of silver plates and utensils, the plates of each separate set bearing a thousand rupees in silver. There were, besides, with each set, shawls, broadcloth, tusser silk, and silk dhuties.

and chādars (clothes for men). These articles were all arranged on the east side of the quadrangle; on the south were heaps of brass utensils of every description, symmetrically arranged. There was also a palanquin and a horse.

"All these were dedicated to the service of the family idol, Gopināthji (*i.e.*, Krishna), who was brought out and placed on a silver throne over the musmid (or platform), to hallow the service with his sacred presence. Nearly 4,000 Adhyapaks, or Professors of Hindu Logic, Philosophy, &c., were invited to the convocation from the principal *tols*, or educational institutions of Bengal, Behar, and Orissa. Besides these, invitations were issued among 1,600 of the Maharājah's friends and acquaintances in different parts of Bengal, amongst whom 482 were of the Kāyastha caste. . . . The hour fixed for the service was 8 a.m., and by that time the streets in the vicinity of the Rājbāri presented a scene of animation and bustle." Then follows a long list of the principal guests invited.

"The company having been seated, Rāja Harendra Krishna, being the oldest of the Mahārāni's grandchildren, obtained leave with folded arms, according to Hindu custom, from Maharājah Komul Krishna Bāhādur, as the head of the family, to perform the Shrādha ceremony. The Maharājah, before according permission, had himself to obtain the leave of the convocation. During the performance of the ceremony, which lasted about half an hour, the whole assembly remained standing. The Vedic benediction having been pronounced by all the Brāhmans present in a body, the assembly slowly dispersed. In the evening some ten to twelve thousand beggars received charity in the shape of a small coin. On the second day over 2,000 Brāhmans were fed; on the third day the Kāyasthas had a feast; whilst some 3,500 ladies partook of a banquet on the fourth day. The fifth and last day the tenants and domestics were entertained." The Maharājah of Travancore, in writing to excuse himself from the ceremony, said, "It is a source of satisfaction to you that she died attended with all the observances prescribed in your holy Sāstras." The Maharājah of Doomraon, writing on the same occasion, refers to her as "according to our holy Sāstras, she has been able to breathe her last on the banks of the Hoogly whilst reciting the name of her god."

CHAPTER III.

JUDGMENT—REWARDS AND PUNISHMENT.

THE belief in life after death is universal amongst the Hindus; and the opinions as to its nature do not differ materially in the different sects. In brief, it is as follows: When the soul forsakes the body, according as the conduct has been good or evil, it ascends to heaven to enjoy the rewards, or sinks into hell to suffer the penalties attached to the deeds committed. After a longer or shorter period it returns to the earth in a lower position than in the previous life if the evil preponderated, or rises to a higher condition than formerly if the good outweighed the evil; and again is rewarded or punished, until finally it attains to that condition wherein it is fit to return to the Supreme Spirit whence it came, and of whom, all unconsciously, it was but a part throughout the ages of its separate existence. However low in the scale a soul may be, by faithfully fulfilling the duties of that condition it will in due time rise, though the process may extend over millions of years. As all have come out from God, to Him they must eventually return. In the case of some there may be an uninterrupted rise from the lowest to the highest; in others there may be a much more protracted course, owing to the evils committed in certain stages, which have caused them to sink in the scale of being; which failures must be counteracted by penance and good works in succeeding stages. I shall now give the teachings of Hinduism on this subject at length.

In the Vedas the doctrine of the immortality of the soul is not very prominent. The great desire of men in that age was worldly prosperity; the "powers of the world to come" did not exert any great influence upon the community. Agni and Soma, two of the great gods of that age, are in some hymns spoken of as givers of immortality to mortals; and liberality in bestowing gifts was considered as the most certain means of attaining it. Still, in speaking of the departed, they are said to ascend to the Pitris, or *fathers*, as though it was believed that those who had passed away from the world were still living in other worlds.

Yama is regarded in these hymns as the king of the spirit-world, and the rewarder of the faithful, but not as the punisher of the guilty; in fact "there is very little mention of hell in the Veda." There is a reference to the dogs of Yama which guard the way to his abode, and the worshippers are exhorted to hurry past them with all speed. This Yama is at once the lord of the spirit-world, and the first of mortals who passed through death to glory, and is consequently addressed by men as the guide to immortality. He was the son of the Sun, and Saranya, the daughter of Tvashtri, the architect of the Vedic gods. When Yama and Yami, his twin-sister, were born, their mother, in terror of the intense brightness of her husband, left a beautiful woman—a counterpart of herself—with her children in her husband's house, and, transforming herself into a mare, hoped to remain unknown. But her husband, penetrating through her disguise, transformed himself into a horse, and they became the parents of the Asvins (the Twins). She then changed herself into other forms, with a similar result; they became the progenitors of the various classes of animals.

Reference is made to the way in which Agni, as the god of Fire, whilst consuming the bodies of the dead, did not destroy them, but sent their several parts to heaven, there to form another body, all which parts are said to go to heaven by different routes: "Do thou, Agni, burn up or consume the deceased; do not dissolve his skin or his body. When thou hast matured him, send him to the Pitris. When he shall reach that state of vitality, he shall fulfil the pleasure of the gods. Let his eye go to the sun, his breath to the wind. Go to the sky, and to the earth, according to the nature of thy several parts; or go to the waters, if that be suitable to thee; enter into the plants with thy members. As for his unborn part, do thou, Agni, kindle it with thy heat, let thy flame and thy lustre kindle it; with those forms of thine which are auspicious, convey it to the world of the righteous. Give up again, Agni, to the Pitris, him who comes to be offered to thee with oblations. Putting on life, let him approach his remains, let him meet with his body." *

In the following quotation from the Brāhmana portion of the Veda, it is taught that the gods, once mortal, have become immortal; and further, that death is the only way of obtaining immortality left to mortals:

> "The gods lived constantly in dread of Death,
> The mighty Ender; so with toilsome rites
> They worshipped and performed religious acts
> Till they became immortal. Then the Ender
> Said to the gods, 'As ye have made yourselves
> Imperishable, so will men endeavour
> To free themselves from me; what portion, then,
> Shall I possess in man?' The gods replied,
> 'Henceforth no being shall become immortal
> In his own body; this his mortal frame
> Shalt thou still seize; this shall remain thine own.
> He who through knowledge or religious works
> Henceforth attains to immortality,
> Shall first present his body, Death, to thee.'" †

As noticed above, Yama, in olden time, was regarded as the rewarder of those who had faithfully discharged their duties in life; now, in addition to this, he is worshipped as Death, ever on the watch for victims, by whom his kingdom

* "The Vedic Religion," p. 55.
† "Indian Wisdom," p. 34.

may be filled with subjects, and as the cruel judge who condemns the wicked to receive the penalties of their evil doings in the various hells over which he reigns. The following description of Yama on his judgment throne is from the Padma Purāna:

"At the extremity of the earth southward, floating on the waters, is Sangryamani, the residence of Yama, the judge of the dead, and of his recorder, Chitragupta, and his messengers.

"Those who perform works of merit are led to Yama's palace along the most excellent roads, in some parts of which the heavenly courtezans are seen dancing and singing, and gods and heavenly choristers are heard chanting the praises of other gods; in others, showers of flowers fall from heaven. There are houses containing cooling water and excellent food, pools of water covered with flowers, and trees which afford fragrance and shade. The gods are seen riding on horses or elephants, or carried in palanquins and chariots, some of whom, from the glory emanating from their bodies, illumine the ten quarters of the world. Yama receives the good with much affection, and feasting them with excellent food, thus addresses them: 'Ye are truly meritorious in your deeds; ye are wise; by the power of your merits ascend to an excellent heaven. He who, born in the world, performs meritorious actions is my father, brother, friend.'

"The wicked have 688,000 miles to travel to the palace of Yama to receive judgment. In some places they pass over a pavement of fire; in others, the earth in which their feet sink is burning hot; or they pass over burning sands, sharp stones; also burning hot showers of brass instruments, burning cinders, scalding water, and stones, fall upon them. Burning winds scorch their bodies; now they fall into hidden wells, or pass through narrow passages in which snakes lie concealed. Sometimes they are enveloped in darkness, their road winding through trees with thorny leaves; or they have to walk over broken pots, bones, putrefying flesh, or sharp spikes; whilst tigers, jackals, giants, &c., beset them. They travel naked, their hair is disordered, their throats and lips are parched, and their bodies are covered with blood and dirt. As they walk some are wailing, some weeping; horror is depicted on every countenance. Some are dragged along by leathern thongs round their necks, waists, or hands; some are dragged by their hair, ears, or feet; others, again, are carried with their heads and feet fastened together.

"On arriving at the palace they behold Yama clothed with terror, 240 miles in height, his eyes distended like a lake of water, with rays issuing from his purple body. His voice is loud as thunder, the hairs of his body are as long as palm-trees, a flame proceeds from his mouth. The noise of his breathing is greater than the roaring of the tempest; his teeth are exceedingly long, and his nails like the fan for winnowing corn. In his right hand he holds an iron club, his garment is formed of animals' skins, and he rides on a terrific buffalo. Chitragupta also appears as a terrible monster, and makes a noise like that of a warrior about to rush into battle. Sounds terrible as thunder are heard, as punishments suited to offences committed are ordered on the offenders.

"Addressing the criminals before him, Yáma says, 'Did you not know that I am placed above all, to award happiness to the good, and punishment to the wicked? Have you never given your minds to religion? To-day with your own eyes you shall see the punishment of the wicked. From age (yuga) to age stay in these hills. You have pleased yourselves with sinful practices, endure now the torments due to these sins. What will weeping avail you?' Yama next calls on Chitragupta, the recorder, to examine into the offences of the criminals, who demands the names of the witnesses; let them give their evidence in our presence. Yama, smiling, though full of rage, commands the Sun, Moon, Wind, Fire, the Heaven, Earth, Waters, Day, Night, Morning, and

Evening, and Religion, to appear against the prisoners, who, hearing their evidence, are struck dumb, and remain trembling and stupefied with fear. Yama then, gnashing his teeth, beats the prisoners with his iron club till they roar with anguish; after which he drives them to different hells." *

There are four kinds of happiness for the faithful after death.

1. *Entrance into the heaven of one of the gods.*

Most of the gods are said to have a heaven of their own to which they raise their worshippers after death. Here they remain to enjoy the fruit of their meritorious acts for a longer or shorter time, according to the amount of merit they have acquired by their good deeds. The works which raise a man to share in the glories of one of the heavens for a number of years are the following: honouring, serving, giving gifts to Brāhmans, repeating the names of the gods, especially that of their own special deity. Visiting or residing at holy places, and performing the worship that prevails there. Performing Shrādhas for deceased ancestors. Bathing in the Ganges and other sacred streams. Offering sacrifices, building temples, cutting roads, excavating tanks, planting trees, especially sacred ones; making and setting up images for worship. Reading and hearing read the Veda if a Brāhman; reading or hearing the Purānas, if not entitled to the privilege of reading the Veda. Honouring a guru, or religious preceptor. Hospitality to guests. Burning with a deceased husband. Dying in a sacred place.

2. *Deification.*

It is taught that by the performance of certain sacrifices, *e.g.*, the Asvamedh, or horse sacrifice, mortals could attain to the position of Indra, or king over the gods: but this position could be held only for a certain time; they were in danger of being compelled to yield their throne to any who by virtue of greater austerity or costliness in sacrifice proved themselves more worthy of the honour.

* Ward, vol. iii. p. 376.

3. *Dwelling in the immediate presence of the gods.*

Though myriads may through their good works gain entrance for a time into some heaven, it does not follow that all would be equally honoured there. As there are gradations in the quality and quantity of good works done by men on earth, so the position of those who enter heaven is graded, and also the duration of their stay in heaven. Those who have performed the greatest number of the best works not only will remain through a more lengthened period, but will obtain nearer access to the god who has received them into his abode.

These three forms of heavenly bliss are terminable, and when the years of bliss to which the recipient is entitled pass away, he must be re-born into the world, and pass through another trial, starting from a higher level than at the commencement of the previous life, the reward of which he has now enjoyed. None of the low-caste people have any immediate hope of attaining the highest blessedness of heaven. This is exclusively for the Brāhmans; at any rate, the highest bliss of all can only be reached by them. The Sudra's hope is that by reason of his good works he may perhaps have a little term of enjoyment in heaven, and then reappear on earth in a higher caste, until at length, coming here as a Brāhman, he may know the Vedas, and then pass to the summit of bliss attainable by mortals. It is, indeed, a long vista that opens out to the view of the low-caste people, as the Sāstras speak of thousands of lives that must be spent, even by those whose onward march is uninterrupted by a single failure.

4. *Absorption.*

This is the final end, the *summum bonum* of the Hindu religion, when the soul, losing its identity, is re-absorbed into Divine Essence, as a drop of water falling into the sea loses its separate existence. This comes chiefly through knowledge. Good works may raise a man from the lower stages of existence, and bring him into that state where the sources of knowledge are available to him; but knowledge—*i.e.*, knowledge of the soul's identity with God, and the destruction of Māya—*i.e.*, the illusion that the soul and God are separate—is *the* way of obtaining this inestimable boon. I have seen men who profess to have found this knowledge, and who expect when they pass away from this world never again to be born into it. The end of their course has now nearly come. Generally they are intoxicated with hemp, or their minds, through utter neglect, have become a perfect blank. As by not using a limb it becomes incapable of action, so, by ceasing to think, they have become incapable of thought. Pleasure and pain, cold and heat, hunger and thirst, they have ceased to know; they are just animated matter, or little more. These have attained to the height of perfection, according to the system of Hinduism, and are now fit for absorption into deity; and once absorbed, they have no longer to endure birth and death, and all the pains and vicissitudes of life. Their course is honourably ended.

That I have not overstated the condition of the "perfect" being, the following quotation from the Bhagavata Gita will show. Krishna is represented as speaking to his friend and companion Arjuna in praise of the man "who forsaketh every desire that entereth his heart, who is happy in himself, who is without affection, who rejoices neither in good nor evil, who, like the tortoise, can restrain his members from their wonted purpose, to whom pleasure and pain are the same."

The Vishnu Purāna, describing the condition of those in heaven, says: "Not in hell alone do the souls of the deceased undergo pain; there is no cessation even in heaven; for its temporary inhabitant is ever tormented with the prospect of descending again to earth, and again must he die. Whatever is produced that is most acceptable to man becomes a seed whence springs the tree of sorrow." And asks, Where could men, scorched by the sun of this world, look for felicity were it not for the shade afforded by the tree of emancipation? This is *the* remedy for the ills of life, for it only is absolute and final. It goes on to teach that this blessedness is attainable by knowledge and works. Knowledge is of two kinds—that derived from Scripture, and that which results from meditation: knowledge obtained from Scripture or any extraneous source being compared to the light of a candle, whilst that which comes from reflection is as the light of the sun. In one place men are urged to obtain light from both sources, as they together form a pair of *eyes* by which a man is able to see the Supreme. The superiority of meditation, or Yoga, is explained in the following story: "There were two kings, one most spiritually-minded, intent by knowledge to obtain final liberation; and the other seeking the same end by good works. These two fought, the one possessed of divine knowledge conquering the one more given to good works. It happened one day that a cow of the conqueror was killed by a tiger in the forest, but the king not knowing how to make expiation for the offence was most miserable; and to add to his difficulty he was told that none but the king whom he had just conquered could enlighten him. So to this king he went, and though his counsellors urged him, in revenge, to slay his conqueror and regain his kingdom, he refused to do so on the ground that by this he would regain a mere earthly kingdom, whilst he would lose a heavenly. He decided, therefore, to forgive his foe, and give him the desired information. When the king had made the penance prescribed he was still uneasy in his mind, and found out that this arose from the fact that he had paid no fee to his preceptor. So he again repaired to his former foe and offered to give a fee. The only one that the king could consent to accept was this: that he should give him instruction in meditation—how to effect it, and the benefits that would arise from it. The king complies and assures him that he who devotes himself through several successive lives to meditation on the Divine Being will at length lose himself in the ocean of deity. The two kings obtained absorption; the one who conquered the world handed over the whole to his son, and went to live a hermit's life in the forest, to carry on the life of meditation he had commenced years before; the other, ceasing from trusting in his own good works, lived amidst objects of sense without regarding them, and instituted religious rites without expecting any advantages to himself. Thus by the two different roads the two rivals finally were admitted into the ocean of deity."

I shall now pass on to give the description of some of the heavens wherein those who have done things worthy of reward expect to enjoy the blessedness attached to these works.

Swarga, the heaven of Indra, is thus described in the Mahābhārata. It is situated on Mount Meru, which the Hindus regard as the centre of the earth. It is supposed to be somewhere to the north of the Himālayahs. The heavens of the other deities are situated near to it. It has beautiful houses for its happy inhabitants to occupy, and its splendour is unequalled in the universe. Its gardens are stocked with trees, which afford a grateful shade, yield the most luscious fruits, and are adorned with beautiful and fragrant flowers. Most beautiful nymphs (apsarasas) charm the inhabitants; whilst choristers and musicians, unrivalled in the universe, discourse the sweetest music. The city, which was built by Visvakarma, is 800 miles in circumference and 40 miles high. Its pillars are diamonds; its palaces, thrones, and furniture, pure gold.

Vaikuntha, the heaven of Vishnu, is similarly described in the same book. It is 80,000 miles in circumference, and has streets of gold, its buildings being formed of jewels, the pillars and ornaments of which are precious stones. The crystal waters of the Ganges fall from the higher heavens on the head of Druva, from thence into the hair of the Seven Rishis, and from there they flow as a river through the city. There are five pools bearing blue, red, and white lotuses. On a seat glorious as the meridian sun, sitting on white lotuses, is Vishnu, and on his right hand Lakshmi, his wife, who shines like a continued blaze of lightning, and from whose body the fragrance of the lotus extends 800 miles.

Kuvera's * heaven is much the same, and is described by the same writer. It is 800 miles long and 560 broad. The wind, perfumed by ten thousand odours, blows in soft breezes; and the palace, adorned with gold and jewels, displays a glory like the rays of the full moon. Here are canals of pure water filled with fish, water fowl, lotuses, &c., with ghâts made of gold; and forests in which Kuvera and his courtezans divert themselves. From his treasury the other deities supply themselves with ornaments. Kuvera is there surrounded with gods and goddesses, and hosts of other beings, such as musicians, singers, and dancers. All the pleasures of the other heavens are to be found here.

With the same Oriental extravagance employed in the description of the various heavens, the several hells are also painted. It is said that there are 100,000 hells, each class of offenders being cast into one place, where the appropriate punishment is given. I shall briefly mention some of the many forms of punishment threatened, with the offences for which they are to be inflicted. This list is from the Sri Bhāgavata. Those guilty of fornication and adultery, and those guilty of stealing children, are to be cast into Tāmisra, or the hell of darkness. The proud, who neglect the ceremonies of religion, are to go to Rowrava, where they will be tormented with animals called rurus. The glutton is to be cast into a hell of boiling oil. He who disregards the Veda and Brāhmans is to be punished in a hell of burning metal for 3,500,000 years. He who injures a man of superior caste is to be torn by swine. The unmerciful are to be tormented by snakes, flies, wasps, lice, &c. The Brāhmans (male and female), the saint, Vaishya, or king, who drinks spirits will be

* The god of wealth.

thrown into pans of liquid fire. He who despises a religious mendicant shall be punished by sticking fast in mud with his head downwards. He who kills a man and offers him to the gods, and he who eats an animal that has not been sacrificed to the gods, are to be fed on flesh and blood. He who betrays and then destroys a person is to be pierced with spears and arrows. He who is inhospitable to guests must have his eyes torn out by vultures. The covetous are to be fed with impure food. The person who professes different religions, and is familiar with people of other castes than his own, is to be punished by being continually thrown down from lofty trees. Highway robbers and poisoners are to be bitten by ravenous dogs. False witnesses are to be cast from rocks 800 miles high.

It must be borne in mind that these punishments are inflicted only on those who have not offered the atonements provided for all these classes of sins, or have not accumulated merit by the performance of good deeds, by which the sins with their punishments could be wiped off. Punishment awarded by a magistrate is a sufficient atonement for most offences. Sins atoned for in this life will not bring punishment in the next.

There is an interesting story in the Mahābhārata to show the impossibility of escape from the punishments inflicted by Yama on those who come under his authority. Rāvana, the demon king of Ceylon, who carried off Sita, the wife of Rāma, had gained such power by his religious acts as to have become a universal conqueror. One day he thought of the suffering souls in hell, and determined to go there and effect their release. As soon as the news of his approach reached Yama he sent offers of submission to the great conqueror, who, seeing the condition of the lost, and his ears being pierced with their cry, said: "I have conquered the three worlds; there is nothing which my power has not performed. It will be a glorious thing to set all these wretches at liberty." He spoke to the miserable souls, and hope sprang into their breasts; but when he called them to come forth, and with his twenty arms tried to assist them to escape, as fast as he pulled them out they fell back. At length he saw that even he could not reverse the decree by which they were doomed to suffer.

Having considered the rewards of the righteous and the punishment of the wicked, so far as their condition in another world is concerned, we come now to speak of the teaching of Hinduism concerning a further reward or punishment, viz., the re-birth of human souls into the world for further trial, either in a better or worse position than that they occupied in the life for which they have either been rewarded or punished by Yama—the transmigration of souls.

The teaching of Manu is most explicit on this subject. In order to understand it clearly it will be necessary to give rather fully his views of man's organism and also his classification of morals. I shall give as briefly as possible an outline of his scheme.

Actions are of three kinds—mental, verbal, and corporeal; and they bear good or evil fruit according as they are good or evil. "From the actions of men proceed their various transmigrations in the highest, mean, and lowest degrees." These three classes of actions are illustrated as follows: *mental actions* are, "planning to appropriate another's wealth, resolving on some forbidden deed, and conceiving notions of atheism or materialism;" *verbal actions* are, "scurrilous language, falsehood, backbiting, and useless tattle;" *corporeal actions* are, "taking goods not given to us, hurting sentient creatures without the sanction of law, and adultery." As the acts are either mental, verbal, or corporeal, so are the punishments for those acts. For corporeal sins a man will assume after death a vegetable or mineral form; for verbal, the form of a bird or a beast; and for mental, the lowest of human conditions. But a man who exerts this threefold self-command with respect to all animated creatures, wholly subduing both lust and wrath, shall by these means attain beatitude.

Man has two souls—the one answering to the living soul, the other to the spirit. At death the soul takes to itself another body, like the one that is burned, by means of which it can enjoy the rewards or suffer the penalties of the actions of life. According as good or evil deeds preponderate will the after condition of men be determined.

There are three qualities—viz., goodness, darkness, and passion, one or other of which is the prevailing character of every soul. Goodness is true knowledge; darkness, gross ignorance; and passion, all emotions of desire or aversion. The soul in which goodness prevails is given to the study of the Scriptures, devotion, corporeal purity, command over the organs, meditation on the Divine Spirit. The soul in which darkness prevails is given to covetousness, indolence, avarice, detraction, atheism, a habit of soliciting favours, and inattention to necessary business. The soul in which passion prevails is given to possess interested motives for acts of religion or morality, perturbation of mind, selfish gratification.

These qualities determine the position the possessors of them must occupy in their following birth. "Souls endued with goodness attain always the state of deities; those with passion the condition of men, and those immersed in darkness the nature of beasts." Each of these classes is again subdivided into three minor classes, and according to the amount or force of the prevailing quality will their position be higher or lower in the grade into which they are born. The gradation of these classes is given as follows:—

I. Darkness.	Class 1.	Vegetable and mineral substances, worms, insects, and reptiles.
	,, 2.	Elephants, horses, men of mlecha (*i.e.* non-Hindu) nations.
	,, 3.	Dancers and singers, birds and deceitful men, and savages.
II. Passion.	,, 1.	Actors. Those addicted to gaming and drinking.

	Class 2.	Kings, warriors, controversialists.
	,, 3.	Heavenly musicians and servants of gods.
III. Goodness.	,, 1.	Hermits, religious mendicants, Brāhmans, and lower gods.
	,, 2.	Sacrificers, sages, deities of the lower heaven.
	,, 3.	Brahma, the genius of virtue.

Then follows a most minute account of sins, and the form the soul will receive in its next birth as a punishment for committing them. After *torture* for a number of years they re-enter the world, and a new start in their almost infinite career is given them. Thus a Brāhman slayer must, according to the circumstances of his crime, enter the body of a dog, boar, ass, camel, bull, goat, sheep, stag, bird, or a chandāla (outcaste). A priest who has drunk spirits shall migrate into the form of a worm, or insect, or of some ravenous animal. He who steals the gold of a priest shall pass 1,000 times into the bodies of spiders, snakes, or chameleons. If a man steal grain in the husk he shall be born a rat (there is some sort of analogy between the crime and the punishment). If a man steal water he shall be born a diving bird; or flesh-meat, a vulture. Women who have done similar evil deeds incur a similar taint, and shall be mated with those male beasts in the form of their females. Failure to discharge religious duties will be punished by migration into sinful bodies and servitude to their foes.

After separation from the material body the spiritual body assumed answers all the purposes the other would serve; and the pains endured by the soul are the same as they would be if it were still united to it.

According to Manu the knowledge of God is the best of all sciences, because it insures immortality, and saves the soul from this almost endless succession of births and deaths, whilst ceremonial duty secures prosperity in this life and bliss in heaven. But even ceremonialism, properly performed, may, in the long run, also save a man from the necessity of reappearing on earth. When a man performs acts of worship with the object of obtaining some special benefit, such as rain, or some reward in heaven, he gains only what he seeks—some temporary blessing here, and a temporary residence in heaven; but when he has no special boon to gain, and, moved only by a desire to please the gods, frequently performs ceremonial acts of religion, he too will be rewarded with the highest bliss, and is for ever exempt from a body, the source of all ills to man.

Such, then, is the teaching on this subject as it was given in a book said to contain the essence of the Vedas, and which has been for over 2,000 years the highest religious authority of the Hindus. On this subject, as on others, the imagination of the later writers has exerted itself, and in their books the doctrine has developed to an astonishing length, as the following passage from the Agni Purāna will show. Here we are taught the length of time, or rather the number of births a soul must pass through, before it can reach the highest position. The man must be very sanguine who entertains the hope "in far-off years" to attain to absorption into the Supreme Brahmā.

"A person who loses human birth passes through 8,000,000 births amongst inferior creatures before he can appear again on earth as a human being. Of these he remains 2,100,000 among the immovable parts of creation, as stones, trees, &c.; 900,000 amongst the watery tribes; 1,000,000 amongst insects, worms, &c.; 1,000,000 amongst birds; and 3,000,000 amongst the beasts. In the ascending scale, *if his works be suitable*, he lives 400,000 lives amongst the lower castes of men, and 100 amongst Brāhmans. After this he may obtain absorption into Brahmā."*

Another work, called the Karmavipāka, enters into particulars as follows:—"He who destroys a sacrifice will be punished in hell, will be born again as a fish, in which state

* Ward, vol. iii. p. 324.

he will continue for three years, or, re-assuming the human form, he will be afflicted with disease. He who kills an enemy conquered in war will be cast into the hell Krakacha; he will then successively appear on earth as a bull, a deer, a tiger, a bitch, a fish, a man; in his human form he will die of palsy. He who eats excellent food without giving any to others will be punished in hell for 30,000 years, and then be born as a musk-rat, a deer, and then as a man whose body emits an offensive smell, and who prefers bad to good food. The man who refuses to give his father and mother the food they desire will be punished in hell, and then be born as a crow, then as a man who can relish no kind of food. The stealer of a water-pot will be born as an alligator, and then as a giant. The man who has lived with a woman of superior caste will endure torment in hell through countless ages, after which he will be cast into a second hell, where for 100,000 years he will burn like a blade of grass; he will next be born as a worm, and then as a man afflicted with disease. The stealer of rice will first sink into hell, live eighteen years as a crow, twelve years as a heron, and then regain his human form, but always be afflicted. He who slays an animal not intended as a sacrifice will, in the form of a turtle, suffer in hell, then appear on earth as a bull, and then again as a man with an incurable distemper. He who strangles an animal, or laughs at the reading of a Purāna, will, after punishment in hell, be first born as a snake, then as a tiger, then as a cow, then as a white heron, then as a crow, and then as an asthmatic man. A beautiful woman who despises her husband will suffer a variety of torments in hell; she will then be born again as a woman, and, losing her husband soon after her marriage, will long suffer the miseries of widowhood." *

The belief in previous and successive births is universal amongst the Hindus, though they freely admit as a rule that they bring with them no memory of their former lives. When a parent is distracted with sorrow at the illness or

* Ward, vol. iii. p. 392.

loss of a child, or when his business does not prosper, or tribulation of any kind falls upon him, his first thought is, Which of the many gods have I offended? What religious duty have I neglected? If nothing can be remembered, nor can any one suggest how it is that he is thus afflicted, the common reflection comes—This sorrow is a punishment of some sin committed in a former birth. As it seems to me, this idea must largely tend to make them careless as to morals. Their present condition may be a reward for good conduct, or a punishment for evil. Who can tell? And in conversation with learned and ignorant, priest and people, as I have spoken to them concerning the future, I have received only one answer to the question, What will be your condition in your next life? They say, with sorrow and pain, "God knows; we cannot say. If our present life is good, we shall be happy; if evil, we shall be miserable;" but whether they have reason to hope or fear, they confess they are unable to say. No word of the gospel, as far as my experience goes, meets the wants of the Hindu more than this: "He that believeth on the Son *hath* everlasting life." The assurance that the Christian has of forgiveness of sin, and the certain hope of blessedness in heaven, is certainly one of the most attractive words the Christian can offer to the Hindu.

THE END.

INDEX.

HINDU MYTHOLOGY,

VEDIC AND PURĀNIC.

BY

W. J. WILKINS,

LONDON MISSIONARY SOCIETY, CALCUTTA.

PROFUSELY ILLUSTRATED BY ENGRAVINGS FROM DRAWINGS BY NATIVE ARTISTS.

PRICE 10/6.

THACKER AND CO., 87, NEWGATE STREET,
LONDON, E.C.

CATALOGUE

OF

NEW AND RECENT BOOKS

PUBLISHED BY

MR. T. FISHER UNWIN.

London:
26, PATERNOSTER SQUARE.
1886-7.

MR. UNWIN takes pleasure in sending herewith a Catalogue of Books published by him.

As each New Edition of it is issued, it will be sent post free *to Booksellers, Libraries, Book Societies, and Book Buyers generally—a register being kept for that purpose.*

Book Buyers are requested to order any Books they may require from their local Bookseller.

Should any difficulty arise, the Publisher will be happy to forward any Book, CARRIAGE FREE, *to any Country in the Postal Union, on receipt of the price marked in this list, together with full Postal Address.*

Customers wishing to present a book to a friend can send a card containing their name and a dedication or inscription to be enclosed, and it will be forwarded to the address given.

Remittances should be made by Money Order, draft on London, registered letter, or half-penny stamps.

After perusal of this Catalogue, kindly pass it on to some Book-buying friend.

CATALOGUE

OF

MR. T. FISHER UNWIN'S

PUBLICATIONS.

Autumn-Christmas Season, 1886.

"HISTORIA SANCTÆ CRUCIS." *With Illustrations.*

THE LEGENDARY HISTORY OF THE CROSS: A Series of Sixty-Four Woodcuts, from a Dutch book published by VELDENER, A.D. 1483. With an Introduction written and Illustrated by JOHN ASHTON, and a Preface by the Rev. S. BARING-GOULD, M.A. Square 8vo., bound in parchment, old style, brass clasps . 10s. 6d.

"The mediæva romance of the Cross was very popular. It occurs in a good number of authors, and is depicted in a good many churches in stained glass. . . . . It would seem that it was made up by some romancer out of all kinds of pre-existing material, with no other object than to write a religious novel for pious readers, to displace the sensuous novels which were much in vogue."—FROM THE PREFACE.

This pictorial version of the Legend is taken from a work that is now almost unique, only three copies being known to be in existence. The Editorial portions contain, besides a full paraphrase of the woodcuts, a fac-simile reprint of the Legend from Caxton's "Golden Legends of the Saints," also much curious information respecting the early History of the Legend, the controversies in which it has been involved, and the question of relics. Copies are also given of some Fifteenth Century frescoes of English workmanship formerly existing at Stratford-on-Avon. Altogether the book forms an interesting memorial of the quaint lorė that has gathered round this "religious novel" of the Middle Ages.

Autumn-Christmas Season, 1886.

A VOLUME OF MEDIÆVAL ROMANCES.

EDITED BY JOHN ASHTON.

ROMANCES OF CHIVALRY: Told and Illustrated in Fac-simile, by JOHN ASHTON, Author of "The Dawn of the Nineteenth Century in England," &c. Forty-six Illustrations. Demy 8vo., cloth elegant, gilt tops . 18s.

CONTENTS.

Melusine.—Sir Isumbras.—Sir Degoré.—Sir Bevis of Hampton.—Sir Tryamoure.—The Squyr of Lowe Degre.—The Knight of the Swanne.—Valentine and Orson.—Sir Eglamoure of Artoys.—Guy of Warwick.—Robert the Devyll.—Howleglas.

The "ROMANCES OF CHIVALRY" were the Novels of the Middle Ages, from the 13th to the 16th centuries. They are highly sensational, full of incident, and never prolix. To render these Romances more interesting to the general reader, Mr. Ashton has fac-similed a number of the contemporary engravings, which are wonderfully quaint, and throw much light on the Manners and Costumes of the period.

LEGENDS AND POPULAR TALES OF THE BASQUE PEOPLE. By MARIANA MONTEIRO. With full-page Illustrations in Photogravure by HAROLD COPPING. Square Imp. 16mo., cloth . . 10s. 6d.

CONTENTS.

I. Aquelarre.
II. Arguiduna.
III. Maitagarri.
IV. Roldan's Bugle-Horn.
V. Jaun-Zuria, Prince of Erin.
VI. The Branch of White Lilies.
VII. The Song of Lamia.
VIII. Virgin of the Five Towns.
IX. Chaunt of the Crucified.
X.-XI. The Raids. The Holy War.
XII. The Prophecy of Lara.
XIII. Hurca Mendi.

Fine edition of 100 copies of the above, medium 4to., numbered and signed by the Author, printed on Dutch hand-made paper, with India-proofs of the Photogravures . £1 1s. net.

MODERN HINDUISM: Being an account of the Religion and Life of the Hindus in Northern India. By W. J. WILKINS, of the London Missionary Society, Author of "Hindu Mythology—Vedic and Purānic." Demy 8vo., cloth . . . . 16s.

Autumn-Christmas Season, 1886.

A GIFT-BOOK FOR GIRLS.

IN THE TIME OF ROSES: A Tale of Two Summers. Told and Illustrated by FLORENCE and EDITH SCANNELL, Author and Artist of "Sylvia's Daughters." Thirty-two full-page and other Illustrations. Square Imp. 16mo., cloth . . . . 5s.

CONTENTS.

Capri.
Isolina.
"Good-bye, Capri."
The Yellow Cottage.
The School Treat.
Home Again!
The Garden Party.
Geraldine makes a discovery.
Isolina's Flight.
Wedding Bells.

A CHILDREN'S STORY-BOOK.

PRINCE PEERLESS: A Fairy-Folk Story-Book. By the Hon. MARGARET COLLIER (Madame Galletti di Cadilhac). Author of "Our Home by the Adriatic." Illustrated by the Hon. JOHN COLLIER. Square Imp. 16mo., cloth . . . . 5s.

CONTENTS.

Fairy Folk.
The Great Snow Mountain.
The Ill-Starred Princess.
The Sick Fairy.
Two Fairies.
The Shadow World.
Prince Peerless.
Something New.

A BOY'S STORY-BOOK.

BOYS' OWN STORIES. By ASCOTT R. HOPE, Author of "Stories of Young Adventurers," "Stories out of School Time," &c. Eight Illustrations. Crown 8vo., cloth . . . . 5s.

A series of glimpses into the state of Europe during the great days of our grandfathers, that may serve to illustrate, or perhaps to introduce closer study of, a period rich in facts as strange and moving as any fiction. The materials for the stories have been supplied in each case by the hero of the several narratives, which thus form so many romances of real life. This, in some respects, new departure in juvenile literature will, it is hoped by the author, give the youngsters an opportunity of realising the fact that "truth is stranger than fiction."

Autumn-Christmas Season, 1886.

By Author of "How to be Happy though Married."

"**MANNERS MAKYTH MAN.**" Imp. 16mo., cloth, 6s.; fine edition, bevelled edges, in box . . 7s. 6d.

SOME OF THE CONTENTS.—Good Manners—"God Almighty's Gentlemen"—Matrimonial Manners—A Husband-and-Wife Mutual Improvement Society—Family Government—Keeping up Appearances—Conversation—Tippling—Travelling with Advantage—Are our Manners and Morals Perfect?—Misapplied Virtues—Vital Force—Success in Life—Distinguished Service in Passion—What is Religion?—The Wisdom of the Foolish—The Wise Man's Conclusion.

EXTRACT FROM PREFACE.—"I am showing my gratitude to the public for their very kind reception of 'How to be Happy though Married' by now presenting to them another little book with my best 'manners!' It is not a book of etiquette, for I am by no means a master of ceremonies; nor does the motto of Winchester College, 'Manners Makyth Man,' refer to those social rules and forms which are often only substitutes for good manners, but rather to manners in the old sense of the word which we see in the text, 'Evil communications corrupt good manners.'"

A COMTIST LOVER, and Other Studies. By ELIZABETH RACHEL CHAPMAN, Author of "The New Godiva," "A Tourist Idyl," &c. Crown 8vo., cloth . . . 6s.

CONTENTS.—Part I.—A Comtist Lover: Being a Dialogue on Positivism and the Zeitgeist—The Extension of the Law of Kindness: Being an Essay on the Rights of Animals. Part II.—The Delphine of Madame de Staël—Some Immortality-Thoughts—Some Novels of William Black.

"LAYS OF A LAZY MINSTREL."

THE LAZY MINSTREL. By J. ASHBY-STERRY, Author of "Boudoir Ballads," "Shuttlecock Papers," &c. With vignette frontispiece. Fcap. 8vo., cloth, printed on hand-made paper . . . . 6s.

Fine Edition of 50 copies of the above, crown 4to., printed on Dutch hand-made paper, each copy numbered and signed by the Author . . . £1 1s. net.

SOME OF THE CHIEF CONTENTS.—Hambledon Lock—Spring's Delights—My Country Cousin—A Common-Sense Carol—Saint May—Doctor Brighton—Symphonies in Fur—Lawn Tennis in Winter—The Music of Leaves—In My Easy Chair—Two Naughty Girls—In Strawberry Time—In an Old City Church—The Pink of Perfection—A Traveller's Tarantella—Henley in July—The Baby in the Train—Love Locks.

CHERRY-STONES. A Book of Sonnets and Miscellaneous Pieces, mostly of Anglo-Indian subjects. By GREECE C. DUTT. Crown 8vo. 6s.

Autumn-Christmas Season, 1886.

ADDRESSES TO CHILDREN.

THE BIRD'S NEST, and Other Sermons for Children of all Ages. By Rev. SAMUEL COX, D.D., Author of "Expositions," "Salvator Mundi," &c. Crown 8vo., cloth . . . . 6s.

EXTRACT FROM PREFACE.—"I have often been urged to print these Discourses by those who heard them. . . . I can only hope that, in them, these pages may revive many happy memories; and that God may deign to use the Sermons to which they listened so attentively for the good of many who did not hear them. . . . This volume advances for itself, at least, one modest pretension. It is the only volume of *expository* sermons addressed to children of which I am aware: and if it brings out the meaning and applies the lesson of words given by inspiration of God, it can hardly fail to do some good to the children who read it.'

CHRISTIAN EVIDENCES.

THE BIBLE AND THE AGE; or, An Elucidation of the Principles of a Consistent and Verifiable Interpretation of Scripture. By CUTHBERT COLLINGWOOD, M.A., and B.M. Oxon, Author of "New Studies in Christian Theology," "A Vision of Creation," &c. Demy 8vo., cloth . . . . 10s. 6d.

THE BERWICK HYMNAL. Edited by the Rev. A. W. OXFORD, M.A., Vicar of St. Luke's, Berwick Street, Soho. Imp. 32mo. . . . . 2s.

THE PAROUSIA. A Critical Inquiry into the New Testament Doctrine of Our Lord's Second Coming. By the Rev. J. S. RUSSELL, M.A. New and cheaper Edition. Demy 8vo., cloth . . . . 7s. 6d.

ANNE GILCHRIST: Her Life and Writings. Edited by HERBERT HARLAKENDEN GILCHRIST. Containing 8 Illustrations, and an Introductory Preface by WILLIAM MICHAEL ROSETTI. Demy 8vo., cloth . . . 16s.
[*In preparation.*

THE STORY OF THE NATIONS.

"The series is likely to be found indispensable in every school library."—
Pall Mall Gazette

A Series of Short Popular Histories, printed in good readable type, and forming handsome well-bound volumes. Crown 8vo., Illustrated and furnished with Maps and Indexes, price 5s. each.

ROME. By ARTHUR GILMAN, M.A., Author of "A History of the American People," &c. Second Edition.

"We heartily commend this volume."—*Schoolmaster.*
"A clear and complete view of the rise and progress of the Roman nation."—
Congregationalist.

THE JEWS: In Ancient, Mediæval, and Modern Times. By Prof. J. K. HOSMER.

"The story of the Jews, when well told, as it is here, is one of thrilling satisfaction, and fruitful in instruction."—*Educational Times.*

GERMANY. Rev. S. BARING-GOULD, Author of "Curious Myths of the Middle Ages," &c. [*In September.*

CARTHAGE. By Prof. ALFRED J. CHURCH, Author of "Stories from the Classics," &c. [*In October.*

THE MOORS IN SPAIN. By STANLEY LANE POOLE, Author of "Studies in a Mosque," &c. [*In November.*

EGYPT. By Prof. GEO. RAWLINSON, Author of "The Five Great Monarchies of the World," &c. [*In December.*

ALEXANDER'S EMPIRE. By Prof. J. P. MAHAFFY, Author of "Social Life in Greece," &c. [*In preparation.*

HUNGARY. By Prof. VAMBÉRY, Author of "Travels in Central Asia," &c. [*In preparation.*

SPAIN. By Rev. E. E. and SUSAN HALE. [*In preparation.*

Other Volumes in preparation.

Autumn-Christmas Season, 1886.

POLITICAL WORKS.

Ireland and Home Rule.

THE MAKING OF THE IRISH NATION: AND THE FIRST-FRUITS OF FEDERATION. By J. A. Partridge, Author of "Democracy: Its Factors and Conditions," "From Feudal to Federal," &c. Demy 8vo., cloth . . . . 6s.

"This is a complete handbook on the Irish question. . . . The whole case is stated by Mr. Partridge in the clearest and most cogent fashion. As a piece of literary workmanship, the book is for the most part of the highest class. The style is lofty, the tone is often passionate and extreme, but the argumentation is throughout sound."—*Lancaster Guardian.*

LABOUR, LAND, AND LAW: A Search for the Missing Wealth of the Working Poor. By William A. Phillips, Member of the Committee on Public Lands, Forty-third Congress, and on Banking and Currency, Forty-fifth Congress. Demy 8vo., cloth . . . 9s.

"He writes in a clear, brisk American style, which leaves his readers in no doubt as to what he means. He is evidently a man of considerable ability and a student of social and economical problems. . . . There is a great deal of statistical information to be found in 'Labour, Land, and Law.'"—*St. James's Gazette.*

THE BALKAN PENINSULA. By M. Emile de Laveleye. Translated by Mrs. Thorpe. Edited and Revised for the English public by the Author. With a new chapter bringing events up to date. 8vo., cloth.

[*In preparation.*

THE BRIDE OF GREENLAWNS; or, William Woodman's Trust. A Parable of Mr. Gladstone and Ireland. Fcap. 8vo. . . . . 6d.

"DOTTINGS OF A DOSSER." Being Revelations of the Inner Life of Low London Lodging Houses. By Howard J. Goldsmid. Fcap. 8vo. . . . . 1s.

Autumn-Christmas Season, 1886.

NEW EDITIONS.

BRIDAL GIFT EDITION OF

HOW TO BE HAPPY THOUGH MARRIED.

Being a Handbook to Marriage. By a Graduate in the University of Matrimony. White vellum cloth, extra gilt, bev. boards, gilt edges, in box . . . 7s. 6d.

"We strongly recommend this book as one of the best of wedding presents. It is a complete handbook to an earthly Paradise, and its author may be regarded as the Murray of Matrimony and the Baedeker of Bliss."—*Pall Mall Gazette.*

"The author has successfully accomplished a difficult task in writing a clever and practical book on the important subject of matrimony. . . . . This book, which is at once entertaining and full of wise precepts, deserves to be widely read."—*Morning Post.*

"An entertaining volume. . . . . The new guide to matrimonial felicity."—*Standard*, Leader.

ALSO, FOURTH AND POPULAR EDITION.

HOW TO BE HAPPY THOUGH MARRIED.

Being a Handbook to Marriage. Small square 8vo., 3s. 6d.

CHARLES DICKENS AS I KNEW HIM: The Story of the Reading Tours in Great Britain and America (1866-1870). By GEORGE DOLBY. New and cheaper edition. Crown 8vo. . . . . . . 3s. 6d.

"Will certainly be read with interest by all who admire the great writer."—*Daily Telegraph.*

THE DAWN OF THE NINETEENTH CENTURY IN ENGLAND: A Social Sketch of the Times. By JOHN ASHTON, Author of "Social Life in the Reign of Queen Anne," &c. Cheaper ed., in 1 vol. Illus. La. cr. 8vo., 10s. 6d.

"The book is one continued source of pleasure and interest, and opens up a wide field for speculation and comment. No one can take it up in a moody moment without losing much of his discontent, and many of us will look upon it as an important contribution to contemporary history, not easily available to others than close students, and not made into its pleasing and entertaining form without a literary skill which is not by any means common."—*Antiquary.*

A New and Cheaper Edition (being the Fifth) of

THE LIVES OF ROBERT & MARY MOFFAT.

By their Son, JOHN SMITH MOFFAT. With New Preface and Supplementary Chapter by the Author. Four Portraits, Four Illustrations (two of which are new), and Two Maps. Crown 8vo., cloth . . . . 7s. 6d.

"An inspiring record of calm, brave, wise work, and will find a place of value on the honoured shelf of missionary biography. The biographer has done his work with reverent care, and in a straightforward, unaffected style." *Contemporary Review.*

Autumn-Christmas Season, 1886.

NEW EDITIONS—*continued.*

STUDIES OF THE EIGHTEENTH CENTURY IN ITALY. By VERNON LEE, Author of "Ottilie," &c. Demy 8vo., cloth . . . . 7s. 6d.

"These studies show a wide range of knowledge of the subject, precise investigation, abundant power of illustration, and healthy enthusiasm. . . . The style of writing is cultivated, neatly adjusted, and markedly clever."—*Saturday Review.*

"A singularly delightful and very able volume."—*Westminster Review.*

EUPHORION: Studies of the Antique and the Mediæval in the Renaissance. By VERNON LEE, Author of "Belcaro," &c. Cheap Edition in one volume. Demy 8vo., cloth . . . . 7s. 6d.

"The book is bold, extensive in scope, and replete with well-defined and unhackneyed ideas, clear impressions, and vigorous and persuasive modes of writing.—*Athenæum.*

BELCARO: Being Essays on Sundry Æsthetical Questions. By VERNON LEE, Author of "Euphorion," "Baldwin," &c. Crown 8vo., cloth . . . . 5s.

"This way of conveying ideas is very fascinating, and has an effect of creating activity in the reader's mind which no other mode can equal. From first to last there is a continuous and delightful stimulation of thought."—*Academy.*

POETS IN THE GARDEN. By MAY CROMMELIN, Author of "Joy," "In the West Countrie," &c. Cheap and Popular Edition, with Coloured Frontispiece. Square pott 16mo., cloth binding . . . . . . 6s.

This edition is printed on a thinner paper, and more simply bound. The text, however, is identical with the half-guinea edition. [—*Times.*

"Decidedly a happy idea. . . . The volume is finely printed, and gracefully designed."

"Merely to describe this book is to write its commendation. It is an anthology in a double sense."—*Academy.*

Still on sale, a few copies of the First Edition, containing Eight Coloured Illustrations. Square pott 16mo., cloth elegant, fine paper, gilt edges, bev. boards . . 10s. 6d.

POPULAR EDITION OF THE "SHAH NAMEH."

HEROIC TALES. Retold from Firdusi the Persian. By HELEN ZIMMERN, Author of "Stories in Precious Stones," &c. With Etchings by L. ALMA TADEMA, and Prefatory Poem by E. W. GOSSE. Pop Ed. Cr. 8vo., cl. extra, 5s.

"Charming from beginning to end. . . Miss Zimmern deserves all credit for her courage in attempting the task, and for her marvellous success in carrying it out."—*Saturday Review.*

Autumn-Christmas Season, 1886.

NEW EDITIONS—*continued.*

A DIARY OF GOLDEN THOUGHTS FOR THE YEAR. New edition, interleaved with ruled paper. Can be used as a Birthday and Event Book of the Home Life. Cloth boards, 2s.; Parchment . . . . 1s. 6d.

"A little oblong book, very daintily and tastefully got-up, containing admirably selected brief extracts from great writers."—*Academy.*

A ROLL OF GOLDEN THOUGHTS FOR THE YEAR; or, Permanent Diary of Wise Sayings from the Best Writers of all Times and Climes. Contents identical with the above, but arranged in oblong shape. Mounted on gilt wire, and suspended by ribands . . 1s. 6d.

"Choicely and delicately produced."—*Christ.an.*

FAIRY TALES FROM BRENTANO. Told in English by KATE FREILIGRATH KROEKER. Twenty-two Illustrations by F. CARRUTHERS GOULD. Cheap and Popular Edition. Square Imp. 16mo. . . 3s. 6d.

"The extravagance of invention displayed in his tales will render them welcome in the nursery. The translation—not an easy task—has been very cleverly accomplished."—*The Academy.*

"An admirable translator in Madame Kroeker, and an inimitable illustrator in Mr. Carruthers Gould."—*Truth.*

WHEN I WAS A CHILD; or, Left Behind. By LINDA VILLARI, Author of "On Tuscan Hills," &c. Illustrated. Square 8vo., cloth, gilt edges . . . . . 3s. 6d.

"It is fresh and bright from the first chapter to the last."—*Morning Post.*

'A very clever, vivid and realistic story."—*Truth.*

SOUTHWOOD: A Tale. By CATHARINE STURGE, Compiler of "A Diurnal for the Changes and Chances of this Mortal Life," &c. Frontispiece. Sm. cr. 8vo., 2s. 6d.

"A thoroughly healthy and well-written tale. The plot is very good."—*Presbyterian Messenger.*

THE CHILDREN'S BOUQUET OF VERSE AND HYMN. Gathered by AUNT SARAH and COUSIN GRACE. 32mo., red edges, cloth elegant, or wood: maple, cedar, walnut, or cycamore . . . . . . 1s.

"Love for the little ones has clearly been at work in the making of this selection; good taste as well, and a most catholic sympathy."—*Christian Leader.*

NEW TWO-VOLUME NOVELS.

THE TOUCHSTONE OF PERIL: A Tale of the Indian Mutiny. By DUDLEY HARDRESS THOMAS. Two vols. Crown 8vo. (*Ready*) . . . . . £1 1s.

A YEAR IN EDEN. By HARRIET WATERS PRESTON. Two vols. Crown 8vo. (*In October*) . . . £1 1s.

RECENT NOVELS. Two Volumes. Price £1 1s. each.

CAMILLA'S GIRLHOOD. By LINDA VILLARI.

"Brightly written. . . . It is from first to last a favourable and pure-toned specimen of Anglo-Italian fiction."—*Morning Post.*

THE BACHELOR VICAR OF NEWFORTH. By Mrs. A. HARCOURT-ROE.

"Bright and readable."—*Athenæum.*

ICHABOD: A Portrait. By BERTHA THOMAS.

"It is indubitably the work of a clever woman."—*Athenæum.*

A NOBLE KINSMAN. By ANTON GIULIO BARRILI.

"A good translation of a very pretty story."—*Guardian.*

JEPHTHAH'S DAUGHTER. By JANE H. SPETTIGUE.

THE CHANCELLOR OF THE TYROL. By HERMAN SCHMID.

"A clever and original story."—*Daily Telegraph.*

WILBOURNE HALL. By Mrs. CAUMONT.

"An agreeable novel."—*Spectator.*

HENRY IRVING: in England and America, 1838-1884. By FREDERIC DALY. With a Vignette Portrait specially etched by AD. LALAUZE. Second thousand. Crown 8vo., cloth extra . . . . 5s.

"Mr. Daly sets forth his materials with a due sense of proportion, and writes in a pleasing vein."—*Daily News.*

"Conscientiously full, thoughtfully considered, and gracefully written."—*Daily Telegraph.*

THE SEVEN AGES OF MAN. From Shakespeare's "As You Like it." POPULAR EDITION. Illustrated with Woodcuts. Sq. pott 16mo., cl. elegant, bev. boards, gilt edges . . . . 5s.

"Strongly contrast the old and new style of engraving. . . . The various artists have all been well chosen."—*Graphic.*

NEW AND RECENT NOVELS AT SIX SHILLINGS,
Large Crown 8vo., cloth.

MELITA: A Turkish Love-Story. By LOUISE M. RICHTER.

"Her story is interesting on its own account; but its background of Turkish life and character gives it an additional charm of freshness."—*Athenæum.*

MERCIFUL OR MERCILESS? By STACKPOOL E. O'DELL, Author of "Old St. Margaret's."

"Animated pictures of nature. . . . Easy lightness of style. —*Saturday Review.*

THE LAST STAKE: A Tale of Monte Carlo. By MADAME R. FOLI. Illustrated.

"Madame Foli's graphic narrative will do much to lift the veil from the horrors and seductions of the gaming tables of Monte Carlo."—*Academy.*

TARANTELLA: A Romance. By MATHILDE BLIND, Author of "Life of George Eliot." Second edition.

"Told with great spirit and effect, and shows very considerable power."—*Pall Mall.*

VALENTINO. By WILLIAM WALDORF ASTOR.

"A remarkable historical romance. . . . Forcibly written."—*Morning Post.*

GLADYS FANE: The Story of Two Lives. By T. WEMYSS REID. Fourth and popular edition.

"A good and clever book, which few readers who begin it are likely to put down unfinished."—*Saturday Review.*

THE AMAZON: An Art Novel. By CARL VOSMAER. Preface by Prof. GEORG EBERS, and Front. drawn specially by L. ALMA TADEMA, R.A.

"It is a work full of deep, suggestive thought."—*The Academy.*

MAJOR FRANK: A Novel. By A. L. G. BOSBOOM-TOUSSAINT. Trans. from the Dutch by JAS. AKEROYD.

"It is a pleasant, bright, fresh book."—*Truth.*

THE POISON TREE: A Tale of Hindu Life in Bengal. By B. CHANDRA CHATTERJEE. Introduction by EDWIN ARNOLD, M.A., C.S.I.

"The healthiness and purity of tone throughout the book."—*Academy.*

THE 4s. 6d. SERIES OF NOVELS.

Crown 8vo., cloth.

STRUGGLES TO LIVE: A Study of Life, Love and Character in a Country Town. By A. BOWER.

FRANCIS: A Socialistic Romance. Being for the most part an Idyll of England and Summer. By M. DAL VERO, Author of "A Heroine of the Commonplace."

"A very bright, cheery and pretty story."—*Academy.*

THE LAST MEETING: A Story. By BRANDER MATTHEWS, Author of "The Theatres of Paris," &c.

"Mr. Brander Matthews' new novel is one of the pleasantest and most entertaining books that I have read for some time. There is vigorous character-drawing; and the characters are, for the most part, men and women in whose company one is pleased to pass the time. There are many clever and shrewd remarks, considerable humour, and some wit."—*Academy.*

A LOST SON. By MARY LINSKILL, Author of "Hagar," "Between the Heather and the Northern Sea," &c.

"The book's doctrine is wholesome, and its religion free from any trace of cant."—*Spectator.*

"Miss Linskill not only shows a quick power of observation, but writes with good taste and without affectation."—*Athenæum.*

THE BECKSIDE BOGGLE, and Other Lake Country Stories. By ALICE REA. Illustrated.

"The interest of the volume lies in its evidently faithful reproduction of Lake Country speech character, and manners. . . . . . A pleasant one and wholesome."—*Graphic.*

TWO VOLUMES OF SHORT STORIES.

TALES IN THE SPEECH-HOUSE. By CHARLES GRINDROD, Author of "Plays from English History," &c. Illustrated. Crown 8vo., cloth . . . . . 6s.

"We can say honestly to everyone who can lay hands on them—Read them."—[*Scotsman.*

"Sweetly and powerfully told."—*Manchester Guardian.*

THE QUEEN OF THE ARENA, AND OTHER STORIES. By STEWART HARRISON. Illust. Crown 8vo., cloth . . . . 6s.

"Major Harrison has a fresh and lively style, he is so far from being tedious that he rather tends to the opposite extreme, and he shows considerable versatility of powers, with an extensive knowledge of the world."—*Times.*

VERNON LEE'S WORKS.

BALDWIN: Being Dialogues on Views and Aspirations. Demy 8vo., cloth . . . . 12s.

"Worth careful study from more than one side. It has a message for all people, to which only indolence or indifference can be deaf. . . . The subjects proposed are discussed courageously and conscientiously, and often with a compression and force which fills part of the book with pregnant suggestion. . . . One cannot read a page of 'Baldwin' without feeling the wiser for it."—*Academy.*

EUPHORION: Studies of the Antique and the Mediæval in the Renaissance. Cheap ed. Demy 8vo., cloth, 7s. 6d.

"The book is bold, extensive in scope, and replete with well-defined and unhackneyed ideas, clear impressions, and vigorous and persuasive modes of writing."—*Athenæum.*

STUDIES OF THE EIGHTEENTH CENTURY IN ITALY. Demy 8vo., cloth . . . . 7s. 6d.

"These studies show a wide range of knowledge of the subject, precise investigation, abundant power of illustration, and healthy enthusiasm. . . . The style of writing cultivated, neatly adjusted, and markedly clever."—*Saturday Review.*

"A singularly delightful and very able volume."—*Westminster Review.*

BELCARO: Being Essays on Sundry Æsthetical Questions. Crown 8vo., cloth . . . . 5s.

"This way of conveying ideas is very fascinating, and has an effect of creating activity in the reader's mind which no other mode can equal. From first to last there is a continuous and delightful stimulation of thought."—*Academy.*

OTTILIE: An Eighteenth Century Idyl. Square 8vo., cloth extra . . . . 3s. 6d.

"A graceful little sketch. . . . Drawn with full insight into the period described." *Spectator.*

"Pleasantly and carefully written. . . . The Author lets the reader have a glimpse of Germany in the 'Sturm und Drang' period."—*Athenæum.*

"A graceful little picture. . . . Charming all through."—*Academy.*

THE PRINCE OF THE HUNDRED SOUPS: A Puppet Show in Narrative. Edited, with a Preface by VERNON LEE. Illust. Cheaper edition. Square 8vo., cloth . . . . 3s. 6d.

"There is more humour in the volume than in half-a-dozen ordinary pantomimes."—*Spectator.*

SUMMER: From the Journal of HENRY D. THOREAU. Edited by H. G. O. BLAKE. Index. Map. Cr. 8vo., 7s. 6d.

"A most delightful book."—*Times.*

"As pleasant a book as can well be imagined."—*Athenæum.*

ECHETLUS: Considerations upon Culture in England. By GEORGE WHETENALL. Crown 8vo., cloth . 4s. 6d.

"Very thoughtful, earnest, and exceedingly clever. . . . . There is an unquestionable streak of genius in the composition of this small work."—*Christian World.*

THE LIFE and TIMES OF WILLIAM LLOYD GARRISON, 1805-1840: The Story of His Life told by His Children. In two vols., with upwards of 20 Portraits and Illustrations. Demy 8vo. . . . £1 10s.

"The prime mover in the cause of Abolition well deserved an exhaustive biography, and English Literature can well afford to assign a permanent and honourable place to the description of a man who accomplished a great work, and whose right to figure among such men as Wilberforce, Clarkson, Brougham, and others cannot for a moment be disputed."—*Times.*

OLE BULL: A Memoir. By SARA C. BULL. With Ole Bull's "Violin Notes" and Dr. A. B. Crosby's "Anatomy of the Violinist." Portraits. Second edition. Crown 8vo., cloth . . . . . . 7s. 6d.

"Full of good stories. It is difficult to know where to choose."—*Saturday Review.*

"A word of commendation must be offered to the young widow of this distinguished musician for the tact and ability displayed in compiling and arranging the work."—*Morning Post.*

THE LIFE & TIMES OF SAMUEL BOWLES, Editor of *The Springfield Republican.* By GEO. S. MERRIAM. Portrait. 2 vols. Crown 8vo. . £1 1s.

"Its pictures of American journalism, so closely interwoven with party struggles, render it a contribution of some interest to the history of the Union during some of its most critical times."—*Daily News.*

PILGRIM SORROW. By CARMEN SYLVIA (The Queen of Roumania). Translated by HELEN ZIMMERN, Author of "The Epic of Kings." Portrait-etching by LALAUZE. Square Crown 8vo., cloth extra . . . 5s.

"For this nature of literature the Queen appears to have a special gift. . . . And never has she been happier than in her *Liedens Erdengang*, which lies before us to-day." —*Literary World* (Review of the German edition).

ON TUSCAN HILLS AND VENETIAN WATERS. By LINDA VILLARI, Author of "Camilla's Girlhood," &c. Illust. Square Imperial 16mo. 7s. 6d.

"Next to the privilege of visiting these localities, this book is the best thing, and no expense has been spared in making the volume an artistic success."—*Bookseller.*

LONDON AND ELSEWHERE. By THOMAS PURNELL, Author of "Literature and its Professors," &c. Fcap. 8vo. . . . . 1s.

"The book is admirably adapted to the season—light in topic and bright in manner, readable from first to last, and, unlike most holiday literature, worth keeping after it has been read."—*Globe.*

MY STUDY, and other Essays. By Professor AUSTIN PHELPS, D.D., Author of "The Theory of Preaching," &c. Crown 8vo., cloth, bev. edges . . . . . . 6s.

"Marked by practical sense and genial, manly piety, and the book, as a whole, will scarcely be read without interest and profit."—*Methodist Times.*

THE CHRIST OF HISTORY. By JOHN YOUNG, LL.D., Author of "The Life and Light of Men," &c. Seventh and Popular Edition. Crown 8vo. . . . . 3s. 6d.

GENESIS THE THIRD: History, not Fable. Being the Merchants' Lecture for March, 1883. By EDWARD WHITE. Crown 8vo., cloth, 1s.; sewed . . 6d.

PAYING THE PASTOR, Unscriptural and Traditional. By JAMES BEATY, D.C.L., Q.C., Member of the Canadian Legislature. Crown 8vo. . . . . . . 6s.

THE TEMPLE: Sacred Poems and Private Ejaculations. By Mr. GEORGE HERBERT. *New Edition,* with Introductory Essay by J. HENRY SHORTHOUSE. Fourth edition. Small crown, sheep, imitation of original binding, or in paper boards, old style, uncut edges . . . . 5s.

This is a fac-simile reprint by typography of the Original Edition of 1633.

"This charming reprint has a fresh value added to it by the Introductory Essay of the Author of 'John Inglesant.'"—*Academy.*

I'VE BEEN A-GIPSYING; or, Rambles among our Gipsies. By GEORGE SMITH, of Coalville. Illustrated. New and Revised edition. Crown 8vo., cloth . 3s. 6d.

"Mr. Smith's sketches of his visits to the gipsies are graphic and varied, and will, we trust, serve to excite a wider interest in the perplexing question of their amelioration, to which the author has already given yeoman's service."—*Contemporary Review.*

THE ADVENTURES OF ROBINSON CRUSOE, By DANIEL DEFOE. Newly Edited after the Original Editions. Twenty Coloured Illustrations by KAUFFMAN. Fcap. 4to., cloth extra . . . . . . 7s. 6d.

"This is irrefutably the edition of 'Robinson Crusoe' of the season. It is charmingly got-up and illustrated. The type and printing are excellent."—*Standard.*

WORKS ON MISSIONS.

MEDICAL MISSIONS: Their Place and Power. By JOHN LOWE, F.R.C.S.E., Secretary of Edinburgh Medical Missionary Society. Introduction by Sir WILLIAM MUIR, K.C.S.I., LL.D., D.C.L. Medallion Frontispiece. Second edition. Crown 8vo., cloth . . . . . . 5s.

"It would be almost impossible to speak too favourably of this book. It is beautifully written, and deserves to be widely circulated."—*Presbyterian Messenger.*

LIFE AND WORK IN BENARES AND KUMAON, 1839-77. By JAS. KENNEDY, M.A., Author of "Christianity and the Religions of India." Introduction by Sir WM. MUIR, K.C.S.I. Illust. Crown 8vo., cloth, 6s.

"Of what he saw and did he writes agreeably, without obtruding the autobiographical form. . . . The volume is better worth reading than others of much higher literary pretensions."—*Academy.*

MODERN MISSIONS: Their Trials and Triumphs. By ROBERT YOUNG, Assistant Secretary to the Missions of the Free Church of Scotland. Map and Illustrations. Third edition. Crown 8vo., cloth extra . . . . 5s.

"This book should certainly be placed upon the shelves of parish, congregational, and Sunday-school libraries. It is brief and comprehensive."—*Christian World.*

LIGHT IN LANDS OF DARKNESS: By ROBERT YOUNG, Author of "Modern Missions." Illustrated. Second edition. Crown 8vo., cloth extra . . . 6s.

"To those who have read 'Modern Missions,' it will be sufficient to say that the present work forms a worthy successor to that interesting and well-written book."—*Congregationalist.*

THE TREASURE BOOK OF CONSOLATION: For all in Sorrow or Suffering. Compiled and Edited by BENJAMIN ORME, M.A., Editor of "The Treasure Book of Devotional Reading." Cr. 8vo., cl. extra, gilt top, 3s. 6d.

THE SHELLEY BIRTHDAY BOOK AND CALENDAR. Compiled by J. R. TUTIN. Crown 16mo., cloth, bev. boards, gilt edges . . . . 3s.

Large paper, Royal 16mo. (only 100 copies printed), with proof impressions of the portrait . 7s. 6d.

CENTENARY SERIES.

Fcap. 12mo., antique paper, parchment boards, 2s. each. Nos. 1 and 3 may also be had in paper covers, price 1s. each.

1. **JOHN WICLIF,** Patriot and Reformer: his Life and Writings. By RUDOLF BUDDENSIEG, Lic. Theol. Leipsic.

"Mr. Fisher Unwin has printed in delicious old text, with a frontispiece and vellum binding worthy of an old Elzevir, Mr. Rudolf Buddensieg's brief extracts from Wiclif' writings. . . . These are full of interest, and the little volume will be useful for reference."—*Graphic.*

2. **THE TABLE TALK OF DR. MARTIN LUTHER.** By Prof. JOHN GIBB.

"Deserves the very highest praise. Great discrimination has been shown in the choice of extracts, and considerable skill in the grouping of them under appropriate heads."—*Congregationalist.*

3. **DOCTOR JOHNSON:** His Life, Works and Table Talk. By Dr. MACAULAY, Editor of *The Leisure Hour.*

"An exceedingly pretty little book. . . . It gives a good taste of quality."—*Book Lore.*
"It is a charming specimen of typography."—*Globe.*

ABOUT THE THEATRE: Essays and Studies. By WILLIAM ARCHER, Author of "English Dramatists of To-day," &c. Crown 8vo., cloth, bevelled edges, 7s. 6d.

"Theatrical subjects, from the Censorship of the Stage to the most recent phenomena of first nights, have thoroughly able and informed discussion in Mr. Archer's handsome book."—*Contemporary Review.*

LITERARY LANDMARKS OF LONDON. By LAURENCE HUTTON. Second Edition. Crown 8vo., 7s. 6d.

"It is a volume that everyone should possess who takes an interest in the local associations which London is so full of."—*Standard.*
"Abounds with interesting facts concerning the residence of famous men in the apital."—*Daily News.*

CHARLES WHITEHEAD: A Critical Monograph. By H. T. MACKENZIE BELL. Cheap and Popular edition. Crown 8vo., cloth . . . . 5s.

"Mr. Mackenzie Bell has done a good service in introducing us to a man of true genius whose works have sunk into mysteriously swift and complete oblivion."—*Contemporary Review.*

NEW AND RECENT POETRY.

AN ITALIAN GARDEN: A Book of Songs. By A. MARY F. ROBINSON, Author of "The Life of Emily Brontë," &c. Fcap. 8vo., parchment, or half-bound in Japanese paper . . . . 3s. 6d.

"The author has a voice of her own, and her own vision of the world—not a loud voice, not a brilliant vision, but sweet, tuneful, and not unsympathetic."—*Daily News.*

A TIME AND TIMES: Ballads and Lyrics of East and West. By A. WERNER, Author of "The King of the Silver City." Crown 8vo., paper board style, 3s. 6d.

"Deserves to be widely read, and will become a favourite with all who read it."—*Literary World.*

OLD YEAR LEAVES: A Volume of Collected Verse. By H. T. MACKENZIE BELL, Author of "Verses of Varied Life," &c. Cheap edition. Crown 8vo. . . . 5s.

"We have great pleasure, indeed, in commending these poems to our readers."—*Literary World.*

VERSES OF VARIED LIFE. By H. T. MACKENZIE BELL, Author of "Charles Whitehead," &c. Crown 8vo., 3s. 6d.

"There are some pretty lines aod stanzas."—*Graphic.*

MEASURED STEPS. By ERNEST RADFORD. Crown 8vo., cloth . . . . 4s.

"He has imported into his deeper verse the beauty of a half-regretful subtlety and the interest of a real penetratioo. He can think with fineness and record his thoughts with point."—*Frederick Wedmore, in The Academy.*

A MINOR POET: And other Verses. By AMY LEVY. Crown 8vo., paper board style, uncut edges . 3s. 6d.

"Her idea of the character of 'Xantippe' is certainly original, and several of her shorter pieces are simple, heartfelt, and harmonius."—*Whitehall Review.*

HOPE'S GOSPEL, and Other Poems. By ARTHUR STEPHENS. Fcap. 8vo., cloth, bevelled edges . 3s. 6d.

"This bright little volume is full of the movement and vivacity of a thought that comprehends the charm of progress, the hopefulness of effort."—*Literary World.*

ORPHEUS, and Other Poems. By ALFRED EMERY. Fcap. 8vo., cloth . . . . 3s. 6d.

'Of considerable merit."—*Cambridge Review.*

REPRESENTATIVE BRITISH ORATIONS. With Introductions, &c., by CHAS. K. ADAMS. 16mo. Roxburgh, gilt tops, 3 vols., in cloth box . . 15s.
The Volumes may also be had without box . 13s. 6d.

"These three elegantly printed volumes, enclosed in a neat box to imitate cloth binding, comprise an excellent selection of famous speeches."—*Daily News.*

"At once an invaluable companion to the history of the most important centuries of English History, and a fascinating course of study in some of the proudest productions of British Oratory."—*Whitehall Review.*

REPRESENTATIVE AMERICAN ORATIONS. With Introductions, &c., by Prof. ALEXANDER JOHNSTON, of New Jersey. 3 vols. 16mo., Roxburgh, gilt tops, in cloth box . . . . 15s.

"By way of conclusion, we venture once more to strongly recommend it to our readers. It will increase their kowwledge of mankind in general, and will help them to better understand a great and friendly nation."—*Saturday Review.*

DECIMAL TABLES, for Calculating the Value of Government Stocks and Annuities, and of all Stocks of Railway and other Companies where the Capital is converted into Stock, at prices from £50 to £150 for £100 Stock (advancing by eighths). By T. M. P. HUGHES, of the Stock Department, Messrs. Williams, Deacon & Co. Demy 8vo., cloth . . . . 12s. 6d.

UNITED STATES NOTES: A History of the various Issues of Paper Money by the Government of the United States. By JOHN J. KNOX. With Photo-Lithographic Specimens. Demy 8vo., cloth . . . . . 12s.

'A very minute historical sketch of the treasury and other notes issued by the Government. . . . The book should be carefully studied by those who would understand the subject."—*New York Herald.*

THE THREE REFORMS OF PARLIAMENT: A History, 1830—1885. By WILLIAM HEATON, Editor of "Cassell's Concise Cyclopædia." Crown 8vo. . 5s.

"As readable as a novel, and as instructive as an important chapter of history can well be."—*Leeds Mercury.*

"An admirable and accurate summing-up of the great Reform movements of the last half-century."—*Literary World.*

ARMINIUS VAMBÉRY: His Life and Adventures. Written by Himself. With Portrait and 14 Illustrations. Fifth and Popular Edition. Square Imperial 16mo., cloth extra . . . . 6s.

"A most fascinating work, full of interesting and curious experiences."—*Contemporary Review.*

"It is partly an autobiographic sketch of character, partly an account of a singularly daring and successful adventure in the exploration of a practically unknown country. In both aspects it deserves to be spoken of as a work of great interest and of considerable merit."—*Saturday Review.*

"We can follow M. Vambéry's footsteps in Asia with pride and pleasure; we welcome every word he has to tell us about the ethnography and the languages of the East."—*Academy.*

"The character and temperament of the writer come out well in his quaint and vigorous style. . . . The expressions, too, in English, of modes of thought and reflections cast in a different mould from our own gives additional piquancy to the composition, and indeed, almost seems to bring out unexpected capacities in the language."—*Athenæum.*

"Has all the fascination of a lively romance. It is the confession of an uncommon man; an intensely clever, extraordinarily energetic egotist, well-informed, persuaded that he is in the right, and impatient of contradiction."—*Daily Telegraph.*

"The work is written in a most captivating manner, and illustrates the qualities that should be possessed by the explorer."—*Novoe Vremya, Moscow.*

"We are glad to see a popular edition of a book, which, however it may be regarded, must be pronounced unique. The writer, the adventures, and the style are all extraordinary—the last not the least of the three. It is flowing and natural—a far better style than is written by the majority of English travellers."—*St. James's Gazette.*

⁂ Over Eighty other English and Foreign Periodicals have reviewed this work.

BOYS' EDITION.

ARMINIUS VAMBÉRY: His Life and Adventures. Written by Himself. With Introductory Chapter dedicated to the Boys of England. Portrait and Seventeen Illustrations. Crown 8vo. . . . . . . 5s.

This new edition was prepared by M. Vambéry at the suggestion of several of his English friends and critics during his late visit to this country, that the story of his life was one well adapted to form the subject of a book for boys. He has carefully revised it throughout, eliminating all political and other matter that would possess but little interest for boys. A new Introductory Chapter is added, giving a more extensive insight ioto his boy life than the previous volume, and showing how even the humblest, poorest, and most delicate lad can, with perseverance and industry, rise to prosperity and renown. It possesses several additional Illustrations and a new Portrait of the Author.

FRANCE AND TONGKING: A Narrative of the Campaign of 1884, and the Occupation of Further India. By J. G. SCOTT (SHWAY YOE), Author of "The Burman." Map and Two Plans. Demy 8vo. . . . . 16s.

"Very graphic and exceedingly interesting pages."—*Spectator.*

"Will be perused with interest both by military men and by the general reader."—*Globe.*

THE MAHDI, PAST AND PRESENT. By Prof. JAMES DARMESTETER. Illustrated. Sewed, 1s.; cloth, 1s. 6d.

"Pleasant and instructive reading."—*Athenæum.*

INTRODUCTORY STUDIES IN GREEK ART. Delivered in the British Museum by JANE E. HARRISON, Author of "Myths of the Odyssey in Art and Literature," &c. Map and 10 Illusts. Square Imperial 16mo., 7s. 6d.

"Admirable work in every way. The lady has mastered her subject; she writes a good, expressive, moving style; she has a fine talent of exposition; she understands, and her readers have no choice but to understand with her. To students, not only of Greek art, but of art in general, her book is really indispensable."—*Magazine of Art.*

A SHORT HISTORY OF THE NETHERLANDS (HOLLAND AND BELGIUM). By ALEXANDER YOUNG, Author of "The Comic and Tragic Aspects of Life," &c. Seventy-seven Illustrations. Demy 8vo., cloth . . . . 7s. 6d.

"It will be found a very valuable manual of the history of the Netherlands by all young men who, for any reason, have to become students of it."—*Spectator.*

"A careful and readable history."—*Daily News.*

LETTERS FROM ITALY. By M. EMILE DE LAVELEYE. Translated by Mrs. THORPE. Revised by the Author. Portrait of the Author. Crown 8vo. . . . 6s.

"Read . . . the second series of 'Letters from Italy,' lately published by E. de Laveleye, a man of European fame in regard to political and social economy."—*Christian World* of August 27, 1885, in leader reviewing the original edition.

THE TRUE STORY OF THE FRENCH DISPUTE IN MADAGASCAR. By Capt. S. P. OLIVER, F.S.A., F.R.G.S., late R.A., Author of "Madagascar and the Malagasy," &c. With a Chapter by F. W. CHESSON, Hon. Sec. of the Malagasy Committee. Map. Demy 8vo. . . . . 9s.

"A very straightforward and ungarnished account of the dispute between France and Madagascar."—*Contemporary Review.*

"Captain Pasfield Oliver's very interesting and informing book."—*Nonconformist.*

CENTRAL ASIAN QUESTIONS: Essays on Afghanistan, China and Central Asia. By DEMETRIUS C. BOULGER, Author of "The History of China," &c. With Portrait and Three Maps. Demy 8vo., cloth . . . . 18s.

"Ought to be read by everybody interested in the Central Asian question. . . . Mr. Boulger's essays are a magazine of information relating to the people and country of Central Asia, Afghanistan and China."—ARMINIUS VAMBÉRY, in *The Academy.*

THE WRECKERS OF LAVERNOCK. By ANNIE JENKYNS. Crown 8vo. . . . . 5s.

"In delineation of character the authoress is extremely clever."—*Schoolmaster.*

THE ROMAN STUDENTS; or, On the Wings of the Morning. A Tale of the Renaissance. By the Author of "The Spanish Brothers," &c. Illustrated by G. P. JACOMB HOOD. Cheaper ed. Imp. 8vo., cloth, 4s. 6d.

"One of the best stories of the year."—*British Quarterly Review.*

THE HOUSE BY THE WORKS. By EDWARD GARRETT, Author of "Occupations of a Retired Life," &c. Frontispiece. 3rd edition. Crown 8vo. . . . 3s. 6d.

SETTLING DAY: A Sketch from Life. By SOPHIE ARGENT. Crown 8vo., cloth . . . . . 3s. 6d.

"A charming story of real life, and one that is as true to human nature as it is true to facts."—*Congregationalist.*

"A pleasant and wholesome little novelette. . . . It is agreeably written."—*Society.*

OFF DUTY: Stories of a Parson on Leave. By CHARLES WRIGHT. Crown 8vo., cloth . . . . . 2s. 6d.

MARGARET THE MOONBEAM: A Tale for the Young. By CECILIA LUSHINGTON, Author of "Over the Seas and Far Away." With Illustrations by M. E. EDWARDS. Second Edition. Small 8vo., cloth extra, gilt edges, 2s. 6d.

BEAUTIES AND FRIGHTS, with THE STORY OF BOBINETTE. By SARAH TYTLER, Author of "Papers for Thoughtful Girls," &c. Illustrated by M. E. EDWARDS. Second edition. Small 8vo. . . . 2s. 6d.

THE STARRY BLOSSOM, & OTHER STORIES. By M. BETHAM-EDWARDS, Author of "Minna's Holiday," &c. Illustrated. Small 8vo., cloth extra . . . 1s. 6d.

THE

"LIVES WORTH LIVING" SERIES

OF POPULAR BIOGRAPHIES.

Illustrated. Crown 8vo., cloth extra, 3s. 6d. per vol.

1. **LEADERS OF MEN:** A Book of Biographies specially written for Young Men. By H. A. PAGE, Author of "Golden Lives." Fourth edition.

"Mr. Page thoroughly brings out the disinterestedness and devotion to high aims which characterise the men of whom he writes. He has done his work with care and good taste."—*Spectator.*

2. **WISE WORDS AND LOVING DEEDS:** A Book of Biographies for Girls. By E. CONDER GRAY. Sixth edition.

"A series of brightly-written sketches of lives of remarkable women. The subjects are well chosen and well treated."—*Saturday Review.*

3. **MASTER MISSIONARIES:** Studies in Heroic Pioneer Work. By ALEX. H. JAPP, LL.D., F.R.S.E. 3rd ed.

"An extremely interesting book. The reader need not be afraid of falling into beaten tracks here."—*The Guardian.*

"A really excellent and readable book."—*Literary Churchman.*

4. **LABOUR AND VICTORY.** By A. H. JAPP, LL.D. Memoirs of Those who Deserved Success and Won it. Third edition.

"We should be glad to see this volume in the hands of thousands of boys and young men."—*Leeds Mercury.*

5. **HEROIC ADVENTURE:** Chapters in Recent Explorations and Discovery. Illustrated. Third edition.

"Gives freshness to the old inexhaustible story of enterprise and discovery by selecting some of the very latest of heroes in this field."—*Daily News.*

PLANT LIFE: Popular Papers on the Phenomena of Botany. By EDWARD STEP. 148 Illustrations by the Author. Third edition. Crown 8vo., cloth extra, 3s. 6d.

"More delightful reading for the country at this season of the year authors and publishers have not provided for us."—*Pall Mall Gazette.*

THE WAY TO FORTUNE: A Series of Short Essays, with Illustrative Proverbs and Anecdotes from many sources. Third Edition. Small 8vo., cloth extra, 2s. 6d.

AMERICAN DISHES, and How to Cook Them. By an American Lady. Crown 8vo., cloth extra, 2s. 6d.

"A smart little tome."—G. A. S., in *Illustrated London News.*

A CUP OF COFFEE. Illustrated. Fcap. 8vo., boards, 1s.

"This pleasant, gossiping monograph."—*Daily Chronicle.*

THE QUICKEST GUIDE TO BREAKFAST, DINNER AND SUPPER. By AUNT GERTRUDE. Paper boards . . . . 1s.

"A capital manual for housewives."—*Literary World.*

ADULTERATIONS OF FOOD (How to Detect the). By the Author of "Ferns and Ferneries." Illust. Crown 8vo., sewed . . . . 9d.

"This little work before us offers many useful hints to householders as to the detection of everyday adulteration."—*Pall Mall Gazette.*

THE ILLUSTRATED POETRY BOOK for Young Readers. Small crown 8vo., cloth, 2s. 6d.; gilt edges, 3s.

"It s the best book of the kind which has passed through our hands for some time." *Bookseller.*

INDUSTRIAL CURIOSITIES: Glances Here and There in the World of Labour. Written and Edited by ALEX. HAY JAPP, LL.D. Fourth ed. Crown 8vo., 3s. 6d.

"Nowadays boys are so fed upon story books and books of adventure that we welcome a book which tells them something about the facts of the world they live in."—*Graphic.*

FOOTPRINTS: Nature seen on its Human Side. By SARAH TYTLER, Author of "Papers for Thoughtful Girls," &c. Illust. Third edition. Crown 8vo. . 3s. 6d.

"A book of real worth."—*Spectator.*

GUDRUN, BEOWULF, and ROLAND. With other Mediæval Tales. By JOHN GIBB. Illust. Second and cheaper edition. Crown 8vo., cloth extra . 3s. 6d.

"A safer or more acceptable gift-book it would be difficult to find."—*Academy*

ARMY EXAMINATION SERIES.

Crown 8vo., cloth, 2s. 6d. each.

1. GEOMETRICAL DRAWING: Containing General Hints to Candidates, Former Papers set at the Preliminary and Further Examinations, and Four Hundred Questions for Practice in Scales and General Problems. By C. H. OCTAVIUS CURTIS. Illustrated.
2. A MANUAL OF FRENCH GRAMMAR. By LE COMPTE DE LA HOUSSAYE, Officier de la Légion d'Honneur, French Examiner for Military and Civil Appointments.
3. GEOGRAPHY QUESTIONS: Especially adapted for Candidates preparing for the Preliminary Examination. By R. H. ALLPRESS, M.A., Trin. Coll., Camb.

STOPS; or, How to Punctuate. With Instructions for Correcting Proofs, &c. By PAUL ALLARDYCE. Fourth and Revised edition. Demy 16mo., parchment antique, 1s.

"We have hardly any words but those of praise to give to his very thoughtful, very dainty little book."—*Journal of Education.*

"We can conceive no more desirable present to a literary aspirant."—*Academy.*

EASY LESSONS IN BOTANY. By EDWARD STEP, Author of "Plant Life." 120 Illustrations by Author. Third edition. Linen covers . . . . 7d.

Also in two parts, paper covers, each . . . 3d.

AN ENGLISH GRAMMAR FOR SCHOOLS. Adapted to the Requirements of the Revised Code. In Three Parts. Price 2d. each, or complete in one cover, 6d.

Adopted by the London School Board.

FIRST NATURAL HISTORY READER. For Standard II. In accordance with the requirements of the Revised Code. Illustrated. Crown 8vo., cloth, 9d.

'Written in a simple and pleasant style."—*School Guardian.*

POETICAL READER FOR THE USE OF SCHOOLS. Illust. In Two Parts, each . . 1s. 3d.

Or in sections separately.

LIST OF BOOKS ARRANGED IN ORDER OF PRICE.

LONDON: T. FISHER UNWIN, 26, PATERNOSTER SQUARE, E.C.